QUANTITATIVE METHODS FOR TRADE-BARRIER ANALYSIS

Also by Alexander Yeats

SHIPPING AND DEVELOPMENT POLICY
TRADE BARRIERS FACING DEVELOPING COUNTRIES
TRADE AND DEVELOPMENT POLICIES: Leading Issues for the 1980s

Quantitative Methods for Trade-Barrier Analysis

Sam Laird
Senior Economist
The World Bank, Washington, DC

and

Alexander Yeats
Principal Economist
The World Bank, Washington, DC

NEW YORK UNIVERSITY PRESS
Washington Square, New York

First published in the U.S.A. in 1990 by
NEW YORK UNIVERSITY PRESS
Washington Square
New York, N.Y. 10003

Library of Congress Cataloging-in-Publication Data
Laird, Sam.
    Quantitative methods for trade-barrier analysis/ Sam Laird and
    Alexander Yeats
        p.   cm.
    Includes bibliographical references.
    ISBN 0–8147–5049–4
    1. Nontariff trade barriers—Econometric models.   I. Yeats,
    Alexander J.   II. Title.
    HF1430.L34   1990
    382'.5'015195—dc20   89– 49635
                                                              CIP

Printed in Singapore

Contents

v

Contents

List of Tables

List of Figures

Acknowledgements

In the preparation of this book we incurred numerous individual and institutional debts. Over 1986–8, UNCTAD and the World Bank co-sponsored two seminars on nontariff barriers and we greatly benefited from the discussion and material presented in these meetings. In particular, a paper by Professors Allan Deardorff and Robert Stern (University of Michigan) on conceptual problems with the quantification of nontariff barriers provided background material for Chapter 2. A second study by Professor Richard Snape (Monash University) contributed to our analysis of the economic effects of nontariff barriers, while a paper prepared by Dr Andrzej Olechowski (National Bank of Poland) and one of this book's authors (Dr Alexander Yeats – then of UNCTAD) provided background for the analysis of nontariff barrier inventory studies.

Several sections of the book draw on previously published research by the authors in co-operation with individuals at different institutions. We would like to acknowledge past collaborations with Dr Gary Sampson (GATT), Dr Andrzej Olechowski (National Bank of Poland), Dr Vernon Roningen (US Department of Agriculture) and Dr J. Michael Finger (World Bank). In addition, Guy Karsenty (UNCTAD) assisted in computerising the trade simulation model described in Chapter 3, and also was a co-author of several subsequent policy studies. Finally, we would like to thank the editors of the following journals for permission to utilise parts of our previously published studies: *Weltwirtschaftliches Archives*, *Review of Economics and Statistics*, *Journal of Business and Economics*, *Economia Internazionale*, *Journal of Political Economy*, *American Journal of Agricultural Economics*, and *Journal of Developing Economies*.

We received helpful comments from numerous individuals in the preparation of this book. We must express special thanks to Dr Carl Hamilton (University of Stockholm) who made suggestions for material to be included in Chapter 5, while Mr Nicolas Marian (International Textiles and Clothing Bureau) reviewed sections of this chapter dealing with the Multifibre Arrangement and provided additional material for inclusion. Dr Harsha Singh (GATT) and Dr Harmon Thomas (UNCTAD) made helpful suggestions on sections of this book dealing with agricultural nontariff barriers. We also profited from working with Dr Ingo Walter (New York University),

Dr Tracy Murray (University of Arkansas) and Dr Craig MacPhee (University of Nebraska) on some of UNCTAD's first applications of the NTB inventory approach in the 1970s, and with Rene Vossenaar (UNCTAD) in the 1980s. Finally, co-operative studies with Dr Refik Erzan (World Bank) and Dr Ho Dac Tuong (UNCTAD) were used in several sections.

SAM LAIRD
ALEXANDER YEATS

1 Policy Issues Involving Nontariff Trade Barriers

Without doubt the major accomplishment of seven multilateral trade negotiations (Mtns) that began in the late 1940s was the reduction of tariffs as trade barriers. Estimates relating to the period prior to the MTNs indicate the average tariff in industrial countries was approximately 40 per cent, but these duties were progressively lowered to under 8 per cent through concessions made in the Geneva (1947) (1956), Annecy (1949), Torquay (1951), Dillon (1962) and Kennedy Round (1968). During the most recent Tokyo Round (1979) negotiations, the General Agreement on Tariffs and Trade (GATT) estimates that developed country most-favoured-nation (MFN) tariffs on manufactures were reduced by about one-third, and now average about 5.5 per cent since the final concessions have been implemented. A further liberalisation of tariffs will undoubtedly occur in the Uruguay Round negotiations which are scheduled for completion in 1990.

While tariffs have been steadily reduced, the relative importance of nontariff trade barriers (NTBs) has increased. Aside from their incidence, concern has been expressed about the NTBs' changing nature since they involve a growing tendency for non-discriminatory trading policies to be replaced by bilateral or other discriminatory arrangements. As a result, the most-favoured-nation (MFN) principle, that is a cornerstone of the GATT, has been eroded by an increasing reliance on nontariff barriers directed at specific countries or country groups.[1] The spread of these measures is often seen as a threat to the functioning of the General Agreement.

As one illustration of this concern, a Commonwealth Secretariat (1982) expert panel concluded that 'nontariff measures have emerged as a major challenge to the entire GATT system' and convincingly listed reasons for this view. First, the panel noted there has been increased use of 'formally permissible' instruments of nontariff protection, particularly in agriculture. Here it was found there are few competing agricultural products supplied by developing countries for which world markets are not distorted by nontariff barriers or concessional sales from developed countries. The EEC, for example, has become the world's second largest exporter of sugar after Cuba, and of beef after Australia, due to the production-increasing effects of high internal price supports that are based on nontariff protection. Second, authorised nontariff measures within the GATT, such as the Multifibre Arrangement (MFA), are becoming increasingly discriminatory against products of importance to developing countries.[2] Third, the panel found there has been increasing resort to new instruments of nontariff protection such as orderly marketing arrangements, 'voluntary' export restraints, import levies, and various forms of discriminatory intervention. Since the multilateral trade negotiations have greatly reduced available options for utilising tariffs, developed countries now employ a wide range of NTBs for industrial protection, particularly in sectors that are experiencing long-term structural adjustment problems. These measures, unlike tariffs, represent a breakdown of order in the trading system since they normally involve a lack of transparency and *de facto* discrimination among trading partners.

As a result of these developments, a high share of world trade now takes place outside the most-favoured-nation principle. Discriminatory trade barriers are applied at a general level between members of different trading blocks, particularly in the case of developed market economy countries and socialist countries of Eastern Europe, and selectively against individual countries and industries. There is a widespread abuse of GATT principles and rules, particularly in the case of quantitative restrictions which are authorised only for balance-of-payments problems or for some agricultural products. In cases, bilateral arrangements have been substituted for multilateral approaches to trade negotiation and dispute settlement. As nontariff measures proliferated, transparency has been reduced, making monitoring, surveillance, and assessment of these trade barriers' effects more difficult. Due to these departures from GATT and free trade principles the international community is experiencing major trade, welfare, employment and other economic losses.

INFORMATIONAL NEEDS FOR CORRECTIVE POLICY ACTION

While there has been growing concern about the spread of NTBs, corrective policy action has been frustrated by the fact that the empirical information on these restrictions often is fragmentary, and is in a form that does not facilitate quantitative analysis. This is due, in part, to the fact that NTBs frequently involve a lack of transparency in their usage and economic effects. Attempts to derive measures for the incidence of NTBs have been hampered by the diverse nature of these restrictions, and the fact that there is no established procedure for quantification without apparent shortcomings. This inability to derive *ad valorem* equivalents for nontariff barriers contributed to the failure of past multilateral negotiations to make progress on their reduction since participants could not easily assess associated gains and losses.[3]

In recognition of the major problems posed by nontariff barriers, and the difficulties connected with the lack of information on their application and incidence, initiatives were made in the early 1980s to establish comprehensive NTB inventories for developed and developing countries. The most extensive project was undertaken by the United Nations Conference on Trade and Development (UNC-TAD), although related efforts were initiated by GATT. The UNCTAD records have been expanded to the point that they contain tariff-line-level statistics on over 100 types of NTBs in most developed countries, and similar information for about 80 developing countries. A useful feature of the UNCTAD records is that they show the year any given restriction was first imposed, modified, or removed. This allows some time series analysis of changing patterns of nontariff protection. Chapter 4 presents empirical evidence on the nature of these changes for developed market economy countries.

While nontariff barrier inventories have many useful policy and research applications, their underlying methodological approach has recognised shortcomings. One major difficulty is that an NTB inventory only records the existence of nontariff barriers, but it tells nothing about their restrictive effects. For many policy needs, such as estimating trade, employment and other economic effects, *ad valorem* equivalents of NTBs are required. However, one reason why work has concentrated on the inventory approach is that recognised problems exist in empirical procedures for estimating NTBs' nominal equivalents. For example, one approach, which involves comparisons between a good's domestic and international prices, can be biased by cross-country differences in supply and demand elasticities, transportation costs, or differences in the ability of foreign and domestic firms to appropriate rents from nontariff restrictions. Measurement problems have also been compounded by exchange rate volatility that makes the translation of 'representative' foreign and domestic prices into a common unit for comparison difficult.

THE COSTS AND CONSEQUENCES OF PROTECTIONISM

Any evaluation of the importance of nontariff barriers should consider certain basic points. Criteria such as the overall value and share of trade subject to these restrictions are clearly relevant. Other relevant questions involve the incidence or nominal equivalents of NTBs, the extent to which they discriminate against different exporters, or whether they have adverse economic effects not associated with trade barriers such as tariffs. For proper evaluation, one would also want to know the magnitude of associated costs from trade, employment, and welfare losses. Perhaps a key question is whether other measures are available that could replace NTBs and achieve the desired policy objective more efficiently.[4]

While the evidence is incomplete, many empirical investigations which consider such points also support the view that NTBs are a major international problem. For example, UNCTAD estimated that approximately 20 per cent of world trade now encounters nontariff barriers and that the trade coverage of these measures has been growing. However, sectorial studies indicate the importance of NTBs is often far greater in industries like textiles, clothing, ferrous metals, automotive products and agriculture where developed countries appear to be losing a comparative advantage in production. Studies that show that these measures' *ad valorem* equivalents may reach several hundred per cent also highlight their importance.

The findings of studies that quantified the trade and other economic losses from current protectionist practices stress the need for international initiatives to deal with nontariff barriers. Among the points that emerge from these investigations are that NTBs significantly reduce developed and developing countries' export earnings; they involve major welfare losses; NTBs frustrate commodity-producing countries' efforts to shift from exports of primary commodities to semi-finished or processed goods; and often discriminate against products in which developing countries have a comparative advantage. These studies also show consumers in protected markets often bear major costs since NTBs limit access to lower-priced foreign goods. In addition, evidence indicates border protection from nontariff barriers is a costly and inefficient way of preserving jobs, and that alternative, less harmful instruments are often available for achieving policy goals. Table 1.1 summarises the findings of several representative analyses that document these points. A more detailed survey and evaluation of such studies is presented in Chapter 5.

Table 1.1   Findings of empirical studies relating to the economic costs and effects of contemporary protectionism

---

A. General Studies

World Bank (1979)
Protectionist measures imposed by the United States between 1975 and 1977 on goods imported from Asia and Latin America resulted in a loss to consumers of $1200 million for footwear, $60 million for sugar, $400 to $800 million for meat and $500 million for television sets or over $4 billion for these five items. (Robert McNamara, 'The High Cost of Protectionism,' *Institutional Investor*, September 1979)

U.S. Federal Trade Commission (1980)
Estimated that the cost of protectionism against all foreign exporters of footwear, clothing and sugar was approximately $7.7 billion over the period 1975–9. (M.E. Morkre and D.G. Tarr, *Effects of Restrictions on United States Imports: Five Case Studies*, Staff Report of the Bureau of Economics to the Federal Trade Commission, June 1980)

UNCTAD (1968)
Demonstrated that trade barriers in industrial countries have a consistent tendency to increase or 'escalate' with the degree of commodity processing. Further demonstrated that escalating tariffs and other forms of trade barriers are a major constraint to the export of fabricated goods from developing countries. (*The Kennedy Round Estimated Effects on Tariff Barriers* (TD/6/Rev.1) United Nations publication, sales no. E.68)

UN Economic Commission for Asia and the Far East (1972)
Estimated nominal and effective rates of protection for a selection of developing countries and demonstrated that in almost all cases a major need for rationalisation existed. High tariffs and trade barriers on production inputs were found to have an important adverse effect on a number of potential export industries. (*Intra-regional Trade Projections, Effective Protection and Income Distribution, vol. II – Effective Protection*, United Nations publication, sales no.E.73.II.F.12)

B. Studies Relating to Manufactures

Consumers Association of the United Kingdom
Concluded that the Multifibre Arrangement had increased prices of 60 per cent of all British clothing imports by between 15 and 40 per cent and had created shortages of many lower prices items. A similar investigation for the European Communities estimated that the MFA raised clothing prices by some 30 to 40 per cent. (*The Price of Protection: A Study of the Effect of Import Controls on the Cost of Imported Clothing*, London, Consumers Association)

(continued on page 6)

Table 1.1   *continued*

B. Studies Relating to Manufactures

North–South Institute (1980), Canada
Placed the annual cost to consumers of bilateral quotas on clothing
applied in 1979 at $Canadian 198 million, while the costs of tariffs and
quotas was put at $Canadian 467 million. The study estimated that only
6000 man/years employment was created by this protectionist policy at an
annual cost to the Canadian consumer of $Canadian 33 000 per job. (Glen
P. Jenkins, *Costs and Consequences of the New Protectionism: The Case of
Canada's Clothing Sector*, North–South Institute, Montreal, July 1980)

Australian Industries Assistance Commission (1980)
Estimated that the total annual cost of protectionism in the clothing sector
was $A 235 per household. At the retail level it was estimated that
consumers pay $A 1.1 billion more per year for clothing, drapery and
footwear than they would if all assistance to industries was withdrawn.
(Australian Industries Assistance Commission, *Report on Textiles,
Clothing and Footwear*, Canberra, 1980)

C. Studies Relating to Agriculture

UN Food and Agricultural Organization (1979)
Subsidies for domestic production and higher prices due to international
trade barriers for three products (wheat, sugar and dairy products) were
estimated to have cost European Community consumers some $27 billion
in 1978. In Japan the extra costs for consumers of rice alone was
estimated to over $10 billion, while in the United States consumers of
sugar and dairy products were paying nearly $4 billion in excess of world
prices. (FAO, *Commodity Review and Outlook: 1979–1980*, Rome, 1979)

International Food Policy Research Institute (1980)
Estimated that the agricultural exports of 56 developing countries would
increase by $3 billion annually if the OECD countries would lower
agricultural trade barriers by 50 per cent. The largest sectoral gains were
projected for sugar ($1.1 billion), oilseeds and products ($378 million) and
meat ($336 million). (A. Valdes and J. Zietz, *Agricultural Protection in
OECD Countries: Its Cost to Less Developed Countries*, Washington,
IFPRI, December 1980)

UNCTAD (1972)
Estimated that a comprehensive liberalisation of trade barriers for ten
major agricultural products (wheat, rice, coarse grains, sugar, vegetable
oils, beef and veal, lamb, pork, poultry and milk) would (i) raise the
annual net foreign exchange earnings of developed and developing
countries by about $8 billion; (ii) raise international prices for these
commodities by about 30 per cent on average, and thus reverse the
decline in their terms-of-trade; and (iii) raise the gross domestic product
of developing countries by about 6 per cent once all linkage effects were

Table 1.1 *continued*

C. Studies Relating to Agriculture

accounted for. (*Agricultural Protection and the Food Economy*, Research Memo. No. 46, Geneva, 1972)

World Bank (1981)
Conducted an analysis of the effects of international trade restraints facing eight processed agricultural products and concluded that their removal could increase total value added in developing country processing activity by 20 per cent or more. Such a liberalisation would increase developing countries' export revenues by more than the GSP had done. (*World Development Report*, 1982. New York, Oxford University Press, for the World Bank, 1981)

UN Food and Agricultural Organization (1980)
In a sectorial study for beef trade, FAO estimated that if rates of protection had been reduced by 25 per cent exports would have been 22 per cent higher than their actual 1977–9 level, and that average prices would have been 7 per cent higher. Furthermore, the study indicated that exports of Latin America and Oceania would have been $3.8 billion, as opposed to an actual figure of $2.8 billion over this three-year period. (*Protectionism in the Livestock Sector*, CCP: ME 80/4, Rome, October 1980)

UN Food and Agricultural Organization (1981)
Estimated that if OECD countries reduced protectionism for oilseeds and related products by 50 per cent, the potential increase in export revenues of developing countries would be about $400 million, a rise of some 7 to 10 per cent, and that world trade in these products would increase by about $1 billion in 1977 prices. (*Protectionism in the Oilseeds, Oils and Oilmeals Sector*, CCP: OF 81/2, Rome, January 1981)

Commonwealth Secretariat (1982)
Estimated the removal of European and Japanese trade barriers facing five agricultural products (wheat, maize, barley, sugar and beef) would raise imports of these items by approximately 60 to 70 per cent with even greater increases expected for beef. Much of the benefit of such increased exports would accrue to developing countries in the case of sugar and maize. (*Protectionism: Threat to International Order*, London, Commonwealth Secretariat)

IMPLICATIONS OF NTBs FOR TRADE AND DEVELOPMENT POLICIES

While the studies cited in Table 1.1, and much of the related debate, focus on the direct economic losses from NTBs, situations exist where nontariff barriers are one of several key elements in a broader policy problem. As an example, instability in domestic and international commodity markets has harmful effects ranging from volatile induced changes in export earnings of countries dependent on these products, a fact that makes rational development planning difficult, to the generation of 'cobweb' cycles in agricultural prices and production. As a result, national and multinational programmes, such as the Common Agricultural Policy (CAP) and international (buffer stock) commodity agreements, have been adopted to offset this instability. However, NTBs like the European Community's variable import levies destabilise international prices and production through their perverse effect on import demand. Specifically, when world prices for agricultural goods fall, variable levies rise to keep landed (European) prices constant. If levies had not risen, and reduced import demand, increased European imports would constrain the price decline. Conversely, when world prices rise variable levies fall. This increases European imports and, consequently, world prices rise to higher levels than if these charges had not fluctuated in a perverse manner.

Recent empirical investigations indicate nontariff barriers are a major obstacle to resolving the international debt crisis. For example, Laird and Yeats (1987a) show over 40 per cent (by value) of the most heavily indebted developing countries' exports (i.e. Argentina, Brazil, Taiwan, Venezuela, Turkey, Republic of Korea, etc.) encounter 'hard-core' NTBs in developed countries that reduce opportunities needed to service existing debts. Projections by these authors show a NTB liberalisation could increase the present value of export earnings by an amount equal to one-half of these countries' debts. Such a trade liberalisation would apparently make many developing countries' debts broadly manageable and would also provide an opportunity to reflate their depressed economies.

A number of studies by international organisations have expressed concern about the need for positive structural adjustment policies. A key element of these policies is the transfer of certain industries where developed countries have lost their comparative advantage (i.e. textiles, clothing and other labour-intensive products) to more efficient developing-country producers. As part of this restructuring process, UNIDO proposed the 'Lima Target' under which approximately 25 per cent of world industrial production would originate in developing countries by the year 2000 (from about 12 to 14 per cent in the early 1980s). However, supplementary studies by UNCTAD and UNIDO indicate that such a transfer cannot occur without greatly expanded export opportunities. These analyses conclude that NTBs are one important constraint working against the required trade expansion. A related point is that many developing countries have a major interest in shifting from exports of raw materials to semi-processed or processed products.[5] These efforts are often frustrated by NTBs that, like tariffs, increase or 'escalate' with product processing. As such, these trade barriers lower the overall level of developing countries' exports and also prevent a shift to higher-value-added products that would facilitate industrialisation.

For several reasons many economists believe 'outward looking' or 'export oriented' growth strategies are best for countries attempting to industrialise. Keesing (1967) argues, for example, that by capitalising on export opportunities, and subjecting domestic industries to competition from foreign suppliers, increasing returns to scale and market size, learning effects and the improvement of human capital, beneficial results from competition and close communication with advanced countries (including the familiarisation with advanced technologies from abroad) should result. Historically, these benefits have served as an 'engine of growth' for the developed market economy countries. Recent empirical studies by Balassa (1982; 1983) which show that developing countries that pursue export-oriented growth strategies generally had higher growth rates and reacted better to unfavourable external developments, stress the continuing importance of the relationship between trade, industrialisation and growth.

Major concerns have been expressed that current protectionism now effectively limits the trade and growth prospects of developing countries. In the analysis that follows, detailed empirical information relating to this point – such as the value of individual developing-country exports subject to NTBs, the industries that are most seriously affected, and the *ad valorem* incidence of these restrictions – is examined. In addition, time-series information on the spread of NTBs is analysed to determine if basic changes have occurred in their level and pattern of use. Quantitative evidence is also examined on the extent to which nontariff barriers discriminate against developing-country exports.

NTBs AND THE URUGUAY ROUND

Given the extensive adverse effects of nontariff barriers, effective corrective action must be taken in the Uruguay Round. However, in previous multilateral trade negotiations little progress was made either in liberalising NTBs or in establishing a general approach for dealing with these measures. In the early stages of the Kennedy Round it was decided that the negotiations 'should deal not only with tariffs, but also with nontariff barriers'. A major negotiating committee was established to focus specifically on nontariff barriers, while a second dealt with agriculture where NTBs were a central problem. An early attempt to devise a general approach for removing nontariff barriers proved unsuccessful and negotiators opted for a liberalisation on a barrier-by-barrier basis. In the end, the only NTB agreements were the GATT Anti-Dumping Code and the package in which the United States agreed to abolish the American Selling Price (ASP) customs valuation procedures.[6] In the Tokyo Round, difficult negotiations produced several codes for specific practices (government procurement, technical barriers to trade, subsidies and countervailing duties, customs valuation practices, and import licensing procedures), but these fell far short of the objectives established at the start of the negotiations. Indeed, little progress was made in sectors like agriculture and textiles where nontariff restrictions are most heavily applied.[7]

In the Uruguay Round, certain key problems must be resolved to deal effectively with nontariff barriers. Perhaps the major difficulty is to formulate a viable strategy for liberalising these restrictions. The barrier-by-barrier approach, in which negotiators focus on the elimination of a specific type of restriction (like quotas) across industry sectors and then turn to a second type of barrier, encounters problems where multiple NTBs are 'stacked' on a product. Here, the removal of one restriction could be offset by tightening others. A sectorial approach has problems, including the fact that restrictions such as general industrial or fiscal policies cut across different industries. If sectors are not dealt with uniformly, a disproportionate liberalisation in one might actually raise levels of 'effective protection' (i.e. the protection for value added in a production process) in others. Such would be the case if protection in an industry that largely supplied production inputs were cut more than that in sectors producing final consumption products. (See Appendix 2 for a graphical illustration of this point.)

Given these potential problems, some negotiators have proposed that NTBs be converted to tariffs and Kennedy or Tokyo Round procedures used to liberalise these duties. Techniques are available for approximating the trade effects of tariff cuts and they would facilitate such an approach.[8] However, a major if not insurmountable problem is that every methodology used to estimate *ad valorem* equivalents for NTBs can incorporate important biases (see Chapter 2 on this point). Due to this estimation problem, and the diversity of types of NTBs, it seems likely that agreement could not be reached on initial conditions, that is, what nominal levels of protection are afforded by existing nontariff barriers.

It is clear that negotiators could have incentives to misstate their nontariff barriers' nominal equivalents. If NTBs were converted to tariffs and a linear reduction formulae applied for their reduction, an incentive would exist to generally overstate all nominal equivalents by equal magnitudes. If other tariff-cutting formulae were employed, such as one that 'harmonises' tariffs or produces greater percentage cuts in higher duties, the incentive to bias NTB *ad valorem* equivalents could vary among different products.[9] Difficulties could also be expected from exporters who appropriated premiums from the nontariff barriers since they would object to the conversion unless compensation for the lost rents were offered.[10]

Perhaps more than on any other single problem the success of future multilateral negotiations will hinge on an agreement being reached for a viable negotiating strategy for NTBs. In choosing among alternatives, accurate information on nontariff measures is needed to make an optimal selection. Questions such as the importance of NTBs in national protectionist profiles, the variance in their use across industries, the extent that discriminatory measures are employed, the likely trade, welfare and economic effects of NTBs all have an important bearing on the liberalisation strategy to be used. In addition, negotiators must have an understanding of the potential biases and omissions in available information relating to these points. It is toward these basic issues that the present book is addressed.

THE TRADE POTENTIALS OF THE SOCIALIST COUNTRIES

Several analyses of the 'openness' of national trading practices tried to assess the import performance of the Socialist Countries of Eastern Europe (SCEEs) using empirical procedures that have been employed for quantifying nontariff barriers. One potentially useful approach involves 'gravity' flow models where potential SCEE bilateral trade is projected using variables like distance between the trading partners, size (measured by population or GDP), and dummy variables for language and cultural characteristics. Where actual trade falls significantly below projected trade this may reflect the effects of nontariff barriers or biases in state trading. Also, SCEE trade performance variables have been compared with similar measures from other countries to roughly quantify differences between actual and potential trade.

Studies that have employed the latter approach accent the need for objective standards for the SCEE's trading practices. According to Yeats (1982), roughly 25 per cent of United States imports of manufactures originate in developing countries while the corresponding ratio for the USSR and other Eastern European countries is under 3 per cent. The ratio of manufactured imports from developing countries to gross domestic product exceeds 0.75 per cent for Australia, Belgium, Denmark, Federal Republic of Germany, Sweden, Switzerland, United Kingdom and United States, but in the SCEEs it ranged between 0.01 to 0.07 per cent. On a per capita basis, the average imports of manufactures from developing countries was between $2 to $4 for the socialist countries, while it ranged between $80 to $120 for the developed market economy countries. If the SCEEs brought their trade performance ratios up to the latter's average an expansion of developing country exports of approximately $7 billion would ensue.

Given the implications of these statistics, there is an abvious need for objective trade performance measures for the socialist countries. This book will propose and evaluate several procedures. Aside from gravity flow models and the 'performance' variable approach, trade intensity indices or procedures for quantifying biases in government procurement practices may be useful. In addition, product classification schemes – where goods are grouped by level of fabrication or other basic production – and end-use characteristics are examined (see Appendix 1) and discussed since they can identify structural biases in SCEE trade.[11]

OUTLINE AND PLAN OF THE BOOK

As far as practical policy and research needs are concerned, this book focuses on four main elements of the NTB problem. The first, which is considered in Chapter 2, examines the technical and theoretical basis for quantifying nontariff barriers. This chapter evaluates potential biases in alternative approaches for estimating these measures' *ad valorem* equivalents and tries to establish guidelines for their application. Since a number of studies have attempted to quantify NTBs using data on international price differentials for standardised products, the chapter discusses the difficulties that can be encountered using this approach. Several methodologies for estimating the quantity effects of NTBs on trade are evaluated, including the use of industry econometric models. As background to this discussion, the procedures employed in constructing nontariff barrier inventories, and implications of results from inventory studies, are assessed.

If *ad valorem* equivalents can be derived using the procedures presented in Chapter 2, the trade, welfare, and other economic effects of NTBs can be estimated. As such, Chapter 3 describes the conceptual foundation, and practical applications, of partial equilibrium trade projection models that have been employed for this purpose. These models have been used by UNCTAD, the World Bank, Brookings Institution, International Monetary Fund and a number of independent research organisations for a wide range of policy studies. Examples of results from these analyses are provided and further possible applications discussed. Next, Chapter 4 employs an inventory of nontariff barriers to analyse basic cross-country and cross-industry information on the use of these restrictions. Data is also examined on the overall level and share of world trade subject to NTBs, as well as trends in their general application. Since these inventories appear to have considerable unutilised potential for empirical analysis, several possible directions for future research are suggested.

The theoretical chapters dealing with quantification of nontariff barriers (Chapter 2) and procedures that can be employed for projecting the costs and effects of these restrictions (Chapter 3) lay the foundation for Chapter 4 and Chapter 5 which present basic NTB inventory results or survey the results of studies that estimated nominal equivalents for NTBs and quantified their economic effects. These chapters have a fourfold objective: to assess the overall implications of available evidence on NTBs for liberalisation efforts; to identify sectors and countries where a liberalisation should have a high priority; to evaluate empirical information on the trade, welfare and other economic costs of nontariff barriers; and, in addition, these chapters are intended to facilitate further research and policy analyses by drawing together and evaluating the findings of previous empirical studies. References are also provided where the reader can locate additional related information on nontariff barriers in the professional literature.

Throughout the book an effort is made to suggest priority areas for further research on nontariff barriers. In offering these suggestions we have benefited from discussions with numerous colleagues at the World Bank, UNCTAD, GATT and various universities in the United States and Europe on priority needs for research and policy purposes. The topics considered are wide-ranging, covering proposals for extensions of the NTB inventory approach to the development of new measures for quantifying the effects of nontariff barriers. It is hoped that these proposals, coupled with the related material in the book, will be of particular interest to government officials, research workers, and university students who are planning studies on contemporary protectionism. However, it is our belief that the material presented in this book should also be of considerable interest to all individuals attempting to broaden their understanding of issues relating to the costs and effects of contemporary protectionism.

2 Quantitative Approaches to Trade-Barrier Analysis

A point that must be addressed before any analyses can be undertaken is to define what constitutes a 'nontariff barrier'. This problem is complicated by the fact that different definitions have previously been advanced. Robert Baldwin (1970), for example, suggests that a nontariff trade distortion is 'any measure (public or private) that causes internationally traded goods and services, or resources devoted to the production of these goods and services, to be allocated in such a way as to reduce potential real world income'. Potential world income is defined as that level attainable if resources were allocated in the most economically efficient manner. Clearly difficulties exist for applications of this definition since it requires an estimate of 'potential real world income' or, at a minimum, knowledge of directional movements in income under alternative policy measures. While there may be agreement on the directional movement for removal of (say) a rigorously enforced quota there are measures whose effects may be more difficult to assess. For example, it may be difficult to determine if removal of some sanitary requirements for imports would increase or decrease income if the resulting trade expansion was accompanied by a decline in health standards and rising medical costs.

In search of a workable definition, Ingo Walter (1972) proposed that NTBs broadly encompass all private and government policies and practices that distort the volume, commodity-composition or direction of trade in goods and services. Walter recognises that this is a weak operational definition, however, in that it requires judgement on what constitutes a 'trade distortion'. Specifically, firms may influence the volume and composition of trade by actions which affect supply and demand conditions. Measures aimed at lowering production costs and prices, or increasing product differentiation through advertising may reduce imports if practised by domestic firms. Most economists would not classify such actions as NTBs since they are normally not assumed to convey and 'unfair' competitive advantage. However, firms may engage in practices, such as dumping or predatory pricing, which should be classified as nontariff distortions due to their intent. Similarly, government policies may influence the

15

volume and composition of trade, sometimes as a remote side-effect not connected with the primary purpose of the action. In other cases, a specific policy measure may be implemented solely to control the level of international trade.[1] As such, Walter proposed that the intent of different measures be a factor used for the identification of non-tariff barriers.

While the difficulty in defining a nontariff barrier may be partially reduced by adopting Walter's suggestion that NTBs be classified on the basis of their intent, there are various measures like standards requirements, liberal licensing procedures, or labelling and packaging regulations that can be used to affect the level of imports depending on how they are applied. In other words, there are regulations whose intent cannot be determined without a difficult and potentially inconclusive investigation of their nature and actual operation. In recognition of this point, UNCTAD found it convenient to distinguish between nontariff measures (NTMs) and nontariff barriers. The term 'measures' is wider than 'barriers', since it encompasses all trade instruments which may be used as barriers, although their restrictive effects, if any, may vary between countries, or even at different points of time in a specific country. Moreover, the restrictiveness may lie in the way the measure is applied rather than in the basic properties of the measure itself.[2] In the UNCTAD scheme, product-specific nontariff measures (i.e. those that are applied to specific items down to the level of the tariff line) are grouped into five broad categories depending on their method of operation: fiscal measures, volume restraining measures, import authorisations, measures to control price levels, and a miscellaneous group of restrictions. Table 2.1 provides the broad outline of the UNCTAD classification scheme for product-specific NTBs, while a glossary for these measures is given in Appendix 4. Separate records are also maintained by UNCTAD for measures like state trading, general entry and exit control procedures, or foreign exchange controls that influence the general level of imports.

While the preceding discussion shows it is generally necessary to distinguish between nontariff measures and nontariff barriers, it should be noted that two different approaches have been employed for these instruments' quantification. These alternative approaches differ considerably in their methodology and in the nature of their empirical results. The first, often referred to as the 'inventory' approach, has been used primarily to produce descriptive statistics on the kinds, pattern and frequency of use of NTMs. The second general approach attempts to quantify the trade and other economic effects

Table 2.1   The UNCTAD classification scheme for nontariff trade control measures of a product specific nature

---

1. Fiscal measures
  1.1. Import-specific charges
    1.1.1. Tariffs
      1.1.1.1. Tariffs with quota
        1.1.1.1.1. *Ad valorem* tariffs with quota
        1.1.1.1.2. Specific tariff with quota
        1.1.1.1.3. Combined tariff with quota
      1.1.1.2. Seasonal tariff
        1.1.1.2.1. Seasonal *ad valorem* tariff
        1.1.1.2.2. Seasonal specific tariff
        1.1.1.2.3. Seasonal combined tariff
      1.1.1.3. *Ad valorem* tariff with specific minimum
    1.1.2. Charges applied on the basis of declared value
      1.1.2.1. *Ad valorem* charges
      1.1.2.2. Specific charges
      1.1.2.3. Combined charges
    1.1.3. Charges applied on the basis of decreed value
      1.1.3.1. Variable import duties
        1.1.3.1.1. Variable levies
        1.1.3.1.2. Variable component
      1.1.3.2. Transaction-specific charges
        1.1.3.2.1. Countervailing duties
        1.1.3.2.2. Anti-dumping duties
  1.2. Product-specific taxes
    1.2.1. *Ad valorem* taxes
    1.2.2. Specific taxes
    1.2.3. Combined taxes

2. Volume-restraining measures
  2.1. Prohibitions
    2.1.1. Total prohibitions
      2.1.1.1. Prohibition of a general nature
      2.1.1.2. Health and safety prohibitions
      2.1.1.3. Wildlife prohibitions
      2.1.1.4. Prohibitions (censorship)
      2.1.1.5. Seasonal prohibitions
    2.1.2. Conditional prohibitions
      2.1.2.1. General conditional prohibitions
      2.1.2.2. Prohibition on basis or origin
      2.1.2.3. Prohibition (except certain purchasers)
        2.1.2.3.1. State monopoly of imports
        2.1.2.3.2. Sole importing agency
      2.1.2.4. Prohibition for certain use
    2.1.3. Quotas
      2.1.3.1. General quotas
      2.1.3.2. Global quota

(continued on page 18)

Table 2.1   continued

---

2. *Volume-restraining measures*

        2.1.3.3. Quotas by country
        2.1.3.4. Seasonal quota
        2.1.3.5. 'Voluntary' export restraints

3. *Import-authorisations*
    3.1. Non-automatic authorisations
        3.1.1. Authorisations to control entry
            3.1.1.1. Discretionary authorisations
                3.1.1.1.1. General import authorisations
                3.1.1.1.2. Discretionary licensing
                3.1.1.1.3. Automatic licensing
                3.1.1.1.4. Declaration with visa
                3.1.1.1.5. Select purchaser authorisation
                3.1.1.1.6. Import permit required
            3.1.1.2. Conditional import authorisations
                3.1.1.2.1. Export dependent authorisation
                3.1.1.2.2. Supply dependent authorisation
                3.1.1.2.3. Dependent on domestic purchase
                3.1.1.2.4. Dependent on foreign financing
        3.1.2. Authorisation to control standards compliance
            3.1.2.1. Health and safety authorisation required
            3.1.2.2. Technical standard authorisation required
            3.1.2.3. Censorship authorisation required
    3.2. Automatic authorisations
        3.2.1. Licence for surveillance purposes
        3.2.2. Liberal licensing
        3.2.3. Automatic licensing
        3.2.4. Declaration without visa requirement
        3.2.5. Intra-community surveillance system

4. *Control of the price level*
    4.1. Minimum price systems
        4.1.1. Minimum general import price requirement
        4.1.2. Reference import price requirement
        4.1.3. Basic import price requirement
        4.1.4. Trigger price system
    4.2. Price investigations
        4.2.1. Anti-dumping investigation
        4.2.2. Countervailing duty investigation
    4.3. Price surveillance
        4.3.1. Price surveillance system

5. *Other measures*
    5.1. Technical requirements
        5.1.1. Health and safety regulations

Table 2.1   continued

---

5. *Other measures*

       5.1.2. Technical standards
       5.1.3. Marking and packaging requirements
    5.2. Measures to assist import-competing production
       5.2.1. Production subsidies
           5.2.1.1. Subsidies to material inputs
       5.2.2. Subsidies to labour
       5.2.3. Subsidies to capital
           5.2.3.1. Investment grants
           5.2.3.2. Research and development grants
           5.2.3.3. Product-specific accelerated depreciation
       5.2.4. Product-specific tax concessions
    5.9. Other import measures
       5.9.1. Multifibre Arrangement
           5.9.1.1. MFA quota
           5.9.1.2. MFA consultation level
           5.9.1.3. MFA export control
       5.9.2. Additional customs formalities
       5.9.3. Import deposits

---

of nontariff measures, often through the estimation of their *ad valorem* equivalents. Given that the two approaches differ significantly, it is important to recognise their advantages and limitations.

THE NONTARIFF MEASURE INVENTORY APPROACH

The most notable example of the 'inventory' approach to nontariff measure analysis is the Data Base on Trade Measures UNCTAD maintains for most developed market economy countries (full information is not available for Spain, Portugal, Sweden, Australia and the Republic of South Africa) and about eighty developing countries. The Data Base, generally available at the national tariff-line level, identifies each NTM and briefly describes its nature, identifies the country imposing the restriction, indicates the official source of information on the measure, and exporting countries affected by it. The latter information is particularly useful for analysing 'discriminatory' measures like bilateral quotas, 'voluntary' export restraints (VERs), the Multifibre Arrangement, or prohibitions applied against specific countries. In addition, the date(s) that the restriction was first imposed, modified or removed are recorded (if the latter actions occurred) along with the value of imports in the tariff-line item. For some countries like the United States, Japan and European Community the records are quite detailed and extend back to the mid-1960s. This permits some time-series analysis of changes in the level and structure of NTM use. A point to note, however, is that the inventory was compiled from official publications such as national customs schedules or GATT notifications. The reliance on official sources may cause the importance of some NTMs to be understated, especially in cases where a lack of 'transparency', or where measures like VERs are not reported in official publications. However, UNCTAD has endeavoured to check the accuracy of all entries in the data base by having these records verified by governments imposing the measures.[3]

A. Technical Aspects of the Data Base

Several technical points should be stressed concerning the Data Base and its applications. First, the information in the Data Base does not provide any indication of changes in the intensity of application of a measure. If, for example, quantitative restrictions are eased to permit increased imports this is not reflected in the basic statistics. Similarly, if the administration of health and safety regulations, or technical standards, becomes less rigorous it is not possible to incorporate this fact in the Data Base. Another problem is that the entries are usually made from national sources which utilise the tariff classification of the year the measure was introduced. This means that if changes in tariff classification occur, the Data Base contains a mixture of entries relating to tariff numbers from different years. This problem could be resolved if concordances existed for year-to-year changes in classification systems, but these are not available for most countries. Third, very little information is contained in the Data Base on measures that might be classified as nontariff 'distortions' to trade. These instruments, like export subsidies or special export rebate schemes, seek to improve the competitive position of domestic producers in foreign markets. These export incentives have been a major source of contention, particularly in agriculture (wheat, sugar and dairy products) as well as ferrous metals.

For empirical analysis involving NTM inventories several indices have been used. One measure is a frequency index (F_j) showing the percentage of tariff lines covered by some pre-selected group of nontariff measures,

$$F_j = (\Sigma D_i N_i \div N_t) \times 100 \tag{2.1}$$

where N_i is tariff line i, D_i is a dummy variable that takes a value of unity if one or more NTMs is applied to the item or zero otherwise, and N_t is the total number of lines in the product group. The above summation is made over all countries exporting to the importing country j. Given that matched tariff-line-level import statistics are available, in which individual countries of origin for shipments are identified, a second index showing the share of total imports subject to NTMs can be computed. This trade coverage measure (C_j) is defined as,

$$C_j = ((\Sigma D_{i,t-m} \times V_{i,t-n})/\Sigma V_{i,t-n}) \times 100 \tag{2.2}$$

where $V_{i,t-n}$ represents the value of imports in tariff-line item i in year $(t-n)$, and $D_{i,t}$ is a dummy variable that takes a value of unity if an NTM is applied to the item and zero otherwise.[4] If n and m are zero the index is based on current trade values, otherwise it is expressed in a base year trade weights. Holding n constant and varying m will measure the effects of changes in protection with constant trade weights. Since concordances exist between the UNCTAD inventory data and the SITC and CCCN systems, equations (2.1) and (2.2) can be computed for any product group in the latter classification systems.

B. Illustrative Empirical Applications

As an illustration of the empirical results produced using the UNCTAD Data Base, Table 2.2 shows the 1981 NTM 'own' trade coverage ratios for selected developed countries.[5] Coverage ratios based on total imports weights (excluding petroleum) are shown in column 2, while the ratios in column 1 are based on imports from developing countries. For comparison, NTM frequency ratios (column 3) are also shown. All three indices suggest NTMs are most prevalent in New Zealand, followed by Switzerland, Japan, Norway and Italy. The United States has one of the lower trade coverage ratios shown in the table (11.4 per cent), but these results are sensitive to the treatment of petroleum. When fuels (SITC 3) are included in the trade base both the United States and Finland produce much higher ratios.[6] Whether or not restrictions on fuels are included, however, New Zealand registers the highest NTM ratios due to an extensive

Table 2.2   Extent of industrial countries' nontariff measures in 1981

Importer	Trade coverage ratio[1] Developing countries	All imports	Frequency ratio[1]
European Community	21.7	13.4	11.4
Belgium-Luxembourg	12.4	12.6	8.4
Denmark	20.9	6.7	9.0
France	15.5	15.7	13.5
Germany, Fed. Rep.	24.3	11.8	11.1
Greece	12.5	16.2	10.4
Ireland	15.6	8.2	6.3
Italy	21.2	17.2	18.1
Netherlands	27.0	19.9	11.0
United Kingdom	25.4	11.2	10.1
Finland	15.3	7.9	3.4
Japan	17.4	24.4	12.7
New Zealand	35.3	46.4	45.0
Norway	46.9	15.2	19.8
Switzerland	18.1	19.5	9.7
United States	15.5	11.4	4.8

[1] Excludes petroleum products.

Note: The ratios shown in this table include: variable import levies and product-specific charges; quotas; prohibitions; non-automatic import authorisations; import licensing requirements (restrictive); 'voluntary' export restraints; and trade restraints under the Multifibre Arrangement.

quota and licensing scheme for most manufactured imports. The results for Norway (i.e. an overall trade coverage ratio of 15 per cent and a frequency index of almost 20 per cent) is largely due to NTBs on agricultural products, while Japan's 24 per cent coverage ratio is heavily influenced by global quotas on coal. In most cases, the trade coverage ratios are higher for developing-country products, although there are a few situations where the 'all' country ratios are higher.

While Table 2.2 illustrates how NTM inventories can be employed for analysis of restrictions in importing markets, they have also been used to assess measures facing specific exporting countries. As an illustration, Table 2.3 shows NTM 'own' trade coverage ratios (and tariffs) for eight Latin American countries which had external debts of over five billion dollars in 1986 (Argentina, Brazil, Colombia, Chile, Ecuador, Mexico, Peru and Venezuela), as well as eight heavily indebted countries outside the region.[7] The NTM coverage ratios range from zero, in the case of Venezuela's exports to Austria, to

Table 2.3 Tariff and nontariff barriers facing imports from selected heavily indebted developing countries in major developed country markets

Exporter	1980 value of imports (US$ mill.)							Average tariff rate							Share of imports subject to NTBs						
	Austria	EEC(9)	Japan	Norway	Sweden	Switz-erland	USA	Austria	EEC(9)	Japan	Norway	Sweden	Switz-erland	USA	Austria	EEC(9)	Japan	Norway	Sweden	Switz-erland	USA
1. Latin America																					
Argentina	24	2435	293	25	54	70	739	3.4	4.2	3.2	1.8	0.8	1.7	4.2	16.2	34.0	21.1	71.3	33.3	82.4	0.6
Brazil	153	5705	1558	141	257	157	3969	1.2	2.3	6.5	0.5	0.6	4.2	2.6	40.7	27.7	6.3	6.5	69.8	45.3	10.2
Colombia	41	1498	175	54	150	69	1326	0.5	5.2	2.6	1.3	1.0	5.2	1.8	75.8	73.3	2.0	5.1	98.7	37.6	5.5
Chile	22	1818	650	3	67	7	536	0.8	0.4	1.1	1.1	0.1	1.2	1.1	11.9	12.7	12.6	36.5	7.1	50.6	8.3
Ecuador	19	250	247	1	36	9	850	0.1	6.9	14.6	0.0	0.1	6.2	0.4	34.4	2.8	5.0	2.6	15.0	95.8	3.6
Mexico	19	1463	934	6	42	50	12715	3.5	3.8	11.9	1.8	2.6	2.4	3.7	15.4	8.1	8.6	2.1	4.3	41.8	5.8
Peru	17	707	480	2	34	27	1425	0.8	0.7	1.0	0.9	1.2	0.7	0.4	4.2	15.2	1.5	0.4	1.5	18.1	1.9
Venezuela	38	2276	683	56	396	9	5547	0.0	2.2	2.1	0.0	0.0	0.3	0.6	0.0	7.5	0.7	0.0	0.0	71.0	0.1
2. Other indebted developing countries																					
Algeria	143	5579	451	1	11	40	6881	2.7	0.0	1.9	0.0	0.0	1.3	0.8	0.0	8.9	7.1	0.0	0.0	99.9	0.0
Egypt	29	2806	142	2	4	43	487	1.2	1.2	0.3	3.9	3.7	1.9	1.1	3.5	22.4	0.2	2.0	17.8	27.6	7.0
Rep. of Korea	69	2993	2744	38	152	68	4428	13.4	8.9	7.4	2.9	8.6	5.0	10.6	0.3	32.7	27.5	25.1	40.4	19.1	33.6
Morocco	3	1641	85	21	29	28	41	2.0	1.3	1.2	0.2	0.1	2.5	4.1	25.5	40.1	49.9	1.3	2.0	39.3	1.0
Pakistan	28	1145	1951	14	31	18	1910	3.7	1.3	14.8	3.6	1.6	7.9	3.7	0.0	30.1	21.1	3.2	37.0	9.4	71.1
Turkey	61	1377	39	7	40	68	186	3.9	1.6	69.3	0.7	1.7	1.6	7.5	1.3	28.2	1.1	2.8	4.3	41.0	2.1
Yugoslavia	199	3540	41	16	87	104	448	6.7	5.5	53.0	5.6	5.8	4.6	2.7	22.9	39.9	1.2	20.9	41.6	35.2	19.8

Note: The tariff rates shown are the average of tariffs actually applied to each individual exporting country (i.e. the average of the MFN or preferential import duty). The NTB coverage ratios include the following types of non-tariff measures: voluntary export restraints; prohibitions; quantitative restrictions; import authorisation systems; restrictions under the Multifibre Arrangement; tariff quotas; variable import levies; anti-dumping and countervailing investigations and duties; minimum import price regulations; and import surveillance systems.

Source: Laird and Yeats (1987a).

over 95 per cent for Colombia's exports to Sweden. The table also indicates considerable variation in the application of nontariff measures in seven industrial markets, with the average NTM ratio for the United States and Japan's imports standing at 11 per cent, as opposed to 26 per cent in the EEC and 48 per cent in Switzerland. Finally, countries like Republic of Korea and Argentina that export a relatively high share of labour-intensive or temperate-zone agricultural products encounter higher trade coverage ratios than other indebted developing countries.

While Chapter 4 provides more detailed results from the Data Base, it should be noted that the inventory approach appears to have a limited potential for analysis of socialist countries' trade regimes. The import decision of firms in market-economy countries is affected to a great degree by tariffs and NTMs on foreign goods. However, in socialist countries, these measures do not have the same importance since imports depend largely on the State planning authority. The greater the degree of planning the less important are product-specific measures like those used in market economies. As such, the compilation of product-specific NTMs in a uniform format would not be of the same utility as is such information for market economy countries. What would appear to be useful, however, are objective measures of potential trade for these countries that could be compared with the actual value of imports. Balassa (1986), Yeats (1982) and Linnemann (1966) have developed empirical procedures that may prove useful for this purpose.

ECONOMIC EFFECTS OF NTBs: A GENERAL ANALYSIS

For many research and policy studies more precise information is needed on the trade and economic effects of measures operating as barriers (NTBs) than can be derived from existing inventories. In this respect, Figure 2.1 provides a framework for analysing the influence of a nontariff barrier in a country that imposes the measure. Panel 2.1a examines the effects of a NTB that influences foreign demand, such as a quantitative restriction or variable import levy, while panel 2.1b deals with measures like 'voluntary' export restraints or the Multifibre Arrangement that primarily affect import supply.

In Figure 2.1a, *DD* represents the free trade import demand curve for a foreign good while the supply curve for exports from abroad is *SS*. Initially, the equilibrium price and quantity is P_0 and Q_0, respectively, and then a volume-restraining NTB, say a quota, is imposed

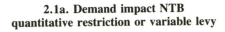

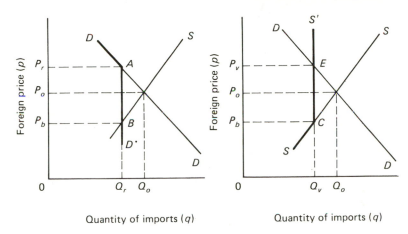

Figure 2.1   The general price and quantity effects of a nontariff barrier

that limits imports to the quantity Q_r. The quota causes import demand to become vertical at the restricted volume. That is, to foreign suppliers the demand curve seems to have shifted from DD to $DABD'$. The quantity imported under the quota falls by Q_0Q_r while the price of the good on the domestic market rises initially to OP_r and the world (foreign) price falls to P_b. Since consumers now pay P_r, while foreign exporters receive P_b, the difference P_bP_r represents a premium that will be collected by exporters, importers, or the government, depending on how the quota is administered.[8]

In contrast to a nontariff barrier which affects import demand, Figure 2.1b examines the effects of measures like VERs that influence the supply of exports. Here, P_0 and Q_0 represent the free trade price and quantity of the good imported and then a 'voluntary' agreement is reached with foreign suppliers to limit exports to Q_v. In this case, domestic consumers perceive the foreign supply curve as having shifted to $SCES'$ and becoming vertical at the agreed export limit (Q_v). The export restraint produces a premium of P_bP_v, with P_b and P_v representing prices received by foreign producers and paid by domestic consumers respectively. As was the case with an export quota, the price differential P_bP_v will be appropriated by importers, exporters or the government as an NTB rent.

As these examples show, nontariff barriers influence import

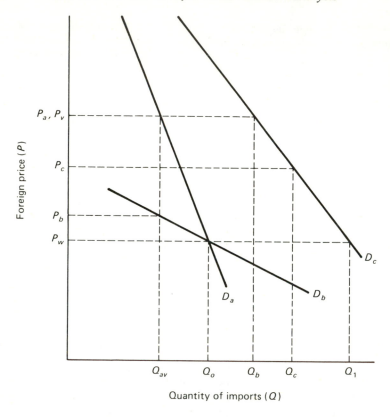

Figure 2.2   Analysis of the influence of different demand conditions on price impact measures for NTBS

demand or supply curves and this fact could be useful for analysing their effects. Specifically, Figure 2.1 suggests that a price impact measure could quantify the effects of nontariff barriers. That is, if information were available on the change in consumer prices $(P_0 P_r)$, exporter prices $(P_0 P_b)$, or differences between domestic and foreign prices of the good $(P_r P_b)$ this may be useful for measuring the restriction's incidence. One problem with this approach, however, is that price impact measures incorporate the combined influence of the NTB and the supply and demand schedules. Two identical NTBs, applied in two almost identical markets, could have very different price and quantity effects if demand or supply conditions differ.

Figure 2.2 illustrates how differences in supply and demand may bias NTB price impact measures. Here, the import demand schedules for a given product in countries A, B, and C are shown while exporter's supply is assumed to be perfectly elastic and represented by the horizontal line P_w. In a free trade situation, A and B both import the same quantity of the good (Q_0). However, if identical absolute and percentage quantitative restrictions (Q_0Q_{av}) are applied the resulting price increase is higher in A than in B (P_aP_w is greater than P_bP_w) because internal demand in the former is more price inelastic. The higher price impact measure in A than B is misleading since import barriers are the same in both countries.

Additional problems with the use of price impact measures can arise when import markets are not equal in size. Consider two countries, A and C, which import different quantities of a commodity. In Figure 2.2, D_c and D_a are these countries' demand curves which are assumed to have the same elasticity at each price. If C reduces imports by a quota of the same absolute amount as A, i.e., Q_0Q_{av} equals Q_1Q_c, the resulting price increase in the former (P_cP_w) will be less than that in A ($P_a' \ P_w$). On the other hand, since the elasticities of D_c and D_a are equal, identical percentage reductions in imports (Q_1Q_b, and Q_0Q_{av}) lead to identical price increases, that is P_aP_w equals P_vP_w. These two examples demonstrate that, given different volumes of imports, with identical demand elasticities, price impact measures accurately reflect different percentage reductions in imports but not different absolute reductions.[9]

Since Figures 2.1 and 2.2 show an NTB influences both the price and quantity of imports, the effects of the restriction could be assessed by a quantity impact measure. The difficulty with this approach, however, is that there is generally no reliable (free trade) quantity figure with which to compare the quantity of imports under a restriction. Importers generally have some advance notification of a NTB's imposition so prior trade could be inflated. Also, the longer the interval after the restriction was imposed the more difficult it is to even roughly approximate the 'free trade' import volume since this will be altered by changing tastes, changing incomes, new sources of supply, or the availability of new substitute products. For specific barriers that are alternatively applied and removed, like a seasonal quota, it may be possible to construct a time-series econometric model and approximate what imports would be without the restriction. However, most quantity reducing nontariff barriers are not applied in such an 'on and off' fashion, so these procedures have a limited utility. Alternatively, efforts have been made to 'fit' econometric models using data from a period prior to an NTB's imposition and then project quantities (and prices) in the period when the barrier was operative. Differences between actual and projected imports could provide a quantity impact measure of the NTB's effects. (See OECD, 1985b and 1985d for illustrations of this approach.) However, the possibility always exists that residuals in econometric projections will be influenced by factors other than the trade restriction.

The preceding discussion shows major conceptual and operational problems are often encountered in attempting to derive price and quantity impact measures for nontariff barriers.[10] Even when reliable estimates of price and quantity changes resulting from NTBs are available they may not be useful for cross-country or cross-industry studies since they incorporate the influence of additional factors like supply and demand differences. Aside from these conceptual problems, other practical difficulties could be a major problem in efforts to actually compute NTB impact measures. Volatile exchange rate changes, for example, could make it difficult to translate import prices into domestic currency equivalents required for estimating price impact measures. Third-country protectionist practices may also have a significant influence on the foreign supply curve for exports, and thus affect differences between domestic and import prices. For some agricultural products world prices have been significantly affected (lowered) by export subsidies, so domestic–foreign price differences would be a biased (upward) indicator of actual protection levels.

A. Formulation of Price Impact Measures for NTBs

In spite of their limitations, several studies attempted to quantify NTBs by computing price impact measures.[11] These investigations have

$$R_p = (P_r \div E_{xi} P_b) \times 100 \tag{2.4}$$

utilised differences in domestic and foreign prices, e.g. P_r and P_b in Figure 2.1a, and have taken the form of price relatives (R_p), or were expressed as a percentage difference between the prices,

$$T_e = ((P_r - E_{xi} P_b) \div E_{xi} P_b) \times 100 \tag{2.5}$$

$$= ((P_r \div E_{xi} P_b) - 1) \times 100$$

where E_{xi} is the exchange rate between the currency of the exporting and importing country.[12] Estimates derived from equation (2.4) have been called 'nominal protection coefficients' while those from equation (2.5) are referred to as 'implicit tariffs' or 'tariff equivalents' of the nontariff barriers.

Several operational problems often arise in applying the above equations with a major difficulty centering on which prices should be used. Imported goods are often not identical to those produced domestically so there may be several possible price combinations involving different qualities or grades of products. Ideally, equations (2.4) and (2.5) should employ the price of the closest domestic substitute as a proxy for P_r, while P_b should be the c.i.f invoice price of the foreign good facing the NTB inclusive of tariffs and any special taxes. In some cases, unit values calculated from national tariff-line-level import statistics for homogenous items like steel, cement or some agricultural produce can be used for the latter, but generally this data is too aggregate to be employed for price comparisons.[13] Another complication is that price comparisons are often not able to account for transport costs inside the country. Domestic wholesale prices are normally recorded at or near consuming centres whereas border prices are normally compiled at ports of entry. Westlake (1987) demonstrated that sampling domestic and import prices at different locations in the same country could significantly bias nominal protection coefficients derived from such data. In addition, the domestic–foreign price ratio for any one year could be distorted by transitory factors such as a bad harvest. Finally, the comparisons utilise world prices that prevail under protection and these may be significantly lower than prices under free trade.

A further operational problem associated with equations (2.4) and (2.5) is that this approach can be biased by the degree of substitutability between domestic and foreign goods. If domestic and foreign goods are close substitutes, and if foreign producers are in a position to appropriate most of the NTB rent, a very restrictive barrier may produce only a small foreign and domestic price differential. In this case, the alternative is to collect wholesale prices of the good in several countries and take the lowest observed price as the standard for comparison (i.e., as a proxy for P_b in Figure 2.1). After the influence of transport costs, tariffs and quality differences have been accounted for this 'minimum' price could be employed in equations (2.4) and (2.5) for the computation of NTB price impact measures.

As an illustration of this empirical approach, Roningen and Yeats (1976) compiled price statistics for ninety finely specified products known to face nontariff barriers in fifteen developed countries.[14] This analysis took the comparison or 'world' price (P_b) to be the lowest observed price in any country after the influence of domestic sales and excise taxes, tariffs and other charges were eliminated and allowance was made for transport costs. After these adjustments, residual elements were assumed to reflect NTBs although it was recognised that differences in supply and demand elasticities could bias the results. The findings for France, Japan, Sweden and the United States, aggregated to 21 two-digit BTN product groups, are summarised in Table 2.4. Pre-Tokyo tariff averages are also shown in the table as are NTB frequency indices (equation (2.1)). Separate tests indicate the latter were not significantly correlated with the price impact measures.

Overall, Table 2.4 shows Japan and Sweden had the highest price impact measures (equation (2.5) results average about 70 per cent) followed by France and the United States at 40 and 35 per cent respectively. However, these figures still incorporate the influence of international transportion charges which produce price differences between countries. Using estimates of United States and German freight costs as a guide, the average relatives in Table 2.4 were reduced by about 10 to 15 percentage points to arrive at a 'pure' NTB residual.[15] The resulting figures suggest that the average *ad valorem* equivalent of NTBs facing these products ranges from 20 to 25 per cent in the United States and France and from 50 to 60 per cent for Japan and Sweden.

B. Quantity Impact Measures for NTBs

Figures 2.1 and 2.2 show that quantity impact measures could be employed for empirical analysis of NTBs, except that it is often difficult to approximate the 'free trade' volume of imports needed for these comparisons.[16] However, there are several empirical approaches that could produce potentially useful information. One procedure could utilise 'gravity flow' trade models which are based on the proposition that bilateral exports can be explained by a relatively few variables such as: (a) the gross national product of the exporting country (Y_i); (b) the GNP of the importing country (Y_j); and (c) the distance between the two countries (D_{ij}). The relevance of these variables is the proposition that the quantity of exports a country can supply depends on its economic size or GNP; the absorptive capacity for imports is determined by the size of the country's

Table 2.4 Estimated nominal equivalent for nontariff barriers in France, Japan, Sweden and the United States, 1973
(per cent)

BTN	Product group	France Nominal tariff	France NTBs Reported frequency	France NTBs Price impact	Japan Nominal tariff	Japan NTBs Reported frequency	Japan NTBs Price impact	Sweden Nominal tariff	Sweden NTBs Reported frequency	Sweden NTBs Price impact	USA Nominal tariff	USA NTBs Reported frequency	USA NTBs Price impact
02	Meat products	15	100	67	13	17	161	0	83	133	7	50	54
03	Fish and seafood	10	33	34	8	100	72	0	66	64	1	100	78
04	Dairy products	18	83	15	35	50	10	0	–	23	10	66	0
07	Vegetables & products	12	66	30	12	17	72	7	17	80	13	100	50
08	Edible fruits & nuts	14	46	22	14	23	180	4	23	51	7	69	128
09	Coffee, tea & spices	10	–	83	6	–	155	1	–	100	1	30	38
10	Cereals	13	100	11	11	43	16	0	100	12	5	43	0
11	Mill products	21	100	40	25	44	158	0	18	85	8	33	57
15	Fats & oils	7	29	0	8	–	50	18	80	94	5	12	0
17	Sugar & products	38	20	9	66	20	68	5	–	51	6	80	23
18	Cocoa & products	12	17	0	16	–	157	19	–	47	2	50	2
19	Cereal preparations	10	63	94	23	57	92	11	14	113	5	88	47
20	Vegetable preparations	23	86	63	23	10	76	8	40	54	13	86	3
22	Beverages	28	50	0	47	100	0	14	–	73	5	20	19
24	Tobacco & products	74	100	0	352	100	0	20	–	72	20	–	0
48	Paper & products	7	5	67	13	–	33	5	100	75	5	–	39
60	Knitted goods	13	100	92	16	–	44	28	100	15	28	100	61
61	Apparel	15	100	16	19	–	0	21	36	0	21	100	32
64	Footwear[1]	17	–	28	18	17	11	15	–	62	15	–	70
82	Tools & cutlery	7	–	41	12	–	59	17	–	121	17	7	82
92	Instruments & recorders	6	–	25	10	–	32	6	–	41	–	–	0
	All item average	17	45	40	32	19	70	7	22	70	9	41	35

Note: The figures on reported NTB frequencies show the percentage of tariff-line-level products in the two-digit BTN product group that face major forms of nontariff barriers. These statistics have been computed using data contained in the UNCTAD Inventory of Non-Tariff Measures. The statistics shown under 'price impact' have had the effects of tariffs and other special taxes netted out of the gross margins.

Source: Roningen and Yeats (1976).

market (i.e. the GNP of the importing country); and the volume of trade will depend on transportation costs which are assumed to correspond roughly to the distance between the two countries. The distance term has also been taken as an (inverse) index of available information about export markets. The trade flow equation expressed in its simplest form is then,

$$\log E_{ij} = a_1 \log Y_i + a_2 \log Y_j + a_3 \log D_{ij} \tag{2.7}$$

where E_{ij} represents exports of country i to country j.[17]

Projections of 'expected' trade from equation (2.7), or some related version of the model, are taken as proxies for the free trade import volumes, e.g., Q_f in equation (2.6) (see note 17) and situations are 'flagged' where estimated trade deviates from actual trade by a sizeable margin. Large positive deviations (projected minus actual) have been interpreted as possible evidence of trade restrictions although no previous attempts have been made to determine if there were specific nontariff measures where such differences occurred. Obviously, the utility of the approach depends on how accurately the gravity model can project 'free trade' import volumes.

A logical extension of the model would be to include variables reflecting trade intervention in equation (2.7) and statistically test their effects. Roningen (1978) conducted such an analysis using a cross-section model of fourteen OECD countries' aggregate annual bilateral trade flows over 1967–73. The model's explanatory variables included gross domestic product, country surface area (to reflect the potential size of the domestic and foreign sectors), distance, and dummy variables for preferential trading arrangements and common language. A general index of restrictiveness for each country's exchange, payments, and trade regimes was also employed. This measure was a simple count of twelve specific restrictions listed in the IMF *Annual Report on Exchange Restrictions* (e.g. more than one exchange rate, restrictions on current transaction payments, import surcharges, advance deposit requirements, etc.). Separate indices were also constructed when these restrictions were classified as applying primarily to exchange controls, payments requirements, or the control of trade levels.[18] Two regressions were tested. In the first, the aggregate restriction index was used, while in the second the three partial restriction indices were employed as explanatory variables.

Roningen's 1970 to 1973 results for all countries combined are given in Table 2.5. The regression coefficient for the general restriction index takes the expected negative sign and is statistically significant for the exporting, but not for the importing, countries. This was the case as well in the individual country results. The results employing separate restriction indexes were generally inconclusive since, in several cases, the regression coefficients were statistically significant, but with the opposite directional sign predicted by theory. Although the equations were able to 'explain' 80 to 90 per cent of the variation in trade flows the 'trade restriction' indices do not appear to have emerged as major explanatory variables.

A second related empirical approach for analysis of NTBs was undertaken by McCulloch and Hilton (1983) for the Federal Reserve Bank of New York. This study regressed bilateral trade flows across commodities on variables which measure bilateral production costs. The model took the form,

$$\ln T_j = a_1 + a_2 C_j \tag{2.8}$$

where T_j is the ratio of exports to imports between two regions for commodity j, and C_j is the relative difference in production costs for j. Equation (2.8) was applied to US trade with eight major countries or country groups (Canada, UK, France, Germany, Italy, South Asia, East Asia and Japan) in some 296 industries defined in terms of the United States input–output table. The relationship between relative costs and relative input prices for two countries producing the jth good was expressed as,

$$C_j = \Sigma \theta_{ij} w_j \tag{2.9}$$

where θ_{ij} is the value share of factor i in the production of commodity j and W_i is the relative difference in the price of five endowment variables: unskilled labour, skilled labour, capital, land and natural resources.

The predicted trade ratios from equation (2.8) were compared with the actual ratios and a large difference was taken as possible evidence of a nontariff intervention. A confidence interval was established for the 'normal' variation in T_j, and it was found that in about 20 per cent of the cases the export/import ratio fell below this designated range. These cases identified US 'under performance' and the possibility that NTBs were a factor restraining this trade. The smallest number of these distortions occurred in trade with Canada, Federal Republic

Table 2.5 Regression results for bilateral trade flows between OECD countries, 1970 to 1973

Variable	1973 Coefficient	t value	1972 Coefficient	t value	1971 Coefficient	t value	1970 Coefficient	t value
Constant term	-6.92	(12.7)	-7.05	(11.4)	-5.95	(10.3)	-5.96	(9.89)
Exporting country GDP (Y_i)	0.90	(28.1)	0.91	(24.9)	0.88	(26.7)	0.92	(26.1)
Importing country GDP (Y_j)	0.85	(26.7)	0.86	(23.5)	0.79	(24.0)	0.88	(24.8)
Exporting country area (A_i)	-0.07	(2.43)	-0.09	(2.53)	-0.07	(2.18)	-0.10	(2.82)
Importing country area (A_j)	-0.07	(2.21)	-0.04	(1.19)	-0.07	(2.00)	-0.14	(3.95)
Distance (d)	-0.76	(15.3)	-0.78	(14.5)	0.75	(14.3)	-0.72	(12.6)
Preference dummy (m)	0.67	(6.11)	0.79	(6.79)	(0.83)	(7.39)	0.72	(5.78)
Language dummy (l)	0.66	(5.34)	0.58	(4.31)	(0.69)	(5.28)	0.72	(4.99)
General restriction index								
Exporting country (r_i)	-0.08	(5.02)	-0.09	(4.70)	-0.12	(6.54)	0.11	(5.57)
Importing country (r_j)	-0.01	(0.84)	-0.02	(0.91)	-0.04	(2.00)	-0.05	(2.56)
R^2	0.89	–	0.88	–	0.89	–	0.87	–

Source: Adapted from Roningen (1978).

of Germany and the United Kingdom, and the most with East and South Asia. Apparent NTBs affecting US trade with Germany were concentrated in agricultural products and processed foods, while they were clustered in office, computing and accounting machinery, motor vehicles and some other transport equipment in trade with Japan.

While gravity-flow and related regression models have the potential to be useful for NTB analysis, they probably have not been developed sufficiently that they can be used without major reservations. The fact that these models attribute all departures of actual from predicted trade to NTBs weakens their utility since the less precise the specification the greater these residuals will be. However, there are several lines of empirical analysis involving these models that could be potentially important. Specifically, an attempt should be made to extend Roningen's regression model to include comprehensive NTB frequency and coverage indices as explanatory variables. Such an approach could overcome some of the major shortcomings of the IMF restrictions information. Chapter 4 provides detailed NTB coverage and frequency indices that could be employed in these tests. Second, it appears useful to independently test these models' projections against entries in existing NTB inventories. For example, it would be useful to know if there is a strong correlation between projections of trade 'underperformance' and entries in the UNCTAD Data Base on trade measures. Research aimed at resolving this question would serve a dual purpose: it would assist in verifying the models' projections and it could also assist in providing a quantitative dimension to some of the entries in the inventory. That is, it could be useful in ranking the relative importance of the individual entries and assist in distinguishing between nontariff measures and nontariff barriers.

C. A Control Group Approach to NTB Measurement

Apart from the use of gravity-flow and related regression models, in some situations a control-group approach may help in estimating the quantity impact of a nontariff barrier. This methodology might be used where a product had an NTB applied to it at a specific point in time while a related item, with similar supply and demand characteristics, continued to be traded freely. In this case, the quantity effects of the NTB could possibly be approximated by comparing subsequent import growth rates for the product facing the restriction and the control group items. Specifically, an equation of the following form could be used,

$$dQ = ((G_{c,t+n} - G_{a,t+n}) - (G_{c,t} - G_{a,t})) \times Q_{a,t} \qquad (2.10)$$

where G_a and G_c are annualised import growth rates for the affected product and control group, t is a period before and $t+n$ a period after the NTB is applied, $Q_{a,t}$ is the quantity of imports of the affected product, and dQ is the estimated trade loss due to the NTB. Aside from growth rates, other performance variables, like changes in import-penetration ratios, changes in per capita imports, or changes in the ratio of imports to GNP could be employed in equation (2.10). In each case, the objective would be to determine how the performance variables for the control group differed from those of the affected product.[19]

The difficulty with the control-group approach is that it assumes the NTB on the affected product will not influence the performance variables of the items that continue to be traded freely. Since the two were chosen on the basis of similar supply and demand characteristics, imports of the control group should increase if consumers can switch from restricted items to these products. However, an offsetting effect could result if the NTB increases uncertainty in trade of substitute items. Foreign suppliers of the control-group products might feel that the restriction could spread to their own related items and react to this threat by holding exports below their potential. Thirdly, the performance variables may have been distorted by importers anticipating the NTB prior to its official enactment. That is, abnormally large imports could have occurred if consumers attempted to beat the restriction and this would have distorted the normal relation between the control group and affected products. Finally, it is possible that factors such as changing tastes, incomes or supply conditions could alter the previous relation between the control group and other products after the NTB's imposition. Any of these developments could produce major biases in the control-group approach.

METHODS FOR QUANTIFYING SPECIFIC NONTARIFF BARRIERS

Several important nontariff barriers such as quotas, variable import levies, 'voluntary' export restraints, and government procurement regulations can be quantified using specific methodologies relating to these restrictions. While these approaches may be subject to the same potential biases as the general NTB price and quantity impact measures, which of course can also be computed for these restrictions, they appear to be useful for providing 'order-of-magnitude' estimates for these NTBs' effects. The following sections examine these empirical approaches and also indicate some of the difficulties that may be encountered in their actual application.

A. Variable Import Levies

Variable levies are used primarily to protect agricultural products in the European Community and some EFTA countries (particularly Sweden), although the United States has applied similar charges on sugar imports. Levies are designed to achieve domestic price stability by imposing a charge on imports which varies to hold the landed prices of foreign goods constant. The levy may change daily, with the customs official responsible for collecting the difference between the domestic (target) and the foreign (world) invoice of the product. Alternatively, it may be fixed for as long as three months. In cases where domestic prices are higher than foreign prices the levies reverse sign and become a subsidy on exports. However, EEC and Swedish levies are generally positive with several studies suggesting their *ad valorem* equivalents may often range between 50 to 100 per cent or more. See Sampson and Yeats (1976; 1977) for estimates of the *ad valorem* incidence of European variable levies.

While regulations differ according to commodities, the basic elements of the EEC levy system are as follows. First, a target price, (P_t) is established each year in advance of the following crop year. This price is intended to serve as a guide for producers in allotting future acreage. Since transportation charges influence price differentials within the EEC, the target price is set as the delivered c.i.f. price in Duisberg, Germany, the greatest grain deficit (production minus consumption) region in the Community. Next, an intervention price (P_i) is established (generally not more than 10 per cent below the target price) which is guaranteed to farmers. Finally, threshold prices (P_h) are used to insulate domestic prices from fluctuations in world price (P_w) levels. The threshold price equals the target price minus transport costs from each port of entry to the centre of largest deficit. Imports are subject to a variable levy (L_i) that equals the excess of the threshold over the world price.[20]

Empirically, an approximation of a variable levy's nominal equivalent, or, for that matter, any nontariff barrier expressed as a fixed monetary charge per unit of import, may be derived using procedures employed to convert specific tariffs to nominal equivalents. (See Yeats, 1976, for an analysis of potential biases associated with these approaches.) For example, GATT has published tariff-line-level estimates of _ad valorem_ equivalents for levies (N_{11}) by computing the following ratio,

$$N_{11} = (R_i \div M_i) \times 100 \qquad (2.14)$$

where R_i is the revenue collected by the levy over a specific interval and M_i is the total value of imports to which the levy is applied. UNCTAD estimated nominal equivalents by taking the ratio,

$$N_{21} = (L_i \div U_i) \times 100 \qquad (2.15)$$

where L_i is the average value of the levy over a given period and U_i is the unit value of the product covered.

Table 2.6 summarises the results of an analysis that employed equation (2.14) to estimate nominal equivalents for Sweden's variable levies. As shown, levies are extensively applied to imported agricultural products in SITC 4 (animal and vegetable oils) and SITC 0 (food and live animals). Perhaps the most striking point from the table concerns the relative height of the average nominal tariff and average _ad valorem_ equivalent of the variable levies. In SITC 0, for example, a nominal tariff of 3.6 per cent is coupled with a levy of more than ten times this figure. In SITC 4, tariffs emerge as being almost negligible, but levies average close to 80 per cent. However, for sugar and honey preparations (SITC 06) and soft animal fats and oils (SITC 4) the _ad valorem_ equivalents of variable levies averaged 100 per cent. Table 2.6 also shows that over 50 per cent of the tariff line items in the meat (SITC 01), cereal (SITC 04) and fixed animal and vegetable oil (SITC 42) faced variable levies. Sampson and Yeats (1977) reached similar conclusions concerning the incidence and extent of application of EEC variable levies.

B. Quotas

An import quota is a government-imposed quantitative restriction on imports. That is, a country wishing to restrict imports of a particular good determines the amount to be admitted during a given period and then prohibits additional trade. The forced scarcity raises the

Table 2.6 Comparison of coverage and rates of protection from Swedish tariffs and variable levies

Description and SITC	Value of Sweden's imports ($000)	% coverage by levies[a]		Estimated average nominal rate[b]	
		Value of imports	Tariff line items	Tariffs	Levies
Food and live animals (0)	627 275	29.5	40.6	3.6	39.8
Meat preparations (01)	54 970	94.9	79.4	0.0	62.0
Dairy products and eggs (02)	15 471	100.0	100.0	0.0	77.3
Cereals and preparations (04)	33 385	41.2	48.0	6.3	65.9
Sugar, honey and preparations (06)	21 215	62.1	59.3	8.7	105.8
Misc. food preparations (109)	18 590	34.6	35.8	4.1	20.2
Beverages, tobacco and fuels (1+3)	826 185	0.0	0.0	12.2[c]	0.0
Crude materials, inedible (2)	614 485	1.8	2.8	0.3	77.3
Animal and vegetable oils (4)	39 855	63.2	50.0	0.2	78.7
Animal oils and fats (41)	8 619	5.6	44.5	0.0	116.2
Fixed vegetable oils (42)	22 885	90.0	77.3	0.1	77.7
Chemicals and plastics (5)	570 154	1.0	2.5	5.2	30.9
Machinery & manufactures (6+7+8)	3 314 553	0.0	0.0	8.9	0.0

[a] The value of imports covered by levies has been estimated using equation (2.2) while the average of tariff line items was computed using equation (2.1). See the text for a description of these indices.
[b] The ad valorem equivalents of Swedish variable levies have been estimated by taking the ratio of revenue collected by the levies to the value of imports in the product group to which they are applied. These estimates are made at the level of the tariff line and have been aggregated to one and two-digit SITC groups.
[c] Excluding fuels.
Source: Sampson and Yeats (1976).

domestic price of the good by the amount necessary to reduce demand. This, in turn, means that somewhere along the distribution chain from the foreign producer to the domestic consumer, a premium is added to the restricted good's price (see Figure 2.1a). Who receives the premium depends on how the quota is administered.

The administration method generally held to be the most efficient involves the auctioning of import licences. Under such a system the government annually prints licences to import the quantity set by the quota and sells the licences in competitive bidding. If these licences can be resold on a secondary market, competition should equate their price with the anticipated difference between the price of the good on the domestic (import) market and world market. In such a situation, the ratio of the quota licence's price to the value of authorised imports provides a measure of the restriction's incidence. It should also be noted that this method of administration allows the government to collect the quota's premium as revenue in contrast with a procedure where import rights are freely distributed to domestic firms.[21]

As far as NTB price impact measures are concerned there are several reasons why quotas may pose difficulties. First, if quotas are allocated directly to consuming firms, who are discouraged from reselling these rights, the price P_r in Figure 2.1a will not occur in any actual market transactions. In this situation, a price impact measure like equation (2.4) or (2.5) could not be computed. Second, measurement problems may arise due to foreign supply response to the quota. If foreign firms (or governments) can raise the supply price for the good after the quota is imposed, possibly through counter-actions such as an export tax, it would be in their advantage to do so. In this case, the invoice price for imports could be raised close to P_r even though the quota may be quite restrictive. Price impact measures would, therefore, understate the true incidence of the quantitative restriction in such a situation.

The tendency for foreign suppliers facing a quota to upgrade their product and export a higher-quality and higher-priced item will reduce the utility of price impact measures.[22] An upgrading would enable exporters to increase returns within the quantity limits and cause the post-quota prices to rise even more than if such a product-shift did not occur. In some cases, so-called 'hedonic' or quality corrected price indices may be useful for separating the price effect of the quota from that due to product upgrading, but these procedures have not yet been employed in tests involving nontariff barriers.

While the methodologies are also as yet untested, 'limit pricing' models developed in the industrial organisation literature may be useful for assessing the effects of some nontariff trade barriers. These models are based on the proposition that pricing and other business practices of established firms are influenced by the threat of entry into the market by outside suppliers. Since a quota or other nontariff barrier reduces the threat of entry, analysis of pre- and post-restriction pricing practices (i.e. levels, frequency of change, cyclical behaviour, etc.) could yield useful information on the importance of the barrier and its economic effects.[23] The difficult problem is, of course, to develop an analytical framework that isolates the effects of the nontariff barrier from other external factors that would influence pricing policy.

C. Voluntary Export Restraints

A 'voluntary' export restraint (VER) is an agreement by an exporting-country government to restrict exports of a good to a specific importing country. Normally, the 'agreement' is reached through actual or implied economic pressure on the foreign suppliers. A very simplistic diagrammatic model of the VER's operation was given in Figure 2.1b where it is assumed that one exporting country provides the good, the free trade supply and demand curves for imports are SS and DD respectively, while the equilibrium price and quantity are P_0 and Q_0. If a VER restricts exports to Q_v this results in a new kinked supply curve $SCES'$. The foreign supplier's price falls to P_b while the price on the domestic market rises to P_v. If export quotas are auctioned by the government, Figure 2.1b suggests their prices could be used to quantify the VER's rent element. Such sales would also allow the government to collect these premiums as revenue.

Previous efforts to quantify the effects of VERs follow Hamilton's (1984a; 1984b; 1985) studies for Asian textile exporters. In these investigations, data were collected on monthly prices of Hong Kong export licences for different clothing articles shipped to Austria, Denmark, Finland, France, Federal Republic of Germany, Italy, Sweden, United Kingdom and the United States. These MFA export quota prices, which were assumed to measure the VER's rents, were then expressed as a ratio to the export product's unit value. Table 2.7 shows the average tariff equivalents of the VERs estimated by this procedure over 1981 to 1983, the average import tariff, and the combined trade barrier (tariffs plus VER) in each market. Hamilton's

Table 2.7   Estimated levels of tariff and NTB protection for clothing in
selected industrial countries, 1981–3
(*ad valorem* equivalents)

Country	Average tariff	Import licence tariff equivalent	Estimated total trade barrier (%)[a]
Sweden (EFTA)	14	29	47
Benelux (EEC)	17	14	33
Denmark (EEC)	17	14	33
Finland (EFTA)	35	6	43
France (EEC)	17	13	32
Switzerland (EFTA)	13	n.a.	n.a.
United Kingdom (EEC)	17	15	35
Germany, Fed. Rep. of (EEC)	17	14	33
Austria (EFTA)	33	4	38
EEC-EFTA Average	17	15	35
USA	23	23	51

[a] Derived from (1 + tariff rate) × (1 + import tariff equivalent) to produce
an estimate of the total trade barrier.
Source: Hamilton (1984b) p. 104.

estimates suggest that the VER has an *ad valorem* equivalent ranging
from approximately 3 to 4 per cent for Italy and Austria with highs of
26 to 27 per cent for Sweden and the United States.

While the quota-price approach provides useful empirical information about the incidence of VERs, there are potential limitations.
First, it requires statistics on the export licence prices and this
information is available in relatively few countries. Second, for
cross-country comparisons supply and demand elasticities must be
equivalent or else the export quota rents may not provide an accurate
ranking of the relative size of the barriers (see the analysis connected
with Figure 2.2). Third, the approach assumes that exporters capture
all, or most of the VER's rent. If rents somehow accrue to importers,
export licence prices will understate the true effects of the restriction.
A bias could be caused by an 'upgrading' of products within the quota
as this would distort both quota licence prices and export unit values.
Two further complications could make it difficult to assess the influence of VERs or the extent of their application. Voluntary export
restraints are normally negotiated with a limited number of exporters, and they may stimulate increases in exports from other
sources of supply. This could depress the prices of the export licences

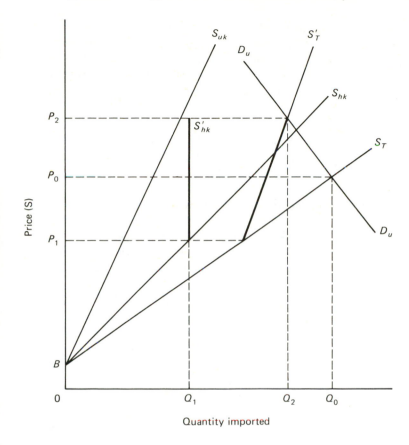

Figure 2.3   Analysis of the use of quota premium prices to estimate tariff
equivalents for voluntary export restraints

and cause the effects of the VER to be understated. Finally, since
VERs are often not reported in official documents, the 'inventory'
approach probably understates these measures' true frequency of
application and trade coverage.

Under certain conditions, import supply and demand relationships
can bias estimates of a VER's effects that are derived through the
quota price approach. Take, for example, the situation depicted in
Figure 2.3 where import demand is represented by D_u, and S_t is the
total supply curve. The latter is the sum of two individual countries'
export supply curves S_{hk} and S_{uk}, depicting (say) Hong Kong and the
United Kingdom respectively. If Hong Kong agrees to a VER limiting

its exports to OQ_1 its supply curve appears to become vertical at that point (it shifts to BS_{hk}') while the total supply curve becomes more inelastic at price P_1 (it becomes BS_T'). Figure 2.3 shows that the true price-increasing effects of the VER in the domestic market is ($P_2 - P_0$), or expressed as an implicit tariff ($P_2 - P_0$) ÷ P_0. However, an approach that employs observed quota prices utilises the ratio of the premium ($P_2 - P_1$) to the unit value of the export product (OP_1). The latter provides an upward biased estimate of the VER's true price effect in the domestic market if import supply is not perfectly elastic.[24]

D. Government Procurement Regulations

Procurement regulations which have been established in many countries may require government purchasers to favour domestically produced goods. For example, there may be a requirement that domestic goods be purchased unless their prices exceed those of similar foreign products by more than a stated percentage. While the Tokyo Round produced a code on government procurement practices it is still not uncommon for government purchasers to favour domestic suppliers. As such, it is important to develop objective standards for quantifying the magnitude of the associated trade bias.

Suppose government purchasers must purchase domestically produced goods unless imports can be obtained for (say) at least 20 per cent cheaper. Given this requirement, government procurement decisions will be made as though there were a 20 per cent tariff on imports. However, there are important differences between a procurement regulation and a tariff. First, unless the government is the sole purchaser of the good the implicit tariff relates to only a portion of total national consumption. Thus, when government and non-government consumers are aggregated, the size of the implicit tariff will be equal to 20 per cent times the share of government in total demand for the good. Also, depending on the characteristics of the good, the differential government and private sector demand may cause domestic firms to increase imports and resell the good to the government after sufficient further processing to qualify for the government preference. If this happens, the implicit tariff is further reduced. Accordingly, the size of the official procurement preference may overstate the true trade bias.

A difficulty often encountered in efforts to quantify the trade bias in government procurement is that the competing foreign and domestic good prices are often not made public for inclusion in price impact measures such as equations (2.4) or (2.5). However, Lowinger (1976) developed a useful model that overcomes some of these short-comings. The Lowinger approach first projects what government imports would be if the government had the private sectors' import propensities. In the absence of any discrimination, it is assumed that the government and private sector propensities would be equivalent since the latter attempt to maximise utility subject to their budget constraints. As such, the difference between actual and hypothetical government imports under equivalent import propensities may be a useful measure of discriminatory government purchasing practices (D),

$$D = M_a - \Sigma m_i Y_i \qquad (2.20)$$

where m_i is the private sector propensity to import good i, Y_i is total government purchases of i, and M_a is actual government imports aggregated over all the manufacturing sectors. To facilitate cross-country comparisons an overall index of discrimination (I_d) can be defined as,

$$I_d = (M_h \div M_a) \times 100 \qquad (2.21)$$

where M_h is the 'hypothetical' level of imports that would occur without the government preference.

The above procedure can also be further extended to derive a rough measure of the implicit tariff connected with government procurement. This approach attempts to estimate the incremental tariff rate that would cause a reduction of imports equal to the difference between hypothetical and actual government imports,

$$\Delta t = (M_h \times e \, \Delta t) \div (1 + t) \qquad (2.22)$$

which reduces to,

$$\Delta t = \Delta m \div (M_h \times e) \qquad (2.23)$$

if the tariff on government imports were initially zero.

While there appears not to have been any previous empirical tests, a question of some importance is whether Lowinger's approach could be used to assess biases in state trading of the socialist countries of

Eastern Europe. Specifically, a control country (say Austria, Sweden or Finland) might be selected and import propensities calculated on a sectorial basis. These propensities could then be utilised in equations (2.22) and (2.23) to calculate the state trading bias of socialist countries. However, it must be recognised that there are potential difficulties with the Lowinger approach. In some sectors, such as armaments, the government may be the sole national purchaser with the result that there are no observable private sector import propensities. Other factors, such as economies of scale in purchasing or size rebates, could cause government and private sector import propensities to differ. In these cases, equations (2.22) and (2.23) could be misleading as to the true magnitude of the trade bias in government procurement practices. Finally, tariffs and NTBs may have a major impact on private sector purchasing patterns and be a further reason why government and non-government import propensities should differ.

E. Countervailing and Anti-Dumping Duties

The most common measure to counteract dumping in an importing country is the imposition of a countervailing import duty.[25] Such a duty is normally part of a country's national tariff legislation, but its imposition often requires formal proceedings to prove that dumping occurred. For example, in the United States anti-dumping cases involve a two-step investigative procedure. First, the US Treasury Department determines whether an imported product is being sold at prices below those prevailing in the exporting country ('sales at less than fair value'). In cases of positive findings, the US International Trade Commission institutes an investigation to determine whether the American industry 'is being, or is likely to be injured, or is prevented from being established' due to such imports. In cases of affirmative determination, an anti-dumping duty is imposed by the Treasury. Such duties are assessed in addition to the normal tariff, and their size can vary depending on the magnitude of the underpricing.

While the above procedures may appear relatively straightforward, fluctuations in monetary exchange rates have greatly complicated the problem of determining whether imported goods are being sold below prices prevailing in the domestic markets of the exporting countries. In some cases a Treasury Department affirmative finding

Table 2.8   Analysis of the final outcome of anti-dumping and countervailing actions in the Developed Market Economy Countries (1979–82)

Information on actions	Total[d]	USA	EEC	Australia	Canada
Number of actions	824	295	159	217	148
Concluded actions[a]	740	275	144	189	128
Type of outcome:					
1. Claim not upheld	223	84	26	67	44
2. Duty levied[b]	245	43	39	93	68
3. Undertakings and other arrangements[c]	123	27	74	19	3
4. Termination or withdrawal	149	121	5	10	13

[a] Including actions for which information on the type of outcome is not available.
[b] Including actions when the claim was only partially upheld.
[c] Including price and volume undertakings by exporters (also in cases when claim was not upheld), suspended agreements, etc.
[d] Including actions initiated in Austria, Finland and Sweden

has been seemingly invalidated shortly afterward by sizeable movements in the relevant exchange rates. However, once imposed, anti-dumping duties can be quantified by procedures used for converting variable levies to *ad valorem* equivalents (see equations (2.14) and (2.15)) although a formal procedure for applying these duties can have trade distorting effects. As an example, the US steel trigger-price mechanism established a predetermined downward limit on the extent that import prices could fall without official action being taken. Foreign exporters would, therefore, charge higher prices than they might otherwise offer to avoid anti-dumping penalties. In such a situation, the established anti-dumping mechanism might have an important influence on foreign prices, although the fact that it was not actually operative precludes empirical assessment of its effects.

In some cases charges have been made that anti-dumping actions are initiated with the intent of 'harassing' foreign exporters. Related empirical evidence is presented in Table 2.8 which examines the outcomes of anti-dumping cases initiated in the early 1980s.[26] Out of 824 actions, results for final outcomes were available for 740 proceedings when the compilation was made (1983). In the remaining cases, the investigations were not completed or the published information was too ambiguous to determine a final outcome. In a few cases, information on the outcome could not be obtained. However, of the 740 actions for which information was available, 33 per cent resulted in the imposition of anti-dumping or countervailing duties, while 16.6 per cent resulted in price undertakings, export restraints or other commitments by exporters. Almost 20 per cent of the cases were terminated, generally because the petition was withdrawn, and 30 per cent of the cases were dismissed because the dumping claim was not substantiated.

The high share of dismissed cases may be interpreted either as evidence of the objectivity of the investigations, or as an indication that an excessive number of weak cases were filed. UNCTAD's (1984) cross-country comparisons show Australia had the highest share of cases where the claim was not upheld, while most EEC cases resulted in a positive finding. For further analysis, the continual tabulation of data on initiations and outcomes of anti-dumping actions (as in Table 2.8) should be useful for assessing their importance as trade harassment measures. In addition, 'case studies' which examined exporters' response to anti-dumping actions could help quantify these actions' trade effects. In one such analysis, Messerlin (1988) demonstrated that three years after the initiation of investigations, EEC anti-dumping measures reduced imported quantities by 40 per cent on average. In addition, the duties had average *ad valorem* equivalents of 23 per cent, which were added to existing protection. Further research is needed to determine if Messerlin's findings for the effects of EEC anti-dumping actions parallel those for other industrial country markets.[27]

SPECIAL PURPOSE ESTIMATION PROCEDURES

Aside from the general methods for quantifying NTBs, other procedures may be useful in special situations. For example, Deardorff and Stern (1985) show that many NTBs change the elasticity of import demand for affected products. This suggests that a cross-country analysis of elasticity estimates for specific products could provide a basis for quantifying nontariff barriers' effects. Employing cross-country elasticity estimates for given products, regression models may be able to 'explain' variations in these estimates in terms of country characteristics like level of development, availability of domestic substitutes, or the size of the market. The regression residuals could be used to 'flag' industries where the demand elasticities differ significantly from predicted values, possibly because of nontariff barriers.[28] As a supplementary test, it would be useful to cross-check the 'flagged' sectors with information in available inventories to see if NTBs were recorded for the industry. Similarly, time-series estimation of import demand elasticities in situations where an NTB was changing could help in quantifying the measures' effects.[29]

A. Econometric Modelling of Nontariff Barriers

In cases, industry econometric models may be useful for simulating the effects of nontariff barriers. This approach is most reliable when an industry model can be 'fitted' using data from a period in which trade was free of the nontariff restriction. Projections for prices, quantities consumed, total expenditures, or import volumes can be made for the interval in which the NTB was operative. Deviations of actual from projected values have then been attributed to the trade barrier.[30] The difficulty with this approach, however, is that such deviations may be due to structural shifts in underlying relationships, errors associated with the basic specification of the model, as well as the trade restriction. If the nontariff barrier was 'anticipated' this could also distort the model's coefficients and bias projections of the NTB's effects. In addition, there are generally difficulties in determining how much of the deviation between actual and predicted values is due to random variations in the data, i.e., the normal forecast error, and how much is due to the effects of the nontariff restriction. It should also be noted that many economists have a basic conceptual difficulty with the econometric approach in that all deviations of actual from predicted values are attributed to nontariff barriers and, the less precisely is the model specified, the greater will these unexplained residuals be. Several practical examples of studies that attempted to utilise industry econometric models for quantifying the price and quantity effects of nontariff barriers can be found in OECD (1985b) (1985d).

B. Decomposition of Export Unit Values

In situations where discriminatory nontariff barriers produce rents that are largely appropriated by exporters, it may be possible to quantify the NTB's effects through analysis of export unit values.

Specifically, if shipments to a given market are subject to measures like a 'voluntary' export restraint or bilateral quota, while trade with other destinations is unrestricted, differences between f.o.b unit values for exports to the restricted and free market may reflect the NTB rent. This approach is based on the assumption that f.o.b. unit values for homogenous products exported freely to all markets would be equal. However, those destined for restricted markets will be higher by an amount that reflects the NTB rent element. Greenaway (1985b) employed this approach for quantification of 'voluntary' restraints on non-leather footwear exports from Republic of Korea and Taiwan to the UK, but noted that there may be potential difficulties with its application. In particular, care must be taken to ensure that the unit value differences do not reflect factors like quality differentials, variations in importer's countervailing power, differences in international transportation costs, or basic errors in the compilation of trade data. Since the approach has been employed in relatively few studies, efforts should be made to verify its accuracy. Where data on export licence prices are available, this could be done by comparing these statistics with the unit value differentials to determine if equivalent magnitudes were involved. Stated differently, tests should attempt to verify that the export licence prices were comparable to the difference in unit values for similar goods exported to restricted and non-restricted markets.[31]

C. The Cost Element in Protection Systems

Although the approach differs from that normally employed for derivation of NTB price and quantity impact measures, compilation of information on the cost of administering protectionist measures may be a useful way to increase transparency. In one such study, Jackson (1984) estimated the quantifiable costs of the US import regulation system to be roughly $240 million per year. This figure includes the budgetary costs of US government agencies that administer customs regulations, the costs of private attorneys and consultants who handle trade-related cases, the in-house costs of firms that have to comply with the regulations. The total excludes, however, what Jackson terms 'nonquantifiable costs of the import regulatory system', i.e., induced foreign policy rigidity, use of the system for manipulation and harassment (through such actions as trade embargoes or anti-dumping measures), or what Jackson sees as a tendency for important cases to be mishandled. The United Nations Food and

Agricultural Organization has also developed related methodologies for approximating the total costs of farm support programmes in developed countries (see Table 5.16 in Chapter 5). These analyses clearly improve transparency and show the burden placed on consumers and taxpayers by protectionism and support measures.

Aside from administrative costs, some studies have attempted to estimate other costs of protection for countries imposing trade restrictions. In general, these investigations recognise that the costs of protection have several components: deadweight losses, inefficiency losses, and other ancillary losses.[32] While these analyses have often differed in their methodological approach, such investigations assist in quantifying the burden protectionism places on national producers and consumers. Chapter 5 in this book surveys the findings of some representative studies that attempted to approximate the magnitude of costs associated with trade restrictions. However, these loss calculations are likely to understate the actual cost of protection. They ignore, for example, the fact that free trade can offset a national monopoly whereas protection sustains it. When this happens the cost of protection must include: (i) losses resulting from the monopolist's profit maximizing behaviour, and (ii) any further efficiency losses from constraints to competition. Other 'dynamic' element costs such as the lack of incentives to adopt technological innovations in a timely fashion, failure to capitalise on opportunities for 'learning by doing', or the inability of exporters to achieve potential scale economies are also generally excluded.

D. Producer and Consumer Subsidy Equivalents

There are empirical producers which can be used to assess the overall cost–benefit effects of tariff or nontariff barriers, as well as additional policy variables not normally thought of as trade barriers. These procedures employ what might be termed a 'balance sheet' approach in that they sum the estimated producer and consumer costs and benefits of different policy measures. For example, producer subsidy equivalents (PSEs) and consumer subsidy equivalents (CSEs) are measures designed to reflect the monetary value of all policies that assist or tax producers or consumers of a specific product.[33] However, it should be noted that PSEs and CSEs are static measurements of assistance at a point in time, the secondary or dynamic effects of assistance are not included, and no account is taken of national policies' effects on world prices or production.

Analyses based on the PSE and CSE concept start by classifying relevant measures in three groups: those generally affecting producers; those generally affecting consumers; and those that impact in varying degrees on both consumers and producers. The next problem is to derive 'subsidy equivalents' for these measures which are the most accurate estimate of consumer and producer costs (or benefits) from each policy element and then sum up these individual values. Table 2.9 provides an illustrative example of what measures might be included and how overall PSEs and CSEs are derived. The table shows that price support payments are a positive element in the calculation of producer subsidy equivalents since these payments raise producers' incomes. Nontariff barriers, like variable import levies, are also positive elements in the calculation of PSEs since they raise producer prices and incomes, yet since they raise prices consumers have to pay they are negative elements in the calculation of CSEs. In contrast, domestic donations (like food aid programmes or consumption subsidies) will generally enter the calculation as a credit to consumers (a positive element in the calculation of consumer subsidy equivalents). Table 2.9 also indicates that some programmes like transportation subsidies will influence consumers or producers differently depending on how they are administered. Their proper treatment first requires determination of whether they are positive or negative elements for producers and consumers and then to derive estimates of their monetary costs or benefits.

In practice, there are two basic methods for measurement of producer or consumer subsidy equivalents. The first sums the direct or implicit budgetary payments to producers and consumers and then tries to account for any effects on market prices. The second method measures subsidy equivalents by comparing the supported domestic market price with another external reference price. Import tariffs, levies and quotas, export subsidies and restraint agreements are major trade policy instruments whose effects are measured in this way.[34]

To obtain producer or consumer subsidy equivalent estimates three distinct steps are followed. In calculating PSE, the first step is to derive the value to the producer of the year's production of the commodity. This is normally done by multiplying the production volume times the producer price. In some cases, however, the producer price does not include grants that are made by the government so these payments are added to obtain total producer value. The second step is to list all policies affecting the producer and derive the

Table 2.9   Elements entering the calculation of producer and consumer
subsidy equivalents: an illustrative example

General measure	Normal or assumed effects
A. *Measures primarily affecting producers*	
1. Price-support payments	A specific payment per unit of output paid to producers regardless of the market price. In the absence of other policies this would induce an increase in supply and a fall in market price, and consequently part of the payment would also go to the consumer as a subsidy.
2. Diversion payments	All payments for the purpose of limiting output are treated as a direct producer subsidy. No account is taken of the effect of these programmes on the market price of the commodity.
3. Input subsidies	Where production inputs are subsidised the producer's expenses are reduced and assuming no change in market price of the commodity the entire government expenditure is treated as a producer subsidy equivalent. Several problems exist: increased use of the subsidised input may influence production levels and prices; also there is the problem of how to attribute usage to one single commodity since the input may be employed for several different items.
4. Storage subsidies	Involve subsidies on the storage of producer owned crops or products. They generally have no significant price effects and are entered as a producer subsidy equivalent.
5. Deficiency payments	A direct producer subsidy. The government establishes guaranteed prices on various commodities and if the market price is lower makes a direct payment to producers. No effect on market price is assumed.
B. *Measures primarily affecting consumers*	
1. Domestic donations	All programmes which subsidise domestic consumption are assumed to have no effect on producers. The programmes are usually directed at specific sectors of the population: children, the elderly, poor.

(continued on page 54)

Table 2.9   *continued*

General measure	Normal or assumed effects
	Enters the calculation as a direct consumer subsidy.
2. Excise taxes	An excise tax on a commodity with a relatively inelastic demand (like sugar in the United States) is assumed to be paid entirely by consumers and not affect producers.
3. Denaturing premiums	Mainly for the treatment of wheat to direct it to the feed grain market. The question of who receives the benefit is complex since the payment maintains wheat prices and depresses feed grain prices. The producer subsidy equivalent is calculated from the difference of the market price and import c.i.f. price. A similar approach is taken for the consumer except that the total expenditure is treated as a consumer subsidy.
C. *Measures affecting producers and consumers* 1. Tariffs	A tariff raises the price which domestic producers can command for their production (a positive entry in the PSE) and which domestic consumers will have to pay (a negative entry in the CSE).
2. Variable levies and other NTBs	A variable levy is treated like a tariff which changes in response to fluctuations in c.i.f. import prices. Since other NTBs (quotas, prohibitions, etc.) generally raise domestic prices they have the same effects on PSEs and CSEs as tariffs. The magnitude of these effects are estimated by taking domestic–world–price differentials.
3. Transportation subsidies	The impact of subsidies on the transport of a commodity depends on whether or not the market price of the commodity is affected. Normally, such a subsidy would benefit distant consumers.
4. Export credit and subsidies	The impact depends on how the operative price for the commodity is determined. If the relevant price is an export price determined on world

Table 2.9 *continued*

General measure	Normal or assumed effects
	markets, the expense of financing the purchase is one less item to be deducted from the export price, and the return to the producer is increased. This is a producer subsidy. There is also a consumer tax since the domestic price of the product increases due to reduced availability of the item on local markets.

Source: Adapted from a discussion in UN Food and Agricultural Organization (1975).

value of the PSE attributable to each one. The sum of these (positive and negative) amounts is the total PSE, and the third step is to state the subsidy as an amount per metric ton produced, or as a percentage of total producer value. (See Table 5.21 in this book for PSEs calculated for OECD agricultural production of major temperate zone crops.)

The calculation of CSE follows a parallel series of operations with the first being to calculate consumer value from consumption volumes and an appropriate wholesale price. Where the wholesale price does not reflect a particular policy induced expense, such as a milling tax, this is deducted to obtain total consumer value. Similarly, the second step is to list all policies affecting the consumer and indicate whether they are taxes or subsidies. These figures are summed to obtain total CSE, and in the third stage this is divided by volume of consumption and total consumer value to obtain CSE per metric ton and CSE in percentage terms respectively. (See the UN Food and Agricultural Organization (1979) study reviewed in Chapter 5 for one example of an application of the CSE concept.)

ANNEX TO CHAPTER 2

A Note on Nominal and Effective NTB Tariff Equivalents

Before considering actual applications of the empirical procedures discussed in this chapter, it is useful to distinguish between 'nominal' and 'effective' rates of protection from nontariff barriers. Nominal rates, which are calculated from price impact measures such as equation (2.5), reflect the protection for a specific good while effective rates measure protection for the entire manufacturing process (value added) for the good. As such, the latter accounts for the joint effect of NTBs (and tariffs) on the final product as well as on the production inputs.

The effective rate of protection of industry j (E_j) is normally defined as the percentage difference between the industry's value added per dollar of output under protection (V_j'), and its value added per dollar of output in the absence of protection (V_j).[35]

$$E_j = (V_j' - V_j) \div V_j \tag{2.33}$$

The model can be developed as follows. If a_{ij} is the input value of factor i per dollar value of output j, in the absence of all trade barriers, value added can be expressed in terms of the m inputs,

$$V_j = 1 - \Sigma a_{ij}. \tag{2.34}$$

Now, if imports which are perfect substitutes for the final product j are subject to a nontariff barrier with an *ad valorem* equivalent (t_j), the price of j can rise by this amount on the domestic market. Since production inputs are assumed to be in perfectly elastic supply, none of the price increases will be observed in the values for the a_{ij}, but will be reflected in an increase in value added.[36]

This formulation can be expanded to account for *ad valorem* equivalents of any NTBs applied to the production inputs,

$$V_j' = 1 + t_j - \Sigma a_{ij} (1 + t_i), \tag{2.36}$$

which can also be expressed as,

$$V_j' = V_j + t_j - \Sigma a_{ij} t_i \tag{2.37}$$

Finally, it is possible to express the effective rate of protection in terms of the input coefficients and ad valorem equivalents for NTBs facing the intermediate and final products.[37]

$$E_j = (t_j - \Sigma a_{ij} t_i) \div (1 - \Sigma a_{ij}) \tag{2.38}$$

One modification is required before the above can be employed in the calculation of effective rates of protection. Equation (2.38) calls for the use of free trade input coefficients (a_{ij}), but what is typically observed are these coefficients distorted by trade restrictions on the intermediate inputs and final product. However, by deflating these observed shares (a_{ij}) by nominal rates for tariffs and NTBs on inputs and the end product,

$$a_{ij} = a_{ij}' [(1 + t_j) \div (1 + t_i)] \tag{2.39}$$

the needed 'free trade' coefficients can be approximated. Appendix 2 presents a graphical procedure that can simplify many of the basic calculations.

The implications of the effective rate model for empirical analysis and policy formulation for nontariff barriers should be carefully noted. Even in cases where unbiased estimates of nontariff barriers' nominal equivalents can be derived (say from one of the price impact measures) the effective rate model shows that such information still has the potential to be an inaccurate gauge of the true levels of protection accross industries or countries. Consider, for example, a situation where a specific industry has the same nominal rate of NTB protection in two countries, but protection for production inputs differs substantially. In the country where production inputs were (relatively) highly protected, the NTB on the final product will be having a relatively less important protective effect for value added in the manufacturing process. This would have been completely missed if comparisons were only made of nominal rates of NTB protection. The point that follows is that the structure of protection from trade barriers can be of vital importance and must be examined in any attempt to assess the true incidence of nontariff or tariff barriers.

3 Simulating the Effects of Trade Liberalisation

While estimates of *ad valorem* equivalents for nontariff barriers have important independent uses, such as the provision of a standard for assessing concessions in multilateral trade negotiations, they also constitute a key input into empirical analyses that quantify their trade and other economic effects. In other words, once nominal equivalents of NTBs have been derived using the procedures discussed in Chapter 2 this information can be utilised in general or partial equilibrium trade models to empirically assess the likely effects of their modification on policy variables such as employment, welfare, balance of payment and exchange rates, imports and exports, or prices and incomes. Since many of the studies surveyed in Chapter 5 deal with the influence of NTBs on these policy variables, it is important to understand how these effects have been estimated.

To illustrate how empirical procedures can be employed for quantifying the effects of NTBs, this chapter describes the operation of the fully computerised Trade Policy Simulation Model developed by the authors for the World Bank and UNCTAD secretariat.[1] This model, which has been used to estimate the effects of changes in tariff and nontariff barriers, may be described technically as an *ex ante* partial equilibrium model which measures the first-round effects of trade policy changes (see the annex to this chapter for a full technical description). The model is similar to those used by the Brookings Institution to analyse the effects of Tokyo Round tariff cuts, by the International Monetary Fund to quantify the influence of tariffs and nontariff barriers on developing-country export earnings, and by several academic researchers to analyse the effects of changes in trade preferences for developing countries.[2] The description that follows is intended to assist interested readers in establishing independent trade simulation procedures for research or policy analysis. The need for such an analytical capacity will likely increase significantly as the current round of multilateral trade negotiations proceed, or as new liberalisation measures are proposed. Since access to required data on parameters such as tariff rates, elasticities, or concordances may be a problem, the following discussion also indicates where potentially useful sources of information can be found.

BASIC FEATURES OF PARTIAL EQUILIBRIUM TRADE MODELS

Partial equilibrium models have the limitation that they do not fully account for economy-wide effects of trade changes, although they can be extended to approximate inter-industry effects and the maintenance of equilibrium in the balance of trade. Theoretically, general equilibrium models are preferable since they can account for second-round effects and other factors like the influence of exchange rate changes on imports and exports.[3] As such, they provide insights into the interaction of sectors not directly affected by the trade changes. However, general equilibrium models are vulnerable to criticisms regarding many underlying assumptions, and results obtained using such models have a number of obvious difficulties. As an example, some of the most well-known general equilibrium models are unable to account for trade diversion, the effects of discriminatory trade barriers, or linkages between industries classified in the same broad product group. There are also problems associated with working versions of general equilibrium models, with the loss of detail, due to their high level of aggregation, posing major difficulties.

Although the partial equilibrium approach has the drawback that it cannot account for economy-wide effects of trade policy changes, it has the advantage that it can be applied at very low levels of product detail. For example, in most empirical analyses undertaken with the Trade Simulation Model tariff-line-level information is used for the basic simulations. This is extremely detailed data which allows projections to be made for well-defined products. As an illustration, United States tariff-line import statistics for one year contain roughly 4000 individual products and approximately 150 000 different product–country combinations. Working at this level of detail permits a high degree of precision in identifying specific products and trading partners affected by trade policy measures. Other importers provide even more detail with several Scandinavian countries distinguishing between 10 000 to 12 000 tariff line products.

The most frequent policy projections involving the model generally focus on direct trade effects of tariff and nontariff barriers. Here, two distinct effects are estimated: (i) trade creation: resulting from a change in overall demand for imports whose price has changed relative to domestic substitutes (it is assumed that tariff and NTB changes are reflected fully in consumer price changes); and (ii) trade diversion, or the substitution of goods imported from one or more foreign suppliers for similar goods from other exporters. This latter substitution results from changes in relative import prices (after payment of duties) of goods from different foreign suppliers due to differential changes in tariff rates or nontariff barriers. For tariffs, this can occur through changes in the MFN rate, the preference rate, or both. If a preference rate for one group of exporters is introduced, or an existing rate is lowered, while other suppliers continue to face the MFN rate, there is (positive) trade diversion in favour of the preference receivers and (negative) trade diversion for other countries.[4]

While the model's projections are made at the level of tariff-line products, the trade creation and diversion effects can be summed to arrive at the total effects of the trade-barrier changes for each partner country. This summation can also be made to predetermined product groups like the two or three-digit level of the SITC. However, in simulating the effect of tariff changes an important assumption is that other restrictions, such as quotas or GSP ceilings, would be sufficiently relaxed to permit the full tariff-induced trade expansion to occur. If these limitations were maintained, trade volumes would not rise to the extent predicted and NTB rents would increase.

THE DATA AND PARAMETERS

For simulations involving the model, basic data from a number of established sources must be employed. To simulate the effects of nontariff barriers, nominal equivalents for these measures must first be derived using the procedures outlined in Chapter 2. These estimates can either be derived independently or compiled from published sources (Chapter 5 provides a survey of studies from which such data could be compiled). Information is also needed on tariffs in the markets for which the simulations are to be run, data on price and substitution elasticities, and statistics on actual trade levels. Technical concordances are needed between the different systems for compiling trade and trade-barrier data because the latter information is recorded at a level where no two countries have identical classifications – i.e. the national tariff schedules.[5]

A. Tariffs

In simulations involving tariff changes it is assumed that modifications in import duties are directly translated into changes in consumer prices for the affected products. For the compilation of basic information on tariffs two sources have been used. For most developed market economy countries, tariffs are drawn from computer files compiled by the GATT Secretariat.[6] These magnetic tapes contain highly detailed information which indicates: the national tariff number (the number of digits varies from country to country); corresponding import data (by product by country) at the same level of detail; the pre-Tokyo Round base-rate tariffs; other tariffs such as temporary or applied rates; general tariffs (which are applied to some socialist country products); various preferential rates where they exist; the post-Tokyo Round MFN rate; and codes showing the legal binding of the latter tariff.[7] Individuals not having access to these records can compile similar information directly from national customs schedules, but corresponding price or unit value data is needed to compute the *ad valorem* equivalents of specific or mixed tariff rates.

In simulations involving MFN tariff cuts, the rates normally used are post-Tokyo Round statutory bound tariffs or, in the absence of a binding, the applied rates.[8] In cases where preferences exist, under the GSP or through other arrangements, the appropriate preferential rate for each individual country is used for projections. While the preferential tariffs may change irregularly, the rate used in simulations normally corresponds to the year for which trade data have been drawn.

In the simulations, attempts are made to account for ceilings or quotas in the operation of the preferences, although a lack of required information sometimes makes this difficult. In other words, if imports from a particular beneficiary have exceeded a preferential quota the MFN rate will influence any further expansion of trade. In this situation, the most-favoured-nation tariff is employed in the simulations. Unfortunately, it is often difficult to determine precisely if such ceilings have been exceeded as needed tariff-line-level information is only provided by a few countries like Australia and the United States. Other developed countries provide GSP 'utilisation' rates for broad groups of products (e.g., the share of imports under preferential tariffs) and it has been necessary to apply these overall rates to each component tariff line item.

The second major source of tariff data that has been employed with the model are UNCTAD computerised files which record information on import duties in developing countries. However, there are some major differences between these records and the GATT files.

UNCTAD only lists the MFN rate and does not report preferences extended by regional groups such as ASEAN. This, of course, makes it impossible to quantify the effects of 'erosion' of developing-country preferences due to MFN cuts. The problem of converting developing-countries' specific duties to *ad valorem* equivalents is often encountered and the procedure normally employed here is to take the ratio of the specific tariff to the unit value of the four-digit SITC group in which the items are classified. Since tariff-line trade data are not readily available for developing countries, even though import duties are recorded at this level, it is necessary to compute unweighted tariff averages for products up to the four-digit SITC group. This is the lowest level at which developing country projections can be made, although those for developed countries are made at the level of the tariff-line aggregation. Unlike the *GATT Tariff Study* data on developed countries, the UNCTAD Trade Information Service (TIS) data on developing countries is publicly available.

B. Nontariff Barriers

In projecting the effects of a nontariff barrier liberalisation two assumptions are made. First, it is assumed that changes in these measures will, like tariffs, have a direct effect on consumer prices in the importing market.[9] Second, it is also assumed that simulations of the trade effects of these measures can be computed using estimated NTB *ad valorem* equivalents. Since no central records exists for nominal equivalents, they must be independently estimated using procedures discussed in Chapter 2 or drawn directly from the professional literature. (See Chapter 5 for a survey of published studies which contain such information.) Concerning the nominal equivalents compiled from published sources, several specific points should be noted. First, many estimates reflect the 'general' or average level of protection against all exporters and do not measure any differential incidence on specific foreign countries. Biased trade projections could result if the average (overall) NTB nominal equivalents were employed in simulations for individual exporting countries.[10] Another problem occurs with NTBs for which no estimates of *ad valorem* equivalents can be found. In such cases, it is not possible to simulate the trade effects of the barrier unless an independent effort to derive nominal equivalents were made. Finally, some *ad valorem* equivalents for nontariff barriers in the agricultural sector are quite volatile due to wide year-to-year variation in these products' prices. Here, it is often necessary to make a decision as to what constitutes an average or 'normal' level of protection based on information for several previous years. However, there is no assurance that these 'average' levels for the past will prevail in the future.

C. Imports

Statistics on the actual level of imports in specific countries are of key importance since they constitute the 'base' from which the trade projections are made. For the developed market economy countries, actual import data used in simulations are drawn from computer tapes made available from national statistical offices. This information is recorded at the tariff-line level so tariff and trade statistics can be matched directly. The import statistics in this series are recorded at the point of clearing customs, even though they may have been imported earlier and held in bond. In the case of the United States, Canada, Australia and New Zealand, imports are valued on a free-on-board basis (f.o.b.) while other developed countries use a cost-insurance-freight (c.i.f.) valuation. As a result, trade projections vary between countries in terms of f.o.b. and c.i.f. values. In most countries tariff-line trade data are not published – data are usually published in the national classification corresponding to the UN Standard International Trade Classification system. However, the data are normally made available to researchers on tape for the costs of preparation.

For projections involving a liberalisation of trade barriers in developing countries, required import statistics can be taken from the United Nations Commodity Trade Statistics, Series D, which employs the UN Standard International Trade Classification Revision 1 and Revision 2 (although Revision 1 still is used by the majority of developing countries).[11] Import data in this series are recorded on arrival in the importing country, even though some time may pass before the goods clear customs. For the most part, these statistics are tabulated at the level of four-digits in SITC Revision 1 or five-digits in SITC Revision 2. An additional point is that the developing-country trade data are normally three or four years out of date, although statistics for developed countries are available with about a one-to-two-year lag.

D. Elasticities

Demand elasticities play a key role in the model's projections since they indicate the proportionate change in consumption of a foreign good that would accompany a given (tariff or NTB induced) change in price. Information on elasticities of demand is normally taken from published sources. A compendium prepared by Stern *et al.* (1976) is particularly useful, while additional data can be found in studies by the Brookings Institution and the Kiel Institute for World Economics.[12] Information on elasticities of export supply has not yet been used explicitly in the model since reliable information on these parameters is not available. Given this data deficiency, the simulations normally use infinite elasticities and 'sensitivity' tests based on a plausible 'range' of supply elasticities are conducted.

One potentially important effect that is not taken into account may occur where elasticities of supply are known to be non-infinite. This could be important in the case of a simultaneous trade liberalisation in a number of markets, as might happen following multilateral negotiations. Such a multilateral liberalisation in the presence of non-infinite supply elasticities may cause a smaller expansion of trade volumes than are projected by the model due to international price changes. However, the resulting price increases should offset the smaller trade volumes in estimating revenue effects. This problem does not arise under the assumption of perfectly elastic supply since, in this case, there is no effect on world prices.

Explicit values for the elasticity of substitution between goods from different sources are necessary for the model to estimate trade diversion. An implicit assumption in estimating trade diversion is that products from different suppliers (e.g. from developing countries or from industrial countries) are imperfect substitutes.[13] However, if relative prices change there will be shifts in purchases among different foreign suppliers goods. Another approach for estimating trade diversion is needed if the elasticity of substitution between alternative suppliers is not known. This procedure, using import penetration ratios, was developed by Baldwin and Murray (1977).[14] They assume that the substitutability between a country's product and a similar product produced in non-beneficiary countries (i.e. developed countries, in the GSP context in which they were writing) should be similar to the substitutability between a developing country's product and a similar product produced in the (GSP) donor (importing) country. However, Pomfret (1986) argues that there is no economic foundation for this assumption and that it ensures that trade creation is inevitably greater than trade diversion. This is not, *ipso facto*, the case with the formulation with explicit elasticities of substitution.[15]

E. Concordances

Accurate concordances are needed since they provide the basis for utilising the diverse statistical material in producing the model's projections. These data are classified under different systems such as the SITC, ISIC or national tariff classifications. Most, but not all, of the latter are based on the Customs Cooperation Council Nomenclature (CCCN) and employ this system down to the four-digit level. Since the ISIC, SITC and CCCN do not concord on a one-to-one basis there are sometimes errors in cross-classifying data, particularly at the detailed level.[16] The concordances of the national tariff classification of the United States (TSUSA) and of Canada, which are not CCCN based, pose particular problems which are amplified by a frequent reclassification of items from one year to the next.

ILLUSTRATIVE POLICY APPLICATIONS

Several examples will assist in showing how simulation procedures can be employed for practical policy studies. In one such application, Laird and Yeats (1987a) employed the partial equilibrium trade projection model described in this chapter's annex to assess the potential contribution of trade liberalisation initiatives for alleviating developing countries' debt burdens.[17] Drawing on an earlier IMF (1984) study, the authors compiled NTB *ad valorem* equivalents from the sources listed in Table 3.1 and then employed this data in the model to simulate the effects of both a preferential and most-favoured-nation liberalisation of trade barriers (tariffs plus NTBs) facing indebted countries' major export products.[18] Their results show that an MFN removal of tariffs and NTBs could increase developing-country exports by some $32 billion annually, while a preferential trade liberalisation would increase these exports by $35 billion. The present value of such a recurring annual increase in export earnings were estimated to be roughly $700 billion.[19]

The Laird–Yeats projections indicate that the effects of a preferential trade liberalisation would be dispersed among developing countries. For the Republic of Korea, the Philippines, Turkey and Yugoslavia the present value of the export expansion exceeded these countries' debts, while Morocco's trade gains equalled about 70 per cent of existing debt. For Brazil, the country with the largest debt,

Table 3.1   Information collated by IMF on tariff equivalents of tariff and nontariff barriers for seven sectors in four OECD markets (percentages)

Sector	United States	EEC	Japan	Canada
Meat	49(a), 16(b) 6(c)	118(a), 50(b) 104(d), 37(c)	328(a), 297(b) 219(c)	52(a)
Cereals	20(e), 55(c)	81(h), 35(e) 73(b), 51(d) 34(c)	175(b), 70(e) 139(c)	–
Sugar	27(f), 18(c)	31(d), 46(b) 33(c)	44(b), 53(c)	–
Textiles	59(e), 9(g)	50(e)	18(c)	39(j)
Iron and steel	6(g), 5(i)	6(i)	3(i)	–
Clothing	70(e), 9(g)	50(e)	23(e)	39(j)
Footwear	2(g), 9(i)	12(i)	16(i)	–
All sectors	33(e)	39(e)	62(e)	–

Note: The averages shown in the 'All sectors' row are only for products which encounter hard-core nontariff barriers.

Sources: (a) FAO, 'Protectionism in the Livestock Sector', Rome, 1980. Estimates refer to beef for 1977–9.

(b) S.J. Anjaria, *et al.*, 'Developments in International Trade Policy', *IMF Occasional Paper No. 16* (Washington, D.C., 1982). Meat estimates refer to beef for 1977–9. Cereal estimates refer to a simple average for rice, maize and wheat for the United States; maize and wheat for the European Communities, and rice, wheat, barley and soybeans for Japan, in 1979–80.

(c) Japan Economic Institute, 'Agricultural Protectionism' (Tokyo, 1983). Estimates for meat refer to beef; for cereals, to grains for the United States and the European Communities, and to a simple average for rice, wheat and barley for Japan in 1978–80. Estimates for sugar also refer to 1978–80.

(d) Commonwealth Secretariat, *Protectionism: Threat to International Order* (London, 1982). Estimates for meat refer to beef; and for cereals to a simple average for rice, maize and wheat in 1979–80. Estimates for sugar refer to the same time-period.

(e) A.J. Yeats, *Trade Barriers Facing Developing Countries* (New York, 1979). All estimates are for 1973. For cereals, estimates refer to grains and grain products; for textiles, clothing and manufactures, estimates are the sum of post-Kennedy Round tariffs and tariff equivalents for nontariff barriers. Tariff equivalents for nontariff barriers refer to apparel for both textiles and clothing.

(f) Derived from US Department of Agriculture, 'Sugar and Sweetener: Outlook and Situation' (Washington, D.C., 1981).

Table 3.1 *continued*

Estimates refer to 1979–80. Transport costs were assumed at 6 per cent of the c.i.f. price.

(g) P. Morici and L.L. Megna, *U.S. Economic Policies Affecting Industrial Trade* (Washington, D.C., 1983). The tariff equivalent for textiles reflects the impact of the Multifibre Arrangement; for iron and steel, it reflects the effects of several orderly market agreements with Japan, and quotas against other producers; for footwear, it reflects orderly market agreements with Taiwan and Korea between 1977 and 1979.

(h) U. Koester, 'Policy Options for the Grain Economy of the European Community: Implications for Developing Countries', *IFPRI Research Report No. 35* (Washington, D.C., 1982). Estimates refer to a simple average for wheat, barley and maize for 1979–80.

(i) Pre-Tokyo Round tariffs calculated in A.V. Deardorff and R.M. Stern, 'The Effects of the Tokyo Round on the Structure of Protection'. Paper presented at the Conference on the *Structure and Evolution of Recent U.S. Trade Policy* (National Bureau of Economic Research, Cambridge, Mass., December 1982).

(j) M. Wolf, 'Managed Trade in Practice: Implications of the Textile Arrangements', in W.R. Cline (ed.), *Trade Policies in the 1980s* (Washington, D.C., 1983). The simple average of total protective rates for 16 products in 1979 was employed.

the projected trade expansion equalled one-half of this nation's debt, while the corresponding ratio is between 50 to 75 per cent for Colombia and Pakistan. For developing countries as a whole, the simulations show that the present value of the increased export earnings (before the resource cost of exports or exchange rate effects are accounted for) would be about $700 billion. Even though these results vary under different assumptions concerning the discount rate, sensitivity tests show that trade expansion would, in all cases, make a major contribution towards alleviating developing countries' debt burdens. As a result, both the World Bank and UNCTAD utilised these figures in policy documents linking a resolution of the debt crisis to a liberalisation of market access for developing countries' exports.

Laird and Yeats identify the product groups that would have to be the focus of the liberalisation for it to be effective. Information relevant to this point is presented in Table 3.2 which tabulates the trade expansion projections for one-digit SITC products. The table

Table 3.2 Analysis of the simulated increase in developing country export earnings in terms of major SITC product groups

SITC	Description	EEC Japan & US 1980 imports from developed countries ($ mill.)	Average applied tariff			Types of NTBs applied	Projected export		Percentage of total expansion[a]
			US	EEC	Japan		Value ($ mill.)	Increase (%)	
0	Food and live animals	32 395.3	1.8	5.2	5.6	HS, GQ, V, L, TQ, ID, OM, SR	6 197.1	19.1	17.8
0813	Vegetable oil-seed & cake	1 733.6	3.2	0.0	0.0	HS, L, V, ID	761.5	43.9	2.2
0313	Crustacea and molluscs	1 790.7	2.1	9.5	4.7	HS, GQ, L	610.7	34.1	1.8
0311	Fresh or frozen fish	1 657.4	0.0	10.2	4.8	HS, TQ, L, OM, SR	561.0	33.9	2.6
0320	Preserved fish	1 594.4	0.7	13.5	12.6	HS, TQ, L, OM	556.2	34.9	1.6
0112	Meat of sheep and goats	1 799.1	1.8	2.9	4.9	HS, TQ, L, V, ID, GQ, OM	551.2	30.9	1.6
0539	Prepared fruits and nuts	838.1	1.9	20.2	27.1	HS, GQ, V, L, TQ, ID	334.7	39.9	1.0
1	Beverages and tobacco	1 072.7	11.5	0.0	355.0	HS, ST	37.6	3.5	0.1
2	Crude materials except fuels	13 744.9	0.3	0.2	0.2	MFA, HS, SR, GQ, L, S	200.3	1.5	0.6
3	Mineral fuels	184 958.7	0.3	0.1	1.1	TQ, S	3 044.3	1.6	8.8
3310	Crude petroleum	139 877.2	0.3	0.0	1.1	TQ, S	1 377.5	1.0	4.0
3411	Natural gas	8 857.6	0.0	1.3	2.3	TQ, S	346.1	3.9	1.0
4	Animal and vegetable oils	1 726.8	0.1	6.6	6.0	HS, V, L, ID	644.5	37.3	1.9
4223	Coconut oil	1 298.8	0.0	6.9	6.1	HS, V, L, ID	574.6	44.2	1.7
5	Chemicals	3 684.1	4.7	4.9	3.1	GQ, S, Q	358.7	9.7	1.0
6	Manufactures classified by material	32 936.5	4.8	5.6	4.4	BQ, TQ, MFA, L, SV, OM	5 994.1	18.2	17.2
6412	Other printing paper	7 846.4	0.0	5.6	4.3	TQ	592.3	7.5	1.7
6575	Carpets	1 093.3	5.3	7.2	7.3	MFA	490.2	44.8	1.4
6715	Other ferro-alloys	944.6	1.1	4.4	3.2	L, TQ, SV, OM	480.2	50.8	1.4

SITC	Description								
6535	Fabrics of synthetic fibre	818.7	19.3	8.5	7.2	TQ, MFA, L	368.4	45.0	1.1
6569	Textile articles, n.e.s.	701.4	6.0	9.5	8.3	L, MFA	306.6	43.7	0.9
6727	Iron and steel coils	471.3	4.2	3.2	3.0	SV, OM	290.4	61.6	0.8
6513	Cotton yarn and thread	782.2	6.5	4.5	3.4	TQ, MFA	289.7	37.0	0.8
7	Machinery and transport Equipment	19 871.7	4.2	7.4	2.9	SV, L, GQ	2 091.0	10.5	6.0
7249	Telecommunications Equipment	4 025.5	4.4	8.4	2.5	SV	829.4	20.6	2.4
7323	Lorries and trucks	1 176.8	2.5	8.4	3.0	SV	266.8	22.7	0.8
8	Miscellaneous manufactured articles	21 241.6	9.0	7.8	8.5	S, MFA, SV, GQ, BQ	16 195.0	76.2	46.6
8411	Clothing or textiles	8 632.9	18.0	10.3	10.8	MFA	10 752.4	124.6	30.9
8510	Footwear	2 027.6	10.0	8.7	9.1	SV, GQ	1 744.5	85.0	5.0
8210	Furniture	1 732.3	1.9	4.2	3.2	SV	1 030.1	59.5	3.0
8310	Travel goods	956.5	17.0	4.2	8.8		580.0	60.6	1.7
8942	Toys and games	1 801.7	3.8	5.6	4.6	HS	489.4	27.2	1.4
8420	Fur clothing	605.0	4.2	4.5	14.3		348.3	57.6	1.0
0 to 8	All Core Products	311 632.2	3.6	2.0	4.1	(See above)	34 762.6	11.2	100.0

Key: Restrictions applied in whole or in part to the SITC group. The key to symbols applied is as follows:

PHS, HS = prohibitions due to health and sanitary reasons or health and sanitary regulations;
Q = quotas (method unspecified) or bilateral quotas;
TQ = tariff quotas;
GQ = global quotas;
OM = other price distorting measures;
SV = surveillance;
S = standards;
ID = import deposits;
MFA = Multi-fibre Arrangement.

SR = seasonal restrictions;
BQ = bilateral quota;
DL, L = import licensing (method unspecified);
V, MP = variable levy or minimum import price restriction;
R = restrictions (method unspecified) or special seasonal restrictions;
PLR = special labelling requirements;
ST = state trading.

[a] The figures shown for the projected export expansion are estimated effects of a complete preferential removal of tariffs and NTBs facing exports of indebted developing countries to the EEC, Japan and United States. Ad valorem equivalents for nontariff barriers were drawn from the sources listed in Table 3.1. In all cases, projections were made at the tariff-line level and then summed up to the different levels of aggregation shown in Table 3.2. The model described in the annex to this chapter was used to make the projections summarised in this table.

Source: Laird and Yeats (1987c).

indicates the actual value of EEC, Japan and United States imports and shows the simulated increase for each group following a full preferential trade liberalisation. In addition, it shows the average post-Tokyo Round tariff in each industrial market and indicates the types of NTBs applied. For more detailed analysis, similar information is also given for those four-digit products registering the largest projected trade gains.

Table 3.2 shows the key importance of the clothing group (SITC 8411) in a debt-related trade liberalisation. Over 30 per cent of the estimated total increase in developing countries' export earnings occur in this sector (again of about $10.9 billion), while footwear (SITC 8510) adds another 5 per cent or $1.7 billion. Table 3.2 indicates close to 18 per cent of the total export increase occurs for the food and live animals group, with vegetable oilseeds and cake (SITC 0813) accounting for about 2 per cent of the increase. Although iron and steel products (SITC 67) have encountered a growing number of restrictions (often on other developed countries' exports), the simulations suggest this sector has a relatively modest role to play (under 10 per cent of the total) in any aggregate developing-country trade expansion.

Aside from trade-debt issues, a second policy area in which there have been applications of trade simulation models, such as that listed in the chapter's annex, is in the design or evaluation of preferential trade measures. In one such analysis, Erzan et al. (1986) simulated the potential influence of preferences for developing countries' intra-trade on exports, imports and trade balances of selected major countries or country groups. The simulations assumed that preferences were generated through 10, 20, and 50 per cent tariff cuts, and that supply was infinitely elastic.[20] The results of these simulations are summarised in Table 3.3. The major policy implications concern the relatively limited potential that such preferences appear to have for stimulating intra-trade. Fifty per cent preferential margins, for example, increase trade by some $7.2 billion (about a 9 per cent expansion), while 10 per cent preferences produce an increase of less than $1.5 billion. The authors note that the simulations assume that any nontariff barriers also applied to these exports will be relaxed to allow the full effects of tariff preferences to be achieved. If nontariff barriers are not liberalised, the trade gains would be even smaller than projected.

While trade policy simulations can be run for total exports or imports of individual countries, the results can also be aggregated over countries for specific commodities or industry sectors. Table 3.4, which is drawn from a Laird and Yeats (1987c) study, summarises projections of the effects of full tariff preferences (100 per cent preferential margins) on the commodity intra-trade of developing countries. The table shows the projected change in the value of total commodity trade, and also gives a breakdown for specific products. Three different assumptions are made concerning supply conditions in the simulations (perfectly elastic supply, unitary elastic supply, and a case where export prices rise by one-third of the corresponding change in volumes is tested). Among other points, these simulations illustrate the importance of supply factors on commodity trade as the projections with unitary supply elasticity are about half the value of those assuming perfectly elastic supply prevail.

Trade simulation models have been of major importance in evaluating results of previous multilateral trade negotiations, and should also be extensively applied for similar policy analyses in the Uruguay Round. Cline *et al*. (1978), for example, provide an illustration of one such study in which a trade simulation model was employed for quantifying the effects of the Tokyo Round results. In a related analysis, Yeats (1987) indicates how such procedures could be employed for quantifying the likely effects of Uruguay Round tariff-cutting proposals. International organisations such as UNCTAD and the World Bank have come under increased pressure to provide technical expertise for utilising such models to assist developing countries formulate strategies for the multilateral negotiations.

Other policy studies utilising trade simulation models have involved attempts to quantify the effects of trade barriers (tariffs as well as NTBs) in specific sectors such as agriculture. For example, Valdes and Zietz (1980) simulated the effects of an agricultural trade liberalisation and concluded that, if OECD countries reduced agricultural protection by 50 per cent, export earnings of fifty-six of the largest developing countries (see Table 3.5 for a listing) would increase by at least $3 billion a year over trend growth.[21] This represents an annual increase of approximately 11 per cent above total developing-country agricultural exports in 1975–7. These simulations also show that the hypothetical reduction in protection would increase world agriculture trade by approximately $8.5 billion. Among OECD countries, the largest increases in imports are projected for Japan ($1.6 billion), Germany ($1.5 billion), the United Kingdom ($1.5 billion), and Italy ($1.4 billion), while the largest export expansion occurs for the United States ($2.1 billion), Canada ($0.5 billion), Australia ($0.5 billion), New Zealand ($0.1 billion), and Sweden ($0.1 billion). France and Italy experience a substantial reduction in exports,

Table 3.3 Actual values and projected changes in exports and trade balances for selected developing countries due to the adoption of a GSTP (million US$)

Country or market	1981 trade values					Projected trade change due to GSTP					
	Exports to		Imports from			10% preferences		20% preferences		50% preferences	
	Developing countries	All sources	Developing countries	All sources	Trade balance	Exports	Trade balance	Exports	Trade balance	Exports	Trade balance
Algeria	1 060.0	14 981.6	898.1	10 698.3	4 283.3	7.0	−3.7	14.0	−7.4	34.9	−18.7
Bangladesh	193.6	504.3	615.3	1 591.0	−1 086.7	4.9	−23.7	9.8	−47.4	24.3	−118.7
CARICOM	871.0	4 747.6	1 629.6	4 527.4	220.2	21.0	6.0	42.0	11.8	104.1	28.8
CEUCA	598.5	5 097.6	161.3	2 454.0	2 643.6	4.9	2.8	9.9	5.0	24.6	13.7
Côte d'Ivoire	328.3	2 499.1	646.1	2 092.6	406.5	7.6	−14.5	15.2	−29.0	37.5	−73.1
Egypt	369.7	5 108.5	721.8	7 444.5	−2 336.0	5.0	−16.5	10.1	−33.1	25.0	−82.8
India	1 922.7	6 883.7	3 176.5	9 326.2	−2 442.5	54.8	−17.4	109.4	−35.1	271.1	−110.3
Indonesia	1 484.9	23 316.5	3 544.7	12 178.8	11 137.7	21.0	−32.5	42.0	−65.1	104.4	−163.4
Kenya	312.3	905.7	779.3	1 973.1	−1 067.4	5.6	−22.9	11.2	−45.2	27.7	−115.2
Korea, Rep. of	4 536.9	17 219.8	8 248.8	24 464.1	−7 244.3	167.0	101.8	332.8	202.5	824.2	498.5
Malaysia	5 608.3	13 292.5	3 443.7	10 659.4	2 633.1	55.9	33.3	111.5	65.4	277.4	164.6
Mexico	2 220.7	22 288.8	749.2	11 952.0	10 336.8	44.0	69.5	87.9	50.3	218.3	125.4
Morocco	304.2	2 149.7	1 199.8	3 977.4	−1 827.7	6.2	−23.6	12.4	−47.2	30.7	−118.4

Nigeria	1 343.4	18 628.7	562.0	9 076.0	9 552.7	14.7	-6.3	29.3	-12.8	73.0	-31.8
Pakistan	896.8	1 977.0	2 260.3	4 968.7	-2 991.7	11.8	-37.4	23.5	-74.8	58.1	-189.6
Philippines	1 166.5	6 368.2	2 841.4	6 958.8	-590.6	28.8	-25.7	57.5	-51.5	142.4	-130.2
Saudi Arabia	22 983.3	110 745.7	4 101.3	32 705.2	78 040.5	152.2	133.9	304.2	267.6	759.2	667.7
Singapore	7 697.7	14 414.1	12 618.6	25 079.9	-10 665.8	165.9	163.0	331.0	325.3	822.2	808.0
Sri Lanka	264.2	840.4	693.8	1 540.9	-700.5	4.9	-8.5	9.6	-17.1	23.7	-43.1
Tanzania, United Republic of	247.9	540.3	147.5	937.4	-397.1	6.8	4.4	13.5	8.8	33.1	21.2
Thailand	2 094.5	6 100.5	3 392.3	8 816.6	-2 716.1	31.7	9.0	63.2	17.8	156.1	42.8
Tunisia	246.0	1 751.3	569.7	3 580.3	-1 829.0	4.9	-3.9	9.7	-8.0	24.1	-20.1
Yugoslavia	767.7	4 139.2	1 753.8	11 169.8	-7 030.6	36.2	27.0	72.2	53.8	179.1	133.2
Other developing Africa	2 470.6	21 365.5	2 348.4	14 482.0	6 883.5	21.7	-21.1	43.4	-42.1	134.8	-105.8
Other developing America	11 704.4	60 066.3	18 536.4	65 863.8	-5 797.5	357.4	89.6	713.0	177.5	1 769.5	430.6
Other developing Asia	13 271.3	67 930.2	9 325.4	45 802.6	22 127.6	216.7	66.6	432.4	132.4	1 046.9	301.5
All developing countries	84 965.4	433 862.8	84 965.4	334 320.8	99 542.0	1 458.6	449.2	2910.7	803.8	7 226.4	1 781.6

Notes: The actual trade values may be understated due to problems in reporting, and for some countries the data may be for 1979. Also, the projections do not account for supply constraints that may arise in some of the countries. The 'other' developing-country groups shown here are assumed to have average tariff profiles that are similar to the 23 countries or markets listed in the table.

Source: Erzan, Laird and Yeats (1986). The projections reported in this table were made at the four-digit level of the SITC and then summed to the country totals. The annex to this chapter describes the model used to make these projections.

Table 3.4 Projected changes in the structure of developing countries' intra-trade in primary and processed commodities under preferential tariffs

Processing chain	1981 value of intra-trade ($ million)		Share of processed products	Projected change in developing country intra-trade in processed commodities under tariff preferences[a]					
				Value ($ million)			Processed products' share		
	Primary stage	Processed products		$e_s = \infty$	$e_s = 3.0$	$e_s = 1.0$	$e_s = \infty$	$e_s = 3.0$	$e_s = 1.0$
All commodities	51 644.8	13 874.9	21.2	2 529.5	1 894.4	1 365.0	2.4	1.8	1.3
All commodities (excl. petroleum)	6 871.0	6 182.7	47.4	1 491.4	1 132.1	845.7	3.9	3.0	2.1
of which:									
Meat	547.7	49.8	8.0	12.6	9.8	8.1	1.8	1.5	1.2
Fish	260.4	125.6	32.5	36.0	29.4	23.6	4.1	3.1	2.4
Fruit	857.9	157.3	15.5	23.9	19.2	15.2	1.1	0.8	0.5
Vegetables	555.6	73.7	11.7	9.8	9.6	9.3	0.6	0.6	0.6
Vegetables oils[b]	70.0	147.5	67.8	9.3	6.9	4.8	0.1	-0.1	-0.3
Coffee, cocoa and sugar	1 798.9	121.5	6.3	38.2	30.9	24.5	1.4	1.1	0.9
Leather	54.8	123.7	69.2	43.8	30.2	22.1	8.1	4.3	3.3
Rubber	1 295.3	262.3	16.9	151.8	91.0	63.4	7.1	4.3	3.0

Wood and paper	69.6	2 107.0	96.8	258.7	217.3	157.9	-0.5	-0.5	-0.5
Wool	25.5	26.7	51.1	25.9	21.1	17.1	12.7	10.6	8.7
Cotton	486.7	348.2	41.7	258.9	186.8	132.4	13.0	9.9	7.3
Iron	314.4	1 235.2	79.7	300.1	233.9	186.2	3.1	2.4	2.0
Copper	183.2	697.7	79.2	157.3	115.2	79.4	2.8	2.0	1.3
Bauxite	35.4	306.0	89.6	87.9	71.6	57.6	2.1	1.8	1.5
Lead	11.0	51.2	82.3	6.8	5.2	3.9	1.5	1.1	0.8
Zinc	26.4	85.7	76.4	15.2	12.2	9.8	2.4	1.9	1.6
Tin	56.9	128.5	69.3	28.7	20.5	13.6	4.0	2.9	1.9
Phosphates	221.3	135.1	37.9	26.5	21.3	16.8	2.7	1.9	1.4
Petroleum	44 773.8	7 692.2	14.7	1 038.1	762.3	519.3	1.3	0.9	0.6

Note: The projected trade changes shown in this table are based on the assumption that any nontariff barriers applied to these products are also liberalised to an extent that the full effects of the tariff preferences can be realised. Trade diversion estimates, which are incorporated in the total figures, are based on an assumed elasticity of substitution of 1.5 between preference-receiving and other products. See Cline *et al*. (1978) for a discussion covering this latter point.

[a] Processed commodities are defined as all items other than the stage one goods listed in table 1 of Laird and Yeats (1987c).

[b] Including groundnuts, copra, palm kernel oil and oilseeds.

Source: Laird and Yeats (1987c). Since NTB *ad valorem* equivalents were not available the trade projections only include tariff effects. The annex to this chapter describes the model used for the projections.

Table 3.5   Potential trade effects on developing countries from reducing trade barriers for agricultural exports

Country	Change in export revenues	Change in agricultural import expenditures	Increase in agricultural export revenues	Most affected export commodity in absolute terms
	(US $1000)		(percent)	
Sub-Saharan Africa				
Angola	11 623	−2 452	3.9	Coffee
Cameroon	21 391	−552	4.8	Cocoa
Ghana	31 152	−1 945	4.4	Cocoa
Guinea	245	−102	2.7	Coffee
Ivory Coast	49 581	−2 101	4.2	Cocoa
Kenya	18 415	−5 884	5.9	Beef
Madagascar	16 925	−1 185	8.4	Sugar
Malawi	9 686	−220	6.3	Beverages/tobacco
Mali	2 955	142	10.0	Vegetable oils
Mozambique	12 251	−1 219	17.1	Sugar
Niger	1 045	311	7.7	Vegetable oils
Nigeria	19 840	829	3.9	Cocoa
Rwanda	1 597	59	2.9	Coffee
Senegal	20 500	649	7.1	Vegetable oils
Tanzania	11 653	−4 371	5.8	Beef
Uganda	13 369	−64	3.1	Coffee
Upper Volta	195	−387	2.1	Pulses
Zaire	9 879	−4 802	4.3	Coffee
Zambia	943	−449	8.2	Beverages/tobacco
Asia				
Bangladesh	2 017	−5 511	5.3	Beverages/tobacco
Burma	6 344	−466	3.0	Rice
Hong Kong	723	−16 168	16.2	Fats
India	254 872	−181 576	18.4	Sugar
Indonesia	42 461	−29 256	6.1	Vegetable oils
Malaysia	49 314	3 626	6.4	Vegetable oils
Nepal	1 034	−605	2.3	Rice
Pakistan	14 850	−52 631	4.5	Beverages/tobacco
Philippines	154 356	−12 480	10.7	Sugar
South Korea	34 986	1 739	22.9	Sugar
Sri Lanka	14 841	3 823	4.1	Beverages/tobacco
Thailand	105 518	−106	6.6	Sugar
North Africa/ Middle East				
Afghanistan	14 084	−291	32.8	Temperate fruits
Algeria	78 899	−34 873	28.5	Beverages/tobacco
Egypt	17 392	−63 160	12.4	Temperature fruits
Iran	190	−107 955	−	Temperature fruits
Iraq	914	−11 828	9.7	Wheat
Morocco	28 681	−17 810	10.1	Vegetable oils
Saudi Arabia	−	5 425	−	−
Sudan	6 947	−1 767	3.0	Oilseeds
Syria	4 933	−11 515	17.6	Coarse grains
Tunisia	35 944	−9 059	22.2	Vegetable oils

Table 3.5 continued

Country	Change in export revenues	Change in agricultural import expenditures	Increase in agricultural export revenues	Most affected export commodity in absolute terms
	(US $1000)		(percent)	
Turkey	81 026	−10 117	23.1	Beverages/tobacco
Yemen, Arab Republic of	156	2 618	5.1	Coffee
Latin America				
Argentina	568 009	1 516	17.3	Beef
Bolivia	14 508	−1 427	22.6	Sugar
Brazil	773 788	−20 584	12.8	Sugar
Chile	39 731	−10 949	40.1	Temperate fruits
Colombia	99 702	−3 109	8.5	Sugar
Dominican Republic	79 384	−1 194	11.7	Sugar
Ecuador	28 930	−652	5.8	Sugar
El Salvador	25 228	−38	5.8	Coffee
Guatemala	39 608	−2 088	7.6	Sugar
Haiti	5 572	−87	8.4	Sugar
Mexico	87 379	−46 810	16.8	Coffee
Peru	38 419	−5 819	14.1	Sugar
Venezuela	3 898	−39 816	5.9	Coffee

Note: The projected trade expansion is based on estimates for the individual commodities listed in Table 3.6. The estimates are based on a removal of tariffs and those nontariff barriers for which NTB *ad valorem* equivalents could be found in published sources. The model employed for making these projections was similar to that specified in the annex to this chapter.

Source: Valdes and Zietz (1980).

largely to other EEC members, due to the removal of the 'common' trade barriers of the Community.[22]

As far as developing-country exports are concerned, their potential gains under the liberalisation scenario represent an increase in real income of approximately $1 billion a year, which is equivalent to about one-third of the gains in export revenues. The difference reflects the cost of domestic resources used to generate additional exports. Table 3.6 examines this increase in developing-country export revenues for selected major agricultural products and also shows their projected change in trade shares for each commodity. The major gains occur for raw and refined sugar (approximately $1 billion annually) with beef and green coffee exports also projected to expand by over $200 million annually.

Valdes and Zietz find potential welfare losses arise from world price increases of imports following a trade liberalisation. (See annex

Table 3.6 Potential absolute and percentage increase in exports of selected developing countries after trade liberalisation, by commodity

Commodity	Increase in LDC export revenues	LDC increase as percentage of initial export revenues	LDC share of total increase in world exports	LDC share of total world exports Initial	Post liberalisation
	(US $1000 1977)		(percent)		
Raw sugar	682 766	25.2	42.9	38.0	38.9
Refined sugar	334 202	46.1	a	34.8	51.4
Beef and veal	243 488	74.9	42.7	19.2	25.1
Green coffee	210 168	3.1	88.8	88.8	88.8
Wine	161 028	46.3	29.0	28.0	28.3
Tobacco	139 628	11.8	43.3	53.0	51.8
Maize	83 361	7.9	14.9	14.9	14.9
Wheat	78 570	13.2	8.5	6.7	6.9
Soy cake	77 631	8.3	30.2	50.1	47.7
Cocoa butter oil	56 492	18.6	90.5	90.5	90.5
Pork	51 018	104.4	7.8	7.8	7.8
Tea	50 646	5.0	90.5	90.5	90.5
Molasses	49 493	21.8	71.3	72.0	71.9
Palm oil	43 580	4.9	96.7	96.7	96.7
Cocoa beans	40 899	2.1	92.3	92.3	92.3
Copra oil	40 695	9.7	91.3	91.4	91.4
Roasted coffee	38 099	94.9	55.6	61.1	58.3
Olive oil	36 100	22.0	56.3	56.3	56.3
Potatoes	32 875	53.0	16.0	19.0	17.8
Soybeans	32 028	3.6	22.2	18.6	18.7
Soy oil	30 278	10.0	a	33.6	35.8
Barley	29 302	85.7	8.2	2.9	4.1
Coffee extracts	28 930	10.7	73.5	80.0	79.3
Apples	28 878	22.9	17.0	25.2	23.2
Groundnut oil	28 617	9.3	74.4	82.5	81.8
Grapes	28 412	76.4	14.1	14.9	14.6
Cocoa paste cake	27 814	19.1	100.0	100.0	100.0
Wheat flour	25 263	86.9	a	2.9	6.5
Cocoa powder	21 703	39.9	a	36.3	46.1
Bananas	21 267	4.3	53.1	53.1	53.1
Milled rice	16 713	1.3	a	45.0	45.5
Groundnut cake	16 014	7.3	93.0	93.0	93.0
Beef preparations	15 181	5.6	52.4	57.0	56.7
Mutton and lamb	13 345	28.2	14.7	6.1	7.0
Oranges	13 028	6.4	15.1	23.5	22.8
Copra cake	12 834	13.8	95.5	95.5	95.5
Malt	12 196	63.8	39.4	3.9	6.0
Beans, dry	11 528	7.0	46.4	50.2	49.9
Groundnuts, shelled	11 438	4.0	62.1	60.8	60.8
Chicken	8 597	28.3	a	4.1	5.4
Sugar, confectionary	7 634	95.1	21.9	28.8	25.0

Table 3.6   *continued*

Commodity	Increase in LDC export revenues	LDC increase as percentage of initial export revenues	LDC share of total increase in world exports	LDC share of total world exports	
				Initial	Post liberalisation
	(US $1000 1977)		(percent)		
Castor oil	6 559	6.4	98.0	98.0	98.0
Lemon and lime	6 382	18.7	18.9	16.6	16.9
Oats	6 091	51.8	5.4	7.5	6.7
Sorghum	5 853	1.3	27.8	33.9	33.8
Copra	5 512	2.7	80.5	80.5	80.5
Sunflower cake	5 151	11.4	76.3	76.3	76.3

[a] Total world exports for this commodity would decrease.
Source: Valdes and Zietz (1980). See the explanatory notes which accompany Table 3.5.

equation (20) for information on how welfare effects are estimated.) The welfare losses to the poorest developing countries originate predominantly from cereals markets (mainly wheat) due to their dependance on foreign suppliers for these products. If no change in the volume of developing-country agricultural imports occurs in response to higher world prices, the current protectionist policies of developed countries 'save' developing countries (in total) approximately $660 million per year.

Aside from the Valdes–Zietz study, other investigations have simulated the effects of changes in protectionism or price support policies in agriculture. The results of representative analyses, which have focused on international price effects and employed models similar to that shown in the annex, are summarised in Table 3.7. While these investigations have often been based on different time-periods and on different assumptions concerning national policies, two important conclusions emerge: that protectionism causes major distortions in international prices and trade flows; and that there are often important adverse secondary effects from the protectionist practices such as increased market instability. The simulation model outlined in this chapter's annex has also been used to quantify the influence of NTBs and tariffs applied to manufactured goods. The results accent the importance of nontariff barriers and show that they generally involve major costs at the national and international levels. Chapter 5 summarises findings of some representative major studies that simulated the costs and effects of nontariff trade barriers.

Table 3.7 Summary of the main results of recent simulation studies on agricultural trade liberalisation

Reference	Basic assumptions	Policy implications
Sarris and Freebairn (1983)	Adoption of free trade by all wheat trading countries except the Soviet Union and other socialist countries of Europe.	World wheat prices rise approximately 11 per cent and the year-to-year variability of wheat prices declines 35 per cent.
" " "	Full liberalisation of wheat trade by the EEC alone.	World wheat prices rise 9 per cent and price variability reduced by 20 per cent.
Koester (1982)	Full liberalisation of EEC grains trade.	World wheat prices rise by 10 per cent and maize prices by 2 per cent.
Sampson and Snape (1980)	Elimination of the EEC variable levies.	World wheat, barley and maize prices rise by 3 to 11 per cent.
Anderson and Tyers (1983)	Full agricultural liberalisation by all developed market economy countries.	Wheat prices rise 20 per cent, coarse grains by 16 per cent, rice by 14 per cent, beef and veal by 24 per cent. Price variability is reduced considerably.
Koester and Bale (1980)	Elimination of EEC sugar protection.	World prices rise by 12 per cent.

Parikh *et al.* (1986)	Removal of all OECD agricultural protection.	Compared to 1970s trend wheat prices rise by 18 per cent, rice 21 per cent, coarse grains 11 per cent, dairy products 31 per cent and bovine products 17 per cent.
Thomson (1985)	Elimination of all EEC agricultural protection.	Increased grain and reduced livestock and sugar production (due to resource shifts from more to less protected sectors) influencing world prices in opposite directions.
Sarris (1985)	World free trade adopted for rice and wheat.	World wheat price falls by 9 per cent and rice by 34 per cent, both prices more stable under free trade.
World Bank (1985)	Full liberalisation of all OECD trade in sugar, beef and veal.	Increased export earnings by developing countries of over $10 000 million annually in terms of 1979–81 prices.
Tyers (1982)	Full liberalisation of grain trade in major producing or consuming developed and developing countries.	Moderately higher prices for wheat and coarse grains but 10 per cent fall in rice prices as compared with prices under a continuation of the protectionist policies of the late 1970s.

Source: Adapted from United Nations Food and Agricultural Organization (1987).

ANNEX TO CHAPTER 3

Technical Description of the Trade Policy Simulation Model

The basic model can be described in a series of equations and identities from which the formulation for the simulations is derived. First the notation is given:

Notation

M – imports
X – exports
P – price
W – welfare
Y – national income

Mn – imports from non-preference-receiving countries
V – output in the importing country
R – revenue
t – tariff rate or non-tariff distortion in *ad valorem* terms

Em – elasticity of import demand with respect to domestic price
Ex – elasticity of export supply with respect to export price
Es – elasticity of substitution with respect to relative prices of the same product from different sources of supply
TC – trade creation
TD – trade diversion
i – subscript denoting commodity
j – subscript denoting domestic/importing country data
k – subscript denoting foreign/exporting country data
  (In certain expressions the subscript K is used to denote data for an alternative foreign/exporting country)
d – prefix denoting change

Examples:
P_{ijk} – Price of commodity i in country j from country k
  (i.e. domestic price in j)
P_{ijk} – Price of commodity i from country k to country j
  (i.e. export/world price j)
M_{ijk} – Imports of i by j from k
X_{ikj} – Exports of i by k to j

The Basic Model

The importing country j's import demand function for commodity i produced in country k may be expressed as:

$$M_{ijk} = F(Y_j, P_{ij}, P_{ik})$$ (1)

The producer/exporting country k's export supply function for commodity i may be expressed as:

$$X_{ijk} = F(P_{ikj})$$ (2)

Expressions (1) and (2) are related by the following identity:

$$M_{ijk} = X_{ikj} \tag{3}$$

Assuming that in a free trade situation the domestic price of the commodity i in the importing market j will be equal to exporting country k's export price plus transport and insurance charges, it follows that this price will rise by an amount equivalent to the *ad valorem* incidence of any tariff or nontariff distortion applied to the good. Thus:

$$P_{ijk} = P_{ikj} (1 + t_{ijk}) \tag{4}$$

It is also clear that the export revenues earned by k are:

$$R_{ikj} = X_{ik}.P_{ikj} \tag{5}$$

Trade Creation

The trade-creation effect is the increased demand in country j for commodity i from exporting country k resulting from the price decrease associated with the assumed full transmission of price changes when tariff or nontariff distortions are reduced or eliminated.

Given the basic model consisting of expressions (1) to (5), it is possible to write the formula for trade creation. First, from expression (4) the total differential of domestic price with respect to tariffs and foreign price is:

$$dP_{ijk} = P_{ikj}.dt_{ijk} + (1+ t_{ijk}).dP_{ikj} \tag{6}$$

Now, the standard expression for the elasticity of import demand with respect to the domestic price can be rearranged as follows:

$$dM_{ijk}/M_{ijk} = Em.(dP_{ijk}/P_{ijk}) \tag{7}$$

Substituting from expression (4) and (6) into expression (7) gives:

$$dM_{ijk}/M_{ijk} = Em.(dt_{ijk}/(1 + t_{ijk}) + dP_{ijk}/P_{ikj}) \tag{8}$$

The standard expression for the elasticity of export supply with respect to the world price can be rearranged as follows:

$$dP_{ikj}/P_{ikj} = (dX_{ikj}/X_{ikj})/Ex \tag{9}$$

From expression (3) it follows that:

$$dM_{ijk}/M_{ijk} = dX_{ikj}/X_{ikj} \tag{10}$$

Substituting expression (10) into (9) and the result into (8) produces the expression that can be employed to compute the trade-creation effect. From equation (3) this is equivalent to exporting country k's growth of exports of commodity i to country j. The expression for trade creation can be written:

$$TC_{ijk} = M_{ijk}.Em.dt_{ijk}/((1 + t_{ijk}).(1 -(Em/Ex)) \tag{11}$$

It may be noted that if the elasticity of export supply with respect to the world price is infinite then the denominator in expression (11) becomes unity.

Trade Diversion

Following standard practice, the term 'trade diversion' is used to account for the tendency of importers to substitute goods from one source to another in response to a change in the import price of supplies from one source, but not from the alternative source. Thus, if prices fall in one overseas country there will be a tendency to purchase more goods from that country and less from countries whose exports are unchanged in price. Trade diversion can also occur not because of the change in the export price as such, but because of introduction or elimination of preferential treatment for goods from one source (or more) while treatment for goods from other sources remains unchanged. Again there could be simply a relative change in the treatment of the goods from different sources in the importing country by differential alterations in the treatment of different foreign suppliers.

(i) Without Explicit Values for the Elasticity of Substitution. If the elasticity of substitution between alternative suppliers is not known then it is still possible to compute the trade-diversion effect using a formulation developed by Baldwin and Murray (1977). However, for this approach it is necessary to be able to calculate the level of import penetration by non-preference-receiving countries, i.e. the level of imports from non-preference-receiving countries in apparent domestic consumption (defined as domestic output of commodity i plus imports less exports of commodity i). The formulation for trade diversion can then be written:

$$TD_{ijk} = TC_{ijk}.(Mn_{ij}/V_{ij}) \tag{12}$$

This formulation assumes 'the substitutability between a developing country product and a similar product produced in non-beneficiary i.e. non-preference-receiving countries should be similar to the substitutability between a developing country product and a similar product produced in the donor importing country'.

(ii) With Explicit Values for the Elasticity of Substitution. If explicit values are available for the elasticity of substitution between goods from different sources then it is not necessary to use the approach outlined above. Alternatively, if there are no market penetration data available then there may be no option but to assume values for the elasticity of substitution (and conduct simulations across a range of reasonable estimates).

It is possible to define the elasticity of substitution as the percentage change in relative shares associated with a 1 per cent change in the relative prices of the same product from alternative sources. That is:

$$Es = \frac{d(\Sigma M_{ijk}/\Sigma M_{ijK})/(\Sigma M_{ijk}/\Sigma M_{ijK})}{d(P_{ijk}/P_{ijK})/(P_{ijk}/P_{ijK})} \tag{13}$$

where k denotes imports from one (group) of foreign supplier(s), K denotes imports from another (group) of foreign supplier(s), and the summation is only across the country group k or K but not across product groups (i) nor across imports (j).

From this expression it is then possible to express the percentage change in the relative shares of the alternative suppliers in terms of the elasticity of substitution, the percentage change in relative prices and the original relative shares of imports from the alternative sources. By extensive expansion, substitution and rearrangement, it is possible to obtain the following expression for the change in imports from one country – or trade diversion (TD) gain or loss, as the case may be – as a result of the change in duty-paid prices relative to the prices from other sources resulting from a commercial policy change:

$$TD_{ijk} = \frac{M_{ijk}}{\Sigma M_{ijk}} \cdot \frac{\Sigma M_{ijk}.\Sigma M_{ijK}.Es.\dfrac{d(P_{ijk}/P_{ijK})}{P_{ijk}/P_{ijK}}}{\Sigma M_{ijk} + \Sigma M_{ijK} + \Sigma M_{ijk}.Es.\dfrac{d(P_{ijk}/P_{ijK})}{P_{ijk}/P_{ijK}}} \tag{14}$$

The term in expression (14) for the relative price movement is specified in terms of the movements of the tariffs or the *ad valorem* incidence of nontariff distortions for the two foreign sources. Expression (14) is the equivalent of the final expression for trade diversion given by Cline *et al.* (1978). Similar expressions can be derived to obtain separate results for the different groups of foreign/exporting countries. Alternatively, the results can be summed for one group, and this sum can be distributed among members of the alternative group of foreign suppliers in accordance with their prior share in the imports.

The Total Trade Effect

The total trade effect is obtained simply by summing together the trade-creation and trade-diversion effects. Results can be summed for the importer across product groups and/or across sources of supply. Results can be summed across groups of importers for single products or groups of products as well as for single sources of supply or for groups of suppliers. Results can also be summed for suppliers across product groups. Finally, results can be summed for groups of suppliers either for individual products or across product groups.

The Price Effect

If the export supply elasticity is infinite then there is no price effect on exports. Otherwise the price effect can be obtained by substituting expression (10) into (9), giving:

$$dP_{ikj}/P_{ikj} = (dt_{ijk}/(1 + t_{ijk})).(Em/(Em - Ex)) \qquad (15)$$

The Revenue Effect

Expression (15) may be directly applied in estimating the revenue effect for the exporting country. If the export supply elasticity is infinite, there is no price effect – as noted above – and consequently revenue increases in proportion to the increase in exports. Otherwise the percentage increase in revenue is equal to the percentage increase in exports plus the percentage increase in prices. This can be shown by taking from expression (5) above the total differential of revenue with respect to export price and the volume of exports:

$$dR_{ikj} = P_{ikj}.dX_{ikj} + X_{ikj}.dP_{ikj} \qquad (16)$$

Dividing the left-hand side (LHS) of (16) with the LHS of expression (5) and the right-hand side (RHS) of (16) with the RHS of (5) gives

$$dR_{ikj}/R_{ikj} = (P_{ikj}.dX_{ikj} + X_{ikj}.dP_{ikj})/(P_{ikj}.X_{ikj}) \qquad (17)$$

Reducing the substituting from expression (10) gives:

$$dR_{ikj}/R_{ikj} = (dM_{ikj}/M_{ijk}) + (dP_{ikj}/P_{ikj}) \qquad (18)$$

Alternatively, this can be written:

$$dR_{ikj}/R_{ikj} = (dt_{ijk}/(1 + t_{ijk})).Em.((1 + Ex)/(Ex - Em)) \qquad (19)$$

The Welfare Effect

The welfare effect arises from the benefits consumers in the importing country derive from the lower domestic prices after the removal or reduction of tariffs or the *ad valorem* incidence of nontariff distortions. As noted by Cline *et al.* (1978), 'for the pre-existing level of imports, any price reduction to the consumer merely represents a transfer away from the the government of tariff revenue formerly collected on the import and therefore no net gain to the country as a whole. But for the increase in imports, there is a net welfare gain equal to the domestic consumers' valuation of the extra imports minus the cost of extra imports at supply price (excluding tariffs).' Thus, the net welfare gain is normally estimated as the increase in import value times the average between the *ad valorem* incidence of the trade barriers before and after their elimination. This welfare gain can also be thought of as the increase in consumer surplus. It can be written:

$$W_{ijk} = 0.5(dt_{ijk}\, dM_{ijk}) \tag{20}$$

In the case where the elasticity of export supply is less than infinity the supply price is higher than previously. The new domestic price of imports does not decline to the full extent of the tariff change and import expansion is less than in the case of infinitely elastic export supply. Welfare can still be computed using expression (20) but needs to be interpreted as a combination of consumer surplus and producer surplus.

4 The Implications of NTB Inventory Studies

Although the procedure does not provide basic information for simulating economic effects of nontariff barriers (as do most of the studies surveyed in Chapter 5), the 'inventory' approach has been widely used in NTB studies. However, a problem that must be resolved before any 'inventory' analysis of trade restraints is undertaken is to determine which nontariff measures will be included in the empirical analysis. One potential approach is to base an empirical study on all entries in the inventory, but there are acknowledged problems with such a line of analysis. The major difficulty is that it would include measures like health and sanitary requirements or automatic import authorisation systems that may often have no, or relatively unimportant, trade effects. As such, NTM frequency or trade coverage indices which included such regulations would likely overstate the importance of nontariff measures.

In recognition of the potential problems, a more selective approach has often been employed in inventory studies of nontariff measures. This approach recognises that certain types of measures, like quotas or variable import levies, normally are imposed with the specific intent of modifying or restricting international trade. These 'hard core' nontariff measures are frequently defined to include: variable import levies and other similar product-specific charges; non-automatic import authorisation requirements such as restrictive licensing regulations; 'voluntary' export restraints for both prices and quantities; trade restrictions negotiated under the Multifibre Arrangement (MFA); prohibitions; and various quantitative restrictions such as global and bilateral quotas. Since the present chapter is primarily concerned with trade effects, the empirical analysis focuses on these 'hard core' restrictions. Measures like health and sanitary regulations, packaging and labelling requirements, or technical standards, all of which can be applied in ways that restrict trade, are excluded from the analysis.[1]

THE GLOBAL IMPORTANCE OF NONTARIFF MEASURES

A question of obvious importance for any assessment of nontariff measures concerns their overall or global influence on world trade.

For an initial evaluation, Table 4.1 shows NTM frequency and trade coverage indices for OECD imports from the world and three major groups of exporters, namely, developed, developing and socialist countries of Eastern Europe. To assist in evaluating changes in the application of these measures the NTM (hard core) indices have been computed for three years: 1981, 1983 and 1986.[2]

Overall, Table 4.1 shows that in 1981 'hard core' nontariff measures were applied to approximately 15.1 per cent of OECD non-petroleum imports, a point which indicates that about $80 billion in trade (excluding EEC intra-trade) was affected.[3] However, there is some variation in the incidence of hard-core NTMs on different exporters. Table 4.1 shows, for example, that in 1981 approximately 14.3 per cent (or $49 billion) of OECD imports from other developed countries were affected by nontariff measures, while the trade coverage index for developing countries was 4.5 points higher or 18.8 per cent (which implies $26 billion in affected trade). The relatively low NTM coverage ratio for the socialist countries' exports (9.3 per cent) is due largely to the high share (about 22 per cent) of natural gas (SITC 34) in total exports to the OECD area and the fact that these products did not encounter hard-core trade measures.

The statistics in Table 4.1 show the importance of NTMs increased from 1981 to 1986. Overall, the hard-core trade coverage ratio rose by 2.6 percentage points over 1981–6, which implies that these barriers spread to approximately $14 billion in previously unaffected trade. The increase was spread unevenly among the different groups of exporters, with the 3.2 percentage point increase for developed countries being the largest in the table. Analysis of the underlying statistics shows that 'voluntary' export restraints were a major element in this expansion of protectionism (particularly in the United States – See Table 4.9), and that their use was largely concentrated in several specific sectors like ferrous metals, agriculture and transportation equipment.

Table 4.2 examines changes in the use of hard-core nontariff measures in sixteen individual OECD countries over the 1981 to 1986 period. For each country, NTM frequency and trade coverage ratios are shown for 1981, 1983 and 1986, and their change (in points) over the period is computed. The country breakdown indicates that the United States had the greatest expansion in new trade restrictions as its NTM trade coverage ratio rose 5.9 points to 17.3 per cent. This increase was almost two-and-a-half times that of the European Community (where the index rose by 2.4 points) and more than doubled

Table 4.1   Frequency ratios and the share of OECD country non-petroleum imports subject to hard-core nontariff measures,[1] 1981, 1983 and 1986

Importers/Partners[2]	1981 OECD Imports[2] (million)	Frequency ratio[3]				Trade coverage ratio[4]			
		1981	1983	1986	1981–6 Change (points)	1981	1983	1986	1981–6 Change (points)
OECD/World	521 300	12.2	12.5	12.0	−0.2	15.1	16.7	17.7	+2.6
OECD/Developed	344 300	8.4	8.6	8.2	−0.2	14.3	16.3	17.5	+3.2
OECD/Developing	136 600	18.7	19.0	18.4	−0.3	18.8	19.6	20.6	+1.8
OECD/Socialist	40 400	17.7	18.0	17.8	+0.1	9.3	10.2	9.8	+0.5

[1] Hard-core nontariff measures include: Variable import levies and product specific charges (excluding tariff quotas); Quotas; Prohibitions (including seasonal prohibitions): non-automatic import authorisations including restrictive import licensing requirements; quantitative 'voluntary' export restraints; and trade restraints under the Multifibre Arrangement. Not included are measures like health and sanitary regulations, packaging and labelling requirements, technical standards, minimum price regulations and tariff quotas. In subsequent tables an attempt may be made to assess the importance of these additional measures.

[2] OECD importing countries include: Belgium-Luxembourg, Denmark, France, German Federal Republic, Great Britain, Greece, Ireland, Italy, Netherlands, Finland, Japan, New Zealand, Norway, and the United States. Trade data exclude EEC intra-trade. Australia, Canada and Sweden were excluded from the computations due to technical problems experienced in compilation of these countries NTM files.

[3] The percentage of tariff-line-level products subject to hard-core nontariff measures. See equation (2.1) in Chapter 2.

[4] The share of total imports (by value) subject to hard-core nontariff measures. See equation (2.2) in Chapter 2. In computing this index, 1981, 1983 and 1986 nontariff measures are applied to a constant 1981 trade base. This allows one to examine the influence of NTM changes while holding the effects of trade changes constant.

Table 4.2 Frequency ratios and nontariff measure trade coverage ratios for individual OECD countries, 1981, 1983 and 1986

Importer	Frequency ratio[1]				Trade coverage ratio[1]			
	1981	1983	1986	1981–6 Change (points)	1981	1983	1986	1981–6 Change (points)
Belgium-Luxembourg	8.4	8.7	8.6	0.2	12.6	15.4	14.3	1.7
Denmark	9.0	9.1	9.2	0.2	6.7	8.0	7.9	1.2
Germany, Fed. Rep.	11.1	11.2	12.5	1.4	11.8	13.6	15.4	3.6
France	13.5	14.4	14.1	0.6	15.7	18.8	18.6	2.9
Greece	10.4	11.1	10.6	0.2	16.2	21.0	20.1	3.9
Great Britain	10.1	10.1	8.1	-0.2	11.2	13.4	12.8	2.4
Ireland	6.3	6.5	6.5	0.2	8.2	9.7	9.7	1.5
Italy	18.1	18.6	18.3	0.2	17.2	18.7	18.2	1.0
Netherlands	11.0	11.2	11.1	0.1	19.9	21.4	21.4	1.5
EEC (10)[2]	11.4	11.7	11.5	0.1	13.4	15.6	15.8	2.4
Switzerland	9.7	9.7	9.7	0.0	19.5	19.6	19.6	0.1
Finland	3.4	3.4	3.4	0.0	7.9	8.0	8.0	0.1
Japan	12.7	12.8	12.5	-0.2	24.4	24.5	24.3	-0.1
Norway	19.8	19.6	17.4	-2.4	15.2	14.7	14.2	-1.0
New Zealand	45.0	45.0	38.8	-6.2	46.4	46.4	32.4	-14.0
United States	4.8	5.2	6.5	1.7	11.4	13.7	17.3	5.9
All above	12.2	12.5	12.0	-0.2	15.1	16.7	17.7	2.6

[1] See the footnotes to Table 4.1 for a listing of NTMs used in the computations of these indices. Petroleum products have been excluded from the calculations.
[2] Excludes EEC intra-trade.

the OECD average. In Japan, the index dropped slightly as barriers were removed in an effort to reduce this country's trade surplus, and in Finland and Switzerland the coverage index was virtually unchanged over 1981–6. Among the major industrial countries there is considerable variation in the overall level of the NTM coverage figures, with Denmark having the lowest (1986) ratio in the table (just under Finland's hard-core NTM coverage ratio of 8 per cent). At the other extreme, the corresponding figure for Japan stood at over 24 per cent while almost one-third of New Zealand's imports were affected by NTMs.[4]

In some instances, Table 4.2 shows there are sizeable differences between 1981 to 1986 changes in the NTM frequency ratios and the trade coverage indices. For Britain, the two measures actually move in opposite directions with the frequency index falling by two points and the trade coverage ratio increasing by almost two-and-a-half points. In these cases, the underlying (tariff-line) data show there was a removal of NTMs for selected items with relatively low import values and new restrictions applied to more important products. As a result, the number of products facing NTMs fell more (or rose less) than the corresponding trade coverage ratio. This selective pattern of NTM removal and application seemingly makes the NTM frequency index less reliable as an indicator of change in protection.[5]

Table 4.3 takes a more detailed look at the level and 1981–6 changes in nontariff measures in the sixteen OECD countries by analysing their overall impact on total imports as well as on imports from developed, developing and socialist countries of Eastern Europe separately. Perhaps the key point to emerge from the table concerns differences in the coverage of the OECD importing country's NTMs on these groups of exporters. In Britain, for example, almost 13 per cent of total imports encountered NTMs in 1986 while the share of developing-country exports facing restrictions (24.7 per cent) was nearly twice as high.[6] In Norway, 'voluntary' restrictions on tropical beverages pushed the coverage ratio for developing countries' exports to over 40 per cent, a figure which is more than three times the Norwegian national average (14.2 per cent).

Overall, Table 4.3 shows that the coverage of hard-core NTMs was higher on developing as opposed to developed countries' exports in both 1981 and 1986, and that this adverse differential was particularly high (about 10 percentage points) in the EEC. In Japan, this pattern is reversed as quantitative restrictions on temperate zone agricultural

Table 4.3 Analysis of the incidence of OECD country nontariff measures on different groups of exporting countries, 1981 and 1986

Importer	1981 trade coverage[1]				1986 trade coverage[1]			
	Developed	Developing	Socialist	World	Developed	Developing	Socialist	World
Belgium-Luxembourg	12.7	12.4	11.8	12.6	14.9	13.2	11.8	14.3
Denmark	4.3	20.9	4.7	6.7	6.1	20.9	4.7	7.9
Germany, Fed. Rep.	7.3	24.3	8.5	11.8	11.5	28.6	9.2	15.4
France	14.5	15.5	27.9	15.7	18.0	17.4	28.1	18.6
Greece	16.0	12.5	24.9	16.2	22.6	12.3	25.2	20.1
Great Britain	9.8	25.4	1.2	11.2	12.9	24.7	1.1	12.8
Ireland	6.8	15.6	14.7	8.2	8.6	15.8	14.7	9.7
Italy	15.6	21.2	14.2	17.2	17.3	21.3	14.1	18.2
Netherlands	17.4	27.0	12.1	19.9	19.7	27.1	12.1	21.4
EEC (10)[2]	11.3	21.7	8.3	13.4	14.4	23.2	8.5	15.8
Switzerland	19.6	18.1	25.2	19.5	19.6	18.1	25.2	19.6
Finland	5.2	15.3	22.2	7.9	5.2	15.9	22.2	8.0
Japan	29.5	17.4	13.1	24.4	29.4	17.4	13.1	24.3
Norway	13.2	46.9	13.0	15.2	12.5	41.2	12.3	14.2
New Zealand	47.8	35.3	30.2	46.4	32.9	29.1	26.0	32.4
United States	9.7	15.5	4.4	11.4	16.6	19.1	12.1	17.3
All above	14.3	18.8	9.3	15.1	17.5	20.6	9.8	17.7

[1] See the footnotes to Table 4.1 for a listing of NTMs used in the computation of these indices. Petroleum products have been excluded from the calculations.
[2] Excludes EEC intra-trade.

products (particularly meat, dairy and cereal products) as well as on coal cause the 1986 NTM coverage ratio for imports from developed countries (29.4 per cent) to exceed that for developing countries by 12 percentage points.[7]

THE SECTORIAL COVERAGE OF NONTARIFF MEASURES

While the previous analysis demonstrated that considerable variation existed in the country coverage of nontariff measures, wide variation also exists in the coverage of specific products. As an illustration, Table 4.4 presents 1986 NTM coverage indices for the European Community and six other developed countries, namely, Switzerland, Finland, Japan, Norway, New Zealand and the United States. These indices have been computed for each two-digit SITC product within the food and agricultural raw materials group. Table 4.5 provides similar information for manufactured products falling in SITC 6 to 8.

Several important points emerge from the agricultural trade coverage ratios given in Table 4.4. First, while there is considerable variation from product to product and country to country the NTM ratios are generally far higher than the overall national averages shown in previous tables. As an example, over 96 per cent of EEC imports of cereals and products (SITC 04) encounter nontariff measures, while the EEC trade coverage ratio for dairy products (SITC 02) is over 99 per cent. In contrast, imports of agricultural raw material such as tobacco, hides and skins, or wood and cork, encounter few or no trade restrictions.[8] Meat, dairy products, cereals and sugar generally have the highest NTM ratios in the European countries and Japan, although 100 per cent of Norwegian imports of coffee and cocoa, beverages, oilseeds and nuts, and other food preparations, encounter one or more forms of nontariff measures. Several studies surveyed in Chapter 5 of this book estimated that some of these European agricultural trade barriers have *ad valorem* equivalents that exceed 100 per cent.

A further point evident in Table 4.4 concerns the major differences in the level of nontariff measure use for agricultural protection in the United States (and to a lesser extent in New Zealand) as opposed to the European countries and Japan. In the USA, quotas on dairy products and a combination of quotas and a variable import levy on sugar imports produce NTM coverage ratios that match European levels for these products, but in almost every other case the United

Table 4.4 The incidence of OECD nontariff measures on imports of foodstuffs and agricultural raw materials,[1] 1986

SITC	Description	EEC (10)[2]	Switzerland	Finland	Japan	Norway	New Zealand	USA
00	Live animals	60.2	100.0	95.3	1.2	98.0	0.0	0.0
01	Meat	77.8	97.8	89.3	65.7	99.7	14.4	0.0
02	Dairy products	99.7	45.5	100.0	73.2	82.1	12.7	87.8
03	Fish and seafood	4.6	58.3	9.7	100.0	80.4	3.6	0.0
04	Cereals and preparations	96.9	87.8	83.4	32.5	100.0	5.1	0.0
05	Fruits and vegetables	36.0	44.8	51.6	18.3	100.0	39.2	0.9
06	Sugar and honey	85.8	0.0	89.1	84.6	100.0	0.9	91.9
07	Coffee and cocoa	17.5	0.0	0.0	0.0	100.0	0.9	2.3
08	Animal feeds	11.9	30.9	5.3	13.7	92.7	16.9	0.3
09	Food preparations	10.2	13.4	0.0	17.3	100.0	73.7	0.4
11	Beverages	24.9	76.4	88.0	70.7	100.0	5.6	0.0
12	Tobacco	0.0	0.0	0.0	84.3	0.0	5.1	0.0
21	Hides and skins	0.0	99.1	0.0	18.1	0.0	0.0	3.2
22	Oil seeds and nuts	24.8	56.0	100.0	4.3	100.0	0.0	74.0
23	Rubber	0.0	0.0	0.0	0.0	0.0	0.0	0.0
24	Wood and cork	0.6	39.6	0.0	0.0	0.0	2.4	0.0
25	Pulp and paper	0.0	0.0	0.0	0.0	0.0	0.0	0.0
26	Silk, wool, cotton, etc.	0.0	24.8	0.0	1.2	4.6	16.4	2.1
29	Crude animal & vegetable matter	9.0						
		19.0	78.0	5.3	51.8	69.1	11.2	11.0

[1] See the footnotes to Table 4.1 for a listing of NTMs used in the computation of this index. Petroleum products have been excluded from the calculations.

[2] Excludes EEC intra-trade. See the annex to this chapter for more detailed information on NTMs facing the imports of individual EEC countries.

States ratios are zero or negligible. In contrast, EEC temperate zone agricultural imports often encounter a wide range of hard-core measures with variable import levies, quantitative restrictions, seasonal tariffs and restrictive licensing regulations combining to produce trade coverage ratios often exceeding 70 or 80 per cent. In many cases, Sampson and Yeats (1977, p. 105) show there is a multiple application or 'stacking' of the EEC's hard-core measures on a specific agricultural product. As an example, imports of sugar and honey into the EEC encounter variable import levies, seasonal prohibitions, licensing requirements and bilateral quotas. Unmilled wheat faces quotas and levies, while some fresh vegetables face levies, quotas and seasonal restrictions.

In contrast to the protection afforded agriculture, Table 4.5 shows that the EEC and other industrial countries' NTM trade coverage ratios for manufactured goods are generally lower and there is less variation between countries and products (see Table A4.2 in the annex to this chapter for details on individual European Community member NTM coverage ratios). Iron and steel (SITC 67), textiles (SITC 65), and clothing (SITC 84), have the highest trade coverage ratios among the manufactured products (from 35 to 65 per cent for the EEC, and 35 to 76 per cent for the USA), but for the latter two product groups the overall statistics do not reflect the discriminatory nature of existing trade barriers. Specifically, under the Multifibre Arrangement (MFA) quotas are set on most OECD imports of textiles and clothing from developing countries while imports from other developed countries are traded freely (except for Japan which, alone among developed countries, is also affected by the MFA). Thus, the coverage ratios in Table 4.5 are a composite for developed and developing countries and do not reflect the true adverse (discriminatory) effects of MFA restrictions on developing countries.[9]

Along with textiles and clothing, the NTM trade coverage ratios for iron and steel are generally among the highest recorded for manufactured products. In the European Community, 46 per cent of all imports of these products encounter hard-core NTMs while the corresponding ratio for the United States is over 76 per cent. Annex Table A4.8 shows that both the EEC and USA have primarily attempted to protect domestic industries through negotiation of 'voluntary' restraint arrangements, and that there have been important changes in the instruments employed to achieve protection over 1981–6. (Table A4.8 indicates, for example, that the USA shifted away from reference prices for iron and steel imports to a greater

Table 4.5 The incidence of OECD nontariff measures on imports of various manufactured products, 1986

		1986 NTM coverage ratio[1]						
SITC	Description	EEC (10)[2]	Switzerland	Finland	Japan	Norway	New Zealand	USA
61	Leather products	7.7	30.8	0.0	47.0	0.0	59.9	0.0
62	Rubber products	9.1	0.0	0.0	13.6	0.7	53.9	0.0
63	Wood and cork	1.0	1.9	0.0	0.0	0.0	53.0	0.0
64	Paper and articles	5.9	0.0	0.0	0.0	0.0	48.6	0.0
65	Textiles	34.7	0.0	1.6	55.5	6.1	27.4	34.5
66	Cement, clay and glass	2.9	0.0	0.0	24.1	0.0	54.5	0.1
67	Iron and steel	46.2	1.0	0.0	0.0	0.0	64.1	76.3
68	Non-ferrous metals	0.8	1.9	3.5	0.4	0.0	8.7	0.0
69	Metal manufactures, n.e.s.	2.1	5.6	0.0	1.0	0.0	35.3	11.0
71	Non-electric machinery	3.1	4.7	0.0	4.4	0.0	35.9	0.0
72	Electric machinery	11.1	0.0	0.0	0.3	0.0	64.0	1.4
73	Transport equipment	23.6	84.7	0.0	17.3	0.0	22.1	41.1
81	Plumbing & lighting fixtures	0.0	0.0	0.0	0.0	0.0	68.2	0.0
82	Furniture	0.3	0.0	0.0	0.0	0.1	0.0	1.1
83	Travel goods	0.9	53.0	0.0	0.0	0.0	100.0	18.9
84	Clothing	65.7	18.6	12.1	11.3	86.5	52.2	76.4
85	Footwear	11.3	74.6	0.0	6.9	0.3	82.9	0.1
86	Instruments	3.8	0.0	0.0	14.1	0.0	5.3	0.0

[1] See the footnotes to Table 4.1 for a listing of NTMs used in the computation of this index. Petroleum products have been excluded from the calculations.

[2] Excludes EEC intra-trade. See the annex to this chapter for more detailed information on NTMs facing the imports of individual EEC countries.

reliance on 'voluntary' restraint arrangements.) Studies that compiled estimates of the *ad valorem* incidence of ferrous-metal barriers in the United States indicate they often take values between 15 to 30 per cent (see OECD, 1985c).

As far as individual countries are concerned, the NTM trade coverage ratios for New Zealand are consistently among the highest in Table 4.5. New Zealand formerly employed a quota-licensing system for all manufactured imports, but has initiated a longer-term programme to liberalise and remove these restraints. Throughout the 1980s, existing quota limits on imports were progressively expanded, and when a point was reached that the quotas were unfilled they were dropped. This procedure produced major changes in import restrictions as approximately 30 per cent of New Zealand's quotas were removed in 1987.[10]

NATIONAL VARIATIONS IN NONTARIFF MEASURE USAGE

Aside from overall differences in the coverage of nontariff measures at the national level, variations in the use of specific types of nontariff measures from country to country are a matter of interest. The question of reliance on different forms of nontariff barriers is potentially important for several reasons, including the fact that there may be differences in the trade, economic and welfare effects of individual nontariff measures. (See Yeats, 1979, ch. 2, for a discussion of these differences.) There are also important implications for liberalisation strategies, as negotiating approaches based on a barrier-by-barrier elimination of trade restrictions could be complicated by major differences in countries usage of specific types of measures.

Table 4.6 examines differences in national patterns of NTM use by comparing statistics on OECD countries' reliance on ten different types of barriers (tariff quotas, seasonal import charges, variable import levies, anti-dumping and countervailing duties, etc.). The table entries indicate the share of imports from other developed countries subject to these restrictions, while Table 4.7 provides similar statistics based on imports from developing countries. Two points should be noted concerning the tables. First, several of the measures like tariff quotas or seasonal tariffs are not included in the groups of 'hard core' NTMs, but are shown due to their importance in some national protectionist profiles. Second, the trade coverage indices continue to be computed using a 1981 trade base. That is, the tables show the share of 1981 trade subject to nontariff measures operating in 1986.

The trade coverage ratios show there are major differences in the reliance on specific types of NTMs in the sixteen OECD countries. For example, quantitative 'voluntary' export restraints cover approximately 7 per cent of OECD imports from other developed countries while quantitative restrictions are applied to approximately 5 per cent of these imports. Seasonal import charges are of far less importance, however (covering about 0.4 per cent of total imports), while tariff quotas, anti-dumping and countervailing duties, and minimum import price requirements each cover between 1.1 to 1.4 per cent of total exports. A somewhat different ranking is established for OECD imports from developing countries; as Table 4.7 shows, MFA restrictions are applied to about 7.6 per cent of this trade while non-automatic licensing regulations and quota restrictions each cover about 5 per cent of imports.

Aside from the variation in these aggregate statistics, Table 4.7 shows that major differences often exist in individual OECD countries' use of specific measures. For example, the United States applies 'voluntary' export restraints to over 15 per cent of its total imports from other developed countries, while Switzerland, Finland, Japan, Norway and New Zealand have not utilised these measures.[11]

Japan applies restrictive quotas to many temperate zone agricultural imports, as well as to various raw material products and some manufactured goods.[12] Quotas on coal and coke (which account for about 11 per cent of Japanese non-petroleum imports) are of major importance in the overall Japanese protectionist profile, but non-automatic import licensing is also used to regulate trade in meat, fish, animal feeds and animal oils and fats. The tables also indicate that considerable diversity exists in the number of nontariff measures used to control imports, into the OECD countries. New Zealand, for example, only applies licensing regulations and quotas to developed-country exports, while the EEC countries use eight different major types of restraints to control North–North trade.

A comparison of the statistics in Tables 4.6 and 4.7 shows that there are some important differences in the imposition of nontariff measures on developing as opposed to developed-country exports. For example, about 9.6 per cent of all developing-country exports to OECD markets encounter MFA restrictions or other textile quotas while, except for some residual United States restrictions on Japan,

Table 4.6 The incidence of OECD country nontariff measures on imports from developed countries

Importer		Share of imports facing alternative forms of NTMs (1986)[1]								
	TARQ	TARS	VARL	DUMP	MINP	NALIC	QRS	VERS	MFA	QRTEX
Belgium-Luxembourg	0.8	0.7	5.0	0.9	1.7	5.4	0.3	9.1	0.0	0.0
Denmark	2.5	0.9	1.2	0.1	2.5	0.8	0.2	5.1	0.0	0.0
Germany, Fed. Rep.	1.7	0.6	1.6	1.0	2.3	2.6	0.3	7.5	0.0	0.0
France	1.1	1.1	1.2	0.3	3.6	7.9	5.9	4.3	0.0	0.0
Greece	2.5	0.0	4.2	0.3	2.1	4.2	9.8	13.8	0.0	0.0
Great Britain	0.4	0.8	5.0	0.3	4.2	5.5	1.2	7.1	0.0	0.0
Ireland	2.0	0.2	1.4	1.0	0.6	1.4	0.1	7.1	0.0	0.0
Italy	1.2	0.0	7.2	0.4	1.4	7.5	7.5	2.8	0.0	0.0
Netherlands	1.7	0.7	4.2	0.7	2.3	14.3	0.3	5.3	0.0	0.0
EEC (10)	1.2	0.7	3.4	0.6	2.8	5.8	2.3	6.3	0.0	0.0
Switzerland	0.0	0.2	0.5	0.0	0.0	2.8	2.3	0.0	0.0	0.0

Finland	0.0	0.8	1.3	0.0	0.0	4.4	0.7	0.0	0.0	0.0
Japan	2.0	0.4	2.3	0.0	0.0	5.7	20.5	0.0	0.0	0.0
Norway	0.0	0.3	0.0	0.0	0.4	0.8	4.3	0.0	0.0	0.0
New Zealand	0.0	0.0	0.0	0.0	0.0	18.1	27.6	0.0	0.0	0.0
United States	1.6	0.0	0.3	2.5	0.0	0.0	0.8	15.5	0.4[2]	0.0
All above	1.3	0.4	1.9	1.4	1.1	3.7	4.8	7.4	0.1	0.0

[1] Horizontal summation of trade coverage ratios for individual NTMs may not equal total 'hard' core ratios shown in previous tables due to the multiple application or 'stacking' of barriers on a specific product. In addition, trade coverage ratios for several additional measures which are 'hard' core NTMs are not shown in this table. The codes for the column headings are as follows: TARQ – tariff quotas; TARS – seasonal tariffs; VARL – variable import levies; DUMP – anti-dumping and countervailing duties (excluding investigations); MINP – minimum import price requirements; NALIC – non-automatic import licensing regulations; QRS – quantitative restrictions (global or bilateral) other than 'voluntary' or MFA restraints; VERS – quantitative 'voluntary' export restraints; MFA – restrictions negotiated under the Multifibre Arrangement; QRTEX – special textile and clothing quotas negotiated outside the MFA.

[2] Restrictions on Japanese textile exports originating in the Short and Long-Term Textile Arrangement.

Table 4.7 The incidence of OECD country nontariff measures on imports from developing countries

Importer	Share of imports facing alternative forms of NTMs (1986)[1]									
	TARQ	TARS	VARL	DUMP	MINP	NALIC	QRS	VERS	MFA	QRTEX
Belgium-Luxembourg	4.7	0.4	5.6	0.1	1.6	6.2	4.3	3.2	4.5	1.6
Denmark	0.8	0.6	3.0	0.0	2.3	3.1	1.0	0.3	13.9	2.9
Germany, Fed. Rep.	2.3	1.3	2.7	0.1	3.6	4.8	2.2	1.8	14.6	4.7
France	0.3	1.4	2.9	0.0	4.7	3.7	9.8	0.6	5.4	1.1
Greece	1.1	0.0	1.7	0.0	2.2	1.9	5.3	0.3	3.1	2.3
Great Britain	1.5	1.0	6.7	0.0	3.7	8.6	2.6	0.2	13.7	1.7
Ireland	2.5	0.9	6.8	0.0	3.2	6.8	0.8	0.5	7.7	1.0
Italy	0.9	0.3	5.9	0.2	3.2	6.5	9.3	0.6	5.4	1.7
Netherlands	0.8	2.0	12.1	0.0	4.3	16.3	8.3	7.6	7.8	2.3
EEC (10)	1.6	1.1	5.1	0.1	3.7	6.8	5.4	1.7	9.9	2.5
Switzerland	0.0	0.4	0.0	0.0	0.0	1.6	4.5	0.0	5.7	0.0
Finland	0.0	9.5	3.8	0.0	0.0	8.2	2.6	0.0	4.8	0.0
Japan	0.2	0.8	0.9	0.0	0.0	11.4	5.0	0.0	0.0	0.0
Norway	0.0	1.7	0.0	0.0	1.9	4.2	11.1	0.0	0.0	0.0
New Zealand	0.0	0.0	0.0	0.0	0.0	7.1	21.6	0.0	0.0	0.0
United States	0.2	0.8	3.7	0.9	0.0	0.0	4.5	2.1	9.7	2.8
All above	0.8	1.0	3.6	1.2	1.6	5.3	5.1	1.5	7.6	2.0

[1] Horizontal summation of trade coverage ratios for individual NTMs may not equal total 'hard' core ratios shown in previous tables due to the multiple application or 'stacking' of barriers on a specific product. In addition, trade coverage ratios for several additional measure which are 'hard' core NTMs are not shown in this table. See Table 4.6 for a description of each NTM listed in the column headings.

these measures are not applied to imports from other developed countries. The trade coverage ratio for variable import levies is also relatively high on developing-country products (3.6 per cent as opposed to 1.9 per cent on imports from other developed countries), while non-automatic import licensing regulations also have a higher incidence on developing-country products (5.3 as opposed to 3.7 per cent). In contrast, VERs are far more important for developed-country exporters, as their trade coverage on North–North trade (7.4 per cent) is more than three times that of developing-country shipments.

Table 4.8 examines, in more detail, differences in usage of various forms of nontariff restrictions on agricultural imports by the United States, European Community and Japan. Table 4.8 shows the incidence of four major types of restrictions (i.e. variable import levies, minimum import price regulations, non-automatic licensing and quotas) on foodstuffs and agricultural raw materials. Tables A4.4 and A4.5 in the annex to this chapter provide similar statistics for chemicals and other manufactured goods.

The key point evident from Table 4.8 is that very different types of nontariff measures are used for agricultural protection in the EEC, Japan and United States. The European Community primarily employs price control measures like variable import levies or minimum import price requirements, with the effects of these measures reinforced by restrictive import licensing requirements. Japan and the United States, in contrast, tend to rely on measures that act on imported quantities (like quotas on tariff quotas), although both have adopted some measures similar to the EEC variable import levies. The United States, for example, now applies a sliding-scale import charge on sugar imports while Japan applies an import levy to some cereals and sugar products.

The use of different trade control measures also extends to chemical and manufactures imports, although the country differences are not as pronounced as in the case of agriculture (see Annex Tables A4.4 and A4.5). Japan applies relatively few trade control measures to manufactured goods (important quotas on leather and rubber products are an exception), while the United States has employed anti-dumping duties in a number of industry sectors (see Table A4.5). In contrast, the EEC makes fairly liberal use of restrictive licensing regulations as well as quantitative restrictions on imports.

Are there important changes in the types of nontariff devices used for protection in the 1980s? Table 4.9 examines relevant information

Table 4.8   Trade coverage of two-digit SITC agricultural imports by NTMs in the EEC, Japan and USA 1986

SITC	Description	EEC (10)[1]				Japan[2]				USA[3]			
		VARL	MINP	NALIC	QRS	TARQ	VARL	NALIC	QRS	TARQ	ANTIDP	TAXES	QRS
00	Live animals	50.2	29.0	58.5	13.1	13.4	1.2	0.0	0.0	29.1	5.9	0.0	0.0
01	Meat	55.0	37.5	70.1	18.1	0.0	37.4	7.1	22.0	0.0	8.5	0.0	0.0
02	Dairy products	99.7	3.0	96.3	0.8	12.9	0.0	0.0	72.9	2.3	0.0	0.0	87.7
03	Fish and seafood	0.0	51.8	1.0	3.6	0.0	0.0	100.0	13.2	14.1	12.0	0.0	0.0
04	Cereals & preparations	98.9	1.1	96.9	0.0	16.3	0.0	0.0	32.5	1.0	1.0	0.0	0.0
05	Fruits & vegetables	13.1	48.6	20.2	18.1	0.0	0.0	2.8	15.6	1.4	3.9	12.3	0.9
06	Sugar & honey	89.8	0.0	85.1	0.7	0.0	84.6	0.0	0.1	0.0	0.1	0.0	91.9
07	Coffee & Cocoa	7.1	0.0	0.2	0.0	0.0	0.0	0.0	0.0	0.0	0.0	0.0	2.3
08	Animal feeds	3.9	0.8	11.5	0.4	4.7	0.0	13.7	0.0	0.0	0.0	0.0	0.3
09	Food preparations	53.4	4.5	6.7	3.2	0.0	0.0	15.6	14.5	0.0	0.3	0.0	0.4
11	Beverages	0.1	73.7	21.9	3.0	0.0	0.0	0.0	0.0	0.0	0.0	96.7	0.0
12	Tobacco	0.0	0.0	0.0	0.0	0.0	0.0	0.0	0.0	0.0	0.0	3.1	0.0
21	Hides & skins	0.0	0.0	0.0	0.0	0.0	0.0	0.0	0.0	0.0	0.0	0.0	0.0
22	Oilseeds & nuts	0.0	0.0	24.0	0.7	0.0	0.0	0.0	4.3	0.0	0.0	0.0	74.0
23	Rubber	0.0	0.0	0.0	0.0	0.0	0.0	0.0	0.0	0.0	0.0	0.0	0.0
24	Wood & cork	0.0	0.0	0.3	0.3	0.0	0.0	0.0	0.0	0.0	0.0	0.0	0.0

25	Pulp & paper	0.0	0.0	0.0	0.0	0.0	0.0	0.0	0.0	0.0
26	Silk, wool & cotton	0.0	0.0	5.4	0.0	1.2	0.0	6.7	0.0	2.1
29	Crude animal & vegetable fibres	0.0	10.7	0.0	0.0	0.0	0.0	0.0	0.0	10.7
41	Animal oils & fats	2.2	7.6	0.0	0.0	8.8	0.0	0.0	0.0	0.0
42	Fixed vegetable oils	8.8	8.8	0.0	0.0	0.0	0.0	0.0	0.0	0.0
43	Refined animal & vegetable oils	0.0	0.0	0.9	0.0	0.1	0.0	0.0	0.0	0.0

[1] Excludes EEC intra-trade. Aside from the entries shown in table, 10.3 per cent of fruit and vegetable (SITC 05) imports are subject to 'voluntary' export restraints while 4.4 and 20.0 per cent of these imports face tariff quotas and seasonal tariffs respectively. Tariff quotas are also applied to 6.1 per cent of live animal (SITC 00) imports; 7.7 per cent of meat imports (SITC 01); 4.1 per cent of dairy (SITC 02); and 16.4 per cent of fish (SITC 03) imports. Approximately 74 and 96 per cent of beverage (SITC 11) and tobacco (SITC 96) imports also face special tariff-type charges.

[2] Aside from the entries in the table, 23.9 per cent of Japan's fruit and vegetable imports (SITC 05) face seasonal tariffs.

[3] Aside from the entries in the table, 17.5 per cent of US dairy imports (SITC 02) encounter seasonal tariffs and 91.9 per cent of sugar and honey imports (SITC 06) face variable import levies.

Note: The NTMs listed in this table are the most extensively applied to agricultural imports. They are designated as follows: VARL – variable import levies; MINP – minimum import price regulations; NALIC – non-automatic licensing regulations; TARQ – tariff quotas; TAXES – special discriminatory import taxes. ANTIDP – anti-dumping or countervailing duties (excluding investigations);

Table 4.9 Analysis of changes in the use of different forms of NTMs in OECD countries, 1981 to 1986

Importer	Share of imports facing NTMs in 1981[1]						Change in the share of imports facing NTMs, 1981–6					
	VARL	MINP	NALIC	QRS	VERS	MFA	VARL	MINP	NALIC	QRS	VERS	MFA
Belgium-Luxembourg	5.2	1.9	5.7	0.3	5.1	1.2	0.0	0.0	0.0	1.1	2.2	0.0
Denmark	1.4	3.5	1.1	0.3	2.6	2.3	0.0	0.1	0.0	0.1	1.2	-0.1
Germany, Fed. Rep.	2.0	2.5	3.0	0.5	3.0	4.9	0.0	0.1	0.0	0.4	2.0	-0.6
France	2.2	4.0	7.1	5.8	1.2	1.8	0.0	0.1	0.0	1.6	1.8	0.0
Greece	3.8	2.5	3.9	8.2	4.8	1.2	0.0	0.1	0.0	0.4	4.4	0.0
Great Britain	4.4	3.5	5.1	2.2	2.0	2.9	0.0	0.0	0.0	-0.9	2.3	0.0
Ireland	2.2	1.0	2.2	0.1	4.6	1.3	0.0	0.0	0.0	0.1	1.5	0.0
Italy	6.6	2.3	7.0	7.5	0.8	1.8	0.0	0.0	0.0	0.6	1.2	-0.1
Netherlands	6.3	3.0	14.0	0.4	2.0	3.0	0.0	0.1	0.0	2.5	3.6	-0.2
EEC (10)[2]	3.7	3.0	5.6	2.6	2.3	3.0	0.0	0.0	0.0	0.5	2.1	-0.2
Switzerland	0.5	0.0	2.8	2.5	0.0	0.4	0.0	0.0	0.0	0.0	0.0	0.0
Finland	1.8	0.0	6.7	0.9	0.0	0.2	0.0	0.0	0.0	0.0	0.0	0.1
Japan	1.8	0.0	7.7	14.2	0.0	0.0	0.0	0.0	0.0	0.1	0.0	0.0
Norway	0.0	0.5	2.2	5.2	0.0	0.0	0.0	0.0	1.1	-0.5	0.0	0.0
New Zealand	0.0	0.0	25.6	25.3	0.0	0.0	0.0	0.0	-8.8	1.6	0.0	0.0
United States	0.0	0.0	0.0	0.5	6.9	3.2	1.4	0.0	0.0	1.5	4.4	0.0
All above	2.0	1.3	4.2	4.0	3.1	2.3	0.4	0.0	-0.1	0.7	2.2	-0.1

[1] See the footnotes to Table 4.1 for a listing of NTMs used in the computation of this index. Petroleum products have been excluded from the calculations.
[2] Excludes EEC intra-trade.

by tabulating separately the 1981 trade coverage by six major NTMs, and then computing the 1981–6 change in these ratios for each of the sixteen OECD countries. Perhaps the most striking point to emerge from these figures concerns the increased use of VERs in several European countries (particularly Belgium, Federal Republic of Germany, Greece, Britain and the Netherlands where the trade coverage ratio for this measure rose by two points or more) and in the United States.[13] In the latter, the trade subject to VERs rose from 6.9 per cent of the US total in 1981 to 11.3 per cent five years later. Two other points are important. First, Table 4.9 shows that several European countries (particularly France and Netherlands) have increased their use of quantitative restrictions over 1981–6 as the trade coverage ratios for these measures rose by as much as two-and-a-half points. Second, the US adoption of a variable import levy (covering 1.4 per cent of total imports) could have important implications for the future given the extensive use of these measures in the EEC and other European countries. The concern here is whether the US use of levies will spread to a similar extent in Europe.

NONTARIFF MEASURES IN DEVELOPING COUNTRIES

While the previous discussion shows nontariff measures constitute major elements in developed countries' protectionist profiles, trade barriers in developing countries generally differ in two important aspects. First, tariffs in many developing countries are often far higher, as Laird and Yeats (1987c) demonstrate that import duties in countries like India, Indonesia, Morocco, Pakistan and the Philippines average 50 per cent or more. Also, tariffs on some specific items may range to over 300 per cent.[14] Second, empirical information shows that many developing countries often rely more heavily on nontariff measures that operate through exchange or currency controls than do developed countries.

Table 4.10 summarises information on nontariff measures in some 35 developing countries by aggregating this information for eight country or regional groups. Entries in the table show the percentage of four-digit CCCN products affected by seven different types of nontariff measures ranging from required import authorisations (i.e. measures like import licensing requirements) to special (differential) technical standards for imports.[15] The table also tabulates the

Table 4.10   The application of product-specific nontariff measures by groups of selected developing countries

Region[1]	Percentage of four-digit CCCNs affected by nontariff measures[2]						
	Import authorisations	Quotas	Prohibitions	Exchange controls	Other finance requirements	Price control measures	Technical standards
CARB	15.7	0.0	1.1	1.3	0.0	0.9	0.0
CEAM	9.7	0.9	12.2	45.9	8.6	4.6	4.1
EASA	19.2	2.5	11.6	0.0	0.0	0.0	2.1
NAFR	35.6	1.8	4.0	0.0	27.5	0.0	2.4
OTHR	1.1	13.1	0.0	0.0	0.0	0.0	0.1
SOAM	48.9	1.2	16.2	0.0	0.0	1.9	21.9
SSAF	52.4	0.3	2.7	12.5	12.3	0.2	0.0
WASA	5.5	1.9	5.4	0.0	0.0	0.0	4.7

[1] CARB includes: Antigua, Barbados, Trinidad and Tobago; CEAM – Costa Rica, Ecuador, Mexico and Nicaragua; EASA – Bangladesh, Rep. of Korea, Malaysia, Pakistan, Singapore, Sri Lanka, Thailand; NAFR – Egypt, Libya, Morocco, Tunisia; OTHR – Romania, Yugoslavia; SOAM – Brazil, Colombia; SSAF – Central African Republic, Congo, Ghana, Nigeria, Sudan, United Republic of Tanzania, Zaire, Zimbabwe; WASA – Bahrain, Iraq, Kuwait, Oman, Qatar, Saudi Arabia, Syria, United Arab Emirates.

[2] NTM information is stored at the tariff-line level in national classifications. These data have been concorded at the four-digit CCCN level. If an NTM affects only two lines within a CCCN containing ten lines then only 0.2 per cent of the four-digit CCCN is considered to be covered.

percentage of four-digit CCCNs affected by exchange control regulations or by various forms of import finance requirements.

Overall, Table 4.10 shows that required import authorisations, like licensing requirements, are the most common form of nontariff measure in most of the regional groups. Approximately 36 per cent of the North African countries' (NAFR) CCCNs are affected by these measures, but the corresponding percentages actually range between 48 and 52 per cent for Central African countries (SSAF) and the Brazil–Colombia (SOAM) group. Over one-quarter of the North African developing countries' CCCNs are affected by special financial requirements for imports (measures like advance deposit requirements or domestic purchase regulations), while approximately 12 per cent of the Central African CCCNs are affected by such requirements. The Caribbean countries make extensive use of selective financial NTMs, as exchange controls and other financial regulations are applied to almost 55 per cent of all import products.[16]

As was stressed in much of the discussion in this book, NTM inventory statistics, such as the information presented in Tables 4.1 to 4.10, may have limited policy or analytical uses since they tell nothing about the restrictiveness or *ad valorem* incidence of different measures. If nominal equivalents for NTMs were available, at least for a representative group of products, it would greatly assist in interpreting and using the inventory statistics for research and policy studies. Chapter 5 attempts to provide such information by compiling (and analysing) many of the major empirical studies that derived nominal equivalents for nontariff measures.

ANNEX TO CHAPTER 4

This annex presents detailed statistics on OECD countries' nontariff trade control measures which is intended to supplement related information provided in Tables 4.1 to 4.10. The additional data provided in this annex should be useful for both research and policy studies involving trade issues. Basically, the statistics in the annex cover three main points. First, since Chapter 4 only examined the aggregate nontariff measure profile of the European Community, Annex Tables A4.1 to A4.3 provide details on the use of NTMs by each of the ten European Community countries.[17] These tables provide NTM trade coverage ratios calculated at the two-digit SITC level for three major groups of products: foodstuffs and agricultural raw materials (Table A4.1); chemical products (Table A4.2); and other manufactured products (Table A4.3) for each EEC (10) country. The methodological approach followed in Chapter 4, i.e. application of NTMs operating in 1986 to actual

1981 trade data, was employed in preparing these data so the results could be compared with tables in the main part of the chapter.

The second major point covered in this annex, which deals with differences in the use of major NTMs by the European Community, Japan and the United States, is examined in Annex Tables A4.4 and A4.5. For example, Table A4.4 provides EEC, Japan and US trade coverage ratios for anti-dumping and countervailing duties, restrictive import authorisation regulations, discriminatory import taxes and quantitative restrictions on imports (excluding 'voluntary' restrictions or quotas established under the Multifibre Arrangement) for each two-digit SITC chemical product, while Table A4.5 gives trade coverage ratios for anti-dumping and countervailing duties, tariff quotas, quantitative 'voluntary' export restraints and global and bilateral quotas on manufactured goods classified in STIC 6 and 8. Table 4.8 (in Chapter 4) provides a similar analysis of the incidences of major nontariff measures on EEC, Japanese and US agricultural imports.

Tables A4.6 to A4.8 examine detailed statistics on the level (1981) and changes (1981 to 1986) of NTM application in three OECD industry sectors experiencing longer-term structural adjustment problems: i.e. agriculture; textiles and clothing; and ferrous and nonferrous metals (including metal ores). Trade coverage ratios are shown in these tables for individual types of nontariff measures (variable import levies, minimum import price requirements, tariff quotas, etc.), as well as for all hard-core NTMs combined. The intent here is to contrast the pattern of NTM use in these 'problem' sectors with that in other industries. (The reader should also note that Chapter 5 conducts a thorough review of analytical studies that derived *ad valorem* equivalents for these three sectors' trade barriers.) As such, Tables A4.6 to A4.8 should provide useful empirical information relating to these additional studies.

Table A4.1 The incidence of individual EEC country NTMs on imports of foodstuffs and agricultural raw materials, 1986

SITC	Description	Belgium-Luxembourg	Denmark	Germany	France	Greece	Britain	Ireland	Italy	Netherlands
		1986 NTM trade coverage ratio[1]								
00	Live animals	94.4	23.4	83.7	53.0	100.0	3.4	1.9	66.7	52.6
01	Meat	44.0	89.7	79.6	60.0	94.6	93.6	100.0	80.2	51.8
02	Dairy products	100.0	95.2	99.9	99.5	100.0	100.0	100.0	99.9	88.6
03	Fish and seafood	0.0	0.0	0.0	13.9	0.0	0.0	0.0	0.0	23.9
04	Cereals and preparations	99.1	53.9	89.0	92.9	94.9	97.7	89.9	99.5	98.0
05	Fruit and vegetables	41.9	15.2	50.3	36.0	69.9	13.3	7.6	15.2	49.7
06	Sugar and honey	65.4	84.4	24.7	95.7	19.2	95.2	94.0	64.0	89.5
07	Coffee and cocoa	0.1	0.8	63.9	1.4	0.0	0.0	0.0	0.1	0.1
08	Animal feeds	15.0	1.3	11.4	3.2	2.5	24.0	22.7	5.7	23.3
09	Food preparations	20.2	5.5	9.2	4.1	2.7	3.0	0.9	3.1	64.6
11	Beverages	71.0	0.0	68.4	22.9	0.0	0.0	0.0	0.3	0.0
12	Tobacco	0.0	0.0	0.0	0.0	0.0	0.0	0.0	0.0	0.0
21	Hides and skins	0.0	0.0	0.0	0.0	0.0	0.0	0.0	0.0	0.0
22	Oilseeds and nuts	0.0	0.1	0.1	0.7	94.5	0.0	0.0	0.2	92.0
23	Rubber	0.0	0.0	0.0	0.0	0.0	0.0	0.0	0.0	0.0
24	Wood and cork	0.0	0.0	0.0	2.1	0.0	0.0	0.0	1.2	0.0
25	Pulp and paper	0.0	0.0	0.0	0.0	0.0	0.0	0.0	0.0	0.0
26	Silk, wool, cotton	3.9	0.0	3.4	2.3	6.1	1.5	0.1	22.7	10.6
29	Crude animal & vegetable fibre	14.3	11.6	28.7	16.7	13.7	6.1	5.9	16.7	15.9

[1] See the footnotes to Table 4.1 for a listing of NTMs used in the computation of this index. EEC intra-trade and petroleum products are excluded from the calculations.

Table A4.2   The incidence of individual EEC country NTMs on imports of chemical products, 1986

					1986 trade coverage ratio[1]				
SITC	Description	Belgium-Luxembourg	Denmark	Germany	France	Greece	Britain	Ireland	Italy	Netherlands
51	Chemical elements	0.5	1.5	0.1	0.4	0.0	0.2	0.0	4.7	1.0
52	Petroleum-based chemicals	0.0	0.0	0.0	10.5	0.0	0.0	0.0	1.5	0.0
53	Dyes and paints	0.0	0.0	0.0	0.4	0.0	0.0	0.0	2.9	6.7
54	Medicinal products	0.0	0.0	0.6	0.0	0.0	0.0	0.0	0.3	0.0
55	Soaps, perfumes & cosmetics	0.0	0.0	0.0	0.0	0.0	0.0	0.0	1.2	0.0
56	Manufactured fertilisers	0.0	0.0	23.2	8.8	99.5	0.0	0.0	3.9	0.0
57	Explosives	0.0	0.0	0.0	0.0	0.0	0.0	0.0	23.9	0.0
58	Plastic materials	1.5	0.2	0.6	0.7	0.3	0.6	8.4	64.4	1.9
59	Chemicals, n.e.s.	0.2	3.8	4.6	13.2	9.8	4.3	1.7	11.1	1.4

[1] See the footnotes to Table 4.1 for a listing of NTMs used in the computation of this index. EEC intra-trade and petroleum products are excluded from the calculations.

Table A4.3 The incidence of individual EEC country NTMs on imports of various manufactured products, 1986

1986 trade coverage ratio[1]

SITC	Description	Belgium-Luxembourg	Denmark	Germany	France	Greece	Britain	Ireland	Italy	Netherlands
61	Leather products	0.0	0.0	0.0	0.0	0.0	0.0	0.0	25.7	0.0
62	Rubber products	0.0	0.0	0.0	0.0	43.5	0.0	0.2	77.5	0.0
63	Wood and cork	0.0	0.0	2.0	0.0	0.0	0.0	0.0	4.3	0.2
64	Paper and articles	0.3	0.0	0.8	19.3	1.6	0.0	0.0	68.8	0.5
65	Textiles	26.9	31.6	36.9	35.7	41.8	29.2	20.5	41.3	41.4
66	Cement, clay and glass	0.2	4.5	2.7	1.9	6.6	0.3	1.3	30.6	22.0
67	Iron and steel	33.6	59.4	48.6	31.4	65.3	39.2	49.8	60.6	39.9
68	Non-ferrous metals	0.7	0.0	0.4	1.7	0.0	0.1	0.0	1.8	0.3
69	Metal manufactures, n.e.s.	1.1	1.0	0.8	4.2	0.0	0.0	0.0	9.6	0.9
71	Non-electric machinery	3.9	1.3	1.5	2.7	10.3	1.3	0.5	14.1	1.1
72	Electric machinery	19.2	5.2	8.6	24.2	19.5	9.1	1.1	9.0	4.8
73	Transport equipment	40.8	12.5	25.8	32.7	24.8	15.4	60.0	6.9	33.5
81	Plumbing & lighting fixtures	0.0	0.0	0.0	0.0	2.4	0.0	0.0	0.0	0.0
82	Furniture	0.0	5.4	0.0	0.0	0.0	0.0	0.1	0.0	0.0
83	Travel goods	2.1	0.0	2.1	0.0	0.0	0.0	0.0	0.0	1.0
84	Clothing	48.1	51.0	67.7	74.8	39.4	63.6	37.5	64.1	62.6
85	Footwear	9.6	11.1	9.2	5.3	0.0	0.2	4.5	83.3	10.8
86	Instruments	0.9	2.9	2.3	9.2	0.6	1.9	0.8	6.7	2.0
89	Miscellaneous manufactures	23.5	12.8	22.6	19.5	24.7	20.2	5.9	16.9	17.7

[1] See the footnotes to Table 4.1 for a listing of NTMs used in the computation of this index. EEC intra-trade and petroleum products are excluded from the calculations.

Table A4.4   Trade coverage of two-digit SITC chemical imports by NTMs in the EEC, Japan and USA, 1986

		EEC (10)[1]				Japan				USA			
SITC	Description	ANTIDP	TAXES	NALIC	QRS	ANTIDP	TAXES	NALIC	QRS	ANTIDP	TAXES	NALIC	QRS
51	Chemical elements	3.1	0.0	0.0	0.9	0.0	0.0	13.8	29.9	1.3	0.0	0.0	0.0
52	Petroleum-based chemicals	0.0	0.0	0.0	1.7	0.0	0.0	0.0	0.0	0.0	0.0	0.0	0.0
53	Dyes and paints	0.0	0.0	0.0	1.1	0.0	0.0	0.0	0.0	0.1	0.0	0.0	0.0
54	Medicinal products	0.0	0.0	0.2	0.0	0.0	0.0	38.1	10.6	6.4	0.0	0.0	0.0
55	Soaps, perfumes, & cosmetics	0.0	0.0	0.0	0.1	0.0	0.0	0.0	0.0	0.0	0.0	0.0	0.0
56	Manufactured fertilisers	4.5	0.0	3.3	7.0	0.0	0.0	100.0	0.0	0.7	0.0	0.0	0.0
57	Explosives	0.0	0.0	0.0	0.5	0.0	0.0	0.0	15.9	0.0	0.0	0.0	0.0
58	Plastic materials	0.1	0.0	0.0	7.5	0.0	0.0	0.0	0.0	6.6	0.0	0.0	0.0
59	Chemicals, n.e.s.	0.0	0.0	2.1	2.4	0.0	0.0	0.0	10.9	1.7	0.0	0.0	0.0

[1] Excludes EEC intra-trade.

Note: The NTMS listed in this table are the most extensively applied to chemical imports. They are designated as follows:
ANTIDP – Anti-dumping and countervailing duties (excluding investigations).
TAXES – Product-specific non-general import taxes.
NALIC – Non-automatic import licensing regulations.
QRS – Quantitative restrictions (global or bilateral) other than 'voluntary' or MFA restraints.

Table A4.5 Trade coverage of two-digit SITC manufactured products by NTMs in the EEC, Japan and USA, 1986

		EEC (10)[1]				Japan				USA			
SITC	Description	ANTIDP	TARQ	VERS	QRS	NALIC	TARQ	VERS	QRS	ANTIDP	TARQ	VERS	QRS
61	Leather products	0.0	0.0	0.0	7.7	0.0	3.7	0.0	10.2	0.0	0.0	0.0	0.0
62	Rubber products	0.0	0.0	0.0	9.1	0.0	0.0	0.0	13.6	4.4	0.0	0.0	0.0
63	Wood and cork	0.0	34.8	0.0	1.0	0.0	0.0	0.0	0.0	1.4	0.0	0.0	0.0
64	Paper articles	1.0	24.5	0.0	5.9	0.0	0.0	0.0	0.0	0.7	0.0	0.0	0.0
65	Textiles[2]	1.1	0.0	0.2	3.2	55.5	0.0	0.0	0.0	7.4	0.0	0.0	0.0
66	Cement, clay and glass	0.1	0.0	0.2	2.0	0.0	0.0	0.0	0.0	0.9	0.0	0.0	0.0
67	Iron and steel[2]	2.5	0.0	41.2	5.0	0.0	0.0	0.0	0.0	13.8	0.0	75.1	2.0
68	Non-ferrous metals[2]	0.0	0.0	0.0	0.5	0.0	0.0	0.0	0.4	0.0	0.0	0.0	0.0
69	Metal manufactures, n.e.s.	0.2	0.0	0.0	1.4	1.0	0.0	0.0	0.0	9.2	0.0	11.0	0.0
71	Non-electric machinery	0.9	0.0	1.3	1.5	0.0	0.0	0.0	4.4	2.7	0.0	0.0	0.0
72	Electrical machinery	0.0	0.0	7.8	3.7	0.0	0.0	0.0	0.0	10.9	0.0	1.4	0.0
73	Transport equipment	0.0	0.0	20.4	3.8	0.0	0.0	0.0	0.0	0.6	5.4	41.1	0.0
81	Plumbing & lighting fixtures	0.0	0.0	0.0	0.0	0.0	0.0	0.0	0.0	2.5	0.0	0.0	0.0
82	Furniture	0.0	0.0	0.0	0.3	0.0	0.0	0.0	0.0	0.4	0.0	0.0	0.0
83	Travel goods	0.0	0.0	0.0	0.9	0.0	0.0	0.0	0.0	39.4	0.0	0.0	0.0
84	Clothing[2]	0.0	0.0	0.8	10.9	0.0	0.0	0.0	0.0	2.0	0.0	0.0	0.3
85	Footwear	0.0	0.0	0.0	11.3	0.0	6.9	0.0	0.0	0.0	0.0	0.0	0.0
86	Instruments	2.4	0.0	3.0	0.8	0.0	0.0	0.0	0.0	0.0	0.0	0.0	0.0
89	Other manufactures	0.0	0.0	19.4	0.7	0.1	0.0	0.0	0.0	0.9	0.0	0.0	0.0

[1] Excludes EEC intra-trade.
[2] For a more detailed breakdown on protectionism in this sector see Table A4.7 or A4.8.

Note: The NTMs listed in this table are among the most extensively applied to manufactured products (see also Table A4.7 or A4.8). They are designated as follows: ANTIDP – anti-dumping and countervailing duties (excluding investigations); TARQ – tariff quotas; VERS – quantitative 'voluntary' export restraints; QRS – quantitative restrictions (global or bilateral) other than 'voluntary' or MFA restraints; NALIC – non-automatic import licensing regulations.

Table A4.6 Analysis of the incidence and changes in EEC, Japan and US nontariff measures against foodstuffs, 1981-6

Product/country[1]	Share of imports facing NTMs in 1981[2]					Change in the share of imports facing NTMs, 1981-6				
	VARL	MINP	NALIC	QRS	TARQ	VARL	MINP	NALIC	QRS	TARQ
Live animals (00)										
EEC	50.2	29.0	58.5	0.0	3.8	0.0	0.0	0.0	13.1	2.3
Japan	1.2	0.0	0.0	0.0	13.4	0.0	0.0	0.0	0.0	0.0
USA	0.0	0.0	0.0	0.0	29.1	0.0	0.0	0.0	0.0	0.0
Meat (01)										
EEC	55.0	37.5	70.1	0.0	6.1	0.0	0.0	0.0	18.1	1.6
Japan	37.5	0.0	7.1	22.0	0.0	0.0	0.0	0.0	0.0	0.0
USA	0.0	0.0	0.0	0.0	0.0	0.0	0.0	0.0	0.0	0.0
Dairy and eggs (02)										
EEC	99.7	3.0	96.3	0.8	4.1	0.0	0.0	0.0	0.0	0.0
Japan	0.0	0.0	0.0	72.9	12.9	0.0	0.0	0.0	0.0	0.0
USA	0.0	0.0	0.0	87.7	2.3	0.0	0.0	0.0	0.0	0.0
Fish (03)										
EEC	0.0	49.9	1.0	0.0	18.1	0.0	1.9	0.0	3.6	-1.7
Japan	0.0	0.0	100.0	13.2	0.0	0.0	0.0	0.0	0.0	0.0
USA	0.0	0.0	0.0	0.0	14.1	0.0	0.0	0.0	0.0	0.0
Cereals and preparations (04)										
EEC	98.9	1.1	96.9	0.0	0.0	0.0	0.0	0.0	0.0	0.0
Japan	0.0	0.0	0.0	32.5	16.3	0.0	0.0	0.0	0.0	0.0
USA	0.0	0.0	0.0	0.0	0.0	0.0	0.0	0.0	0.0	0.0
Fruits and vegetables (05)										
EEC	13.1	47.3	19.9	5.8	0.8	0.0	1.3	0.3	12.3	3.6
Japan	0.0	0.0	2.8	15.7	0.0	0.0	0.0	0.0	-0.1	0.0
USA	0.0	0.0	0.0	0.9	1.4	0.0	0.0	0.0	0.0	0.0

Sugar and honey (06)									
EEC	89.8	0.0	85.1	0.5	0.0	0.0	0.0	0.2	0.0
Japan	84.6	0.0	4.7	0.1	0.0	0.0	-4.7	0.0	0.0
USA	0.0	0.0	0.0	0.0	91.9	0.0	0.0	91.9	0.0
Coffee and cocoa (07)									
EEC	7.1	0.0	0.2	0.0	0.0	0.0	0.0	0.0	0.0
Japan	0.0	0.0	0.0	0.0	0.0	0.0	0.0	0.0	0.0
USA	0.0	0.0	0.0	2.2	0.0	0.0	0.0	0.1	0.0
Animal feeds (08)									
EEC	3.9	0.0	11.5	0.4	0.0	0.0	0.0	0.0	0.0
Japan	0.0	0.0	13.7	0.0	4.7	0.0	0.0	0.0	0.0
USA	0.0	0.0	0.0	0.3	0.0	0.0	0.0	0.0	0.0
Food preparations (09)									
EEC	53.4	4.5	6.7	11.0	0.0	0.0	0.0	-7.8	0.0
Japan	0.0	0.0	15.6	14.5	0.0	0.0	0.0	0.0	0.0
USA	0.0	0.0	0.0	0.4	0.0	0.0	0.0	0.0	0.0
Beverages (11)									
EEC	0.1	73.7	21.9	3.0	0.0	0.0	0.0	0.0	0.0
Japan	0.0	0.0	0.0	0.0	0.0	0.0	0.0	0.0	0.0
USA	0.0	0.0	0.0	0.0	0.0	0.0	0.0	0.0	0.0
Oil seeds and nuts (22)									
EEC	0.0	0.0	24.0	0.7	0.0	0.0	0.0	0.0	0.0
Japan	0.0	0.0	0.0	4.3	0.0	0.0	0.0	0.0	0.0
USA	0.0	0.0	0.0	74.0	0.0	0.0	0.0	74.0	0.0

[1] The EEC figures exclude intra-trade.
[2] The trade coverage ratios may not sum horizontally due to 'stacking' on multiple applications of NTMs on a given product.

Note: The NTMS listed in this table are among the most extensively applied to foodstuff imports. They are designated as follows: VARL – variable import levies; MINP – minimum import prices; NALIC – non-automatic import licensing regulations; QRS – quantitative restrictions (global on bilateral) other than 'voluntary' or MFA restraints.

Table A4.7 Analysis of the incidence and changes in EEC, Japan and US nontariff measures against textiles and clothing, 1981–6

Product/country[1]	Share of imports facing NTMs in 1981[2]					Change in the share of imports facing NTMs, 1981–6[2]				
	VOLPR	NALIC	QRS	MFA	QRTEX	VOLPR	NALIC	QRS	MFA	QRTEX
	(imports from developed countries)									
Silk, wool, cotton fibres (26)										
EEC	0.0	0.0	0.0	0.0	0.0	0.0	0.0	0.0	0.0	0.0
Japan	0.0	0.0	0.0	0.0	0.0	0.0	0.0	0.0	0.0	0.0
USA	0.0	0.0	0.2	0.0	0.0	0.0	0.0	0.0	0.0	0.0
Textiles (65)										
EEC	0.0	1.4	5.9	0.0	0.0	0.0	0.0	-4.1	0.0	0.0
Japan	0.0	54.5	0.0	0.0	0.0	0.0	0.0	0.0	0.0	0.0
USA[3]	0.0	0.0	0.0	18.6	0.0	0.0	0.0	0.0	0.0	0.1
Clothing (84)										
EEC	0.0	1.6	16.2	0.0	0.0	0.0	0.0	-6.1	0.0	0.0
Japan	0.0	0.0	0.0	0.0	0.0	0.0	0.0	0.0	0.0	0.0
USA[3]	0.0	0.0	0.0	30.9	0.0	0.0	0.0	0.0	0.0	0.0

(imports from developing countries)

Silk, wool, cotton fibres (26)										
EEC	0.0	0.0	7.9	10.1	0.3	0.0	0.0	0.0	-1.1	-0.3
Japan	0.0	3.2	0.0	0.0	0.0	0.0	0.0	0.0	0.0	0.0
USA	0.0	0.0	5.4	0.0	0.0	0.0	0.0	0.0	0.0	0.0
Textiles (65)										
EEC	0.1	2.8	5.8	50.1	14.8	0.1	0.0	-1.4	-1.4	1.3
Japan	0.0	56.1	0.0	0.0	0.0	0.0	0.0	0.0	0.0	0.0
USA	0.0	0.0	0.0	35.0	5.7	0.0	0.0	0.0	3.0	0.0
Clothing (84)										
EEC	0.0	0.7	19.5	65.9	13.2	0.0	0.0	-8.4	-5.9	0.7
Japan	0.0	0.0	0.0	0.0	0.0	0.0	0.0	0.3	0.3	0.0
USA	0.0	0.0	0.0	62.8	18.7	0.0	0.0	0.3	0.3	0.0

[1] Excludes EEC intra-trade.

[2] The trade coverage ratios may not sum horizontally due to 'stacking' or multiple applications of NTMs on a given product.

[3] United States MFA restrictions apply to Japan and were negotiated under the Short and Long-Term Textile Arrangement.

Note: The NTMs listed in this table are among the most extensively applied to textile and clothing imports. They are designated as follows: VOLPR – 'voluntary' price restraints; NALIC – non-automatic import licensing regulations; QRS – quantitative restrictions (global or bilateral) other than 'voluntary' on MFA restraints; MFA – restrictions negotiated under the Multifibre Arrangement; ORTEX – special textiles and clothing quotas negotiated outside the MFA.

Table A4.8 Analysis of the incidence and changes in EEC, Japan and US nontariff measures against ores and metals, 1981–6

Product/country[1]	Share of imports facing NTMs in 1981[2]					Change in the share of imports facing NTMs, 1981–6[3]				
	REFPR	VOLPR	NALIC	QRS	VERS	REFPR	VOLPR	NALIC	QRS	VERS
Metal ores (28)										
EEC	0.0	0.0	0.0	0.0	0.0	0.0	0.0	0.0	0.2	0.0
Japan	0.0	0.0	0.0	10.1	0.0	0.0	0.0	0.0	0.0	0.0
USA	0.0	0.0	0.0	0.0	0.0	0.0	0.0	0.0	0.0	0.0
Iron and steel manufactures (67)										
EEC	47.2	2.9	0.6	4.5	40.7	0.0	5.7	0.0	0.5	0.5
Japan	0.0	0.0	0.0	0.0	0.0	0.0	0.0	0.0	0.0	0.0
USA	7.9	0.0	0.0	0.0	0.0	-7.9	0.7	0.0	2.0	75.1
Non-ferrous metal manufactures (68)										
EEC	0.0	0.0	0.3	0.5	0.0	0.0	0.0	0.0	0.0	0.0
Japan	0.0	0.0	0.0	0.4	0.0	0.0	0.0	0.0	0.0	0.0
USA	0.0	0.0	0.0	0.0	0.0	0.0	0.0	0.0	0.0	0.0
Metal manufactures, n.e.s. (69)										
EEC	0.0	0.2	0.7	1.4	0.0	0.0	0.1	0.0	0.0	0.0
Japan	0.0	0.0	1.0	0.0	0.0	0.0	0.0	0.0	0.0	0.0
USA	0.0	0.0	0.0	0.0	0.0	0.0	0.4	0.0	0.0	0.0

[1] The EEC figures exclude intra-trade.
[2] The trade coverage ratios may not sum horizontally due to 'stacking' or multiple applications of NTMs on a given product.

Note: The NTMs listed in this table are among the most extensively applied to metal imports. They are designated as follows: REFPR – import reference prices; VOLPR – 'voluntary' price restraints; NALIC – non-automatic import licensing regulations; QRS – quantitative restrictions (global or bilateral) other than MFA or 'voluntary' restraints; VERS – 'voluntary' export restraints.

5 Findings of Empirical Studies of Nontariff Barriers

This chapter reviews and evaluates findings of previous studies that derived empirical information on the application and incidence of nontariff barriers. Given the basic differences in their methodological approaches, the results of previous 'inventory' studies are examined separately from analyses that estimated quantity or price impact measures for nontariff barriers. The review draws upon the theoretical foundation for quantification of NTBs developed in Chapter 2 in order to identify biases and other potential problems in these investigations' empirical results. In addition, the conclusions of several studies that simulated the trade and other economic effects of a nontariff barrier liberalisation are examined since these analyses have important implications for the Uruguay Round negotiations. Here, several representative analyses that approximated the economic costs of trade intervention measures have been included. Too often, nontariff barriers involve a lack of transparency as far as their costs and economic effects are concerned, and by reviewing several relevant studies their importance can be placed in proper perspective.[1]

In surveying the empirical studies, our intention was to derive 'average' or 'normal' nominal equivalents for nontariff barriers. If the normal level of nominal NTB protection for (say) United States clothing imports were a (known) fixed percentage this would simplify multilateral trade negotiations and also be useful for many research purposes. Unfortunately, the studies surveyed suggest that many NTBs' *ad valorem* equivalents are unstable and vary widely from year to year. For example, domestic and international prices changes for many agricultural products have produced annual swings in NTB *ad valorem* equivalents of 100 percentage points or more. Also, for some manufactured goods like clothing and textiles, NTBs seemingly have been tightened during the 1970s and 1980s with the result that their incidence has changed. This, plus the fact that new trade restrictions have been added, makes it exceedingly difficult to estimate 'normal' levels of nontariff protection. This point has important implications for multilateral negotiations like the Uruguay Round.

Negotiations on tariffs are simplified by the fact that their protective levels are normally fixed (legally bound) at a specific nominal rate. In contrast, nominal equivalents of many NTBs seem to be changing constantly with the result that it is difficult to determine what constitutes equivalent concessions.

Several points should be noted concerning studies surveyed in this chapter. First, a number of important investigations relating to the 1960s or early 1970s have been reviewed in order to provide a 'benchmark' from which subsequent results could be assessed. (See, in particular, the studies by Robert Baldwin, Larry Wipf, Ingo Walter or Gulbrandsen and Lindbeck.) These studies are important since they can be employed, with subsequent analyses, to assess general or sectorial trends in the level of protection. In cases, these earlier investigations are also important for the procedures they develop for quantifying nontariff barriers' effects. Second, for many of the studies surveyed we reference other analyses which supplement key points developed in the principal investigation. This is to assist individuals engaged in related research or policy studies to locate relevant background material. Finally, we have also included several studies whose findings or methodological approach suggest lines of potentially useful research.

STUDIES BASED ON THE INVENTORY APPROACH

Previous empirical analyses that employed the NTM inventory approach often utilised the UNCTAD Data Base on Trade Measures, or a separate inventory compiled by Professor Ingo Walter in the late 1960s. These studies were instrumental in documenting the overall importance of nontariff measures and the extent of their use by individual developed countries. Inventory studies of nontariff measures are a regular part of UNCTAD's work programme on protectionism and structural adjustment, and this organisation prepares annual reports which tabulate new trade intervention measures and analyses their effects. Since these annual reviews present detailed frequency and coverage indices for nontariff measures, and also list newly imposed trade barriers (by product by country), they should provide additional useful information for research and policy analysis. The main findings of these studies, which are summarised in the following section, together with the information presented in Chapter 4, indicate the general conclusions emerging from inventory studies of nontariff measures.[2]

Nogues *et al.* (1985): Developed Country Nontariff Measures

This report represents one of the initial sources of statistics on nontariff measures in developed market economy countries. The study focuses on the use of specific nontariff restrictions, such as quotas, discretionary and conditional import authorisations, 'voluntary' export restraints for prices and volumes, minimum import price systems, tariff quotas, seasonal tariffs, surveillance mechanisms, price and volume investigations, and anti-dumping and countervailing duties over the interval 1981 to 1983. Detailed statistics, such as NTM frequency indices and trade coverage ratios, are presented for sixteen developed market economy countries, namely, Belgium, Denmark, France, Federal Republic of Germany, Greece, Ireland, Italy, Netherlands, United Kingdom, Australia, Austria, Finland, Japan, Norway, Switzerland and the United States.[3]

The major findings of the Nogues, Olechowski and Winters study can be summarised as follows:

Coverage of nontariff measures. Approximately 13 per cent of all tariff-line items in the sixteen DMECs were covered by one or more forms of nontariff barriers in 1981. In value terms, 27 per cent of their imports, which represented some $231 billion of their total trade, faced hard-core NTBs. Hard-core measures were found to be widely applied to agricultural products, textiles, clothing, mineral fuels and ferrous metals where the frequency and coverage ratios were well above national averages. For example, in Switzerland, 73 per cent of all agricultural imports face hard-core measures while between 36 and 42 per cent of EEC and Japanese agricultural imports encounter these restrictions. Over 50 per cent of the EEC and USA textile and clothing imports face NTMs, with the trade coverage ratios reaching 60 per cent in the United Kingdom. However, since these statistics are based on 'own' trade weights, which are downward biased by very restrictive barriers, Nogues *et al.* conclude that the importance of nontariff measures is greater than indicated by these indices. The fact that sizeable differences are often observed between the 'own' and world trade-weighted NTM coverage indices is viewed as supporting this proposition.

Reliance on specific measures. Quantitative restrictions and trade monitoring systems were found to be the most widely applied NTMs as these measures account for over 85 per cent of the reported restrictions in the sixteen developed countries (about one-third of the total are quantitative restrictions). Voluntary export restraints constitute about 11 per cent of all trade control measures, but for various reasons (see Chapter 2) it is felt that this percentage estimate is downward biased. Considerable differences exist in the use of specific nontariff measures in various sectors. Agricultural imports, for example, encounter a far higher number of 'decreed price' barriers than other products, while price control measures (primarily variable levies) are extensively used in the EEC, Sweden and Switzerland to control imports of these products. However, manufactured goods mainly encounter quantitative restrictions and different types of monitoring systems, with import surveillance fairly common in Europe.[4] Another point is that considerable differences in the reliance on nontariff measures are observed within the European Community. For example, almost 10 per cent of France's tariff-line-level imports are subject to NTMs while the corresponding shares for Italy and Denmark are about 2 per cent.

Country comparisons. All statistical indicators suggest Australia, Finland, France and Switzerland are countries where nontariff measures are most important as their 'own' trade coverage ratios exceed 30 per cent (57 per cent for France). The United States results are sensitive to the inclusion of petroleum since these imports faced a surveillance system (suspended in 1984). If energy imports are included, the US trade coverage ratio is relatively high (about 43 per cent), yet if these products are excluded the ratio is relatively low (about 18 per cent). Overall, Austria and Norway have the lowest NTM coverage ratios (5 to 6 per cent), while the corresponding ratio for Italy is about 8 per cent.

Incidence on developing countries. Nogues *et al.* find nontariff measures are more extensively applied to imports from developing countries, both in total and for each of the individual sixteen OECD markets (see our Appendix 1 for an analysis of differences between the World Bank's developed and developing-country classification, which was used by these authors, and those of other organisations). Also, NTMs are applied more frequently to imports from the heavily indebted developing countries (35 per cent of these countries' exports face nontariff measures) than to other developing or developed countries' exports. The underlying data shows this is largely due to a discriminatory application of NTMs on manufactured products since nontariff restrictions are less widely applied to agricultural imports from developing countries than to agricultural products from developed countries.

Trends in NTM application. From 1981 to 1983, nontariff measures spread to approximately $12.8 billion in trade of the developed countries that was previously unaffected. This increase affected approximately 1.5 per cent of their total 1981 trade. According to the coverage ratios, new restrictions were aimed primarily at developed countries' exports, with automotive products and ferrous metals encountering a particularly high incidence of the new barriers.[5]

(*Author's note*: Since publication of the Nogues *et al*. report efforts to verify entries in the UNCTAD Data Base with national governments has produced major changes in some nations' underlying NTM data. As such, some statistics in the Nogues *et al*. study may be incorrect since they do not reflect these revisions. Users of data drawn from the report are advised to cross-check this information with Chapter 4 in this book.)

UNCTAD (February 1983): NTBs in Developed and Developing Countries

This study provides a 1983 status report on the UNCTAD Data Base which identifies technical problems encountered in compiling the inventory. It discusses the NTB classification scheme employed in the Data Base (see Table 2.1 in Chapter 2 of this book), identifies the sources of information used in compiling the Data Base and indicates the country coverage achieved by 1983. Detailed NTB frequency and coverage indices, for both developed and developing countries, are given, and the study illustrates how this information can be used for policy issues. The statistical analysis focuses on nontariff measures facing developing countries' exports to the North and discusses how these restrictions affect their trade and industrialisation prospects. It differs from related studies in that the statistical results are presented for major CCCN groups, whereas other analyses have generally used a SITC format. This study employs data which records trade measures at the four-digit CCCN level, although the UNCTAD Data Base was later shifted to tariff-line-level information.

The UNCTAD study represents one of the first attempts to examine changes in nontariff barriers over commodity processing chains. This made an important contribution to analyses of trade-barrier escalation.[6] Table 5.1 summarises the relevant findings and gives frequency indices for developed and developing countries' nontariff measures facing 24 CCCN products that constitute different stages of commodity processing chains. Out of the total, 14 products encounter escalation in the developed market economy countries, but in only 4 cases do the NTM frequency indices increase for the developing countries. Developed-country escalation occurs for

Table 5.1   Volume-restraining measures facing the exports of developing
countries in selected developed market-economy and developing countries,
incidence on primary and processed commodities (percentage)

Commodity	Stage of processing	CCCN	Measures to restrain volume	
			Developed market-economy countries	Developing countries and territories
Agricultural	primary		25	31
products	processed		26	25
Meat	fresh	0201–04, 06	49	40
	prepared	1601–03	43	21
Fish	fresh	0301–03	35	47
	prepared	1604–05	31	27
Vegetables	fresh	0701–03, 05, 06, 1204–06, 08	39	26
	processed	1704, 1103–06, 1904, 2001–02	48	16
Fruit	fresh	0801–09, 0812	20	31
	processed	0810, 11, 13, 2003–07	54	21
Coffee	green, roasted	0901	11	41
	extracts	2102	17	27
Oils	oil seeds	1201	33	45
	oils	1507	56	50
Sugar	raw	1701	78	50
	processed	1701, 03, 04, 05	56	26
Cocoa	beans	1801	–	14
	processed, chocolate	1803–06	14	13
Tobacco	unmanufctrd	2401	11	45
	manufactrd	2402	22	37
Rubber	natural	4001	–	23
	processed	4005–09, 15	6	22
	rubbr articls	4010–14, 16	14	27
Leather	hides, skins	4101	–	23
	leather	4102–08, 10	13	17
	leath articls	4201–05, 6401–06	26	24
Wood	rough	4403–04	6	25
	simply worked	4405–07, 13	9	25
	manufactures	4408–12, 14–28	12	26
Paper	pulpwood	4403	6	27
	papermkng mat	4701–02	–	25
	paper prodcts	4801–21	8	29
Wool	raw	5301	–	23
	carded, combed	5305	44	23
	yarn	5306, 07, 10	57	20
	woven fabrics	5311	72	37
Cotton	raw	5501	6	32
	carded, combed	5504	44	32
	yarn	5505, 06	61	43
	woven fabrics	5507–09	57	38

Table 5.1   continued

Commodity	Stage of processing	CCCN	Measures to restrain volume	
			Developed market-economy countries	Developing countries and territories
Jute	raw	5703	–	18
	fabrics	5710	33	32
	sacks	6203	44	32
Sisal	fibres	5704	–	19
	cordage	5904–06	56	26
Mineral	primary		8	32
products	processed		12	25
Metallic ores		2601	17	41
Iron, steel	semi-processed	7301, 02, 04, 05	10	25
	processed	7306–18	23	36
Copper	unwrought	7401–02	3	18
	wrought	7403–08	3	24
Aluminium	unwrought	7601	39	27
	wrought	7602–06	16	27
Lead	unwrought	7801	6	23
	wrought	7802–05	6	15
zinc	unwrought	7901	22	23
	wrought	7902–04	9	17
Tin	unwrought	8001	–	18
	wrought	8002–05	–	14
Phosphates	natural	2510	–	23
	phosphoric acids	2810	–	18
	superphosphates	3108	6	41

Notes: Developing countries included in the tabulation are: Algeria, Brazil, Chile, Guatemala, Hong Kong, Indonesia, Ivory Coast, Kenya, Malawi, Mexico, Nigeria, Pakistan, Peru, Philippines, Republic of Korea, Saudi Arabia, Sri Lanka, Thailand, Tunisia, Turkey, United Republic of Cameroon, and Venezuela.

Developed countries included are: Australia, Austria, Canada, EEC (9), Finland, Israel, Japan, New Zealand, Norway, Sweden, Switzerland and United States.

The volume-restraining measures included in the calculation of frequency indices are: all quotas, voluntary export restraints, required import authorisations, discretionary licensing, licensing, declaration with visa, authorisations to select purchasers, import permits, authorisation dependent on export, and other specific authorisations.

Source: UNCTAD (1983).

vegetables, fruit, coffee, oils, cocoa, tobacco, rubber, leather, wood, wool, cotton (up to and including yarn), jute, sisal and phosphates, while the frequency ratios decrease for meat, fish, sugar and aluminium (for copper they are constant over the chain). According to UNCTAD, these data indicate: (i) that most developed countries protect domestic processing industries with both tariffs and NTMs, thus denying developing countries the comparative advantage derived from domestic production of raw materials; and (ii) escalation is less likely in developing countries which produce the raw materials that provide an advantage in commodity processing.[7]

Walter (1972): Barriers in Major Industrial Countries

This study, along with several related investigations by the author, are among the earliest attempts to apply the inventory approach to the analysis of nontariff measures. Walter develops a workable definition of a nontariff barrier, based on the intent of different measures, and then constructs a useful classification scheme for these restrictions.[8] Walter compiles his NTB inventory through a survey of International Chamber of Commerce, GATT, UNCTAD, United States Office of the Special Representative for Trade Negotiations, and US Bureau of International Commerce publications. Using these sources, NTBs are tabulated (at the four-digit SITC level) for nineteen industrial countries (see Table 5.2 for a listing) and then these data are concorded with 1967 import statistics. Walter acknowledged problems with some underlying information on nontariff measures (e.g. no data are available for NTBs covering Irish or Finnish farm imports, while New Zealand's import licensing for almost all industrial goods made it impossible to include these measures in the data base).

Table 5.2 summarises Walter's findings when 1967 trade coverage indices were calculated for the nineteen industrial countries. The results indicate that approximately 18 per cent of all imports, or approximately $24.7 billion in trade, was affected by one or more of these nontariff measures.[9] Walter found that agricultural imports were most heavily affected by NTBs, with over half the 1967 value of developed countries' imports of live animals and meats, cereals, sugar, beverages, tobacco and food preparations encountering trade barriers. As far as industrial goods are concerned, fossil fuels, transport equipment, chemicals and pharmaceuticals generally had higher NTB trade coverage ratios than average. In terms of individual countries, about a third of all 1967 imports encountered nontariff barriers in Japan, Belgium–Luxembourg, United States and Portugal. In contrast, Australia, Sweden, Denmark and Canada were countries with the lowest NTB coverage ratios.

In addition to the trade coverage ratios, Walter presents frequency indices for nontariff barriers (see his table 2 on p. 341) which document the relatively high application of NTBs in the agricultural sectors of all nineteen countries (particularly on dairy products, cereals and prepared foods). These figures indicate that Japan has the highest frequency of nontariff barrier usage (34 per cent of all imported products are affected by NTBs). In contrast, frequency indices for Canada, Sweden and the UK range between 7 to 14 per cent.

Any assessment of Walter's studies should recognise that these investigations have considerable (unutilised) potential for research on the intertemporal spread of nontariff barriers. Specifically, Walter provides 1967 NTB frequency and trade coverage indices for the total imports of individual developed countries, as well as for major two-digit SITC products, while sources such as the UNCTAD Data Base contain statistics with which corresponding measures can be computed for the 1980s. Such information, drawn from different points of time, could be extremely useful for analysing changes in the level and pattern of NTB use in different industries and countries. A major problem, however, is that Walter employs a considerably broader list of measures in his analyses than has been used in more recent studies. This may cause problems in making the data sources comparable.

Olechowski and Yeats (1982): Barriers Facing Socialist Countries

This study illustrates how the inventory approach can be employed to analyse trade barriers facing exports from a given country or group of countries. In this case, the UNCTAD Data Base was used to assess the influence of nontariff barriers on exports from the centrally planned countries (CPCs) of Eastern Europe (Bulgaria, German Democratic Republic, Hungary, Poland, Romania and the USSR) to eight major developed market economy countries or country groups, namely, EEC, USA, Japan, Canada, Sweden, Switzerland, Norway and Austria. In addition to standard frequency and trade coverage indices, the authors employ an 'uncertainty' index to reflect the potential spread of nontariff measures to products not subject to these restrictions.[10] For comparison, these indices are also computed for both developed and developing countries' exports.

Table 5.2 Percent of 1967 imports subject to nontariff restrictions

SITC	Commodity group	USA	Canada	UK	Japan	Belg.-Lux.	France	Germany	Italy	Netherlands	Denmark	Finland	Norway	Sweden	Austria	Switzerland	Portugal	Ireland	Australia	New Zealand	Mean
00	Live animals	n	100	-	49	97	49	98	88	81	11	n	100	69	96	98	-	n	100	100	71
01	Meat	60	64	34	22	85	67	89	94	68	80	n	93	100	97	98	100	n	18	88	67
02	Dairy	97	69	77	42	100	100	100	100	-	2	n	100	100	76	50	81	n	-	-	70
03	Fish	19	-	-	100	-	-	-	100	-	16	n	-	56	-	-	99	n	-	-	17
04	Cereals	2	-	95	99	100	99	100	100	100	91	n	100	49	77	85	94	n	-	82	75
05	Fruit	-	-	28	52	44	63	67	86	43	91	n	43	35	56	46	62	n	37	56	48
06	Sugar	89	-	99	30	83	98	73	54	61	100	n	6	62	19	-	75	n	-	-	52
07	Coffee, tea, cocoa, spices	-	-	-	46	73	7	73	1	44	76	n	4	1	-	-	-	n	-	-	19
08	Feeds	-	4	100	51	79	100	69	75	80	4	n	13	100	100	65	-	n	-	-	49
09	Misc. food preps.	-	-	50	50	95	100	100	92	93	-	n	100	100	17	95	-	n	-	-	56
11	Beverages	79	96	26	96	100	100	100	100	100	99	97	99	99	66	90	-	-	-	-	71
12	Tobacco	5	-	2	100	100	100	98	100	99	99	3	99	60	100	-	-	18	72	96	40
21	Hides and skins	60	-	-	-	-	-	-	-	-	-	-	-	-	-	-	-	-	-	-	3
22	Oil, seeds, nuts and kernels	1	-	-	67	-	-	-	-	-	-	-	-	9	-	100	-	-	9	-	10
23	Crude rubber	-	-	-	-	-	-	-	-	-	-	-	-	-	-	-	-	-	-	-	0
24	Wood and cork	-	37	-	-	-	-	-	-	-	-	-	-	-	-	-	-	-	-	-	2
25	Pulp and waste paper	-	-	-	-	-	-	-	-	-	-	-	-	-	-	-	-	-	-	-	0
26	Textile fibres	67	-	-	-	-	-	-	-	-	-	-	-	6	-	-	82	-	21	2	9
27	Crude minerals and fertilisers	-	-	-	27	-	-	-	17	-	-	-	-	-	-	-	-	-	-	-	2
28	Metal ores and scrap	-	-	-	-	-	-	-	-	-	-	-	-	-	-	-	-	-	-	-	0
29	Misc. crude animal/vegetable materials	-	-	-	-	15	45	49	3	2	16	-	26	-	-	22	-	-	23	61	14
32	Coal, coke and briquettes	-	100	100	100	95	70	100	-	-	100	-	-	-	12	-	-	-	-	A	38

33	Petroleum	100	–	–	19	100	10	–	–	–	–	–	60	–	–	–	–	–	–	–	A 16
34	Gas	–	–	–	–	–	25	–	–	–	–	–	–	–	–	–	–	–	–	–	A 1
35	Electric energy	–	–	71	–	–	100	–	–	–	–	–	–	–	–	–	–	–	–	–	A 6
41	Animal oils and fats	74	71	–	–	–	65	44	–	–	–	–	–	–	–	–	–	–	–	–	A 14
42	Fixed vegetable oils and fats	–	–	–	9	2	10	2	66	1	2	–	–	–	–	–	–	3	100	–	A 11
43	Processed oils and fats, waxes	49	–	–	–	–	–	–	56	–	–	–	–	–	–	–	–	–	–	–	A 6
51	Chemical elements and compounds	49	–	–	96	67	–	24	97	–	–	–	–	–	–	9	–	–	–	–	A 19
52	Tar and crude derivatives	–	–	–	–	–	–	–	–	100	–	–	–	–	–	–	–	–	–	–	A 6
53	Dyes	81	–	–	–	–	–	–	–	–	–	–	–	–	–	3	–	–	–	–	A 5
54	Medicinal and pharmaceutical	38	–	–	100	23	100	–	3	–	–	100	–	–	–	3	–	–	–	–	A 20
55	Perfumes, cleaners, toiletries	19	–	–	74	–	–	–	–	–	32	–	–	–	–	–	30	–	–	–	A 9
56	Manufactured fertilisers	100	–	–	–	68	7	–	–	100	–	100	–	–	–	–	–	–	18	–	A 22
57	Explosives	–	–	–	–	–	100	100	–	–	–	–	–	–	–	–	–	100	–	–	A 17
58	Plastics	100	–	–	–	–	–	–	–	–	–	–	–	–	–	–	–	–	–	–	A 6
59	Misc. chemicals	38	–	–	23	19	11	18	14	–	–	–	19	11	–	8	–	11	–	–	A 10
61	Leather and manufactures	–	–	–	–	–	–	–	–	–	–	–	–	–	–	–	–	–	–	–	A 5
62	Rubber manufactures	95	–	93	–	–	–	–	–	58	–	–	–	–	–	–	–	100	–	–	A 14
63	Wood and cork manufactures	–	–	–	–	–	–	–	–	–	–	–	–	–	–	–	–	–	–	–	A 0
64	Paper and paperboard manufactures	–	–	–	–	–	18	–	12	–	33	25	–	30	30	–	1	–	–	–	A 1
65	Textile manufactures	25	19	35	45	70	69	18	23	–	–	–	–	–	–	–	–	–	–	–	A 24
66	Non-metallic mineral manufactures	3	–	79	–	16	–	–	–	–	5	–	–	–	–	3	–	–	–	–	A 6
67	Iron and steel	73	–	80	–	–	–	–	8	–	–	–	–	13	–	30	–	–	–	–	A 9
68	Non-ferrous metals	–	–	–	–	–	–	–	–	–	–	–	–	–	–	30	17	–	–	–	A 3
69	Misc. metal manufactures	1	–	–	–	–	–	–	–	–	–	–	–	–	–	2	–	–	–	–	A 0
71	Non-electric machinery	1	–	72	–	3	–	–	–	–	–	–	–	–	–	2	11	–	–	–	A 5

(continued on page 132)

Table 5.2   continued

SITC	Commodity group	USA	Canada	UK	Japan	Belg. Lux.	France	Germany	Italy	Netherlands	Denmark	Finland	Norway	Sweden	Austria	Switzerland	Portugal	Ireland	Australia	New Zealand Mean
72	Electric machinery	72	27	–	58	–	15	–	–	12	–	–	–	–	–	–	37	2	–	A 12
73	Transport equipment	73	39	39	65	75	59	70	65	–	–	39	88	35	–	68	76	10	1	A 45
81	Construction equipment	100	–	–	–	–	–	–	–	–	–	–	–	–	–	–	–	–	–	A 6
82	Furniture	–	–	–	–	–	–	–	–	–	–	–	–	–	–	–	–	–	–	A 0
83	Travel goods & accessories	–	–	–	–	–	–	–	–	–	–	–	–	–	–	–	–	–	–	A 0
84	Clothing	92	–	–	–	–	–	51	–	–	–	–	–	3	–	93	–	–	100	A 19
85	Footwear	16	–	3	35	5	16	–	3	–	–	–	–	–	–	–	–	100	–	A 12
86	Precision instruments	–	–	–	–	–	–	–	–	–	–	–	100	–	24	–	53	–	62	A 11
89	Misc. manufactures	10	13	–	3	2	2	26	3	14	7	15	–	26	–	–	–	2	–	A 4
	Total imports	39	11	13	32	30	20	26	19	14	7	n	9	12	12	12	33[a]	n	4	A 18

A: New Zealand applies automatic import licensing to most manufactured goods, with preferences granted to Commonwealth suppliers.

n: Not available.

[a]: Specific commodities covered by NTBs, 62 per cent of all dutiable imports subject to bilateral or multilateral quotas.

Source: Walter (1972).

Table 5.3 summarises Olechowski and Yeats' findings on the incidence of nontariff barriers on total CPC exports to the eight major developed market economy countries. Shown here is the total value of exports from each country group and the share of trade covered by major nontariff barriers (quotas and licensing, minimum import prices, export restraints, variable import levies, other quantitative restrictions including prohibitions, health restrictions, cost-increasing measures including tariff quotas, state trading, and a group of 'other' measures). Frequency and uncertainty indices are given along with a 'partial' NTB frequency index (shown in the far right column of the table) which is based on the number of tariff-line items covered by four specific barriers (i.e. quotas, discretionary licensing, price control measures and variable levies).

The data in Table 5.3 document the differential adverse treatment of CPC exports relative to shipments from developed or developing countries. Over 20 per cent (by value) of CPC shipments are subject to quotas or restrictive licensing arrangements while only 6 per cent of other countries' exports face these retraints. The adverse differential is largely due to the European Community where over 27 per cent of centrally planned country exports face quotas or restrictive licensing arrangements, as opposed to only 8 to 9 per cent of developed or developing country exports.[11] EEC minimum import price restrictions have a higher incidence on the CPCs covering 6.6 per cent of total exports, as opposed to under one-half a per cent of other countries' shipments. In Japan, the normal pattern is reversed, however, as the NTB trade coverage ratios for the centrally planned countries are generally lower than those for the developed market economy countries.

For the eight markets combined, Olechowski–Yeats found trade barriers are applied most often to products from centrally planned countries. Adding the trade coverage ratios for the nine barriers, and making allowance for double coverage by the restraints, shows 46.7 per cent of CPC exports encounter NTBs, but only 21 to 23 per cent of exports from developing and developed countries face these restrictions. This adverse differential is particularly striking in the EEC where over 60 per cent of CPC exports face barriers, while the United States applies NTBs to approximately 48.5 per cent of the CPCs' trade. Aside from this aggregative data, Olechowski and Yeats present NTB indices for Hungarian, Polish and Bulgarian exports in a format similar to Table 5.3 and data on nontariff barriers facing major CCCN product groups (see their table 6 on p. 18).[12] This

Table 5.3 Summary statistics on nontariff barriers facing eight industrial markets' imports

Importing markets	Exporters	1976 value of total imports ($US m.)	Share of imports subject to non-tariff barriers									NTB indices		
			Direct import controls					Other non-tariff barriers				Uncertainty	Frequency	
			Quotas and licensing	Minimum prices	Export restraints	Variable levies	Others	Health and sanitary standards	Cost increasing measures	State trading	Others		Total	Partial
EEC	Developed	78 918.3	.081	.005	.013	.066	.024	.044	.002	.010	.064	.24	.28	.21
	LDC	77 297.6	.093	.004	.003	.025	.014	.025	.000	.126	.055	.23	.28	.20
	CPC	11 612.9	.273	.066	.032	.045	.005	.036	.013	.089	.047	.41	.48	.44
USA	Developed	67 576.6	.026	.024	.010	–	–	.024	–	–	.040	.14	.14	.10
	LDC	52 499.7	.028	.002	.057	–	–	.021	–	–	1.04	.14	.18	.13
	CPC	836.4	.010	.006	.054	–	–	.210	–	–	.205	.13	.17	.12
Japan	Developed	25 796.4	.235	.021	–	–	–	.265	.037	.067	.000	.18	.15	.04
	LDC	35 811.2	.016	.012	–	–	–	.102	.024	.004	.002	.18	.20	.05
	CPC	1 361.5	.179	–	–	–	–	.068	.015	.004	–	.18	.14	.03
Canada	Developed	32 308.2	.005	–	–	–	–	.014	–	.002	.011	.04	.03	.01
	LDC	5 378.1	.060	–	–	–	–	.002	–	.002	.012	.06	.06	.03
	CPC	190.9	.112	–	–	–	–	.010	–	.005	.033	.07	.07	.05

Sweden	Developed	15 341.0	.031	.001	—	.024	.002	.010	—	.005	—	.09	.11	.10
	LDC	2 521.9	.073	—	—	.033	.004	.017	—	.002	—	.08	.14	.13
	CPC	1 121.0	.030	—	—	.019	.001	.016	—	.004	—	.08	.11	.10
Switzerland	Developed	12 815.3	.028	.027	—	.024	.004	.003	.001	.001	.020	.06	.05	.04
	LDC	1 388.3	.039	.052	—	.045	.004	.004	.001	.001	.014	.07	.08	.06
	CPC	497.8	.032	.008	—	.050	.009	.002	.004	.007	.062	.07	.06	.05
Norway	Developed	9 454.4	.015	.005	.000	—	.003	.004	—	.031	—	.13	.11	.07
	LDC	1 205.0	.018	.010	.000	—	.011	.001	—	.016	—	.12	.11	.08
	CPC	341.9	.036	.002	—	—	.000	.002	—	.014	—	.09	.06	.04
Austria	Developed	8 186.8	.015	—	—	.017	.003	.005	—	.004	.003	.07	.07	.05
	LDC	1 057.3	.049	—	.013	.016	.001	.006	—	.008	.001	.08	.11	.09
	CPC	929.1	.036	—	—	.041	.002	.019	—	.007	.002	.06	.07	.05
Total	Developed	250 397.0	.062	.012	.007	.024	.008	.051	.004	.012	.034	.12	.12	.08
Eight	LDC	177 159.1	.056	.005	.018	.012	.006	.038	.005	.056	.029	.12	.15	.10
Markets	CPC	16 891.5	.210	.046	.010	.036	.004	.043	.010	.063	.045	.14	.15	.11

Source: Olechowski and Yeats (1982).

latter information shows agricultural products experience the highest overall frequency of NTB incidence. In the eight industrial markets, 58 per cent of all prepared foodstuffs (CCCN ch. IV) exported by the CPCs are subject to trade restraints and 25 per cent of these are hard-core measures.

STUDIES OF AGRICULTURAL TRADE BARRIERS

Agricultural support programmes in most countries are directed at five basic objectives: stabilising and increasing rural incomes; provision of abundant food supplies at stable prices; improving external trade balances; acceleration of the development of other sectors that have linkages to agriculture; and to facilitate agricultural commodity processing. However, many related studies show these support programmes often involve major costs for society and also cast doubts on their efficiency. For example, Miller (1986) notes that these policies have important anomalies: (i) the budgetary cost of US farm programmes in 1986 was nearly $700 for each non-farm family while the EEC's was more than $900; (ii) Japanese consumers pay about 60 per cent more than they would if internal food prices reflected the fall in world prices and the appreciation of the yen since 1980; (iii) the quarter of the EEC and US farmers with the largest output receive three-quarters of the farm support; and (iv) the annual transfers from consumers (through higher dairy product prices) and taxpayers to EEC dairy farmers represents $410 per cow and in the United States $835 per cow.

More general studies on the costs and effects of agricultural support policies in developed countries reveal four important points. First, the levels of protection for many agricultural goods are very high, particularly in Europe and Japan, with some estimates of NTB *ad valorem* equivalents ranging to several hundred per cent. Second, empirical evidence shows protection levels are often unstable with some NTBs' nominal equivalents registering wide year-to-year changes. This often reflects the fact that relationships between domestic and world prices fluctuate widely due to exchange rate changes and factors affecting supply and demand for agricultural products. Third, wide differences exist in the level of agricultural protection in developed countries with Australia, New Zealand, Canada and the United States having relatively low barriers (exceptions exist for specific products), while Japan, the European Community and EFTA countries are highly protected. Fourth, studies that simulated a liberalisation's effects show agricultural protectionism involves major costs for the highly protected markets, and is an important constraint on export earnings and employment prospects of countries with a comparative advantage in this sector. In addition, recent analyses question whether the objectives of agricultural support programmes could be achieved by alternative policies that have less detrimental international consequences.[13]

To provide background information for policy initiatives and further research, this section surveys previous studies that estimated the level and effects of agricultural protectionism in major markets. However, a troublesome point about most of these investigations is that they are often based on differentials between domestic and world prices. To assess the level of (say) Japanese protection for a specific good, wholesale prices for domestic products have been compared with 'world' prices. The latter, however, can be influenced by protectionism in other major markets. For example, a tightening of trade barriers in Europe could widen the spread between Japanese domestic and world prices due to the influence of the European action on world demand. External influences would (incorrectly) make it appear as if Japanese protection were rising. Ideally, one should use estimates of the 'free trade' world price in the comparisons, but such an approach has not yet been employed. As noted in Chapter 2, domestic world price differences can also be distorted by other factors that would reduce their utility as measures of protection.

Saxon and Anderson (1982): Japanese Agricultural Protection

These authors develop a comprehensive historical series on trends in Japanese protectionism for ten major agricultural products (e.g., polished rice, wheat, barley, soybean, raw sugar, refined sugar, beef, pork, chicken and eggs) during the period 1955 to 1980.[14] The authors compile domestic wholesale and producer prices for the agricultural products and then estimate their 'border' prices. To obtain the latter, the unit c.i.f. value of imports (or unit f.o.b. value of exports) are used for years in which Japan imported (exported) substantial quantities of the product. Where the quantity traded by Japan was small, or unrepresentative of the products consumed, proxy border prices were obtained from trade statistics of comparable countries. In compiling this data, an effort was made to only include items of the same grade and quality so the effect of product variations on prices would be minimal.

Annual *ad valorem* equivalents for Japanese trade barriers were estimated for each product by taking the ratio of the domestic to border price. These results are summarised in Table 5.4. While considerable variation is due to irregular year-to-year changes in border prices, Saxon and Anderson conclude that an upward trend is evident in protection for most products (particularly for polished rice, soybean, refined sugar), and that where a clear trend does not exist protection has remained high throughout the 25-year period. Beef is cited as a product where Japanese long-term domestic prices have been maintained at levels of 200 to 400 per cent or more above border prices. However, rice is the most important single item in Japanese production and trade and there is a strong upward trend in the ratio of domestic to border prices. By the late 1970s, domestic producer prices for rice had risen to three and four times the international price level and were stimulating Japanese production surpluses. Substantial surplus production also occurred for wheat and barley since domestic producer prices rose to more than four times the corresponding border price.[15]

Cline et al. (1978): EEC, Japan and United States

Employing a partial equilibrium trade projection model similar to that presented in Chapter 3, this study simulated the effects of a liberalisation of agricultural trade barriers in the EEC, Japan and United States. For the EEC projections, a GATT (1971) document was employed which derived 1969 *ad valorem* equivalents for variable levies by taking the ratio of the total revenue collected by these charges to the annual value of trade in the product (see equation (2.14) in Chapter 2). Nominal equivalents were also computed for 1972 using an alternative procedure. Specifically, the *EEC Bulletin* regularly publishes values of variable levies as well as 'threshold' prices for individual products. Since the levy equals the difference between the world and threshold price (see equations (2.10) to (2.13) in Chapter 2) the ratio of the levy to the world price can be used for deriving nominal equivalents. The 1972 estimates derived using this procedure are compared with the earlier GATT nominal equivalents in Table 5.5. For products such as wheat, rye, oats and lard, differences of 25 points or more indicate the size of the short-term changes that can occur in the levies' incidence. (See UNCTAD, 1983b, for additional estimates of the *ad valorem* equivalents of NTBs derived by this procedure.)

Table 5.4 Estimated *ad valorem* equivalents for Japanese protection of agricultural products, 1955 to 1980

Year	Polished rice	Wheat	Barley	Soybean	Raw sugar	Refined sugar	Beef	Pork	Chicken	Eggs
1955	142	135	129	122	222	133	174	99	64	134
1956	144	133	129	125	212	143	250	81	85	146
1957	150	131	132	124	150	150	225	80	92	123
1958	155	141	150	154	219	149	227	79	87	128
1959	164	140	143	158	235	156	190	106	111	102
1960	165	142	141	150	278	158	223	153	126	101
1961	150	135	140	132	288	155	232	105	126	102
1962	173	130	134	144	322	172	256	100	129	106
1963	167	133	135	142	161	180	269	139	130	115
1964	157	125	126	145	164	192	230	136	123	110
1965	177	133	122	145	292	206	271	119	122	89
1966	176	127	114	148	345	207	288	95	116	92
1967	132	121	118	142	367	174	260	119	125	95
1968	166	127	129	162	344	201	247	141	131	99
1969	194	130	147	170	279	215	259	141	113	89
1970	247	132	138	219	232	270	254	116	112	93
1971	278	132	114	227	209	310	277	135	141	95
1972	273	146	135	212	194	324	279	131	130	104
1973	169	131	117	264	199	223	244	127	123	109
1974	115	66	69	196	95	152	174	114	110	89
1975	197	74	72	173	82	240	346	134	117	94
1976	304	103	106	258	158	355	385	122	124	83
1977	343	155	134	222	288	394	443	118	127	93
1978	330	173	174	361	407	388	421	113	127	100
1979	360	150	174	352	410	405	327	93	107	108
1980	279	123	128	385	196	n.a.	275	100	108	143

Source: Saxon and Anderson (1982).

Table 5.5   Tariff equivalents of EEC variable levies on selected
agricultural products, 1969 and 1972

Tariff	Category	Product	Tariff equivalent 1969	1972
0202	82	Turkey drumsticks	n.a.	51.9
0405	12	Hatching eggs	7.0	24.5
1001	10	Wheat	76.0	109.5
1001	50	Durum wheat	69.0	99.0
1002	00	Rye	75.0	108.6
1003	00	Barley	98.0	84.6
1004	00	Oats	84.0	109.1
1005	92	Maize	64.0	75.9
1006	10	Paddy rice, round	n.a.	96.1
1006	30	Paddy rice, long	n.a.	107.3
1006	25	Rice, husked, long	n.a.	107.3
1006	27	Rice, husked, round	n.a.	96.1
1006	43	Rice, semi-milled, long	n.a.	154.3
1006	45	Rice, bleached, round	n.a.	104.6
1006	47	Rice, bleached, long	n.a.	186.4
1007	91	Millet	71.0	41.8
1007	95	Sorghum	48.0	72.5
1101	20	Wheat and maslin flower	76.0	99.7
1501	11	Lard	55.0	93.4
1501	19	Lard	n.a.	93.4
1602	22	Prepared meat, minimum of 57 per cent poultry	n.a.	27.9
1602	23	Prepared meat, minimum of 27 to 57 per cent poultry	n.a.	28.1

Note: For the 1972 figures crop years are used for grains while calendar years
are used for other products.
Source: Cline *et al*. (1978).

Using changes in agricultural production costs, Cline *et al*. extra-
polated the nominal equivalents to 1974 and then simulated the
effects of a liberalisation that would result from tariff-cutting formulae proposed during the Tokyo Round. Their results indicate that
reduction of the levies by any of three basic tariff-cutting formulas
would increase agricultural imports from non-EEC countries by
approximately $1.9 billion (1974 dollars) while intra-EEC trade in

these items would decline by about $900 million. The United States is projected to have the largest overall trade gains (about $500 to $600 million annually), with those for Canada ranging from $260 to $317 million (see Cline, table 4.6 on p. 160). The most significant losses would be experienced by France whose EEC intra-trade in agricultural products would decline by about $570 to $700 million annually.

Cline *et al.* approach the problem of estimating *ad valorem* equivalents for Japanese nontariff barriers by computing the percentage difference between domestic and equivalent import prices of the good. Since most agricultural imports facing quotas and other NTBs were also subject to tariffs, the estimates reflect the joint protective effect of these trade barriers. The 1970 results are summarised in Table 5.6 for twenty-four Japan Trade Classification (JTC) products.[16] In some cases, tariff equivalents of over 100 per cent are observed (beef, non-sweetened evaporated milk, powdered milk, butter, cheese), while the level of protection for powdered skimmed milk exceeds 300 per cent.

Cline *et al.* estimate that the removal of trade barriers facing the items in Table 5.6 would increase imports by about 45 per cent, or $311 million over their 1971 trade base. The largest relative trade gains (about 90 per cent) are for Norway, Sweden, Finland, Austria, Switzerland and Denmark due to their concentration on dairy exports and the high import demand elasticities for these products. In contrast, US agricultural exports to Japan are projected to increase by about 44 per cent ($89 million) in total, or about 36 per cent ($7 million) if wheat is excluded from both the projections and the actual trade figures.

As far as United States agricultural nontariff barriers are concerned, Cline estimates that 'voluntary' export restraints on meat products had a tariff equivalent of about 20 per cent, and that NTB nominal equivalents for dairy products classified in SITC 022, 023 and 024 (milk, butter and cheese) averaged about 90 per cent in 1971. A complete elimination of these barriers is projected to increase meat imports by about $100 million (1974 dollars) and dairy product imports by about $76 million. (See Tyers and Anderson, 1986, for more recent estimates on the trade effects and deadweight losses associated with Japanese and United States protection for major agricultural products. These authors estimate Japanese protection for wheat, coarse grains, rice, beef, lamb, pork, poultry, dairy and sugar products involved a deadweight loss of approximately $27 billion in terms of 1980 prices.)

Table 5.6   Import price, domestic price and estimated tariff equivalents for Japanese restrictions on agricultural commodities (prices expressed in yen per kilogram)

BTN code	ITC code	Commodity	1972 price Import	Domestic	Tariff equivalent
02.01	011–110	Beef	345.5	794.5	1.2996
03.01	031–142	Yellowtail	286.0	460.1	0.6087
	–143	Herring	78.8	90.6	0.1497
03.03	031–314	Squid and cuttlefish	259.3	317.4	0.2241
04.02	022–111	Evaporated milk, sugared	121.3	234.9	0.9365
	–112	Skimmed milk, sugared	141.2	150.8	0.0680
	–121	Evaporated milk, not sugared	99.6	277.1	1.7821
	–210	Powdered milk	176.9	423.5	1.3940
	–221	Powdered and skimmed milk	78.5	327.0	3.1656
04.03	023–000	Butter	221.5	591.5	1.6704
04.04	024–010	Cheese	276.8	608.9	1.1998
07.05	054–210	Small red beans	116.0	180.2	0.5534
	–220	Broadbeans	51.8	53.7	0.0367
	–230	Peas	46.2	112.1	1.4264
	240	Green beans	61.2	142.9	1.3350
	–250	French beans	54.7	105.1	0.9214
	–260	Pegrin beans	51.4	139.4	1.7121
08.02	151–110	Oranges	104.5	252.0	1.4115
10.01	041–000	Wheat	24.5	60.2	1.4571
10.03	043–000	Barley	19.5	58.5	2.0000
10.06	042–210	Rice, polished	50.3	149.6	1.9742
11.08	599–51	Starch	27.7	62.8	1.2671
12.01	221–100	Groundnuts (peanuts)	120.9	286.7	1.3714
21.04	099–041	Tomato ketchup	187.0	273.0	0.4599

Note: The figures shown for 'tariff equivalents' have been derived using equation (2.5) in Chapter 2 with the exception that they have not been multiplied by one hundred.

Source: Cline *et al*. (1978).

Commonwealth Secretariat (1982): Alternative Forms of Trade Measures

This study quantifies the effects of replacing some existing nontariff trade barriers with measures thought to have less detrimental international effects. It simulates the expansion of trade in five major agricultural products – wheat, maize, barley, sugar and beef – which could occur if production subsidies replaced other forms of protection in a way that left income support levels unchanged. Using 1976 trade data, the projections are made for Japan, Federal Republic of Germany, France and the United Kingdom. The most dramatic impact is for beef trade, particularly in Japan, with net imports for the four countries projected to rise eighteen-fold. Net imports of sugar, wheat and barley increase about 70 per cent under 'equivalent' production subsidies, while trade in maize increases by about 16 per cent. Developed-country exporters experience the largest trade gains, yet developing-country exporters, particularly in South America and, for sugar, some Commonwealth countries, also record major increases. (See Bale and Lutz, 1979a, 1979b, and Snape, 1981, for other examples of studies that consider the different trade impact of alternative forms of agricultural support measures.)

General Agreement on Tariffs and Trade (1971): EEC and Other Europe

GATT estimates *ad valorem* equivalents for all tariff-line-level products subject to variable import levies in the EEC (6), Sweden, Spain, Switzerland and Greece. Nominal equivalents were estimated from the ratio of the duty collected by the levy to the corresponding value of imports covered by these charges. Separate information is also provided on most-favoured-nation tariffs and other special taxes (droit de douane) applied to products facing levies. Two points should be noted with regard to these data. First, all estimates are for 1969 and the *ad valorem* incidence of variable levies can change significantly from year to year. Second, the GATT figures do not include the protective effect of other trade barriers such as quotas, state trading, licensing arrangements or seasonal quotas that are also applied to EEC agricultural imports. However, even with these ommissions the GATT data show that the protective effect of EEC levies is often very high with nominal rates exceeding 100 per cent for many tariff-line items.

While the GATT report provides statistics on *ad valorem* equivalents for over 400 tariff-line-level products, two studies by Sampson and Yeats (1976; 1977) (reviewed in this chapter – see, in particular Tables 5.13 and 5.14) aggregate this information to one- and two-digit SITC products for the EEC and Sweden. Cline *et al.* (1978) also employs these GATT estimates in simulating the effects of a European agricultural liberalisation. (See Table 5.5.) UNCTAD (1983b) provides estimates of *ad valorem* equivalents of variable levies for selected agricultural products in other years (see Table 5.18), so a time series on changes in nominal equivalents can be compiled from published sources.

Gulbrandsen and Lindbeck (1973): Major Developed Countries

Gulbrandsen and Lindbeck estimated the average level of price support for agricultural products in developed market economy countries (excluding Japan) over selected periods from the mid-1950s to the beginning of the 1970s. Their overall agricultural support estimates are based on wheat, sugar, milk, beef, pork and eggs with the products combined to arrive at an average level of protection for each European country using weights based on Western Europe's production of each commodity. For Australia, Canada and the United States the aggregation employed weights based on national production. The authors also compare the level of each country's agricultural support with that for industrial goods.[17]

In estimating product support levels, the authors utilise differences between (domestic) producer wholesale and world prices. These basic price ratios are then adjusted to account for production incentives, such as subsidised fertiliser or machinery inputs, that would lower domestic producer prices. The resulting estimates of protection levels, which are summarised in Table 5.7, incorporate the combined effect of tariffs, nontariff barriers and production incentives. According to these figures, protection in Western Europe in the late 1960s averaged 50 per cent, compared to about 40 per cent in the mid-1950s. Ireland and Denmark had far lower levels of price support (about 15 per cent) than other European countries, while protection in Norway and Sweden was highest and appeared to be increasing. The table indicates a price support level of about 50 per cent in the EEC, which was somewhat lower than in Sweden. According to Gulbrandsen and Lindbeck's results, Great Britain was one of the few European countries to reduce agricultural protection over the 1950–70 interval.

Gulbrandsen and Lindbeck recognise that the absolute level of agricultural price support may be less important than its size relative to other sectors of the economy since the flow of resources is governed by relative, not by absolute prices. In order to estimate relative price support, Table 5.7 shows average tariffs on industrial products during 1960–62. These estimates, which are rough, suggest that relative price support for agriculture was about 30 per cent in Western Europe as a whole, and was highest in Switzerland, Norway, West Germany and Sweden. Gulbrandsen and Lindbeck also conclude that the relative support for agriculture in the USA and Canada was very low and might even be negative.

For some policy studies there is an obvious interest in linking the Gulbrandsen and Lindbeck support figures to more recent estimates since this would permit an analysis of trends in the cost and levels of protection. Winters (1987) provides a comprehensive survey of more recent studies of the incidence and effects of developed countries' agricultural protectionism that could be employed in such an intertemporal analysis. A direct match could be made with these recent investigations if the data in the Gulbrandsen–Lindbeck analysis were extended to show the costs and trade effects of protection in the 1950–70 period.

Hamilton (1986): Swedish Agricultural Protection

Hamilton estimated the level and trend in Swedish agricultural protection from 1970 to 1980, by year and by commodity. He provides nominal equivalents that incorporate the joint effects of variable levies and subsidies, while effective protection rates are also approximated. In addition, the arguments for national defence and crisis self-sufficiency in agriculture are assessed in relation to actual Swedish food production maintained by the support measures.

Hamilton quantifies agricultural protection levels by comparing Swedish wholesale and 'world' prices of individual commodities. Danish and EEC f.o.b. export prices are employed for the latter since they were similar to items consumed in Sweden and could not deviate greatly from world prices due to the 'the law of one price'. Transport costs from Danish or EEC exports to Sweden were added to each commodity's export price so a true 'border' price could be used in the comparisons. (See Hamilton's appendix on pp. 83–5 for a description of the data and empirical procedures employed.) Table 5.8 summarises the *ad valorem* equivalents for Swedish trade barriers that were derived from these domestic–border price differentials.

According to these estimates, Sweden's agricultural protection increased by about 10 percentage points, from approximately 70 per cent in 1970–72 to 80 per cent in 1976–80. This suggests that the rising protectionist trend observed by Gulbrandsen and Lindbeck (1973) continued through the last decade (see the review of the Gulbrandsen–Lindbeck study in this chapter). Dairy products, beef and veal emerge as the most heavily protected Swedish agricultural commodities with tariff equivalents of over 100 per cent occurring for these items. For beef and veal, the table shows a dramatic increase in protection over 1970–80 while tariff equivalents for eggs exceeded

Table 5.7   The level of agricultural price support in industrial countries

Country	Price support for agriculture 1956/57	Price support for agriculture 1966/67	Price support for agriculture 1968/69	Industrial tariffs 1960/62	Relative support 1966/67
Benelux	25	51	74	13	33
France	34	43	66	19	20
West Germany	40	58	69	8	46
Italy	44	73	78	20	44
EEC	36	53	69	15	33
Great Britain	47	32	31	19	11
Denmark	9	12	19	7	5
Norway	50	70	102	13	50
Sweden	40	63	80	8	51
Switzerland	76	86	103	9	71
Austria	30	32	39	18	12
Portugal	30	74	98	30	34
EFTA	40	39	46	n.a.	n.a.
Finland	97	97	93	n.a.	n.a.
Ireland	6	17	22	n.a.	n.a.
Spain	40	66	60	n.a.	n.a.
Greece	44	66	82	n.a.	n.a.
Western Europe	38	50	62	n.a.	n.a.
USA	21	18	n.a.	21	−2
Canada	25	12	n.a.	16	−3
Australia	n.a.	0	n.a.	10 to 30	−10 to −30
New Zealand	n.a.	0	n.a.	20 to 40	−20 to −40

Source: Compiled from Gulbrandsen and Lindbeck (1973). See the notes on p. 38 of the Gulbrandsen and Lindbeck study for details on how the data were prepared.

100 per cent over 1976–80, and a major decline also occurred in the tariff equivalents for grains. However, even with these diverse movements standard deviations of each year's tariff equivalents did not increase markedly (see Table 5.8), a point that suggests the dispersion in levels of protection did not undergo significant changes.[18]

Table 5.8 also compares Swedish nominal protection coefficients with the rates of protection afforded by the European Community's variable import levies. The figures indicate Swedish protectionism is generally lower than that of the EEC. Hamilton suggests this may be due to a higher capital intensity in Swedish agriculture, particularly relative to a southern European country like Italy. (See Tyers and Anderson, 1986, for supplementary information on the effects and costs of Swedish and EFTA agricultural protectionism in the 1980s.)

International Monetary Fund (1982): Selected Industrial Countries

This IMF study (see the reference to Anjaria *et al.* 1982) derives nominal protection coefficients (the ratio of domestic wholesale to world prices) for maize, wheat, sugar beets, lamb and sheep meat in the EEC, Japan and the United States.[19] For various reasons, the IMF indicates the results of its price comparisons must be treated with caution. For some items, no true 'world' price existed since the commodity is not traded in competitive markets. Here, the comparisons used prices of the dominant suppliers, or prices prevailing at the country's border (e.g. Japan). In other cases, quality differences were thought to distort the price ratios (e.g. US rice), but no corrections for this potential source of bias could be made. Also, the comparisons were not able to account for transportation costs inside each country. As a result, the domestic wholesale prices were normally recorded at or near consuming centres while border prices were compiled at ports of entry. Such differences would cause the degree of protection to be overstated. (Westlake, 1987, provides empirical evidence that internal transport and insurance costs are sufficient to impart significant biases in price comparisons made at different geographic points in an importing country.) In addition, the domestic–world price ratio for any one year could reflect transitory factors. World prices are converted to domestic currency prices using market exchange rates, and the comparisons could be distorted if the exchange rate were not in equilibrium.

Given these potential limitations, the IMF results are summarised in Tables 5.9 to 5.11. For most products the nominal protection coefficients exceed unity, reflecting positive protection in the EEC and Japan. For the United States, the ratios are generally below unity (except for sheep meat). The industrial country domestic–world price ratios are generally higher for essential foodstuffs, such as grains, than for products like sugar where domestic production competes directly with developing countries. The IMF suggests that the US comparative advantage in the production of agricultural products, particularly grains, is shown by its lower domestic–world price ratios relative to the Community and Japan.

Pryor (1966): Barriers in Socialist and Market Economy Countries

Pryor quantifies the effects of trade barriers in ten European 'capitalist' and eight 'communist' countries by comparing domestic with

Table 5.8   *Ad valorem* tariff equivalents of the combination of border protection and consumer price subsidies, 1970–80: Sweden and the European Community

| | Sweden | | | | | | European Community | |
| | | | | | | | | |
Product	1970–72 (average)	1973 (Sept–Nov)	1974 (Sept)	1976 (Jan–Dec)	1980 (Jan–Dec)	1976–80 (average)	1971–72 (average)	1976–77 (average)
Wheat	150.7	–4.0	–13.4	25.1	11.4	27.4	na	204[d]
Rye	150.7	–4.0	12.1	18.4	1.8	15.8	na	na
Sugar	64.9	0.0	–43.6	43.2	–4.7	60.0	174	176
Milk, fresh[a]	57.3	55.7	77.0	96.8	99.1	88.1	na	na
Milk, powder	90.0	43.2	38.8	76.9	51.9	64.4	112[e]	571
Cheese	84.6	123.1	62.2	146.6	113.6	121.7	na	na
Butter	31.9	87.5	79.5	118.0	37.6	92.5	327	401
Cream, thick	27.1	115.0	112.9	118.0	37.6	92.5	na	na
Eggs	217.2	27.8	91.5	129.2	116.6	104.8	182	na
Margarine	na	na	na	22.5	16.6	14.3	na	na
Beef and veal	53.2	41.7	189.6	155.2	195.4	155.2	137	192
Pork	50.0	3.6	37.8	11.3	41.4	26.6	133	125

149

Poultry	na	10.8	45.7	10.4	10.4	8.4	na	na
Consumption weighted average[b]	70.0	45.0	76.0	85.0	82.0	81.0	na	na
Production weighted average[c]	72.0	33.0	77.0	80.0	90.0	78.0	na	na
Standard deviation[f]	–	46.7	63.7	53.2	61.0	–	na	na
Agricultural inputs:								
Oilcake	36.4	na	na	32.7	40.3	31.6	na	na
Soyabean meal	32.3	na	na	28.8	27.3	22.2	na	na
Beet pulp	25.0	na	na	0.0	1.5	0.9	na	na
Pig feed	43.0	na	na	7.1	11.2	24.2	na	na

[a] Figures for fresh milk before and after 1975 are not quite comparable.
[b] Weights are those calculated for the price regulation index. Coarse grains excluded. Milling fee not included.
[c] Weights are those calculated for the farm-gate price index. Excluded are milk powder, cheese, butter, cream, margarine and poultry.
[d] Figures refer to soft wheat.
[e] Figures refer to 1971/72.
[f] Refers to the 11 products available for 1970/72. The variance of the two average periods 1970/72 and 1976/80 are 59.6 and 43.2, respectively.
Source: Hamilton (1986).

Table 5.9 European Community: nominal protection coefficients, 1975–80 (price in terms of ECUs and per 100 kilograms, excluding value-added tax)

	1975			1976			1977		
	Domestic price[1] P_d	World price[2] P_w	$\dfrac{P_d}{P_w}$	Domestic price[1] P_d	World price[2] P_w	$\dfrac{P_d}{P_w}$	Domestic price[1] P_d	World price[2] P_w	$\dfrac{P_d}{P_w}$
Maize									
Germany, Fed. Rep. of	14.53	9.65	1.50	16.97	10.04	1.69	19.02	8.35	2.28
France	12.43	9.65	1.29	14.30	10.04	1.42	15.27	8.35	1.83
Italy	13.14	9.65	1.36	14.63	10.04	1.46	15.11	8.35	1.81
Netherlands	13.38	9.65	1.38	15.72	10.04	1.56	17.70	8.35	2.12
Belgium	14.29	9.65	1.48	16.80	10.04	1.67	18.97	8.35	2.27
Luxembourg	14.80	9.65	1.53	17.28	10.04	1.72	19.58	8.35	2.34
United Kingdom	10.13	9.65	1.05	12.13	10.04	1.21	13.65	8.35	1.63
Weighted avg.[3]	**13.01**	**9.65**	**1.35**	**15.10**	**10.04**	**1.50**	**16.58**	**8.35**	**1.99**
Wheat									
Germany, Fed. Rep. of	14.03	12.03	1.17	16.61	11.89	1.39	17.63	9.04	1.95
France	11.96	12.03	0.99	13.45	11.89	1.13	13.33	9.04	1.47
Italy	13.44	12.03	1.12	15.68	11.89	1.32	16.61	9.04	1.84
Netherlands	12.87	12.03	1.07	15.04	11.89	1.26	15.87	9.04	1.75
Belgium	12.94	12.03	1.07	15.09	11.89	1.27	16.33	9.04	1.81
Luxembourg	12.51	12.03	1.07	15.06	11.89	1.27	15.41	9.04	1.70
United Kingdom	10.12	12.03	0.84	11.65	11.89	0.98	12.85	9.04	1.42
Ireland	11.87	12.03	0.99	12.44	11.89	1.05	14.10	9.04	1.56
Denmark	11.79	12.03	0.98	14.13	11.89	1.19	14.55	9.04	1.61
Weighted avg.[3]	**12.63**	**12.03**	**1.05**	**14.68**	**11.89**	**1.23**	**15.43**	**9.04**	**1.71**

Sugar beets[4]

Germany, Fed. Rep. of	26.69	36.53	0.73	30.37	22.85	1.33	32.44	15.71	2.06
France	24.25	36.53	0.66	24.55	22.85	1.07	22.59	15.71	1.44
Italy	37.76	36.53	1.03	35.16	22.85	1.54	35.64	15.71	2.27
Netherlands	30.86	36.53	0.84	29.86	22.85	1.31	30.13	15.71	1.92
Belgium	26.42	36.53	0.72	29.02	22.85	1.27	31.19	15.71	1.98
United Kingdom	30.61	36.53	0.84	29.28	22.85	1.28	30.60	15.71	1.95
Ireland	31.60	36.53	0.86	30.57	22.85	1.34	35.18	15.71	2.24
Denmark	24.89	36.53	0.78	28.63	22.85	1.25	27.83	15.71	1.77
Weighted avg.[3]	**28.45**	**36.53**	**0.78**	**29.30**	**22.85**	**1.28**	**29.91**	**15.71**	**1.90**

Beef[5]

Germany, Fed. Rep. of	227.46	106.96	2.13	249.80	141.40	1.77	268.10	132.01	2.03
France	199.47	106.96	1.86	223.77	141.40	1.58	226.90	132.01	1.72
Italy	241.94	106.96	2.26	239.97	141.40	1.70	245.99	132.01	1.86
Netherlands	213.41	106.96	1.99	238.90	141.40	1.69	261.06	132.01	1.98
Belgium	234.97	106.96	2.19	259.21	141.40	1.83	285.97	132.01	2.17
Luxembourg	189.45	106.96	1.77	216.10	141.40	1.53	257.08	132.01	1.95
United Kingdom	130.92	106.96	1.22	160.69	141.40	1.14	158.07	132.01	1.19
Ireland	115.26	106.96	1.08	156.31	141.40	1.11	181.05	132.01	1.37
Denmark	178.59	106.96	1.67	205.12	141.40	1.45	225.51	132.01	1.71
Weighted avg.[3]	**204.78**	**106.96**	**1.91**	**226.04**	**141.40**	**1.60**	**236.55**	**132.01**	**1.79**

Lamb and sheep[5]

France	293.65	120.45	2.44	309.83	141.70	2.19	324.20	150.85	2.15
Italy	237.10	120.45	1.97	240.08	141.70	1.69	248.30	150.85	1.65
Belgium	188.73	120.45	1.57	205.28	141.70	1.45	217.60	150.85	1.44
United Kingdom	133.53	120.45	1.11	150.39	141.70	1.06	171.53	150.85	1.14
Ireland	143.31	120.45	1.19	181.97	141.70	1.28	179.76	150.85	1.19
Denmark	164.27	120.45	1.36	222.87	141.70	1.57	239.80	150.85	1.59
Weighted avg.[3]	**224.24**	**120.45**	**1.86**	**239.88**	**141.70**	**1.69**	**254.45**	**150.85**	**1.69**

(continued on page 152)

Table 5.9 continued

	1978			1979			1980		
	Domestic price[1] P_d	World price[2] P_w	$\dfrac{P_d}{P_w}$	Domestic price[1] P_d	World price[2] P_w	$\dfrac{P_d}{P_w}$	Domestic price[1] P_d	World price[2] P_w	$\dfrac{P_d}{P_w}$
Maize									
Germany, Fed. Rep. of	20.05	7.91	2.53	–	8.44	–	–	9.01	–
France	15.89	7.91	2.01	16.29	8.44	1.93	17.54	9.01	1.95
Italy	15.88	7.91	2.01	16.70	8.44	1.98	18.02	9.01	2.00
Netherlands	18.61	7.91	2.35	18.97	8.44	2.25	19.35	9.01	2.15
Belgium	19.63	7.91	2.48	19.92	8.44	2.36	20.53	9.01	2.28
Luxembourg	20.75	7.91	2.63	20.87	8.44	2.47	20.82	9.01	2.31
United Kingdom	16.54	7.91	2.09	17.28	8.44	2.05	–	9.01	–
Weighted avg.[3]	**17.76**	**7.91**	**2.25**	**17.17**	**8.44**	**2.03**	**18.22**	**9.01**	**2.02**
Wheat									
Germany, Fed. Rep. of	19.62	10.03	1.95	–	11.74	–	–	12.35	–
France	16.04	10.03	1.60	16.35	11.74	1.39	17.34	12.35	1.40
Italy	17.00	10.03	1.69	17.67	11.74	1.50	19.18	12.35	1.55
Netherlands	17.70	10.03	1.76	17.79	11.74	1.51	17.72	12.35	1.43
Belgium	17.70	10.03	1.76	17.70	11.74	1.51	17.92	12.35	1.45
Luxembourg	–	10.03	–	–	11.74	–	–	12.35	–
United Kingdom	13.15	10.03	1.31	14.99	11.74	1.28	–	12.35	–
Ireland	–	–	–	–	–	–	–	–	–
Denmark	17.38	10.03	1.73	–	–	–	16.53	12.35	1.34
Weighted avg.[3]	**17.09**	**10.03**	**1.70**	**16.53**	**11.74**	**1.41**	**17.88**	**12.35**	**1.45**

Sugar beets[4]

Germany, Fed. Rep. of	34.55	13.53	2.55	35.29	15.54	2.27	36.09	45.39	0.79
France	23.59	13.53	1.74	25.59	15.54	1.65	–	–	–
Italy	41.95	13.53	3.10	–	–	–	–	–	–
Netherlands	32.16	13.53	2.38	34.86	15.54	2.24	39.01	45.39	0.86
Belgium	31.20	13.53	2.30	30.72	15.54	1.98	–	–	–
United Kingdom	32.28	13.53	2.38	37.28	15.54	2.39	–	–	–
Ireland	37.66	13.53	2.78	39.58	15.54	2.55	39.94	45.39	0.88
Denmark	30.57	13.53	2.56	–	–	–	–	–	–
Weighted avg.[3]	**32.16**	**13.53**	**2.38**	**32.63**	**15.54**	**2.10**	**36.63**	**45.39**	**0.81**

Beef[5]

Germany, Fed. Rep. of	275.42	167.79	1.64	279.19	210.42	1.33	278.11	198.22	1.40
France	239.90	167.79	1.43	246.16	210.42	1.17	267.17	198.22	1.35
Italy	258.10	167.79	1.54	264.62	210.42	1.26	294.57	198.22	1.49
Netherlands	269.78	167.79	1.61	271.41	210.42	1.29	268.09	198.22	1.35
Belgium	303.26	167.79	1.81	301.78	210.42	1.43	303.00	198.22	1.53
Luxembourg	262.05	167.79	1.56	262.14	210.42	1.24	264.10	198.22	1.33
United Kingdom	180.45	167.79	1.08	210.17	210.42	0.99	243.45	198.22	1.23
Ireland	206.19	167.79	1.23	–	–	–	–	–	–
Denmark	234.21	167.79	1.39	233.45	210.42	1.11	236.73	198.22	1.19
Weighted avg.[3]	**248.97**	**167.79**	**1.48**	**257.58**	**210.42**	**1.22**	**271.54**	**198.22**	**1.37**

Lamb and sheep[5]

France	327.19	174.13	1.88	337.25	175.13	1.92	336.35	207.69	1.62
Italy	228.20	174.13	1.31	267.82	175.13	1.53	277.38	207.69	1.33
Belgium	229.17	174.13	1.32	254.28	175.13	1.45	280.06	207.69	1.35

(continued on page 154)

Table 5.9   *continued*

	1978			1979			1980		
	Domestic price¹ P_d	World price² P_w	$\dfrac{P_d}{P_w}$	Domestic price¹ P_d	World price² P_w	$\dfrac{P_d}{P_w}$	Domestic price¹ P_d	World price² P_w	$\dfrac{P_d}{P_w}$
United Kingdom	186.02	174.13	1.07	215.21	175.13	1.23	221.63	207.69	1.07
Ireland	251.47	174.13	1.44	–	–	–	–	–	–
Denmark	256.86	174.13	1.47	270.91	175.13	1.55	245.55	207.69	1.18
Weighted avg.³	**257.38**	**174.13**	**1.48**	**280.39**	**175.13**	**1.60**	**284.73**	**207.69**	**1.37**

[1] For maize and wheat, the marketing stage is from the first buyer, wholesaler, or importer to the trader; for sugar beets, the marketing stage is from producer to industry; for beef and lamb, the marketing stage is from wholesaler (or slaughterhouse) to retailer.

[2] Based on average prices (daily for lamb and sugar, weekly for maize and wheat, and monthly for beef). The sources of these prices are as follows: for maize, US No. 2 yellow, f.o.b. Gulf ports, export price base (*USDA Grain Market News*); for wheat, US No. 2 hard red winter wheat, f.o.b. Gulf ports, export price base (*USDA Grain Market News*); for rice, Thailand white milled, 5 per cent broken, f.o.b. Bangkok, export price (*USDA Rice Market News*); for sugar. International Sugar Agreement prices calculated in accordance with Economic Rule 611.3 (*Journal of Commerce and Financial Times*); for beef, US imported frozen boneless, 85 per cent visible lean cow meat, import price, f.o.b. port of entry (US Department of Agriculture); for lamb, New Zealand Pl's Smithfield Market, London (*Financial Times*). The prices in US dollars were converted to European Currency Units (ECUs) at exchange rates given in *EUROSTAT*.

[3] Using 1979 gross national product at market prices.

[4] Standard quality.

[5] Price per 100 kilograms (carcass weight).

Source: Anjaria *et al.* (1982).

Table 5.10 Japan: nominal protection coefficients, 1975–81

Year/price		Rice[a]	Wheat[b]	Barley[b]	Soybeans[b]	Beef[a]	Beef[b]	Pork[b]	Butter[a]	Sugar[a]	Oranges[a]
					Agricultural commodity						
1975											
	Domestic price	288	43	34	145	1203	1760	989	992	220	240
	World price	109	59	47	84	498	508	734	462	171	149
	Price relative	2.64	0.74	0.72	1.73	2.42	3.46	1.35	2.15	1.29	1.61
1976											
	Domestic price	306	55	46	181	1170	2027	963	1234	187	267
	World price	77	54	44	70	531	527	838	410	122	144
	Price relative	3.97	1.03	1.06	2.58	2.20	3.85	1.15	3.01	1.53	1.85
1977											
	Domestic price	318	55	46	182	1174	1917	969	1233	185	321
	World price	73	35	35	82	436	433	831	327	103	138
	Price relative	4.36	1.55	1.34	2.22	2.69	4.43	1.17	3.77	1.80	2.33
1978											
	Domestic price	319	54	46	201	1140	1945	890	1191	187	326
	World price	79	31	26	56	462	462	834	312	98	145
	Price relative	4.04	1.73	1.74	3.61	2.47	4.21	1.07	3.82	1.91	2.25
1979											
	Domestic price	319	60	51	235	1340	2239	761	1119	222	331
	World price	75	40	29	67	684	685	846	356	145	177
	Price relative	4.24	1.50	1.74	3.52	1.96	3.27	0.90	3.14	1.53	1.87

(continued on page 156)

Table 5.10 continued

Year/price	Agricultural commodity									
	Rice[a]	Wheat[b]	Barley[b]	Soybeans[b]	Beef[a]	Beef[b]	Pork[b]	Butter[a]	Sugar[a]	Oranges[a]
1980										
Domestic price	327	60	51	–	1181	2233	809	1120	239	316
World price	103	49	40	–	811	813	852	452	179	135
Price relative	3.17	1.23	1.25	–	1.46	2.75	0.95	2.48	1.34	2.34
1981										
Domestic price	328	–	–	–	1144	–	921	1204	–	301
World price	110	–	–	–	720	–	853	583	–	188
Price relative	2.98	–	–	–	1.59	–	1.08	2.07	–	1.66

[a] Price data for these products were provided by the Japanese authorities.
[b] Price data for these commodities were provided by the Australia-Japan Research Center, Australian National University. The domestic price for beef is the weighted average of the principal categories of beef at major wholesale markets (yen per kilogram of boneless beef), and the world price is the comparable import price. For grains, the domestic price is the price paid to producers per kilogram, and the world price is the unit c.i.f. value of Japanese imports per kilogram.

Source: Adapted from Anjara et al. (1982).

Table 5.11   United States: nominal protection coefficients, 1975–80

Year/price	Agricultural commodity				
	Maize	*Wheat*	*Rice*	*Beef*	*Lamb*
1975					
Domestic price	3.03	3.88	–	72.55	98.33
World price	3.26	4.06	16.47	60.20	67.99
Price relative	0.93	0.96	–	1.21	1.45
1976					
Domestic price	2.64	3.22	20.03	61.00	99.41
World price	3.05	3.62	11.52	71.71	71.86
Price relative	0.87	0.89	1.74	0.85	1.38
1977					
Domestic price	2.29	2.77	16.97	62.69	104.41
World price	2.59	2.81	12.35	68.33	78.08
Price relative	0.88	0.99	1.37	0.92	1.34
1978					
Domestic price	2.33	3.10	17.84	80.43	120.75
World price	2.74	3.48	16.71	96.99	100.65
Price relative	0.85	0.89	1.07	0.83	1.20
1979					
Domestic price	2.61	3.86	19.73	101.62	125.29
World price	3.15	4.36	15.16	130.82	109.02
Price relative	0.83	0.89	1.30	0.78	1.14
1980					
Domestic price	2.93	4.36	20.47	104.44	126.00
World price	3.42	4.70	19.67	125.19	131.17
Price relative	0.86	0.93	1.04	0.83	0.96

Notes: Maize prices are in terms of US dollars per 56 pounds. Domestic maize prices are wholesale prices for Corn No. 2 yellow – Chicago, and world prices are for US No. 2 yellow, f.o.b. Gulf ports, export price base. Wheat prices are in terms of US dollars per 60 pounds. Domestic wheat prices are for Kansas City, No. 1 hard red winter wheat minus 2 US cents. World wheat prices are for US No. 2 hard red winter wheat, f.o.b. Gulf ports, export price base. Rice prices are in terms of US dollars per 100 pounds. Domestic rice prices are for Houston No. 2 f.o.b. mill price and world prices are for Thailand white milled, 5 per cent broken, f.o.b., Bangkok export price. Beef prices are in terms of US dollars per 100 pounds. Domestic prices are wholesale prices of US Central Markets for steer beef choice, 600–700 pounds. World beef prices are for US imported frozen boneless, 85 per cent lean cow meat import price, f.o.b. port of entry. Lamb prices are in US dollars per 100 pounds. Domestic prices are wholesale prices in Eastern markets for prime choice meat, 55–65 pounds. World lamb meat prices are New Zealand Pl's Smithfield Market, London.

Source: Adapted from Anjaria *et al.* (1982).

foreign prices for specific tropical items: bananas, chocolate (in bars), coffee (unground), oranges, pepper, rice sugar, tea, and tobacco. In collecting price data, an attempt was made to hold quality variations, seasonal differences, or transport cost differentials to a minimum (for details see Pryor, p. 407).

Three technical problems in the preparation of data were resolved as follows. First western European prices were converted to a common standard using official exchange rates, while both the 'official' and 'tourist' exchange rate were employed for the communist countries. Pryor presents all basic price statistics (see Pryor, p. 411) so other exchange rate conversion values can be tested. Second, the lowest price observed in the eighteen countries is employed as the 'world' market price. This means that trade barriers are measured on a relative rather than an absolute basis. Nevertheless, there should not be significant difference from absolute comparisons since several of the European countries had low or zero tariffs on these products, no quantitative restriction, and low domestic sales taxes. Third, Pryor employed weights based on world trade for each commodity to derive aggregate indices of restrictiveness for each country. Finally, the effects of sales taxes was removed by dividing the indices of trade barriers by a factor incorporating net sale taxes (taxes minus subsidies) to net material production for each of the eighteen countries.[20]

Three main conclusions emerge from Table 5.12 which summarises the results of these calculations. First, trade barriers facing tropical foodstuffs are higher among communist nations (excluding Yugoslavia) than in capitalist countries. Also, the communist nations not only have higher barriers, but also had wider differences in protection against individual products. (For the former normalised standard deviations of foreign–domestic price differentials exceeded those of the capitalist countries.) Second, the difference in the range of trade-barrier indices among the capitalist countries (Spain has a value of 123 while the index for Ireland is 236) is much lower than among the communist nations (from a value of 250 for Romania to 844 for East Germany), even when Yugoslavia is omitted. Third, even capitalist countries which had some domestic production of the commodities (Spain and Greece) had lower aggregate barriers than the communist countries. (See Holzman, 1969, for an important critical comment on this study and on the use of price differentials for measuring levels of protection.)

Table 5.12   Average trade barriers against nine foodstuffs exported by tropical underdeveloped countries

| | Index of height of barrier (Base = 100) | | |
| | Official exchange rate: | Tourist exchange rate | |
Country	Average sales tax element Omitted	Average sales tax element Omitted	Average sales tax element Included
Spain	140	140	123
Yugoslavia	151	151	127
United States	163	163	133
Switzerland	164	164	144
France	217	217	155
Austria	196	196	156
United Kingdom	256	256	202
Italy	247	247	214
Greece	257	257	223
West Germany	303	303	228
Ireland	270	270	236
Rumania	792	317	250
Bulgaria	1085	375	279
Hungary	671	338	284
Soviet Union	415	415	346
Poland	2752	429	347
Czechoslovakia	1105	560	437
East Germany	2094	1107	844

Source: Adapted from Pryor (1966).

Sampson and Yeats (1976): Sweden

Sampson and Yeats examine the *ad valorem* incidence of Sweden's variable import levies, which are applied to most agricultural imports, and compare their level with most-favoured-nation tariffs. Basic statistics were drawn from a GATT (1971) report that estimated variable levies' nominal equivalents from the ratio of revenue collected by these charges to the value of imports. While the GATT report derived nominal equivalents at the tariff-line level, Sampson and Yeats aggregated these data to one- and two-digit SITC products. (See Table 2.6 in this book.) The authors also show Sweden's variable levies are frequently applied to SITC 4 imports (animal and vegetable oils) and SITC 0 (food and live animals) where over 40 per cent of the tariff lines are covered by these charges. Approximately 77 per cent of fixed vegetable oil imports (SITC 42) encounter levies, as do all tariff-line items in the dairy product and egg group (SITC 02). Swedish levies are applied with a high frequency to meat products (SITC 01), as 95 per cent of all imports (measured by value), and 80 per cent of tariff-line items face these charges.

Table 5.13 summarises Sampson and Yeats' findings when nominal and effective rates of protection from tariffs and levies were estimated for Swedish agricultural imports. These results indicate that nominal or effective tariffs alone provide an inaccurate gauge of the level and structure of Swedish protection. For example, meat and dairy products both have a slightly negative effective tariff rate, but effective protection from both tariffs and levies is several hundred per cent. The most extreme divergences occur for vegetable oils where low value added in processing, coupled with high *ad valorem* equivalents (35 to 100 per cent) for levies, sends effective protection to over 1000 per cent. (See Appendix 2 in the present volume for an explanation of why this occurs.) Aggregate rates of effective protection exceed 100 per cent for corn milling and flour (and flour products) even though the nominal tariffs on these items average under 1 per cent. (See Hamilton, 1986, or OECD, 1987a, for more recent estimates of Swedish agricultural protection levels.)

Sampson and Yeats (1977): European Economic Community

Sampson and Yeats quantify the effects of the EEC variable import levies, which are applied to most temperate-zone agricultural imports, and also provide information on these charges' product coverage. Basic data for the analysis were drawn from a GATT (1971) report that estimated *ad valorem* equivalents for levies by taking the ratio of the annual revenue collected by these charges to the value of tariff-line-level imports. Sampson and Yeats recognised that the GATT approach has drawbacks, e.g., no nominal equivalents can be derived when levies become prohibitive while falsified transaction prices and traded values will bias the results.

Sampson and Yeats estimate the coverage of EEC import levies in terms of the values of imports and percentage of tariff-line products facing to these charges. These data are tabulated for major two-digit SITC products classified within food and live animals (SITC 0), beverages and tobacco (SITC 1), and animal and vegetable oils (SITC 4). Over one-third of the tariff-line-level imports of live

Table 5.13   Nominal tariffs, variable levies, and the effective rate of protection in Sweden, 1970: selected products of importance to developing countries

Product name	Nominal rate on inputs		Nominal rate on end product		Effective protection		
	Tariffs	Levies	Tariffs	Levies	Tariffs	Levies	Total
Meat products	0.3	9.3	0.0	63.7	−1.0	217.8	216.8
Preserved seafoods	0.6	0.8	4.1	0.1	11.6	−2.3	9.3
Preserved fruits and vegetables	2.6	1.4	13.4	0.0	40.1	−5.3	34.8
Grain and grain products:							
Corn milling	0.2	26.2	0.0	84.3	−0.5	165.8	165.3
Flour and cereal preparations	0.3	36.2	2.9	52.9	13.7	88.0	101.7
Bakery products	0.3	10.0	16.5	0.0	36.0	−22.1	13.9
Prepared feeds	0.2	26.3	0.0	16.0	−1.6	−68.5	−70.1
Prepared and processed foods:							
Animal and marine fats and oils	0.2	1.3	0.0	24.8	−0.9	117.5	116.6
Macaroni and spaghetti	0.5	20.4	54.8	0.0	175.2	−65.9	109.3
Pickles and dressings	2.5	0.0	8.9	0.0	38.8	0.0	38.8
Cocoa powder and butter	0.0	0.0	2.0	0.0	16.8	0.0	16.8
Chocolate products	1.5	2.0	5.2	0.0	12.4	−6.8	5.6
Alcoholic beverages	1.1	6.6	8.7	0.0	15.1	−13.2	1.9
Dairy products:							
Butter	0.1	88.1	0.0	204.0	−1.2	1158.8	1157.6
Cheese	0.1	15.2	0.0	39.7	−0.2	178.5	178.3
Condensed and evaporated milk	0.4	66.3	0.0	76.8	−2.1	58.4	56.3
Vegetable oils:							
Soybean oil	0.1	1.3	0.0	104.9	−1.7	1480.0	1478.3
Groundnut oil, crude	0.1	0.0	0.0	71.7	−0.7	896.5	895.8
Palm kernel oil, crude	0.1	0.0	0.0	50.8	−0.7	635.2	634.5
Rapeseed oil	0.3	0.0	0.0	92.9	−1.9	617.5	615.6
Coconut oil, crude	0.2	0.0	0.0	56.0	−2.2	509.3	507.1
Cottonseed oil	0.2	3.2	0.0	61.8	−2.0	488.0	486.0
Palm kernel oil, refined	0.2	49.7	0.0	35.8	−6.0	−462.7	−468.7
Tobacco products	0.1	0.0	31.5	0.0	59.2	0.0	59.2
Leather and leather products:							
Shoes	2.6	0.0	14.0	0.0	24.5	0.0	24.5
Leather	0.4	0.0	7.3	0.0	23.1	0.0	23.1
Leather manufactures	1.8	0.0	7.0	0.0	12.5	0.0	12.5
Rubber products	0.9	0.0	8.0	0.0	19.7	0.0	19.7
Soaps and detergents	1.1	2.1	8.0	0.0	29.7	−9.1	20.6

(continued on page 162)

Table 5.13   *continued*

Product name	Nominal rate on inputs		Nominal rate on end product		Effective protection		
	Tariffs	*Levies*	*Tariffs*	*Levies*	*Tariffs*	*Levies*	*Total*
Yarns, threads, and fabrics:							
Wool fabrics	2.8	0.0	15.3	0.0	39.1	0.0	39.1
Cotton fabrics	1.7	0.0	13.0	0.0	37.7	0.0	37.7
Cotton clothing	6.4	0.0	17.4	0.0	29.7	0.0	29.7
Jute fabrics	0.1	0.0	9.6	0.0	26.4	0.0	26.4
Wool clothing	7.7	0.0	15.0	0.0	19.7	0.0	19.7
Wool yarn	0.2	0.0	5.5	0.0	19.0	0.0	19.0
Average	1.1	10.5	7.7	29.6	19.4	170.2	189.5

Source: Sampson and Yeats (1976).

animals (SITC 00), meats and preparations (SITC 01), cereals (SITC 04) and sugar and honey preparations (SITC 06) encounter these charges. In addition, the levies' average *ad valorem* equivalents ranged from two to five times the MFN tariffs, and nominal rates of protection from both tariffs and levies often are very high. For example, when levies combine with tariffs the nominal rate of protection for dairy products and eggs is over 170 per cent, for cereals and preparations it is almost 70 per cent, while nominal protection for both meat and sugar imports is about 50 per cent (see Sampson and Yeats, table 1, p. 102).

Table 5.14 summarises Sampson and Yeats' findings when nominal and effective rates of protection were estimated for specific products. For the nine farm gate items, an average tariff of 14 per cent represents an imposing trade barrier, yet the additional protection afforded by levies (45 per cent) is roughly three times higher. Much the same pattern occurs for processed agricultural product, as an average tariff of 18 per cent combines with a nominal equivalent of 75 per cent for levies. Only in one out of twenty-three products with joint coverage (meal and groats) is the nominal tariff rate larger than the levy's *ad valorem* equivalent. Altogether, the comparisons show that levies are a far more important source of protection for EEC agriculture than MFN tariffs.

While the levels of protection in Table 5.14 are imposing, other EEC trade barriers also restrict agricultural imports. The authors provide a listing of products subject to NTBs like seasonal prohibitions, licensing systems, quotas and state trading arrangements (see

Table 5.14   Comparison of nominal and effective rates of protection for selected agricultural products in the European Economic Community

Description	Nominal rate (%)		Effective rate (%)		
	Tariffs	Levies	Tariffs	Levies	Total
Farm gate products					
Oats	13.0	84.2	25.8	177.9	203.7
Rye	16.0	75.8	32.1	160.0	192.1
Wheat	20.0	73.0	40.6	154.1	194.7
Rice	16.0	34.5	32.1	72.8	104.9
Maize	6.0	34.1	10.7	72.0	82.7
Sheep	14.8	a	33.7	−42.7	−9.0
Swine	15.8	26.4	37.7	34.4	72.1
Poultry	12.0	15.9	25.5	3.8	29.3
Bovine animals	15.2	16.0	34.9	5.0	38.9
Meat products					
Bovine meat	20.0	64.2	38.2	215.2	253.4
Pig meat	20.0	30.4	36.7	52.9	89.6
Mutton	20.0	20.0	39.3	80.0	119.3
Poultry meat	18.0	23.3	38.5	51.9	90.4
Preserved fruits and					
vegetables	26.0	26.8	62.5	199.2	161.7
Grain products					
Corn flour	8.0	45.3	10.4	85.6	96.0
Wheat flour	25.0	76.4	98.9	206.8	305.7
Other flour	8.3	37.5	−2.8	41.9	39.1
Rolled cereal flakes	26.9	33.4	94.5	19.5	114.9
Meal or groats	23.0	17.3	75.6	−51.2	24.4
Roasted and puffed cereals	8.0	24.9	−14.9	−52.2	−67.1
Fodder	14.8	35.2	61.2	62.8	134.0
Macaroni and spaghetti	12.0	43.7	6.7	50.6	57.3
Dairy products					
Cheese	23.0	82.5	58.8	217.2	276.0
Butter	21.0	328.0	76.5	1244.2	1322.7
Condensed & evaporated					
milk	21.3	98.5	44.3	290.1	334.4
Tobacco products[a]	87.1	–	148.5	–	148.5
Leather products[a]	7.0	–	21.4	–	21.4
Vegetable oils[a]					
Soybean oil	11.0	–	148.1	–	148.1
Groundnut oil	7.5	–	92.9	–	92.9
Coconut oil	8.0	–	70.3	–	70.3

[a] Variable levies are not applied to this product group.
Source: Sampson and Yeats (1977).

their table 3, on p. 105). The protective effects of these additional measures are not included in Table 15.4 where the estimates refer only to tariffs and variable levies.[21] For supplementary information relating to more recent periods, detailed estimates of the EEC's producer and consumer subsidy equivalents for agricultural products over the 1979–81 period are presented in OECD (1987c) – also see Table 5.21 in this book. In addition, Schiff (1985), Australian Bureau of Agricultural economics (1985) and Buckwell *et al.* (1982) derive more recent estimates of the costs and effects of EEC agricultural protection. Spencer (1985), Stoeckel (1985), Breckling *et al.* (1987), and Burniaux and Waelbroeck (1985) analyse the cost and effects of the Common Agricultural Policy within a general equilibrium framework.

UN Food and Agricultural Organization (1980): Barriers to Meat Trade

Using information on tariffs and tariff equivalents for nontariff barriers, FAO quantified the effects of market protectionism on international trade in beef products.[22] Assuming rates of protection were reduced by 25 per cent, this study estimated that 1977–9 world beef exports would have been 22 per cent greater and that average international beef prices would have been 7 per cent higher. Furthermore, instead of an actual trade value of $2.8 billion over the three-year period 1977–9, the combined beef and cattle export earnings of Latin America and Oceania would have been $3.8 billion. Moreover, with a reduction of 50 per cent, the 1977–9 export earning of these two regions would have increased by $5.3 billion. The FAO also estimated that either the 25 per cent or the 50 per cent liberalisation would have resulted in a moderate expansion of net imports by the United States and a more pronounced rise in net imports by EEC, and other Western European countries, Japan and the Republic of Korea. (See Valdes and Zietz, 1980, for a more general analysis of the effects of protection on approximately fifty major agricultural commodities. Tables 3.5 and 3.6 in this book summarise some of the main finding of the Valdes–Zeitz study.)

UN Food and Agricultural Organization (1979): Major Products

This FAO report employs differences between producer prices and representative 'world' market prices to measure agricultural protectionism in the EEC and Japan over 1974–8. FAO advised caution in

Table 5.15   *Ad valorem* tariff equivalents in Japan and the European Economic Community

Country/product	1974	1975	1976	1977	1978
Japan					
Rice	72.0	238.6	438.3	500.9	305.8
Wheat	100.0	145.0	194.7	378.6	448.9
Barley	130.1	168.4	224.3	322.5	491.1
Beef	36.9	227.9	241.5	285.4	250.7
Pork	28.1	60.2	48.4	105.7	117.3
Sugar	39.7	−10.7	40.3	215.0	329.9
EEC					
Soft wheat	7	24	104	116	na
Hard wheat	20	45	–	–	na
Husked rice	−19	37	66	29	na
Barley	7	17	47	106	na
Maize	6	28	63	103	na
White sugar	−59	9	76	155	na
Beef and veal	62	96	92	96	na
Pigmeat	9	13	25	37	na
Butter	216	220	301	288	na
Skimmed milk powder	39	166	471	394	na
Oilseeds	−20	27	21	53	na

Source: United Nations Food and Agricultural Organization (1979).

interpreting these 'tariff equivalents' for reasons cited by the IMF (1982). None the less, an upward trend in this indicator is viewed as an indication that domestic producers are being increasingly shielded from world supply and demand conditions, even for commodities where the 'free' market accounts for only a small fraction of total trade and production.

Table 5.15 shows that Japanese price differentials moved consistently higher during 1974–8. For all commodities shown, the 1978 price ratios were at least three times the 1974 estimate, and for beef and sugar the increases were much greater. Overall, FAO concluded these figures show agricultural protectionism is very high in Japan and has been on a rising trend. However, part of the apparent increase in tariff equivalents reflects changes in the yen/dollar exchange rate, as well as general declines in c.i.f. import prices in dollar terms. For example, the domestic Japanese procurement price of sugar increased by 38 per cent in national currency, but 91 per cent in terms of dollars, while the c.i.f. price in dollars decreased by 62 per cent. (Related data, i.e. 1978–81 producer and consumer subsidies granted for major agricultural products in Japan, is given in OECD, 1987b. See also the IMF, 1982, study summarised in this chapter.)

Table 5.15 also shows nominal protection coefficients for various commodities in the European Community. From the low levels of 1974, a sharp rise occurred in most tariff equivalents. Given that 1974 and 1975 were years of relatively high world agricultural prices, particularly for grains and sugar, this was to be expected, i.e., the fall in world prices caused the EEC price relatives to raise. Since 1975 the tariff equivalents for cereals and sugar rose 75 points or more, while support for dairy products remained very high (about 200 to 300 per cent) throughout the interval. Butter had the highest level of protection for any product in the table with the 1976 price relative exceeding 300 per cent.

Table 5.16 (panel A) presents FAO estimates of the unit value of subsidies (per ton) to producer, and of the effects on consumer costs arising from support policies in selected countries. Corresponding estimates of the total value of subsidies to producers, and consumer costs, attributed to policy interventions are given in Table 5.16 (panel B). The figures show substantial increases in the producer subsidy equivalents for six of the eight products during the last three years. The 1978 value of sugar subsidies for United States and EEC producers was US $5.1 billion, a figure which exceeded the total value of sugar exported by the developing countries. FAO estimates that the total cost borne to consumers as a result of protection was roughly equal to the value of producer subsidy payments shown in the table.

UNCTAD (March 1983): Major European Countries

UNCTAD estimated the level of protection for nine major agricultural commodities (wheat, coarse grains, potatoes, sugar, beef, pork, poultry, eggs and milk) in Western European countries during the early 1970s. A 'world' or border price was established for each item and differences between these and domestic wholesale prices computed. This difference was expressed as a percentage of the world price and the result used as a rough gauge of domestic protection. Further refinements were made for production incentives, such as subsidies on fertilisers and machinery, that would have an influence (downward) on domestic producer prices and 'implicit' levels of protection. The resulting estimates of protection levels are presented in Table 5.17.

Table 5.16   Cost–benefit analysis of agricultural policy interventions in the USA, EEC and Japan

Country/Product	Producer subsidy equivalent			Additional consumer cost equivalent		
	1976	*1977*	*1978*	*1976*	*1977*	*1978*
Panel A: Measured in US$ per ton						
United States						
Wheat	2.5	18.0	12.6	−0.5	−0.1	–
Milk and products	80.5	98.5	51.0	77.6	96.1	48.4
Sugar	21.1	61.7	149.0	22.5	45.0	132.2
EEC						
Wheat	35.9	109.1	134.6	35.9	109.1	134.6
Milk and products	168.0	194.5	210.7	154.3	177.6	188.3
Sugar	75.6	245.4	398.6	59.8	182.2	259.4
Japan						
Rice	679.6	836.3	1105.5	506.7	682.9	922.4
Milk and products	199.9	234.6	309.6	165.1	192.4	266.8
Panel B: Measured in US$ billions						
United States						
Wheat	0.1	1.0	0.6	–	–	–
Milk and products	4.4	5.5	2.8	4.2	5.4	2.7
Sugar	0.1	0.3	0.8	0.2	0.4	1.2
EEC						
Wheat	1.2	3.9	4.8	1.2	3.7	4.7
Milk and products	15.7	18.7	20.8	14.4	17.1	18.6
Sugar	0.7	2.4	4.3	0.7	2.2	3.7
Japan						
Rice	8.0	11.0	13.9	6.0	7.9	10.6
Milk and products	0.8	1.1	1.5	0.7	0.9	1.2

Note: For the United States sugar prices are for the raw equivalent while in the EEC they are for the white equivalent.
Source: United Nations Food and Agricultural Organization (1979).

The price relatives indicate that sizeable differences exist in the average levels of protection between products and countries. Sugar, potatoes and eggs had average implicit protection rates of over 100 per cent in the European countries, while protection levels for pork and coarse grains were about one-half this figure. Norway and Switzerland register average levels of protection of 142 and 132 per cent for the nine agricultural products, while the corresponding figure for Denmark and Austria ranges between 35 and 42 per cent. The

Table 5.17 Estimated levels of protection for selected agricultural products in Western Europe in the early 1970s

Country and grouping[1]	Wheat	Coarse grains	Potatoes	Sugar	Beef	Pork	Poultry	Eggs	Milk	Average
Austria	79	68	14	97	35	22	72	92	64	42
Denmark	41	33	248	89	37	21	14	60	32	35
Finland	196	34	145	292	89	59	n.a.	146	114	118
Ireland	49	20	190	154	41	10	22	114	12	40
Norway	208	153	275	0	72	48	53	166	150	142
Portugal	119	81	170	0	188	57	120	108	65	113
Sweden	95	90	340	128	90	53	45	118	109	108
Switzerland	205	87	237	167	171	70	61	166	129	132
United Kingdom	33	0	141	104	51	5	1	100	58	53
EFTA	79	39	156	112	62	25	17	104	71	68
Belgium-Luxembourg	85	80	94	125	62	56	30	54	56	62
France	54	51	159	70	110	42	78	67	47	65
Germany, Fed. Rep.	110	106	161	148	136	68	37	150	104	108
Italy	112	98	196	142	97	62	278	148	95	122
Netherlands	90	79	186	105	121	60	16	50	31	83
EEC	86	75	165	114	114	59	110	111	75	90
Greece	81	86	309	146	108	40	61	149	104	105
Malta	79	12	151	0	77	0	128	112	83	85
Spain	86	56	191	161	108	29	44	120	79	88
Yugoslavia	46	28	89	70	6	-17	39	76	n.a.	29
Other Western Europe	70	43	162	130	59	10	45	126	n.a.	59
Western Europe	82	57	162	115	92	43	76	110	70	80

[1] Economic groupings are those existing in the early 1970s before the subsequent enlargement of the European Community.
Source: UNCTAD (1983).

UNCTAD estimates suggest that Yugoslavia has the lowest overall level of protection in Western Europe since domestic prices were about 20 per cent above world levels.

Since significant changes often occur from year to year in the relation between 'world' and domestic wholesale prices for many agricultural products, annual estimates of implicit rates of agricultural protection may be unstable. Recent exchange rate instability has also complicated the problem of estimating implicit protection due to difficulties in translating international prices into a representative domestic price. For such reasons, protection estimates based on a given year's data (such as those shown in Table 5.17) must be regarded with some caution. In recognition of this point, UNCTAD examined the normal change in protection afforded by one major EEC trade barrier, the variable import levy.

By taking the ratio of published values of EEC variable import levies to the average border price of the products to which they are applied, UNCTAD estimated the *ad valorem* incidence of these charges over the seven-year period 1975 to 1981 (see Table 5.18). The results show that levels of protection experience sizeable short-term fluctuations. Year-to-year differences of 50 percentage points or more occur in some levies' nominal equivalents, with raw sugar registering a change of 182 points between 1970 and 1980. However, aside from this volatility, the table shows EEC levies are normally afforded high levels of protection over the whole period and must be regarded as a major barrier to agricultural trade. (Although the data are presented in terms of producer and consumer subsidy equivalents, the OECD (1987a; 1987b; 1987c) provides useful corresponding statistics on EEC protection for the 1978–81 period. Additional empirical information on levels of EEC protection can be found in IMF (1982), Schiff (1985), Bale and Lutz (1981), Australian Bureau of Agricultural Economics (1985), Tyers and Anderson (1986) and Buckwell *et al.* (1982).)

World Bank (1986): Protection in Industrial Countries

The World Bank examined the extent to which industrial countries' protectionist policies raise domestic prices above 'world' market levels. The Bank's estimates of nominal protection coefficients (NPCs), domestic prices divided by border prices, for specific agricultural commodities are given in Table 5.19 for major developed market economy countries. The report advised that the resulting

Table 5.18   Estimated *ad valorem* equivalents for EEC variable import
levies applied to selected agricultural products, 1975–81

Product	Quarter	1975	1976	1977	1978	1979	1980	1981
Wheat	I	22.1	29.0	111.8	115.3	103.0	82.8	36.9
	II	46.7	37.1	135.4	105.6	87.4	72.5	51.0
	III	22.9	48.6	143.5	109.7	56.3	61.2	50.8
	IV	22.7	101.0	112.1	96.7	56.7	39.3	45.2
Oats	I	10.8	15.4	45.9	102.2	150.8	64.0	3.7
	II	48.4	25.9	63.2	109.7	119.8	59.6	15.1
	III	15.7	15.6	97.8	106.6	76.5	48.7	14.0
	IV	18.1	46.8	76.9	125.4	68.6	19.6	29.2
Durum wheat	I	5.0	33.8	146.4	103.0	130.0	62.9	27.9
	II	14.3	53.4	163.7	123.6	113.0	67.2	51.9
	III	8.5	75.0	153.7	130.7	67.1	35.8	67.9
	IV	33.0	139.8	108.6	116.9	53.2	29.8	74.3
Maize	I	17.0	35.8	57.1	104.1	107.6	101.7	41.6
	II	30.5	33.2	81.1	87.5	88.5	95.7	43.2
	III	13.4	31.1	120.7	116.0	76.0	69.7	45.5
	IV	28.5	62.6	103.5	115.3	82.4	53.2	83.0
Barley	I	6.6	23.2	42.1	112.3	152.7	60.7	18.7
	II	40.5	23.7	68.1	98.0	117.2	75.3	43.6
	III	17.8	19.1	112.2	130.7	57.4	57.4	46.3
	IV	11.5	43.1	100.4	141.2	53.3	27.7	54.3
Rye	I	28.3	56.0	71.6	82.5	118.0	54.5	14.2
	II	64.7	51.3	87.1	96.3	113.8	64.8	11.5
	III	35.5	39.4	99.6	113.0	62.2	44.0	19.0
	IV	35.8	61.4	90.7	116.3	53.6	25.5	23.7
Raw sugar[a]	I	na	na	na	na	182.2	25.8	0.2
	II	na	na	na	na	171.3	3.5	27.4
	III	na	na	na	217.2	148.0	0.0	45.4
	IV	na	na	na	173.8	77.7	0.0	79.5

[a] Published statistics on sugar levies are not available before the third
quarter of 1977.
Source: Adapted from UNCTAD (1983b). The authors have made certain
corrections for *ad valorem* equivalents for the 1979 variable levies.

figures be treated with caution and listed several reasons why NPCs
may be biased. (See Chapter 2 in this book for a full discussion.)
With variable world prices but relatively stable domestic ones, nominal protection coefficients vary widely over time. The table shows
NPC values for 1980–2, but those for a year like (say) 1985 would

have been greater because world market prices were generally lower. Also, domestic prices are measured at different stages, such as the farm-gate, the intervention board, or at the wholesale market, and this makes cross-country comparisons difficult. Qualities and varieties of commodities also vary and may bias the price comparison. For example, many types of rice are consumed, and there is no satisfactory way to adjust for this problem from country to country. Because agricultural policies affect world prices, these actual price differentials do not reflect the situation which would prevail if all countries' agricultural protection were abolished.

Even with these potential limitations the World Bank drew certain conclusions from Table 5.19. First, the data indicate dairy farmers are highly protected in all countries, as are rice and sugar producers. Second, Japanese and European farmers are more highly protected than their counterparts in countries like Australia, Canada, New Zealand and the United States. Third, the relative rate of protection between specific agricultural products varies considerably from country to country. This influences the resources (and acreages) allocated to the production of specific commodities in a given country.

Wipf (1971): Barriers in the United States

Wipf estimated US nominal and effective protection for agricultural products at both the farm-gate and processed product level. His effective rate estimates reflect total protection from tariff and nontariff measures and also show the separate effects of these restrictions. The effective protection estimates were derived using 1958 US input–ouput data with information on trade distortions such as tariffs, import quotas and controls, price-increasing provisions of domestic farm programmes, direct subsidy or support payments, American Selling Price (ASP) valuation practices, federal subsidisation of highway transportation, and indirect taxes compiled for 1958, 1963 and 1968. Wipf provides details on data sources used, and how these computations were made, in an appendix to his study.

Table 5.20 presents Wipf's estimated rates of protection for 17 farm-level sectors, 11 processing industries, and 3 composite groups for 1958 and 1963. Columns 1 and 2 show the total nominal and total effective rates for 1958 while effective tariff and effective NTB rates are given in columns 3 and 4. Corresponding rates for 1963 are shown in columns 5 and 8. For the 1958 estimates, the table shows that sizeable differences exist between total nominal and total effective

Table 5.19 Nominal protection coefficients for producer and consumer prices of selected commodities in industrial countries, 1980–82

Product/coefficient	Australia	Canada	EEC[a]	Other Europe[b]	Japan	New Zealand	United States	Weighted average[c]
Wheat								
Producer nominal protection	1.04	1.15	1.25	1.70	3.80	1.00	1.15	1.19
Consumer nominal protection	1.08	1.12	1.30	1.70	1.25	1.00	1.00	1.20
Coarse Grains								
Producer nominal protection	1.00	1.00	1.40	1.45	4.30	1.00	1.00	1.11
Consumer nominal protection	1.00	1.00	1.40	1.45	1.30	1.00	1.00	1.16
Rice								
Producer nominal protection	1.15	1.00	1.40	1.00	3.30	1.00	1.30	2.49
Consumer nominal protection	1.75	1.00	1.40	1.00	2.90	1.00	1.00	2.42
Beef and lamb								
Producer nominal protection	1.00	1.00	1.90	2.10	4.00	1.00	1.00	1.47
Consumer nominal protection	1.00	1.00	1.90	2.10	4.00	1.00	1.00	1.51
Pork and poultry								
Producer nominal protection	1.00	1.10	1.25	1.35	1.50	1.00	1.00	1.17
Consumer nominal protection	1.00	1.10	1.25	1.35	1.50	1.00	1.00	1.17
Dairy products								
Producer nominal protection	1.30	1.95	1.75	2.40	2.90	1.00	2.00	1.88
Consumer nominal protection	1.40	1.95	1.80	2.40	2.90	1.00	2.00	1.93
Sugar								
Producer nominal protection	1.00	1.30	1.50	1.80	3.00	1.00	1.40	1.49
Consumer nominal protection	1.40	1.30	1.70	1.80	2.60	1.00	1.40	1.68

[a] Excludes Greece, Portugal and Spain.
[b] Austria, Finland, Norway, Sweden and Switzerland.
[c] Averages are weighted by values of production and consumption at border prices.
Source: Adapted from World Bank (1986) p. 165.

Table 5.20   Nominal and effective protection in US agriculture, 1958 and 1963

	Total protection				Effective protection			
	Nominal		Effective		Tariffs		NTBs	
Input–output sector	1958	1963	1958	1963	1958	1963	1958	1963
Farm-level sectors								
Meat animals	8.6	9.2	10.8	14.6	14.5	14.7	–3.7	–0.1
Poultry and eggs	0.5	0.3	–28.0	–11.7	–5.2	–6.4	–22.8	–5.3
Farm dairy products	17.6	13.6	41.3	31.9	–5.8	–9.8	47.1	41.7
Other livestock								
products	0.7	0.2	–4.8	–5.4	–1.9	–5.2	–2.9	–0.2
Food grains	40.3	41.3	144.4	158.5	–2.7	–2.8	147.1	161.3
Feed crops	13.2	3.7	22.6	8.8	3.4	7.4	19.2	1.4
Cotton	19.8	32.2	57.1	95.0	–1.2	–1.3	58.3	96.3
Tobacco	11.7	15.0	19.0	24.4	20.5	15.2	–1.5	9.2
Oil-bearing crops	7.2	10.3	9.2	13.6	13.6	–0.5	–4.4	14.1
Vegetables	16.6	16.4	25.5	24.8	26.6	27.7	–1.1	–2.9
Fruits	15.2	14.1	19.8	17.5	21.8	20.2	–2.0	–2.7
Tree nuts	23.0	13.2	32.9	12.4	40.1	22.1	–7.2	–9.7
Legume and grass								
seeds	4.5	4.7	5.1	4.9	7.1	7.5	–2.0	–2.5
Sugar and sirop								
crops	57.4	–6.3	227.7	72.6	34.1	17.5	193.6	55.1
Miscellaneous crops	5.2	8.3	12.1	19.7	13.5	21.9	–1.4	–2.2
Forest products	0.0	0.0	–0.7	–0.9	–0.1	–0.1	–0.6	–0.8
Greenhouse								
products	5.2	4.8	5.1	4.5	6.0	5.7	–0.9	–1.2
Processing industries								
Meat products	5.0	5.1	–4.6	–9.2	–4.5	–7.0	–0.1	–2.2
Dairy products	15.3	19.0	18.2	41.2	–1.3	14.6	19.5	26.6
Fruit, vegetables &								
seafood	12.4	11.6	27.8	21.9	30.2	23.0	–2.4	–1.1
Grain mill products	11.7	16.3	9.8	38.3	–5.2	2.6	15.0	35.7
Bakery products	1.8	1.3	–7.2	–6.9	0.1	–1.2	–7.3	–5.7
Sugar	62.4	–6.9	209.3	–30.3	40.6	20.1	168.7	–50.4
Confection products	24.8	10.6	66.6	27.5	82.9	30.3	–16.3	–2.8
Beverage industries	18.4	9.7	37.9	14.8	47.5	18.7	–9.6	–3.9
Misc. food products	4.3	3.2	–0.2	–9.5	7.7	6.1	–7.9	–15.6
Tobacco								
manufactures	7.0	7.4	4.8	1.6	4.9	8.4	–0.1	–6.8
Fabric, yarn and								
thread	35.7	35.3	103.9	87.5	94.7	60.4	9.2	27.1
Aggregate sectors								
Livestock and								

(continued on page 174)

Table 5.20   continued

Input–output sector	Total protection				Effective protection			
	Nominal		Effective		Tariffs		NTBs	
	1958	1963	1958	1963	1958	1963	1958	1963
products	9.2	8.7	14.6	16.1	8.4	7.5	6.2	8.6
Other agricultural products	17.5	14.2	33.0	29.5	9.5	9.6	23.5	19.9
Food and kindred products	11.5	8.9	17.3	10.5	12.4	7.9	4.9	2.6

Source: Adapted from Wipf (1971).

rates. The former, for example, ranged from zero per cent for forest products to about 62 per cent for sugar processing, while effective rates ranged from minus 28 per cent (poultry and eggs) to 228 per cent for sugar crops. Effective rates for food grains and sugar are almost four times their nominal rates. In contrast, effective rates for meat animals and oil-bearing crops differ little from their nominal rates, indicating that protection for final outputs is approximately equal to that for production inputs. (See Appendix 2 in this book for an analysis of the relation between nominal and effective rates of protection.)

The 1963 effective rates reflect trade policy changes over 1958–63. In particular, the feed-grain results show how changes in one sector alter effective rates in others. Domestic 1958 support prices for feed grains were well above free market levels, leading to an effective rate of 22.6 per cent, yet in 1963 price support was lowered to world levels which caused effective rates to fall to 8.8 per cent. This change influenced effective protection for sectors using feed grains as inputs, i.e. it increased effective nontariff protection for meats, beverages, and poultry and eggs.

Wipf estimated rates of protection for various farm-level sectors in 1968 (see his table 2, p. 427) and these figures were used to analyse the effects of policy changes, such as the 1963–8 revisions in the US cotton programme. By 1968, market support for cotton was lowered to world-price levels while producer incomes were supplemented by measures like acreage diversion payments. This contributed to the rise in the effective protection for cotton, from 57 per cent in 1958 to about 100 per cent in 1968. Wipf also estimated that effective protection declined between 1958 and 1968 for vegetable, fruit, tree nut, greenhouse and nursery products due to lower nominal support for these items.

Individuals planning research on current protectionism that would be linked to earlier studies such as Wipf's should note that there are several other investigations that provide useful data on levels of protection in the 1950s and 1960s. Baldwin (1970), for example, presents similar nominal and effective rates of protection for US manufacturing industries in 1958, 1964 and 1972. For more recent estimates of the costs and effects of United States agricultural support programmes see Anderson (1985), Gardner (1986) and Tyer and Anderson (1986). Related information on Canadian agricultural support can be found in Harling and Thompson (1885).

Other Analyses of Agricultural Trade Restrictions

A useful source of empirical information on developed countries' agricultural trade barriers is OECD (1987a) and the supporting country studies for Australia, Austria, Canada, the European Community, New Zealand and the United States. Each individual country study examines a range of policies which directly or indirectly influence agricultural trade including general macro-economic and specific agricultural policies. The reports include detailed explanations of the methods employed to calculate producer and consumer subsidy equivalents and other indicators used to measure levels of agricultural support. This quantitative analysis for each country is based on a common reference period 1979–81, although the OECD is updating the producer and consumer equivalents for 1982 to 1986.

Table 5.21 summarises the OECD (1987a) estimates of producer subsidy equivalents for major agricultural products. For comparison, results are presented for 'Nordic' countries (Finland, Iceland, Norway, Sweden and Switzerland) as well as a 'Mediterranean' group composed of Portugal, Spain and Turkey. Japan stands out as the country with the highest subsidy element for agriculture (59.4 per cent) which is almost double the EEC average. At the other extreme, the average producer subsidy equivalent for Australia is under 5 per cent, while this support measure averages 16 per cent in New Zealand and the United States. As far as products are concerned, dairy and rice emerge as the commodities with the highest producer subsidy equivalents (the latter largely due to the influence of agricultural support in Japan), while the equivalents for wool and soybeans is about 9 per cent.

While the data presented in Table 5.21 are expressed in terms of producer subsidy equivalents, Hayami and Honma (1983) measure nominal rates of protection in agriculture. The results of their

Table 5.21 Producer's subsidy equivalents by commodity by country, (average 1979–81)

	USA	Canada	EEC[a]	Australia	Japan	New Zealand	Nordic[b]	Mediterranean[c]	Austria	OECD[d]
Dairy	48.2	66.5	68.8	20.8	83.3	18.0	70.8	68.4	77.9	63.5
Wheat	17.2	17.6	28.1[e]	3.4	95.8	-8.2	56.6	10.7	21.1[f]	21.5
Coarse grains	13.1	13.3	27.9	2.9	107.1	5.3	54.7	14.8	19.5	19.0
Beef & veal	9.5	13.1	52.7	4.0	54.9	12.5	61.6	17.6	42.9	30.0
Pigmeat	6.2	14.5	21.7	2.7	14.0	7.4	23.5	16.7	32.2	16.5
Poultrymeat	6.3	25.7	16.4	2.5	20.5	4.7	43.4	19.4	28.4	14.0
Sugar	17.1	12.5	25.0	-5.0	48.4	–	33.4	39.7	39.4	26.6
Rice	5.4	–	13.6	14.4	68.8	–	–	41.9	–	61.0
Sheepmeat	–	–	45.0	3.1	–	18.2	63.5	14.8	–	28.5
Wool	–	–	–	3.9	–	16.3	0.0	26.9	–	9.4
Soybeans	6.9	–	36.2	–	108.1	–	–	21.9	–	9.0
Average, all above commodities	16.0	23.9	42.8	4.7	59.4	15.5	56.1	26.1	42.8	32.1

– Not calculated.
Minus sign indicates a tax on producers.
Different combinations of commodities are included under the headings 'coarse grains' and 'dairy' for different countries.

[a] EEC-10.
[b] Finland, Iceland, Norway, Sweden, Switzerland.
[c] Portugal, Spain, Turkey.
[d] Based on national currencies converted to US dollars at prevailing exchange rates.
[e] Common and durum wheat.
[f] Wheat and rye.

Data concerning PSEs correspond to the average of the years 1979–81. They might be different for more recent years as a result of the evolution in policies and markets which have occurred since then and which have been significant in certain countries.
Source: OECD (1987).

Table 5.22   Estimates of nominal rates of protection for agriculture in ten developed countries

Country	1955	1960	1965	1970	1975	1980
United States	2.3	0.9	8.2	10.9	4.0	–0.1
Japan	17.6	41.4	67.5	72.7	74.5	83.5
Sweden	31.2	40.2	46.4	61.3	40.8	55.3
Switzerland	53.1	55.0	65.0	84.2	86.9	113.2
France	30.4	22.7	28.0	44.1	28.0	29.5
West Germany	28.0	40.6	46.8	44.3	35.9	42.0
Italy	41.8	42.7	53.1	59.0	30.4	49.0
Netherlands	11.1	22.1	30.7	34.6	28.9	25.3
United Kingdom	34.9	34.0	18.9	24.8	5.6	32.1
Denmark	4.5	3.2	4.5	15.7	18.3	24.4
European Community	30.4	32.1	39.0	46.0	26.3	35.1

Note: The 1955–70 figures for the European Community are weighted averages for four countries (France, Federal Republic of Germany, Italy and the Netherlands). The 1975 and 1980 data are weighted averages of six countries (including the United Kingdom and Denmark), summed over the following products: wheat, rye, barley, oats, maize, rice, beef, pork, chicken, milk, sugar beet and potatoes.

Source: Compiled from data published in Hayami and Honma (1983).

analysis are summarised in Table 5.22. Since these figures are based on domestic and international price comparisons they incorporate the joint protective effects of tariffs and nontariff barriers. The general trend is clearly one of rising protection until the mid-1970s. For most Western European countries nominal protection rates then declined, reflecting temporarily high international prices, but they subsequently rose again. In Japan and Switzerland protection rates rose through the 25-year period, while the average United States level of protection declined throughout the 1970s reaching zero or a slightly negative rate in 1980.

Additional studies provide useful data for research or policy analysis on agricultural trade barriers. The United Nations Food and Agricultural Organization (1987) estimated nominal protection coefficients for major agricultural products in more than 25 developing countries (see table 2, on pp. 200–2 of the report), while Monke and Salam (1986) derived similar 1975–80 protection coefficients for wheat, maize and rice in most developed and developing countries. The World Bank conducted several country-specific studies of agricultural price support policies (Bertrand, 1980, for Thailand; Cuddihy, 1980, for Egypt; Gotch and Brown, 1980, for Pakistan), as well as multi-country studies of the influence of agricultural price distortions (Agarwala, 1983; Bale and Lutz, 1979a; Lutz and Scandizzo, 1980; Scandizzo and Bruce, 1980). The majority of the country-specific investigations employed the ratio of domestic farm-gate to border prices to measure distortion, while the cross-country studies used several price distortion measures drawn from studies of factors promoting industrial development (World Bank, 1980; 1982; 1983). FAO (1983) also used the farm-gate to world price ratio to measure distortion, but later shifted (FAO, 1984) to a measure including processing, marketing and transportation costs needed to bring domestic products and imports to exactly the same geographic location in the importing country. (See Westlake, 1987, for a demonstration of the need for making these corrections when estimating nominal protection coefficients.)

STUDIES RELATING TO TEXTILES AND CLOTHING

In 1985, developing and socialist countries' textile and clothing exports to OECD markets totalled approximately $29.5 billion with practically all this trade (excluding minor fibre like coir, sisal and hair fibre) regulated by the Multifibre Arrangement (MFA). Managed trade in this sector was formalised more than twenty years earlier, however, under the 1961 Short-Term Arrangement (STA) and the 1962 Long-Term Agreement Regarding International Trade in Cotton Textiles (LTA). Initially established for five years, the LTA was twice extended and expired in 1973. The LTA's stated aim was to 'encourage orderly development of the international cotton and textile market' and to permit developed countries to restructure their cotton industry. It allowed developed countries to restrict imports from developing countries considered to be a source of market disruption. The restrictions were either bilateral, through negotiated 'voluntary' restraint agreements, or unilateral. Before applying restrictions, the importing country was required to seek bilateral agreement to control trade, accompanying its request for restrictions with a statement justifying the action. Failing agreement within two months, however, the importing country could limit trade unilaterally. While the LTA's guidelines proposed a given per cent annual increase in quotas, the rapid growth of clothing and textile exports of man-made fibres such as nylon, polyester and acrylics produced calls for a broader more restrictive agreement.[23]

The GATT Agreement Regarding International Trade in Textiles, known as the Multifibre Arrangement, tightened existing controls on developing-country exports and expanded the restrictions to non-cotton products. The MFA, which began on 1 January 1974 and was to continue for four years, tried to reconcile two potentially conflicting aims: developing countries were to be guaranteed access to developed countries' markets, but this trade was subject to strict controls to avoid disruption. Countries signing the MFA accounted for over 90 per cent of world textile and clothing trade and, since 1974, most quantitative restraints in this sector have been applied under the Arrangement.[24] Table 5.23 lists the major institutional arrangements regulating international textile trade from the late 1950s to the early 1990s.

As was the case with agricultural barriers the levels of protection for textile and clothing products appear to be increasing. For example, Cable noted that during the last decade

> bilateral agreements have become more restrictive. Annual trade growth rates under MFA quotas has generally been below the prescribed 6 per cent. Controlled product categories have continually been increased. Flexibility has been reduced. Evidence offered to prove that market disruption occurred has become minimal. Very small suppliers have been subject to quotas. The 'basket extractor' and 'anti-surge' mechanisms have been introduced to trigger new or tighter quotas semiautomatically within existing restraint agreements. An essentially temporary arrangement to provide some breathing space to producers has become permanent.[25]

Given the extensive controls applied to textile and clothing imports, it is not surprising that inventory studies and investigations that estimated NTB *ad valorem* equivalents show this sector to be one of the most highly protected in developed countries. In addition, other analyses show protectionism imposes major economic costs and results in sizeable trade losses. According to one simulation study, the removal of tariffs and nontariff barriers could increase developing countries' exports to the main OECD markets by 82 per cent for textiles and 93 per cent for clothing. Similarly, UNCTAD estimates that complete trade liberalisation could raise developing countries' exports of clothing by 135 per cent, and of textiles by 78 per cent. These projections accentuate the importance of the following studies which quantify the effects of textile and clothing restrictions.

Table 5.23 Arrangements affecting trade in textiles and clothing, 1961 to 1991

Agreement	Period	Products	Regulations
STA	1961–2	Cotton products	Short-term quantity restrictions on specific suppliers in case of market disruption.
LTA	1962–4	Textile & clothing products with 50 per cent cotton included.	1. New restrictions permitted where market disruption occurred. 2. Controls either unilaterally (Article 3) or bilaterally negotiated (Article 4). 3. Quota levels not below imports in preceding period. 4. Minimum annual volume growth of 5 per cent within quotas.
MFA1	1974–7	All textiles and clothing of wool, cotton or synthetic fibres.	1. As in LTA but with more specifications of real or threatened market disruption. 2. New provisions for base levels, annual growth rates (not less than 6 per cent) and flexibility of quotas. 3. Special provision for small and new suppliers. 4. Textile surveillance board to monitor bilateral agreements.
MFA2	1978–82	Same as MFA1	1. All MFA1 regulations carried over. 2. Provision for 'jointly agreed reasonable departures' which permitted derogation of MFA requirements (base levels, growth rates, and flexibility provisions).
MFA3	1982–6	Same as MFA1	1. Similar to MFA1. Reasonable departures clause deleted. 2. Introduction of 'anti-surge' procedure to prevent sharp and sustained import growth within quotas.
MFA4	1986–91	Coverage extended to vegetable fibres like flax and ramie and to silk blends	1. As in MFA1 a modified version of 'reasonable departures' restored. 2. Some tightening of Article 3. 3. Special treatment for least developed and wool textile exporters. 4. Commitment to scrap underutilised quotas.

Source: Adapted from Cable (1987).

Cable and Weale (1985): Britain's Textile and Clothing Restraints

Using the Cambridge Growth Project Model, Cable and Weale simulated the direct and indirect economic effects of alternative forms of trade restrictions that would maintain UK textile and clothing import-consumption ratios at their 1980 level of 35 per cent. To stabilise the import-consumption ratio at this level, the annual growth rates of UK textile and clothing imports would have to fall from their actual 6.1 per cent level to about 1.8 per cent.

The simulation procedures Cable and Weale employ for analysis of trade barriers that would reduce import growth to these levels differ from those of a comparative static approach in that they account for factors such as linkages to other (supplying) industries, effects of real income multipliers, terms-of-trade effects and the impact of the trade restrictions on consumer prices.[26] Their results are important since they show that alternative trade barriers, i.e., tariffs, 'voluntary' export restraints and domestically administered quotas that can be employed to achieve a specific policy objective, have different price, employment and production effects.

Cable and Weale start from a proposition that the policy objective is to hold UK import-consumption ratios constant at 35 per cent, and then attempt to estimate the required level of tariff protection needed to achieve this objective. Their findings indicate the required tariffs, roughly 32 per cent for textiles and 55 per cent for clothing above existing rates of protection (see Table 5.24 for data on protection levels), would cause real gross domestic product to decline by –0.4 per cent and consumer prices to rise by 0.3 per cent. Although 110 000 jobs are 'saved' in the textile and clothing sector by this increase in protection, the accompanying exchange rate and terms-of-trade effects cause a loss of approximately 70 000 jobs in other industries. By reducing imports, tariffs put upward pressure on the exchange rate which has an adverse effect on exports of other goods and services. The higher tariffs have a negligible effect on inflation, however, since the exchange-rate appreciation, which lowers import prices, roughly offsets the price-raising effect of the increased import duties.

Rather different results were achieved when the authors simulated the effects of using VERs to limit imports to a 1.8 per cent growth rate. These restrictions cause a decline in real personal disposable income of about two-thirds of 1 per cent, while under tariffs the income reduction effect is negligible. The effects on employment are

Table 5.24   Approximate estimates of the cost to consumers in the EEC
of 1981 tariffs and import quotas on clothing

Level of protection[a]	T-shirts	Knitted jerseys Type I	Knitted jerseys Type II	Parkas and anoraks
F.o.b. price per unit ($HK)	14.8	32.0	25.2	68.0
Landed price in EEC ($HK)	19.1	37.0	29.1	74.0
Tariff ($HK)	3.2	6.3	4.9	12.6
Quota premium ($HK)	5.0	19.0	12.0	9.0
Levels of protection (%)				
Tariffs	17	17	16	17
Quotas	26	51	41	12
Total	43	68	57	29
Memo item:				
Nominal transport costs	29.1	15.6	15.4	8.8

[a] Cost elements are expressed in Hong Kong dollars per unit. Levels of
protection reflect tariff charges or quota premium expressed as a percentage of the landed (c.i.f.) EEC price. The table is based on T-shirts and
knitted jersey (type I) exports from Hong Kong to the Federal Republic of
Germany; type II knitted jerseys exported to Italy; and on parkas and
anoraks to the Federal Republic of Germany.
Source: Adapted from data published in Cable and Weale (1985).

also different since there is a gain of about 125 000 jobs under VERs
(15 000 more than under tariffs) in the protected industries and a gain
of 10 000 jobs in other sectors. Consumer prices rise by 1 to 1 1/2 per
cent due to the increased cost of imports since, under 'voluntary'
restrictions, foreign producers normally appropriate the economic
'rent' from protection. If, however, trade restrictions take the form
of domestically administered quotas the projections become more
tentative depending on who in the UK economy appropriates the
resulting premiums and how these funds are spent. If producers
appropriate these 'rents' the projections suggest that the decline in
disposable income would be more than double that under equivalent
VERs (both VERs and domestically administered quotas could be
designed to hold imports to a 1.8 per cent growth rate), while under
quotas the total jobs saved would be smaller (about 78 000 jobs
preserved in the industry with about 274 000 lost in other sectors of
the economy).

As an input for their projections, Cable and Weale derived 1981

EEC nominal rates of protection from tariffs and nontariff barriers against clothing imports, which were taken as broadly representative for the United Kingdom. This information is summarised in Table 5.24 which shows that total protection (tariffs plus NTBs) ranges from 43 per cent for T-shirts to almost 70 per cent for knitted jerseys. A breakdown of these figures indicates the NTB element, as measured by the quota premium on Hong Kong exports, exceeds the corresponding nominal tariff for each item with the exception of parkas and anoraks. Since both the Hong Kong f.o.b. price and the EEC landed price of each item is given in the table, differences between the two reflect transport and insurance costs for Hong Kong's exports to Europe.

Greenaway (1985a): UK Clothing Restrictions

Greenaway examines the trade and other economic effects of quantitative restrictions imposed under the MFA on three heavily restricted categories of UK clothing imports: woven trousers (Nimexe Category No. 6), woven and knitted blouses (Nimexe Category No. 7), and woven shirts (Nimexe Category No. 8). The three categories together accounted for about 30 per cent of all 1982 UK clothing imports. Nominal equivalents for the MFA estimates were computed from the ratio of the Hong Kong quota price to the 'unrestricted' export price of the goods.[27] In deriving these estimates, Greenaway acknowledges certain biases may influence the estimates, i.e., the potential exists for quota prices to be misleading because only a small proportion of their total number is actually traded; imported and domestically produced clothing may not be perfect substitutes; and that prices for quota transfers tend to vary seasonally and are highest at year-end when quotas are relatively scarce.

For the three clothing import categories, Greenaway sampled five or six monthly prices for Hong Kong quota premiums and computed a simple average price for 1982. To obtain the 'unrestricted' price of the clothing imports, the average quota premium (approximately £0.34) was subtracted from the averaged c.i.f. unit value (£2.67) of the three categories of clothing. *Ad valorem* tariff equivalents for the MFA quotas were then computed from the ratio of the quota premium to the unrestricted product price. This ratio averaged about 15 per cent for the three items combined, while the protection rates totalled about 34 per cent when the joint effects of tariffs and quotas were accounted for.

Employing a partial equilibrium model similar to that described in this book's Chapter 3, Greenaway estimated the economic costs and effects of the MFA restrictions for the UK economy. Assuming that the price elasticity of demand for clothing was slightly over unity (1.086), and that domestic supply elasticity was somewhere between unity and 2.0, Greenaway concluded that the total 1982 annual loss to consumers from protection of the three categories of clothing amounted to over £170 million. More than £21 million of this loss resulted from a (rent) transfer to suppliers in Hong Kong, while a further £37.5 million was transferred to other overseas suppliers (£19 million to those in the EEC and EFTA and £18 million elsewhere).[28] However, these losses are for one year only and will be sustained as long as the import restrictions remain in place. Assuming that they are permanent, and that the losses will recur each year, the present value of the annual consumers' losses were estimated at £3 billion, or over £150 per household.

Hamilton (1984a; 1984b): Developed-Country Textile Barriers

Hamilton provides quantitative evidence on the importance of trade diversion due to discriminatory restrictions under the Multifibre Arrangement and the influence of special European trade regulations. His analysis is based on the proposition that three key factors influence Swedish trade in textiles and clothing: (i) post-Tokyo tariffs which average approximately 14 per cent (nearly three times as high as for other manufactures); (ii) quantitative restrictions under the MFA which discriminate against developing countries; and (iii) the EEC-EFTA free trade arrangement for manufactures. Under the terms of a special protocol, intra-trade in manufactures (broadly defined as items falling in SITC 5 to 9) between EFTA and EEC members face neither tariffs nor quantitative restrictions (Portugal, however, does not fully participate in the arrangement). The free trade arrangement is of major importance since it establishes three distinct categories of textile exporters to Sweden: EEC-EFTA members; other developed countries like the United States, Canada and Japan; and all developing countries including the socialist countries. Since the non-EFTA/EEC developed countries face tariffs on their textile exports to Europe, while developing and socialist countries encounter tariffs plus MFA nontariff barriers, discrimination could cause substantial trade diversion among the different groups of suppliers.

Table 5.25 provides empirical evidence relating to this point.[29] The second column indicates the increase in the share of textile and clothing imports in domestic demand (consumption) between 1970 to 1979, while columns 3 to 8 provide a breakdown of changes in the share of imports in domestic consumption by countries of origin. In France and Sweden, Hamilton suggests the MFA's quantitative restrictions had a sharp trade-diverting effect: 47 per cent and 40 per cent, respectively, of the increased share of imports in consumption came from EEC and EFTA countries. Of the 40 per cent increase in Sweden's imports from EFTA, no less than two-thirds came from Finland alone. This contrasts markedly with the United States and Japanese statistics where the EEC-EFTA share in consumption actually fell (in the USA), or rose by a far more modest extent. It is not clear why EFTA/EEC countries fared relatively poorly in the Federal Republic of Germany and United Kingdom since their exports were also afforded important preferences in these markets.

Aside from the statistics on trade diversion, Hamilton's study provides useful data on average (1981–3) *ad valorem* equivalents of MFA quantitative restrictions in major industrial countries, which have been derived using prices of Hong Kong quota premiums. Table 5.26 reproduces these estimated import tariff equivalents for the Hong Kong VERs on a quarterly basis from 1980 (3rd quarter) to 1983 (1st quarter). The restrictions have nominal equivalents ranging from 4 to 6 per cent in Austria and Finland to about 29 per cent in Sweden. However, when the joint protective effect of tariffs and these nontariff barriers is accounted for the results suggest that fairly uniform levels of protection exists in all EEC and EFTA countries.

Australian Industries Assistance Commission (1980): Australian Apparel Barriers

The Australian Industries Assistance Commission estimated the cost of textile and clothing restrictions by first computing the sum of the gross subsidy equivalent, i.e., the increase in domestic producers' gross revenue provided by assistance. (See Chapter 2 in this book for a discussion of the properties and use of this measure.) Next, the increase in the cost of imports resulting from trade restraints was estimated, and this figure was expressed as a ratio to the value of domestic production to approximate the nominal rate of protection. For clothing, the average 1977–8 nominal rate was 76 per cent while the effective rate of protection was approximately 135 per cent. The

Table 5.25   Empirical evidence on the shift in selected industrial countries' imports of textiles and clothing between 1970 and 1979

Importer	Change in the share of imports in home demand	Distribution of increased share of imports among groups of exporters (%)					
		EEC-EFTA members[1]	Other developed countries[2]	All developed countries	Major developing countries[3]	Other countries[4]	Total
France (EEC)	10.2	47	8	55	20	25	100
Fed. Rep. Germany (EEC)	10.8	5	6	11	54	36	100
Italy (EEC)	12.5	9	20	29	27	44	100
Sweden (EFTA)	16.5	40	-2	38	46	16	100
United Kingdom (EEC)	8.5	-18	16	-2	63	39	100
Japan	5.1	18	6	24	47[5]	29	100
United States (EEC)	2.2	-30	-80	-110	117	93	100

[1] Portugal is excluded since supply restrictions have been used against Portugal by other EFTA countries.
[2] Australia, Canada, Japan, USA and Eastern Europe including the Soviet Union.
[3] Portugal, Greece, Yugoslavia, Spain, Malaysia, Philippines, Singapore, Thailand, Hong Kong, Rep. of Korea, India, Pakistan, Sri Lanka and Indonesia.
[4] Including Taiwan.
[5] Excluding Malaysia.
Source: Hamilton (1984a).

Table 5.26   Import tariff equivalent of Hong Kong VERs in selected
European countries

Country/commodity	1980(3)	1981(1)	1981(2)	1982(1)	1982(3)	1983(1)	Average
Austria							
Men's cotton shirts				2	1	1	1
Blouses, cotton				2	6	9	6
Jeans, slacks, skirts				0	5	6	4
Dresses				6	5	6	6
Average (weighted)				2	5	6	4
Denmark							
T-shirts	27	28	27	11	9	2	17
Sweaters	16	35	19	7	6	22	18
Jeans, slacks	30	18	18	12	13	6	16
Blouses	43	16	14	4	8	3	15
Shirts	30	2	12	4	5	0	9
Parkas, anoraks	23	4	5	2	5	2	7
Average (weighted)	26	13	19	8	9	5	13
Finland							
Men's & boys' underwear				na	4	5	5
Ladies' & girls' underwear				6	7	8	7
Men's shirts				7	3	1	4
Blouses				na	2	1	2
Brassieres				na	4	8	6
Average (weighted)				7	3	4	5
France							
T-shirts	na	45	45	2	25	2	24
Sweaters	na	32	27	21	9	1	18
Jeans, slacks	na	48	23	11	16	10	22
Blouses	na	20	28	6	10	2	13
Shirts	na	24	32	0	8	4	14
Parkas, anoraks	na	22	15	24	28	1	18
Average (weighted)	na	32	27	9	18	4	18
Fed. Rep. of Germany							
T-shirts	15	36	18	21	4	2	16
Sweaters	13	96	25	1	1	2	23
Jeans, slacks	23	27	20	0	6	55	22
Blouses	23	28	21	1	2	0	13
Shirts	18	2	12	0	1	0	6
Parkas, anoraks	7	23	11	0	2	1	7
Average (weighted)	17	31	18	3	3	17	5
Italy[1]							
T-shirts				0	13	0	0
Sweaters				0	11	0	0
Jeans, slacks				0	21	0	0

(continued on page 188)

Table 5.26   continued

Country/commodity	Year and quarter						
	1980(3)	1981(1)	1981(2)	1982(1)	1982(3)	1983(1)	Average
Blouses				0	9	0	0
Shirts				0	9	0	0
Parkas, anoraks				0	4	0	0
Average (weighted)				0	11	0	0
Sweden							
Mens' shirts	29	61	33	na	na	14	34
Night garments	19	71	17	25	21	na	31
T-shirts, underwear	70	90	50	27	12	33	47
Sweaters, jumpers	35	40	18	28	7	11	23
Overcoats	33	65	20	na	na	na	30
Jackets	na	na	na	9	6	48	30
Slacks, jeans	96	32	76	27	16	30	46
Dresses, skirts	20	23	13	6	11	na	15
Blouses	42	27	29	7	23	60	31
Shorts	44	33	32	42	37	27	36
Track suits	36	38	24	na	na	24	31
Average (weighted)	46	43	32	18	13	33	31
United Kingdom							
T-shirts	41	52	24	7	9	0	22
Sweaters	19	28	20	5	4	0	13
Jeans, slacks	54	56	31	32	13	7	32
Blouses	37	16	11	3	8	3	13
Shirts	42	13	15	8	3	4	14
Parkas, anoraks	7	3	6	18	7	2	7
Average (unweighted)	37	35	20	17	8	4	20

[1] The import tariff equivalents shown in the 'average' column for Italy are for the period 1983(3). Hamilton warns that very small volumes are traded for Italy so the estimates may be biased.
Source: Hamilton (1984b).

total annual consumer cost of protection for the Australian clothing industry was put at A\$235 per household while, at the retail level, consumers annually paid A\$1.1 billion more for clothing, drapery and footwear than they would if industry assistance were withdrawn. These findings suggest that Australian costs and levels of protection for textile and clothing may be somewhat higher than for other OECD countries in Europe and North America.

Jenkins (1980): Canadian Clothing Restrictions

Jenkins employed the ratio of quota premiums to the net landed cost for Canada's textile and clothing imports from Hong Kong, Republic

Table 5.27   Protective effects of tariffs and quotas on Canada's imports from Hong Kong, Republic of South Korea and Taiwan in 1979 (per cent)

Garment category	Effect of quotas	Tariff protection	Total protection
Outerwear	34	26	60
Structured suits, blazers	18	25	43
Shirts with tailored collars	54	20	74
Blouses and shirts	10	24	34
Sweaters, pullovers & cardigans	10	23	33
T-shirts and sweatshirts	21	20	41
Trousers & slacks (men & boys)	11	22	33
Trousers & slacks (women & girls)	11	23	34
Overalls and coveralls	21	16	37
Dresses and skirts	8	24	32
Underwear	29	12	41
Shorts	18	19	37
Pyjamas and sleepwear	2	22	24
Foundation garments	7	24	31
Swim wear	15	20	35
Overcoats, topcoats & rainwear	13	25	38

Source: Based on data published in Jenkins (1980).

of Korea and Taiwan to derive nominal equivalents for existing quantitative restrictions. For outerwear, the 1979 quota premiums varied considerably among exporters: from 18 per cent of the f.o.b. value for Hong Kong's exports to Canada, to 34 per cent for Korea's exports, and 36 per cent for Taiwan's. For shirts, the ratio of quota premiums to f.o.b. import values were 43 per cent for shipments from Taiwan, 56 per cent for Hong Kong, and 62 per cent for Korea. Jenkins estimated that the combined quota premiums and tariffs together provide high levels of protection, i.e., total nominal protection was 48 per cent of the landed cost of outerwear exports from Hong Kong, 62 per cent for exports from South Korea, and 64 per cent for exports from Taiwan. For shirts, the corresponding rates were 62 per cent for Taiwan, 76 per cent for South Korea, and 76 per cent for Hong Kong. In sum, quotas and tariffs increased the cost of imports by between 48 and 78 per cent. Table 5.27, which is drawn from Jenkins's study, indicates average rates of Canadian protection from tariffs and quotas for specific textile and clothing products.

As was the case with related analyses for other OECD countries, Jenkins demonstrated that the annual cost to Canadian consumers of nontariff protection in this sector was quite high, approximately

C\$328 million, while the combined cost of tariffs and quotas was about C\$779 million. His estimates show (see Jenkins's table 8, p. 43) that, as a share of total consumption expenditures, the Canadian restrictions cost poorer households almost four times as much as high-income families (measured as a share of total income), due mainly to the greater percentage of income the former spend on apparel. Using observed values of labour input per unit of output, Jenkins estimated the consumer cost of the Canadian tariffs per man year of employment was C\$37 800 and that of quotas was C\$35 500. In addition, the dead-weight loss per man year was estimated at \$2 800 for tariffs and C\$15 500 for quotas.

Koekkoek and Mennes (1986): EEC Textile and Clothing Barriers

This study simulated the likely effects of removing EEC trade barriers (tariffs and MFA quotas) facing textile and clothing imports. The analysis assumed an average EEC tariff of 8 per cent for textiles and 14 per cent for clothing. Three alternative values of tariff equivalents for MFA 'voluntary' restraints were tested, namely, 15, 10 and 5 per cent, while demand elasticities of –1.5 for textiles and –2.5 for clothing were employed.[30] No original estimates were derived for these parameters as the elasticity values and NTB *ad valorem* equivalents were drawn from a literature search. In order to apply their estimation procedures, Koekkoek and Mennes assumed that the MFA acts like a single VER, restricting supply from specific countries and increasing import prices. In other words, it is assumed that the restricted supplier represents all MFA restricted countries, the unrestricted supplier represents the rest of the world.

In projecting the effects of a liberalisation, the authors employ a two-step approach: the first step being the estimation of EEC-wide effects; the second being the decomposition of the total into its regional elements. In the first stage, the following lines of causation are assumed to occur. Elimination of the MFA restrictions (VERs plus tariffs) leads to a decrease in the foreign supply price and thus an increase in the volume of total imports. Imports from formerly VER-restricted suppliers will increase even more in volume, implying a decrease in imports from other sources. These import price and volume movements lead to the following welfare effects. The consumer surplus in the EEC increases while tariff revenues also change. National welfare of the importing countries increases by the sum of these effects. The supplying countries, formerly restricted by the

Table 5.28   Economic effects of the abolition of the MFA by the European Community (millions of US dollars, 1983)

Policy variable	Textiles (Alternative tariff equivalent)			Clothing (Alternative tariff equivalent)		
	0.15	0.10	0.05	0.15	0.10	0.05
	Panel A: Welfare effects for the EEC					
Consumers' surplus	1594	1081	549	1473	983	490
Government revenue	33	27	17	183	138	78
National welfare gain	1627	1108	566	1656	1121	568
MFA rent loss	−401	−279	−146	−665	−464	−243
Other suppliers' loss	−852	−613	−332	−373	−275	−153
Global welfare gain	374	216	88	618	382	172
	Panel B: Additional trade flows					
Additional EEC imports	409	341	210	1304	985	560
Additional MFA country exports	2584	1896	1047	2717	2000	1110
Demand effect	1754	1287	701	2414	1759	966
Substitution effect	1231	897	492	968	705	387
Rent loss	−401	−279	−146	−665	−464	−243
Additional exports other suppliers	−2175	−1555	−837	−1413	−1015	−550
Substitution effect	−1231	−897	−492	−968	−705	−387
Rent loss	−944	−658	−345	−445	−310	−163

Source: Adapted from Koekkoek and Mennes (1986).

VERs, lose a rent transfer, i.e., the quota premiums. The other foreign suppliers also lose a rent transfer, provided their production costs are normally below those of EEC producers. The national welfare gain (minus the transfer from abroad) constitutes the global welfare gain of the abolition of the VER.

Table 5.28 (panel A) summarises the EEC-wide effects of a removal of tariffs and NTBs facing textiles and clothing. The estimated consumer surplus and national welfare gains are roughly equivalent for textiles and clothing, about $0.5 to $1.5 billion, with the variation showing the sensitivity of the projections to differences in the MFA's assumed tariff equivalents (from 5 to 15 per cent). The major difference between the textile and clothing sectors is the extent that the increase in national (EEC) welfare represents a transfer from foreign producers. In textiles, between 75 and 85 per cent of the welfare gain is a transfer from foreign producers, leaving a global gain of between $88 and $374 million. Between 63 and 70 per cent of the national welfare gain for clothing is a transfer from abroad, with the global welfare gain ranging from $172 to $618 million.

Projections of total trade changes resulting from abolition of the MFA are presented in Table 5.28 (panel B). These figures show that such a liberalisation could increase textile exports from MFA restricted countries by $1.2 to $3.0 billion, and from $1.4 to $3.4 billion for clothing. This implies an increase of between 39 to 97 per cent for textiles and 27 to 67 per cent for clothing over actual 1983 trade levels. Employing statistics on direct and total labour requirements per unit of textile and clothing output in MFA countries, Koekkoek and Mennes estimate that such a trade expansion would create between 103 000 to 254 000 jobs in the textile sector and between 122 000 to 303 000 jobs in the manufacture of clothing. In other words, if the EEC abolished the MFA, employment in the textile and clothing industries of countries facing restrictions would rise by an estimated 20 to 45 per cent.

Langhammer (1983a): Developing-Country Import Licensing

Langhammer examines the use of import licensing procedures as a trade control measure in eleven developing countries; Algeria, Brazil, Cameroon, India, Ivory Coast, Kenya, Malaysia, Morocco, Republic of Korea, Taiwan and Tunisia. The countries were selected on the basis of their diverse levels of economic development, while import licensing was chosen for analysis since it is a commonly applied restraint whose use pattern should reflect that of other nontariff restrictions. Langhammer tabulates data on four-digit CCCN products 'affected' by licensing procedures using information from official government sources, which he lists in a statistical appendix. A four-digit CCCN product is judged to be 'affected' if any component item, such as one or more tariff lines, are subject to licensing requirements. The reasoning here is that the restrictions could easily spread to other items in the group, so exporters may have an incentive to restrict actual imports below potential trade.

Between 40 to 50 per cent of all four-digit CCCN products are affected by licensing requirements in Algeria, India and Morocco, while the corresponding share for Cameroon, Ivory Coast, Malaysia and Taiwan ranges between 3 and 7 per cent. However, Langhammer's statistics show licensing requirements are concentrated in five three-digit ISIC industries: food products, industrial chemicals, textiles, non-electric machinery and fabricated metal products.

Langhammer undertakes a detailed analysis of the use of licensing procedures in the textile and clothing sector (defined as CCCN chapters 50 to 65) by computing the share of imports from both developed and developing countries which encounter this restriction. The share of developed countries' exports subject to licensing ranges between 60 and 70 per cent in the eleven markets, while the corresponding coverage ratios for imports from other developing countries are far lower. This leads the author to conclude that licensing procedures are purposely employed in a discriminatory way against developed countries' goods. Specifically, Langhammer suggests (p. 28) that 'a focus of restrictive measures against imports from developed countries is common. Roughly about two-thirds of the imports affected by these measures originate in the developed countries including socialist economies, whereas only one third is against South–South trade.'

OECD (1985b): Textile and Clothing Barriers in OECD Markets

The OECD secretariat analysed the combined trade-depressing effects of tightened quantitative restrictions under the MFA, high tariffs and structural change in the textile and clothing sector through the use of an industry econometric model. The model estimates import demand and supply equations for textiles and clothing for the United States and European Community over the period 1967 to 1981. These equations were then used to simulate import behaviour in 1982 and 1983 when MFA III was being implemented. The OECD suggests that, as with all econometric exercises, the results must be interpreted cautiously. A major problem is that textiles and clothing imports have always been subject to some form of restriction and there is no 'free trade benchmark' against which the impact of protection can be assessed.

Given the qualifications, the OECD suggests that four main points emerge from its analysis. First, subsequent to implementation of MFA I, OECD imports of textiles and clothing became almost totally unresponsive to price behaviour, especially as regards the competitiveness of non-OECD suppliers. Conventional import demand equations, which over the preceding period gave excellent fits, ceased to have any explanatory power. Second, again as of 1973, import prices from non-OECD sources tended to align on domestic prices rather than vice versa despite large and persistent cost differentials. In other words, mark-ups on import prices increased as exporters from restricted countries were able to appropriate larger rents from the MFA quotas. Third, deviations from (estimated) market equilibrium were particularly great, (a) in the United States relative to the European Community, and (b) in clothing relative to textiles. Finally, compression of imports (i.e., shortfalls of actual values below those projected) from non-OECD sources in 1982 and 1983 were estimated at slightly over 10 per cent in volume terms, though the import figures would be much larger had 1966–72 behavioural patterns persisted through the 1970s. If the 1966–72 relations persisted, 1982–3 import volumes from non-OECD sources would be at least twice as great as actually occurred. These volumes shortfalls may be interpreted as quantity impact measures for VERs negotiated under the Multifibre Arrangement.

Silberston (1984): UK Textile and Clothing Restrictions

Silberston contends (p. 31) that removal of MFA restrictions would lower UK retail prices of imported and domestically produced textiles and clothing by about 5 to 10 per cent relative to the prices of other goods and services. This estimate is based partially on an analysis of Hong Kong production data and on quota premiums. Silberston suggests that the latter can be misleading as a guide to the level of protection because only a small proportion of the total number of quota licenses are actually traded over a given period. In 1982, for example, only 18.5 per cent of Hong Kong quotas for the EEC were exchanged. In addition, quota prices can be strongly influenced by exchange rate changes between restricted and non-restricted textile exporters currencies. In cases where import supply is not perfectly elastic the quota price approach will also produce biased estimates of the true price effect of the restrictions (see Figure 2.3 in Chapter 2 of the present volume for an illustration).

Silberston estimates that without the MFA the UK textile and clothing industry would lose some 10 000 to 50 000 jobs by the 1990s with the difference depending on the exact assumptions concerning such factors as import and demand growth. However, the projected job losses from removal of the MFA should be compared with an expected reduction of nearly 20 000 jobs annually even with protection. Moreover, 'saving' a job by continuing MFA protection entails costs considerably higher than the average wage in the textile and clothing industry.

UK Consumers Association: UK Clothing Trade Barriers

In the United Kingdom, the Consumers Association (1979) analysed the effects of restrictions on apparel imports and found that the Multifibre Arrangement, which covered the 60 per cent of British clothing imports originating in 'low-cost' countries, increased clothing prices by 15 and 40 per cent and had created shortages of some products, particularly lower-priced items. The estimates of the price effects of the MFA were derived by taking the ratio of quota licence prices to the average unit values of specific products. In March 1979, the Association found that Hong Kong quota premiums for exports to the UK averaged $2.31 for jeans, $1.24 for a woman's blouse, $1.16 for a man's shirt and $0.98 for an average knitwear item. This study estimated that children's wear doubled in price due to the MFA, jeans prices had risen by 30 to 50 per cent, and prices of men's shirts increased by 50 per cent. Above-average price increases for some lower-value items, like children's wear, were attributed to two distinct effects: shortages due to MFA quotas, and the incentive for exporters to upgrade their products within specific quota lines.

The Consumers Association study further demonstrated how restrictive quota allocations had been to exporting countries. Ten East Asian countries filled 95 per cent of the UK quotas for 'sensitive' clothing products with Hong Kong alone accounting for over 50 per cent of the total. This greatly limited the trade prospects of 'newly emerging' or more efficient textile exporters. Elsewhere, the Foreign Trade Association, a retail organisation based in Brussels and Cologne, found that prices of textile and clothing products of comparable quality were 30 to 40 per cent lower from more efficient producer countries outside the EEC than prices of similar goods made within the Community. (See Table 5.29 in this book for detailed data relating to this point.) The Foreign Trade Association study also noted that, after 1976 when quota protection was tightened, the average price of apparel rose twice as fast in the Federal Republic of Germany as that of all manufactures prices, even though Germany was cited as being relatively liberal in administering MFA quotas.

US Council on Wage–Price Stability: Apparel Restrictions

The Council on Wage-Price Stability (1978) estimated the costs of United States apparel quotas using a trade simulation model similar to that presented in Chapter 3 in this book. According to the projections, which are based on an analysis of barriers facing US apparel imports of $11 600 million, the consumer cost of MFA quotas growing 6 per cent annually would be $369.4 million in the first year and $790.6 million in the fifth year after the restriction's imposition. During the same time-span quotas increasing 3 per cent annually would cost consumers from $427 million to $1 063 million. The increasing spread in costs of a 3 per cent as opposed to a 6 per cent quota is due to the larger discrepancy between potential and re-stricted imports after five years and the effects of this shortfall on domestic prices. The Council's study found that in 1975 a typical family of four paid an extra $175 annually due to the apparel restric-tions; under a quota growing at 3 per cent the consumer's cost of each job saved could be as high as $81 000.[31] These projections are based on the effects of quotas over and above the influence of existing tariffs.

The Council of Economic Advisors (1988) provides more recent statistics on the costs of US textile and clothing protection. The Council estimated that textile and clothing protection costs an American family $200 to $400 annually, and that protectionist legis-lature passed in 1987 by the House of Representatives would add an additional $280 to $420 in costs per household over the first five years that these measures were enacted. Expressed differently, these ad-ditional textile and clothing restrictions would cost consumers be-tween $25 billion and $37 billion in the first five years, above and beyond the $20 to $40 billion annually they pay for existing tariffs and quotas. The Council also estimated (p. 149) that the equivalent rate of protection from actual tariffs and quotas on textiles is roughly 50 per cent, or ten times higher than the average US tariff.

Wolf *et al*. (1984): General Effects of Restrictions

This study surveys major issues relating to textile and clothing pro-duction, employment and trade trends in developed countries from the 1970s to the early 1980s. In addition, the authors review findings of previous studies that quantified the costs of protectionism. Statis-tics are also analysed on income losses of US and Canadian textile workers due to the displacement of domestic production by imports, as well as on their average length of unemployment.

Wolf *et al*. analyse statistics on national differences in textile production costs that are indicative of the levels of protection needed to maintain domestic producers competitive. Table 5.29 reproduces this data which shows the average European landed costs (before VAT and import duties are added) for specific apparel products originating in European countries, the United States and a group of four textile exporting countries (Hong Kong, India, Republic of Korea and Taiwan) that face MFA quotas and other trade barriers. Taking the average landed cost of the restrained countries' products as the base for comparison, the lower half of the table shows the level of protection required for each European country to remain competitive.[32]

While factors like product-quality differentials may cause some variation, the relative cost statistics indicate that high levels of European protection are often required. Table 5.29, for example, suggests that Belgium needs an average nominal protection coefficient in excess of 100 per cent. In Germany, nominal protection levels of over 200 per cent are required for trousers and blouses, while Austrian protection requirements are roughly similar. The United States cost figures are well below those of the European countries, possibly due to the size of its domestic market which permits large production runs, while Greece and Portugal emerge as low cost European producers.

A troubling point is that the coefficients reported in Table 5.29 suggest higher rates of protection are required for European textile and clothing industries than do studies based on MFA export licence prices (see Hamilton 1984a; 1984b). There appears to be no obvious explanation for the differences, but several possibilities warrant further analysis. If importers appropriated some MFA rents this would cause protection estimates based on quota prices to be biased downward. Second, imports may have higher marketing and distribution costs that raise their relative prices at the point of consumption. If this were the case it would offset to some degree foreigners' pure production cost advantages. There is some empirical evidence for primary and processed agricultural products which supports this proposition (see Westlake, 1987).

Other Studies of Textile and Clothing Restrictions

Aside from the studies previously surveyed, other investigations provide useful empirical information on textile and clothing protection. For example, several analyses focused on the effects of relatively high pre-Uruguay Round import duties in OECD countries (see Appendix 3 in this book for relevant statistics). In one such

Table 5.29　Average landed costs of apparel products in Europe and
implied levels of protection against restricted suppliers

Country or market	T-shirts	Jerseys	Trousers	Blouses	Shirts
	(landed costs in European units of account)				
European Community					
Belgium-Luxembourg	4.3	7.0	8.4	6.5	6.2
Denmark	3.3	6.7	8.1	6.1	3.4
France	5.1	9.0	9.5	10.1	7.7
Germany	4.7	8.6	10.5	9.4	5.2
Ireland	2.2	6.5	6.9	7.0	7.2
Italy	2.8	5.1	9.0	6.8	7.2
Netherlands	1.8	5.4	8.6	3.9	4.6
United Kingdom	3.7	10.1	9.6	6.2	7.0
Other Europe					
Austria	5.5	12.0	10.4	11.3	4.0
Greece	1.4	3.5	7.5	4.4	2.5
Portugal	1.5	3.5	7.0	4.4	4.6
United States	1.2	3.0	5.7	4.2	3.0
Restricted Countries					
Hong Kong	2.6	4.8	4.5	4.1	3.5
India	1.1	2.7	3.7	3.0	2.8
Rep. of Korea	2.1	3.1	4.3	2.3	2.7
Taiwan	2.1	3.5	3.7	2.5	2.5
	(implied levels of protection in percent)[1]				
European Community					
Belgium-Luxembourg	115	100	110	117	114
Denmark	65	91	103	103	15
France	155	157	138	237	166
Germany	135	146	263	210	79
Ireland	10	86	73	133	148
Italy	40	46	125	127	148
Netherlands	–	54	115	30	59
United Kingdom	85	189	240	107	141
Other Europe					
Austria	175	243	260	277	38
Greece	–	0	88	47	–
Portugal	–	0	75	47	59

[1] Measured in terms of the difference between landed costs for the country
in question and the average landed cost for the restricted countries. The
figures for landed unit costs are before VAT and import duties.
Source: Estimated from data published in Wolf *et al.* (1984).

analysis, Morkre and Tarr (1980) estimated that the direct cost of US tariffs on several categories of imports were: $2.4 million for yarn; $12.9 million for fabrics; $406.2 million for apparel; and $4.1 million for made-up and miscellaneous textiles. They project that an elimination of US apparel tariffs would result in net welfare gains of $193 million in the first year of the liberalisation, while over four years the cumulative gain would be $1319 million. Morkre and Tarr noted the cost per job of US tariffs was more than double the average industry wage. Bayard (1980), in commenting on the Morkre and Tarr study, estimated terms-of-trade losses resulting from apparel tariffs were $1590 million.

Cline (1987) provides more recent estimates of the consumer and welfare costs of United States protection. Assuming a total protection rate of 28 per cent for textiles (12 per cent rate due to tariffs) and 53 per cent for apparel (22.5 per cent from tariffs), this study projects that a complete liberalisation of trade barriers would increase textile imports by about 30 per cent and apparel imports by 57 per cent. Such a liberalisation would produce consumer savings of approximately $20 billion and cause about 250 000 jobs to be lost. Cline also estimates that apparel prices would decline by about 19 per cent due to the liberalisation, while textile prices would fall by about 3 per cent. Hufbauer *et al.* (1986) published projections broadly similar to Cline's, although they estimate somewhat larger employment losses from elimination of US trade restrictions. The Hufbauer study also published estimates of key industry parameters for textiles and clothing including US supply and import demand elasticities, as well as several cross-elasticities between domestic and foreign prices.

Roningen and Yeats (1976) provide some information on textile and clothing nominal protection coefficients for Japan, France, Sweden and the United States. In this study, international price differentials for standardised products were computed and then decomposed into a tariff, nontariff barrier and transportation cost element. In summarising this information, Yeats (1979, p. 143) reported an average apparel NTB nominal equivalent of 35 per cent in France, 40 per cent in the United States, 15 per cent in Sweden and 5 per cent in Japan. Other studies estimated nominal equivalents for developing-countries' textile and clothing barriers, as well as those for other products, using international price differences. Representative analyses include Baldwin (1975) for the Philippines; Bhagwati and Srinivasan (1975) for India; UN Economic Commission for Asia and the Far East (1972) for several Asian countries; and Balassa and associates (1971) for a selection of developing countries at different stages of industrialisation. The latter two studies derived some effective rates of protection for textile and clothing products. These analyses generally found textiles and clothing were highly protected in developing countries.

Several studies that employed a Heckscher–Ohlin framework provide useful information about 'implied' nontariff barriers in the textile and clothing sector. McCulloch and Hilton (1983) identified industry 'under-achievers' in which US exports were significantly lower than projected on the basis of relative costs. Large differences between actual and projected trade were attributed to possible nontariff intervention. Textiles and clothing figured prominently in these 'under-achievers', particularly in United States exports to Western Europe. Saxonhouse (1977) conducted a related analysis for Japan, but actual textiles and clothing trade did not differ significantly from that projected (see Balassa, 1986, for a comment on Saxonhouse's methodological approach).

STUDIES RELATING TO FERROUS METALS

Although steel trade is not subject to formal multilateral agreements like textiles and clothing, most major steel-consuming nations have imposed fairly extensive import restraints in this sector. The United States, for example, made major efforts to protect domestic producers on three occasions. In 1984 and 1985, the USA negotiated voluntary export restraints with its principal steel suppliers while, previously in the late 1960s, 'voluntary' export restraints were negotiated with the EEC and Japan. These VERs were renewed once and then allowed to expire in 1974. In another effort to restrict foreign competition, the United States established trigger prices for steel imports in 1978. Under this system, imports whose prices were below predetermined levels were subject to automatic anti-dumping proceedings. (See Finger, 1981, for a description of how the trigger price mechanism operated.)

European countries also attempted to restrain steel trade over a period of years. In 1979, as domestic capacity utilisation fell and imports rose, the Commission of the European Communities declared a 'manifest crisis' under terms specified in the Treaty of Paris.

This enabled the Commission to set minimum prices and quotas for steel, and required that European subsidies and capacity expansion plans be approved by the Commission. The EEC also negotiated bilateral agreements with fourteen supplying countries and established minimum import prices for other foreign suppliers.

As was the case with agriculture and textiles, there is evidence that protection levels for steel have changed over time. See, for example, Table 5.30 which presents a chronology of factors affecting United States trade policy. Such changes in trade intervention measures make it difficult to estimate normal or average protection levels. A second important point is that protection coefficients based on international price differences are considered less reliable for steel than for some other sectors due to the subsidy element in some domestic and export prices. Given the key importance of steel as an input into other major industries (autos, construction, shipbuilding, etc.) it appears that the ferrous-industry support measures in OECD markets may best be analysed by estimating cross-country producer and consumer subsidy equivalents. Empirical research along these lines should provide a clearer picture of the true national costs and effects of protection in the iron and steel industry.

Canto (1984): US Steel Restriction

Canto employs a regression model to quantify the influence of the 1969–71 and 1972–4 United States 'voluntary' export restraints on steel imports and prices. Three dependent variables are employed: the percentage change in imports of different steel products; the percentage change in domestic producer prices; and the change in the percentage difference between the average price received by domestic producers and the price of imported steel. Two types of explanatory variables are used. The first includes the percentage change in US real GDP and Japan's real GDP. Three dummy variables are employed for: the 1959 US steel strike; the original 1969–71 VER agreement; and the agreement's 1972–4 extension. The model was fitted using 1956–79 annual data for five different types of steel products: base steel; cold rolled steel; hot rolled steel; plate steel; and structural steel.

The results generally show that the VERs had a significant (upward) impact on United States prices for both imports and domestic steel.[33] In almost all cases, negative significant coefficients were recorded for the VRA dummies when regressions were run on

Table 5.30   The chronology of US steel trade policy

Phase 1: The Voluntary Restraint Agreements

February 1966   American Iron and Steel Institute (AISI, the industry's trade association) advocate temporary tariff on steel imports. The first protectionist move. Subsequently AISI switch to advocating quotas.

Summer 1968   Germany and Japan offer voluntary restrictions on steel exports to USA during Congressional hearings and invite other major foreign producers to join them.

January 1969   Voluntary Restraint Agreement (VRA) setting agreed quotas for bulk steel imports from European Community and Japan comes into effect. Canada and United Kingdom do not join VRA but nevertheless restrict exports to US.

August 1971   Temporary 10 per cent surcharge on all imports into US.

January 1972   VRA extended, with modifications for further 3 years.

May 1975   VRA allowed to lapse.

June 1976   Import quotas imposed on five categories of special steel from Sweden and EEC, initially for three-year period, after attempt to negotiate voluntary 'orderly marketing agreement' in ninety days fails. Japan concludes voluntary restraint agreement for a special steels on last day of ultimatum.

Phase 2: The Trigger Price Mechanism (TPM)

January 1975–
December 1977   Total of 19 separate anti-dumping complaints submitted to US Treasury Department.

December 1977   President Carter accepts recommendation of Task Force (Solomon Report 1977) that: 'Department of Treasury, in administering the Antidumping Act, set up a system of trigger prices, based on the full costs of production including appropriate capital charges of steel mill products by the most efficient foreign steel producers, which would be used as a basis for monitoring imports of steel in the US and for initiating accelerated antidumping investigations with respect to imports below the trigger prices'.

January 1978   Trigger prices for seventeen bulk steel products announced thereby setting de facto minimum prices for bulk steel in US.

February 1980   Import quotas for special steels phased out (bearing steel quota previously dropped June 1977).

Table 5.30 *continued*

Phase 3: The Reinstated Trigger Price Mechanism

March 1980 US Steel Co. alleges steel producers in seven European countries dumping steel below cost. TPM suspended during investigation.

October 1980 Trigger Price Mechanism restored in strengthened form for three to five years and anti-dumping cases dropped. Trigger price based on Japanese costs reinstated. New anti-surge provision prompting investigations in particular product markets whenever US steel industry falls below 87 per cent capacity utilisation and imports reach pre-specified levels.

Phase 4: Voluntary Export Quotas

January 1982 Anti-dumping and countervailing duty petitions filed by the US steel companies against European, Rumanian and Brazilian steel producers. TPM suspended.
In order to reduce trade tension European Commission introduces stricter production quotas for EEC steelmakers limiting output for export to US market.

August 1982 US Commerce Department rules 38 European steel companies received 'illegal' subsidies.

October 1982 Voluntary steel quota arrangement concluded with EEC cutting exports of ten major bulk steel products by 9 per cent. Simultaneous and crucial agreement for limiting sales of EEC tubes and pipes not otherwise precluded under anti-dumping legislation. Threat of penal import duties rescinded.

July 1983 Extra import duties and quotas imposed on European special and stainless steels (not covered by October 1982 agreement) for a four-year period. Canada, Japan and EEC subsequently reject overtures to establish an Orderly Marketing Agreement on Special Steels (OMAS).

March 1984 EEC retaliates against US special steel restrictions after talks with USA, first on their withdrawal and then on compensation, break down. Retaliatory quotas imposed on chemicals (including styrene and polyethelene), some sidearms and sportsgoods, and retaliatory tariffs on other chemicals (including methanol and vinyl acetate) and burglar alarms and other anti-theft devices. Retaliatory measures to last for four years.

March 1984 South Africa announces voluntary restraints on a

(continued on page 204)

Table 5.30   continued

	range of steel products customarily exported to US. Exports to be reduced by 22 per cent to 550 000 tonnes.
April 1984	Brazil concedes voluntary curbs on steel exports to the US to run for three years. Agreement immediately cuts Brazil's steel exports to US from 814 000 tonnes in 1983 back to 430 000 tonnes in the year ending April 1985.
June 1984	US International Trade Commission finds the US steel industry has suffered serious injury in a range of five steel products accounting for 70 per cent of US steel imports. Import injury occurred despite existence of formal and informal export restraints by foreign producers.
July 1984	Following hearings, International Trade Commission recommend five-year import quotas covering these 70 per cent of steel products.
August 1984	US Commerce Department recommends formal division of US steel import market between traditional and new exporting nations as follows: Japan 25%: EC 24%: Canada 14%; South Korea 11%; Brazil 7%; Mexico 4%; Africa 3%.
September 1984	President Reagan rejects International Trade Commission recommendations on quotas in favour of an extended pattern of formal and informal voluntary restraint covering a wider range of countries, to be negotiated within 90 days.
November 1984	US Commerce Department suspends all steel pipe and tube imports from EEC producers after Community proposals to cut shipments from 14.9 per cent to 7.6 per cent share of the US market rejected. The International Trade Commission had earlier failed to find a case for injury to US domestic producers from Community pipe and tube exports.
January 1985	US and EEC finalise an accord limiting Community pipe and tube sales into US market to 7.6 per cent of demand for these products. Import ban lifted.
January 1985	US trade negotiators conclude voluntary restraint agreements with EEC and a range of small producers (Finland, Australia, South Africa and Spain) but agreement still to be finalised with Japan, South Korea, Brazil, Mexico and Argentina.

Source: Adapted from OECD (1985c).

domestic–foreign price differentials, a point that suggests US producers captured a major share of the restrictions's rents. When regressed on the percentage change in imports, the VER dummies take the expected negative sign, but do not achieve statistical significance. These results suggest that the restraint arrangements did not have a significant impact on import volumes, a point which is at odds with the findings of Hufbauer *et al.* (1986).

Hufbauer *et al.* (1986): US Restrictions on Steel Imports

This report provides statistics on industry performance and the effects of various forms of nontariff protection for carbon and alloy steel, ball-bearings and speciality steel products in the United States during periods when 'exceptional' restrictions on imports were in effect. Three separate periods of protectionism are analysed for carbon and alloy steel: 1969 to 1974 when steel imports were subject to 'voluntary' restraint arrangements; 1978 to 1982 when the trigger price mechanism was used; and from 1982 on when anti-dumping and countervailing duty actions were employed extensively. For each period, annual statistics on the volume and value of imports affected by trade restrictions; total imports; apparent consumption; the share of imports in apparent consumption; domestic output and employment in the industry; industry wages and profits; and the level of plant capacity utilisation are given.[34]

In addition to these basic statistics for the 'affected' ferrous-metal industries, the authors provide quantitative information on the price and quantity effects of the trade restrictions as well as their impact on consumer and welfare costs. This information is either compiled from a review of the professional literature, or through original estimates made by the authors. Hufbauer *et al.* estimate, for example, that VRAs decreased carbon steel imports by 4.5 million tons on average over 1969–74; that the induced increase in domestic production over this period was 2.25 million tons; the VRA premiums secured by foreign producers were $330 million in 1974; and that the (1974) welfare costs of the restrictions were $380 million. Separate estimates of the quantity, price and cost effects of trigger prices and anti-dumping and countervailing actions on carbon steel imports are also given. Table 5.31 summarises estimates of the influence of these trade restrictions for the three ferrous-metals industries, i.e. carbon

Table 5.31   Statistics relating to the application of special US trade restrictions on ferrous-metal products

Item	Steel products affected by special trade measures[a]		
	Carbon and alloy steel products	Ball-bearings	Speciality steel
Number of years restraints in force	5 years	4 years	8 years
Induced increase in the price of imported steel	13.3 per cent	12 per cent	25 per cent
Induced decrease in imports due to restraints	$1.42 billion	$6 million	$77 million
Induced increase in domestic production	$465 million	6 million units	40 000 tons
Elasticity of demand for imported steel	2.5	0.25	1.5
Elasticity of supply of domestic steel	2.0	2.0	1.0
Elasticity of demand for domestic steel	1.0	0.1	0.8
Cross elasticity of demand for domestic steel relative to price of imported steel	1.2	0.4	0.9
Cost of restraints to US consumers	$1970 million	$45 million	$520 million
Gains from restraints to US producers	$1330 million	$21 million	$420 million
Tariff revenue and implied average tariff rate of the restrictions	$290 million 6 per cent	$18.0 million 7.8 per cent	$32.5 million 10.2 per cent
Gains from restraints to foreigners	$330 million	negligible	$50 million
Welfare costs of restraints to the USA	$380 million	under $1 million	$80 million
Induced increase in employment in USA	8100 jobs	500 jobs	500 jobs
Cost of restraints to US consumers per job saved	$240 000	$90 000	$1 million
Gain from restraints to US producers per job	$3400	$500	$60 000

[a] The figures for carbon and alloy steel products relate to the imposition of VERs over 1969 to 1974. Hufbauer *et al.* provide additional estimates for the impact of the trigger price mechanism (1978 to 1982) and anti-dumping actions (1982 to the present). The statistics for ball-bearings relate to escape clause relief (1974 to 1978), while the speciality steel action took the form of global quotas (1976 to 1980 and 1983 to 1987). The estimates for carbon steel are either an average for 1969 to 1974 or are for 1974. Estimates for ball-bearings relate to various years from 1973 to 1978. Figures for speciality steels relate to different years during 1983 to 1985.

Source: Adapted from Hufbauer *et al.* (1986).

steel, ball-bearings, and speciality steels. The table indicates that 'special' protectionism for these three products cost US consumers about $2.5 billion annually.

In each of the iron and steel or other industry 'case studies', Hufbauer *et al.* provide empirical information which can be used for original research or policy studies on the effects of the 'special' restrictions. Estimates of industry supply and demand elasticities are compiled, as are estimates of the cross-price elasticity of demand for domestic steel relative to the price of imported steel and the cross-price elasticity of output of domestic steel relative to imported steel quantities.[35] The report also estimates coefficients of domestic price response, e.g. the ratio of any domestic price increase to an induced (by protectionism) increase in the price of imports.

OECD (1985c): US Restrictions on Steel

Although there appear to be few studies that provide corresponding estimates on the influence of European protectionism, useful empirical information on the effects of US steel import restrictions have been compiled and analysed in OECD (1985c). These findings are summarised in Table 5.32. Apart from Crandall (1982), these studies make two simplifying assumptions that abstract from actual conditions. The first is that steel is a homogenous product with a single price, while in fact steel has different grades, qualities and prices. Crandall's analysis, however, distinguishes between five main categories of bulk steel products and specifically excludes speciality steel which were subject to different trade control measures. (See Haufbauer *et al.*, 1986, pp. 193–205, for an analysis of restrictions applied to speciality steels.) This approach allows for the fact that, under quantitative restrictions, foreign producers may alter their US export product mix in order to increase profits. Second, the studies summarised in Table 5.32 assumed imported and domestically produced steel are perfect substitutes and, in effect, argue that there is a single demand function for these items. However, Crandall distinguishes between demand for imported and domestic steel and, with substitution possible, shows that import supply and demand is more responsive to price changes than would be the case where the products were not separately distinguished. For these reasons, the OECD suggest Crandall's analysis may have more credibility than other investigations.

As reported in Table 5.32, Crandall estimates that the US 1972

Table 5.32   Major findings of studies of United States steel trade restrictions

Study[a]	Trade restrictions	Steel prices	Estimated impact on: Imports (Share in apparent supply)
MacPhee (1974)	VRA in 1969	No estimate	−26%
Tackacs (1975)	VRA (general features)	+15 to +18%	No estimate
Crandall (1982)	(1) VRA in 1971/72	+6.3 to +8.3% (import prices) +1.2 to +3.5% (domestic prices)	−15 to −23%
	(2) Trigger price in 1979	+9.1 to 11.5% (import prices) +0.8 to 1.1% (domestic prices)	−41%
Fed. Trade Commission (1977)	(1) 12% import quota and $322 reference price	+3.5%	−7.5%
	(2) As above plus tariff	+9.0%	−18.5%
Jondrow (1978)	VRA plus tariff	+5 to 26% (import prices) No change (domestic prices)	−25 to −58%

[a] Results from the following studies are summarised in this table: Crandall (1982); US Federal Trade Commission (1977); Jondrow (1978); MacPhee (1974); and Tackacs (1975).

'voluntary' restraint arrangements reduced steel imports by 15 to 23 per cent, and the 1978 trigger price mechanism (TPM) cut imports by 40 per cent. These figures are broadly consistent with MacPhee's (1974) estimate for the VER's effects, i.e., an import reduction of 26 per cent, but somewhat lower than estimates made by Hufbauer *et al.* (1986). Both Crandall and MacPhee also conclude foreign producers earned higher margins and profits on steel they sold due to the restrictions although sales volumes were lower. Crandall estimates that, of the resulting transfers from consumers to producers, the redistribution towards foreign firms equalled or exceeded that to the domestic industry.

While there is considerable variation in estimates of the effects of protection on prices and imports, the same is true for the impact of the trade restraints on employment and capacity utilisation. Cran-dall, for example, suggests that the trigger price mechanism increased domestic steel output by some 2 to 3 million metric tonnes, while the previous VERs increased it by 3.2 million tonnes. These estimates suggest that capacity utilisation in the US steel industry rose from 74 per cent to about 77 per cent as a result of 1979 trigger prices. Crandall's data indicate this increase preserved between 8800 and 12 400 jobs (about 2 to 3 per cent of industry employment) that would otherwise have been lost. Hufbauer *et al.* (1986, p. 14) suggest that each job preserved in the carbon and alloy steel sector through protectionism may have cost final consumers as much as one-quarter of a million dollars.

As far as profitability is concerned, the OECD suggests that both foreign and domestic steel companies benefited from the revenue-increasing effects of the protectionist measures. While the domestic price rise induced by protection was relatively small (see Table 5.32), the volume of steel sales affected by higher prices was a key factor in determining revenue effects. Since the short-term price elasticity of demand for steel is relatively low (see estimates provided by Hufbauer *et al.*, 1986), the financial transfer to producers was substantial. Crandall, for example, estimates steel producers received between $371 and $640 million annually extra in rents on existing assets as a result of trigger prices in 1979. Simulation studies by the US Federal Trade Commission (1977) of a $322 reference price with a 12 per cent *ad valorem* duty (relatively close to what actually occurred) suggest an even higher figure for gains to US steel producers of $869 million in 1976.

Estimates of the share of rents going to foreign producers vary widely. Crandall's figure ranges from 43 to 56 per cent, while the Federal Trade Commission put the foreign share as low as 12 per cent. MacPhee estimates approximately two-thirds of the VER premium in 1971 went to foreign producers, while one-third ($88 million) went to domestic steelmakers. Hufbauer *et al.* (1986, p. 159) estimate that the restrictions produced a gain of $1333 million for domestic industry in 1974 and $330 million for foreign suppliers.

STUDIES RELATING TO OTHER MANUFACTURED PRODUCTS

Aside from agriculture, textiles and steel, important empirical analyses have been undertaken on the incidence and effects of trade barriers in other industries. However, there are often several reasons why it is more difficult to utilise these results for research or practical policy studies. First, these investigations may represent initial attempts to quantify the effects of barriers in a particular industry. Since other comparable studies, perhaps using alternative quantification procedures, are generally not available one cannot easily evaluate the potential degree of error (variation) in estimates of the incidence and effects of protection. As an illustration of the nature of this problem, Crandall (1982), Jondrow (1978) and Hufbauer *et al.* (1986) provide a range of estimates of the incidence of US trade restrictions for steel. Since alternative figures are available this assists in developing a 'confidence interval' for the actual effects of the trade restrictions. Second, since similar industry or sector studies are often not available for other countries, it is generally not possible to draw conclusions about differences in national protection levels. This contrasts with the situation in agriculture, for example, where the wide range of available studies permit cross-country comparisons of protection levels. A further problem is that the available studies almost always relate to a specific point of time and offer no evidence on trends in protection.

In spite of these limitations, the studies reviewed in this section are important on at least four different counts. First, they illustrate how specific, sometimes original, methodologies for quantification of nontariff barriers can be applied, and they also show how potentially important data problems may be addressed. Second, these analyses can be used along with 'follow-up' studies to provide required information for tracking changes in protection levels. Results from NTB inventory studies (see Chapter 4) should also provide supporting evidence on this point. Third, several of these studies utilise empirical procedures that may have applications in other areas. Balassa (1986), for example, tests a methodology that could be employed for assessing the trade potentials (and barriers) of the socialist countries of Eastern Europe. Yeats (1976) develops a framework for analysing the discriminatory effects of NTBs like variable import levies that are expressed in fixed-charge-over-unit monetary terms. Finally, several studies for major industries like automobiles and offer insights into the political economy and procedures used to establish new protectionism.

Baldwin (1970): Nontariff Protection in the USA and UK

Professor Robert Baldwin derived nominal and effective rates of US tariff and nontariff protection for 1958, 1964 and 1972. His 1958 effective rate calculations account for tariffs, domestic agricultural price-increasing measures (together with quotas and subsidies that accompany these measures), quotas in other sectors, the American Selling Price system, federal excise taxes, federal transportation taxes, state and local retail taxes, and federal grants for highway transportation. The results are presented (see Baldwin, pp. 158 and 163) for 61 industries defined in terms of the United States input–output table. Similar 1954 and 1972 estimates are presented for the United Kingdom (p. 167), while an appendix (appendix D on pp. 199 to 201) lists the statistical sources employed for these calculations.

Baldwin's estimates for the United States often show considerable differences between nominal and effective rates. In 1958, the average nominal rate of tariff and nontariff protection (weighted by the total domestic supply of each product) was 13 per cent, whereas the weighted average of effective rates was 21 per cent. Furthermore, separate tests show major changes in the ranking of industries by nominal and effective protection levels, and a great dispersion in protection rates when nontariff barriers are included. For some individual industries there are major differences between nominal tariff and total (tariff plus NTB) effective rates. The effective protection rate for food products, for example, is more than double the nominal tariff rate (17 per cent compared to 7 per cent) both because domestic price support programmes (considered in the NTB calculation) raise the total nominal rate to 11 per cent and because value added is slightly less than 20 per cent. A low value added coefficient is a necessary condition for large differences between nominal and effective rates of protection (see Appendix 2 in this book for a demonstration of this point). Broad and narrow fabrics is another sector where a low value-added share (about 15 per cent), plus quotas that raise the nominal rate moderately, increases effective protection to 250 per cent. Effective protection rates for a number of primary product (industries 1 to 10 in the US input–output table) differ little from their low nominal rates because of duties and indirect taxes on some inputs. Higher protection for production inputs than for the final product results in negative effective protection for industries like: forestry and fishery products; iron ore mining; coal mining; stone and clay mining; wooden container; paper and allied products; and farm machinery and equipment.

While Baldwin's nominal and effective rate estimates are now too dated for use in most current policy studies, they are useful in that they provide a base for assessing subsequent change in US tariff and nontariff protection from the late 1950s. Such information would be important for studies attempting to determine how the reliance on different trade measures has evolved, how changes in protection influenced comparative advantage, or how the relative importance of nominal and effective tariff and nontariff protection has changed.

Balassa (1986): Japan's Manufactured Imports

To account for differences in national import levels, Chenery (1960) employed per capita income and population as explanatory variables. The former was used as a proxy for the level of economic development, and the latter for domestic market size. Balassa started with this framework and also included the share of primary commodities in total imports and a variable for transportation costs. The rationale for these additional terms is that a limited domestic availability of natural resources, reflected in the share of primary commodities in total imports, will raise import levels, while imports will be reduced by the cost of transportation.

Balassa employed a regression model based on this framework to examine the relationship between national characteristics and the ratio of imports to gross domestic product in industrial countries. His estimates relate to 1973–83 and involve combining country observations for individual years. Separate calculations were made for total imports as well as for primary products and for manufactured goods. Three separate regressions were tested: the first based on imports from all areas (world imports); the second from industrial countries; and the third from developing countries. The statistical analysis was based on data from eighteen industrial countries which had per capita incomes of $2200 or higher and a share of manufactured goods in total exports of at least 20 per cent in 1973. The group included the United States, Canada, Austria, Belgium, Denmark, Finland, France, Federal Republic of Germany, Ireland, Israel, Italy, Netherlands, Norway, Sweden, Switzerland, the United Kingdom, Australia and Japan.

In the regression tests, a dummy variable was used for Japan to determine if this country's import levels were significantly different from other industrial countries. The introduction of the dummy was warranted because Japan showed the largest deviation of actual from predicted values in the basic equation with an average shortfall of 24 to 30 per cent. The regression results including the dummy show Japan to be an 'outlier' among industrial countries, irrespective if one considers imports from all sources from the industrial countries, or from developing countries. The Japan dummy was significant at the 1 per cent level in all equations and its introduction raised their explanatory power. Separate regressions were also run for primary products, and for manufactured goods. These results also showed Japan to be an outlier. In fact, the Japanese dummy variable took higher values in these tests, and achieved higher levels of statistical significance. (See Carliner (1985), Noland (1987) or Lawrence (1987) for examples of studies that attempted to assess the relative performance of Japan as an import market using comparative statistics on intra-industry trade.)

Analyses such as Balassa's study are useful for determining whether import levels of a specific country conform to established norms, or whether they are significantly different (lower). If the latter is established, however, it must still be determined what factors are responsible for trade short falls. Identification of these factors (barriers) is central in the formulation of effective corrective action. A second point is that Balassa's approach appears to have important policy implications for evaluating the socialist countries' trade performance.[36] Specifically, predictions from a Balassa type regression study would be useful for setting objective standards against which the actual trade performance of the SCEEs could be assessed. (See Yeats (1982) for statistical information on the relative trade performance of socialist Europe and OECD countries.)

Bell (1971): Trade Barriers in the United States

Harry Bell estimated total United States tariff and nontariff protection for selected agricultural and manufactured goods in the early 1970s. As such, this study provides a base from which subsequent protectionist trends can be assessed. Bell's empirical approach employed domestic international price comparisons, although alternative procedures such as analyses of the relationship between price changes of protected products and a control group of freely traded items were also employed. An appendix (see Bell, pp. 479–87) provides details of the estimation procedures and data sources used. Bell's results are presented in terms of total nominal protection coefficients which incorporate the effects of both tariffs and nontariff barriers. Agricultural products like beef and dairy products had nominal protection coefficients of 20 to 90 per cent respectively, while protection for wheat and flour was estimated at between 50 to 60 per cent. Protection for groundnuts was about 70 per cent, while sugar had a nominal protection coefficient of about 100 per cent. Bell stressed that these estimates were for a specific point in time and may be sensitive to underlying supply, demand and price changes.

Bell's estimates for manufactured goods shows that total protection for cotton textiles was approximately 25 per cent, while that for cotton clothing was 33 per cent. For the latter, US tariffs averaged about 23 per cent, which implies that the then existing LTA quotas had nominal equivalents of about 10 per cent. Using information on United States construction subsidies, Bell estimated support for domestic shipbuilding to be about 122 per cent. His analysis of US oil import tickets indicated a protection level of about 60 per cent for petroleum. The American Selling Price (ASP) valuation system, under which foreign goods were valued arbitrarily at corresponding US prices, was estimated to involve a 'true' rate of protection for benzenoid chemicals of about 20 per cent. Very low, or zero tariff and nontariff protection, was reported for the United States aircraft industry.

Boyce and Llewellyn (1982): Support Levels for Australian Industry

This study surveys estimates of support levels for the Australian manufacturing sector made by the Australian Industries Assistance Commission. Although Australian industry is predominantly protected by tariffs, the Industries Assistance Commission estimates include the effects of NTBs and subsidies. In the case of industries subject to special 'sector' policies (clothing, textiles, footwear and passenger motor vehicles), assistance is mainly in the form of quantitative restrictions on imports through the use of tariff-quotas.

Table 5.33 shows the average effective rates of assistance for broad groups of manufacturing industries over six years from 1974–5 to 1980–1. The effective rate is a measure of the net assistance provided, in that it takes account of both the subsidy effect on output and any tax on its inputs (see appendix 2 in this book for an analysis of this relationship). In 1980–1, the average effective rate of assistance was 25 per cent, much the same as in 1974–5, although this was almost 25 per cent lower than 1973–4 due to the Australian 1973 across-the-board tariff cut. Although the average assistance across the manufacturing sector remained virtually constant since 1974, Table 5.33 shows significant change occurred in its structure. In general, sectors with higher than average assistance in 1974–6 received expanded support, while that for the rest of the manufacturing sector declined.

Table 5.33 Average effective rates of assistance for broad groups of manufacturing industries, 1974–5 to 1980–1 (per cent)

ASIC code	Description	1974–5 production weights				1977–8 production weights			
		1974–5	*1975–6*	*1976–7*	*1977–8*	*1977–8*	*1978–9*	*1979–80*	*1980–81*
21	Food, beverages and tobacco	21	20	16	13	8	12	9	9
23	Textiles	39	50	51	57	48	49	51	49
24	Clothing and footwear	87	99	141	149	140	140	130	130
25	Wood, wood products and furniture	18	19	18	18	18	17	15	14
26	Paper, paper products and printing	31	30	30	29	25	28	26	25
27	Chemicals and petroleum products	23	23	21	18	19	19	18	14
28	Non-metallic mineral products	11	10	7	5	6	6	6	5
29	Basic metal products	16	16	15	14	11	12	11	12
31	Fabricated metal products	39	38	34	32	31	32	32	33
32	Transport equipment	45	59	54	61	71	76	91	93
33	Other machinery	24	25	22	21	16	19	20	19
34	Miscellaneous manufacturing	27	26	25	27	24	25	26	27
	Total Manufacturing	27	28	27	26	23	24	24	24

Notes: The statistics in this table reflect net assistance provided to each activity after making allowance for the effects of tariffs and other forms of protection which increase the costs of the activities concerned.
For textiles, clothing and footwear assistance afforded by quotas from 1976 to 1979 were derived from the results of a price disadvantage survey. Estimates for other years were based on a survey of quota transfer prices.
Source: Adapted from Boyce and Llewellyn (1982).

Collyns and Dunaway (1987): US Automative Restrictions

United States automobile quotas were first applied in the early 1980s and were directed mainly at Japan. While they were not 'legitimised' in a formal multilateral process like textiles and apparel, they proved to be long-lasting. Their background can be traced to the 1980 recession which, coupled with rising gasoline prices, contributed to a nearly 30 per cent decline in domestic car sales. During the same year, sales of Japanese imports rose by 40 per cent. In the spring of 1981, a voluntary restraint agreement with Japan was negotiated. Under the terms of this arrangement Japanese auto exports to the United States were reduced by 7.7 per cent from the 1980 level of 1.82 million units to 1.68 million units. Although the arrangement was to be temporary, it was renewed in each of the following three years. Since then, Japan has unilaterally restricted its automobile exports to the United States.

To quantify the effects of VERs on Japanese automobile exports, an econometric model of the US automobile sector was estimated using annual data for the period preceding the restraints (1968–80).[37] This model, which consisted of 6 behavioral equations and 26 identities, was then used to predict 1981–4 price, sales, and imports. The differences between actual and predicted values were taken as a measure of the VER's impact. The authors note that the estimates are, however, subject to a degree of uncertainty because shifts in the model's coefficients, or explanatory variable not included in the model, may affect differences between actual and predicted values. It was also acknowledged that estimation difficulties were caused by the relatively short period for which sufficient (reliable) data were available for fitting the model, and the lack of a quality adjusted price series for imported automobiles.

Differences between actual and predicted change lead Collyns and Dunaway to conclude that new car prices (as measured by the United States Consumer Price Index (CPI) for new cars) were nearly 6 per cent higher in 1984 than they would have been without the VERs. In average dollar terms, the export restraints added about $625 to the base price of a given 1984 model. The export restraints appear to have lowered total United States expenditures on automobiles by about $2.38 billion in 1984, or by over 3 per cent during the 1981–4 period. In terms of units, Collyns and Dunaway's projections suggest the restraints caused one and a half million fewer automobiles to be sold in 1984, and nearly four million fewer sold during 1981–4. (See Hunker, 1984, for a second study of the influence of these trade restrictions.)

Table 5.34 Statistics employed in estimating nominal equivalents and economic losses associated with UK VERs on footwear in 1982

Price data	Pounds
Import unit value of non-leather footwear (Taiwan to the UK)	2.33
Import unit value of non-leather footwear (Taiwan to Hong Kong)	1.80
Freight costs from Taiwan to the UK (per pair)	0.22
Estimated unrestrained price	2.02
VER premium (estimated per pair)	0.31
Unit value plus VER premium plus tariff	2.80
Quantity data	*Pairs*
Apparent consumption of non-leather footwear in UK	149 037 000
UK production	63 971 000
Total imports	85 066 000
Estimated changes	*Pairs*
Changes in consumption due to removal of tariff and VER	+10 379 652
Changes in domestic supply due to removal of tariff and VER	–17 820 989
Change in imports due to removal of tariff and VER	+28 200 641

Source: Adapted from Greenaway and Hindley (1985).

Greenaway (1985b): UK Restrictions on Footwear

Greenaway examined the impact of a UK 'voluntary' export restraint for non-leather footwear first negotiated with Taiwan and the Republic of Korea in the late 1970s and then renegotiated annually.[38] To estimate the value of the 'rent' associated with the restriction, unit values of (restricted) UK footwear imports from Taiwan were compared with Hong Kong's imports from Taiwan. The latter were unrestrained and were similar in composition to British imports. To account for higher transport costs to the UK, a freight factor of 12 per cent (provided by industry specialists) was added to the Hong Kong price. The difference between the resulting figure and the unit value in the UK was taken to reflect the VER premium per unit.[39] In 1982 this estimated rent element amounted to 31p per pair, or 13 per cent of the UK c.i.f. import price. The VER, therefore is estimated to have raised border prices of non-leather footwear by some 13 per cent. A breakdown of how Greenaway derived this figure is provided in Table 5.34.

The lower half of Table 5.34 summarises Greenaway's estimates of the effects of removing the VER and existing tariffs (about a 20 per cent MFN rate) on UK imports and consumption of non-leather footwear products. These projections are made using a partial equilibrium trade model similar to that described in Chapter 3. Consumption is estimated to increase by some 10 million pairs annually, while imports rise by 28 million pairs. (The offsetting factor is a decline in domestic supplies by approximately 18 million.) In monetary units, Greenaway estimated that the consumer savings from removal of these tariff and VERs would be approximately £117 million (see Greenaway, table 5.4, p. 140, for a breakdown of these costs).

An important point to note is that the estimated UK protection levels may be roughly equal to those of other EEC and EFTA countries. Hamilton (1984a) suggested that since manufactured goods are freely traded between these markets the level of external protection should differ only to the extent that intra-European transport costs differ. Hamilton also offers some supporting empirical evidence for this proposition based on comparisons of EEC-EFTA countries' protection for textile and clothing products.

Hufbauer *et al.* (1986): US Restrictions on Manufactures

This report provides detailed industry statistics and estimates of the incidence, costs and effects of 'special' protectionism for the following products which were afforded United States trade restrictions: book manufacturing; benzenoid chemicals; household glassware; rubber footwear; ceramic articles and tiles; textiles and apparel; ferrous-metal products (see the previous review in this book); non-rubber footwear; colour television receivers; citizen band radios; bolts, nuts and screws; automobiles; and heavy-weight motorcycles. Similar information is given for a number of agricultural products (sugar, dairy, meat, peanuts and fish) as well as for petroleum products, lead and zinc. The types of intervention measures analysed range from tariff quotas (motorcycles) and voluntary restraint arrangements (automobiles) to countervailing actions (non-rubber footwear).

A standard format is employed for reporting developments relating to protectionism in each of the above industries. The trade intervention measures being analysed are described and this is followed by 'key statistics' of the protected industry. The latter include value and volume figures for 'affected' imports; the value of total imports' apparent consumption for the industry; the share of imports in apparent consumption; output of the domestic industry; industry employment, wages and profits; and plant capacity utilisation. Hufbauer *et al.* provide estimates of the quantity and price effects of the trade restrictions and also estimate their welfare and consumer costs. This information is either compiled from previously published studies or original estimates by the authors.

Table 5.35 draws from the section of the Hufbauer study on citizen band radios to provide an illustration of the standard format used to summarise statistics for each industry 'case study'. The table first indicates the years that the special trade restriction (temporary higher tariffs in this example) were imposed while the second row estimates the impact of the restriction on import prices. The third column of each row indicates the source of the estimate, i.e., either an original estimate by the authors or a figure compiled from a published source. This information is then followed by additional estimates of the effect of the trade intervention measure including consumer costs, welfare costs, cost of the restriction in terms of jobs preserved, and various estimates of price and demand elasticities for the industry. Each (similar) table in the Hufbauer *et al.* report generally presents comments on how the estimates were derived, their reliability and the data sources used in compiling the estimates. (Morkre and Tarr, 1980, provide related information on the effects of United States trade intervention measures using a 'case study' approach similar to that employed by Hufbauer *et al.*)

McNamara (1979): United States Trade Barriers

McNamara cites estimates of the costs of protectionist measures imposed by the United States between 1975 and 1977 on goods imported from Asia and Latin America. His figures indicate that trade restrictions cost consumers $1250 million for carbon steel, $1200 million for footwear, $660 million for sugar, $400 to $800 million for meat and $500 million for television sets, or over $4 billion for these five items. As a result, the consumer cost per job 'saved' was more than $50 000 per year. Drawing on GATT statistics, McNamara estimated that protectionist measures by industrial countries during 1975 to 1977 affected 3 to 5 per cent of world trade, of $30 to $50 billion a year. He notes (p. 15) that these costs estimates for protectionism are understated since they do not include secondary effects such as efficiency losses or frustrated investment and export opportunities. McNamara's figures are consistent with another estimate that put the cost of protection to United States consumers of

Table 5.35   Estimates of the effects of 1978–81 US trade restrictions for citizen band radios

Item	Amount	Source[a]
Number of years restraints in force (1978–81)	3 years	–
Induced increase in price of imported CB radios	$8 per unit (1980–1) 21 per cent (1978)	Morkre Hufbauer
Induced increase in price of domestic CB radios	same as for imports	"
Coefficient of price response[b]	unity	Hufbauer
Quantity and value of imports (1978)	4.85 million units $194 million	Morkre "
Induced decrease in imports due to restraints (1978)	3.3 million units $132 million	Morkre Hufbauer
Quantity and value of domestic production (1978)	1.10 million units $83 million	Morkre Morkre
Induced increase in domestic production due to restraints on trade (1978)	0.3 million units	Hufbauer
Coefficient of quantity response[b]	0.1	Hufbauer
Elasticity of demand for imported CB radios	2.0	Morkre
Elasticity of supply of domestic CB radios	4.0	Morkre
Elasticity of demand for domestic CB radios	2.0	Morkre
Cross-elasticity of demand for domestic CB radios relative to price of imports	6.0	Hufbauer
Cross-elasticity of output of domestic CB radios relative to price of imports	4.0	Hufbauer
Cross-elasticity of quantity of imports relative to domestic radio prices	1.5	Hufbauer
Cost or restraints to United States consumers	$55 million (1978)	Hufbauer
Gains from restraints to United States producers	$14 million (1978)	Hufbauer
Tariff revenue and implied average tariff rate (1977)	$32 million 6 per cent	Hufbauer Morkre
Gains from restraints to foreigners	negligible	Hufbauer
Efficiency loss from larger domestic production to the USA (1978)	$5 million	Hufbauer
Welfare cost of restraints to the United States	$5 million (1978)	Hufbauer
Employment in the protected industry	2175 (1978) 775 (1981)	Hufbauer Hufbauer

Table 5.35   *continued*

Item	Amount	Source[a]
Induced increase in employment	600 (1978)	Hufbauer
Cost of restraints to US consumers per job saved	$93 000 (1978)	Hufbauer
Gains from restraints to US producers per job saved	$6400	Hufbauer

[a] Some additional estimates of the effects of the trade intervention measures have been omitted from this table. Aside from Hufbauer *et al.*, Morkre and Tarr (1980) has been employed as a source of estimates of barrier effects.
[b] Change in domestic output (price) relative to the change in imports volume (price).
Source: Adapted from Hufbauer *et al.* (1986).

clothing, footwear and sugar at $7.7 billion over a four-year period in the late 1970s. However, he provides little information on the empirical procedures used to produce these cost estimates.

OECD (1985d): US Restrictions on Colour Televisions

This OECD study provides an additional example of how industry modelling can be employed to assess the effects of trade barriers. The OECD estimated an econometric model of US demand for colour television sets, using data prior to the July 1977 orderly marketing arrangement (OMA) for Japanese exports, and then assessed the impact of these restrictions by the extent of the import displacement.[40] The latter was taken as the difference between the predicted levels of imports, domestic prices and final sales under no restrictions, and the level of actual imports.

The OECD model indicates that the OMA led to a significant increase in the mark-up in US import prices over wholesale prices (i.e. the restriction's premium) in the exporting countries. On average, US import unit values were 4 to 8 per cent higher in 1979 than they would have been had the OMA not been in force. Also, on average, US wholesale prices for colour receivers were 4 to 5 per cent higher in 1979 than expected on the basis of prior 1978 behavioural relationships. The OECD found that actual imports in the first three quarters of 1979 were 45 per cent lower than predicted and this figure was taken to be indicative of the volume effects of the restriction.

Roningen and Yeats (1976): Japan, France, Sweden and USA

Roningen and Yeats employed 1973 price statistics compiled by the consulting firm Business International to estimate NTB *ad valorem* equivalents for fifteen developed market economy countries.[41] Business International data were drawn using a 'specification' pricing approach which held cross-country product-quality variation to a minimum. Roningen and Yeats took the lowest observed price in the fifteen developed-country markets (net of any domestic subsidies on the item) as the free market price and then computed 'implicit' nominal protection coefficients for each of the approximately 300 sampled items. These basic results, which are aggregated to two-digit BTN groups, were previously shown in Table 2.5.

Since many of the items included in Roningen and Yeats's study encounter variable import levies, whose *ad valorem* incidence has been derived independently, the authors subtracted nominal equivalent for these charges from the price relative. In addition, several studies had derived nominal freight rates for these products and these factors were also removed. Table 5.36 shows the results of this exercise in which the observed price differentials were decomposed into a transport cost component, a variable levy component, and an NTB residual. These statistics illustrate the importance of variable levies as trade barriers for France and Sweden. In both cases, levies account for over 65 per cent of the food products' price differentials, and a slightly smaller figure for grains. In fact, removal of the transport and variable levy influence from the French data suggest that there are few (if any) remaining NTBs of importance for these product groups. While the Swedish figures also show a considerable decrease, the existence of a positive residual suggests other NTBs have yet to be accounted for. The authors acknowledge, however, that differences in supply and demand elasticities could influence the cross-country price differentials (see Chapter 2 in the present book for a discussion of this point).

Yeats (1976): Barriers Expressed as Specific Charges

Yeats examined the incidence of import barriers expressed as fixed monetary charges per unit on different exporters. Although the analysis utilised US specific tariffs, the results are generalised to NTBs like variable import levies, import deposit requirements, or standards that add a fixed unit cost to imports. The proposition that

Table 5.36 Decomposition of observed price differentials into variable levies, transport costs and nontariff barrier residuals (per cent)

	Estimated ad valorem rate			
BTN Country/Product group	*Average price relative*	*Variable levy*	*Transport cost*	*NTB residual*
France				
0 Food products	40	35	5	0
1 Grains and products	50	35	15	0
2 Beverages, tobacco, etc.	20	10	10	0
3 Pharmaceuticals & detergents	45	0	5	40
6 Apparel	45	0	10	35
Japan				
0 Food products	105	0	15	90
1 Grains and products	90	0	20	70
2 Beverages, tobacco, etc.	25	0	15	10
3 Pharmaceuticals & detergents	80	0	10	70
6 Apparel	20	0	15	5
Sweden				
0 Food products	75	50	5	20
1 Grains and products	70	45	15	0
2 Beverages, tobacco, etc.	65	10	10	45
3 Pharmaceuticals & detergents	115	0	5	110
6 Apparel	25	0	10	15
United States				
0 Food products	60	0	10	50
1 Grains and products	35	0	15	20
2 Beverages, tobacco, etc.	10	0	10	0
3 Pharmaceuticals & detergents	25	0	5	20
6 Apparel	55	0	15	40

Note: The 'grains and products' group excludes sugar and cocoa products while the BTN 2 product group excludes mineral fuels.
Source: Roningen and Yeats (1976) p. 620.

fixed charge per unit barriers generally have a differential adverse incidence on developing countries stems from the fact that unit values of tariff-line products imported from these countries (U_d) are consistently lower than unit values of similar items for developed market economy countries (U_m).[42] If S_i is the trade barrier's specific charge we can state, on average, that,

$$S_i \div U_d = \alpha + (S_i \div U_m) \tag{5.3}$$

where α is the average percentage point difference between the *ad valorem* incidence of the charge on developed as opposed to developing countries.

Employing a sample of 200 US tariff-line products facing specific import charges, Yeats shows that their average incidence is 10.4 per cent on developed and 19.2 per cent on developing countries (α = 8.4). Statistical tests show that α is a significant at the 99 per cent confidence interval. These findings indicate that trade barriers expressed as a fixed charge per unit of import normally have a significantly higher incidence on developing countries and that research is warranted, possibly using nontariff barrier inventories, to determine the extent that specific charge NTBs are employed in developed and developing countries.

Other Analytical Investigations

Aside from the studies previously surveyed, other empirical analyses have documented the costs and adverse economic effects of contemporary protectionism. Table 5.37 lists some representative studies, summarises their main empirical findings, and also indicates where additional information on each investigation can be found. Three points should be made concerning these studies. First the procedures that they employ vary widely from gravity type or related regression models (Lawrence, 1987) to analyses of structural differences in individual country imports (Yeats, 1982). Many of the methodologies employed in these investigations could be usefully applied to other industry sectors and countries. In particular, there appears to be considerable merit in utilising several of these approaches such as Lawrence (1987), Saxonhouse (1983) and the previously reviewed study by Balassa (1986) for an objective evaluation of the trade performance of the socialist countries of Eastern Europe. Second, it also appears useful to update many of these investigations to determine if their basic conclusions concerning the major costs and adverse effects of protectionism have altered with the passage of time. Finally, the studies listed in Table 5.37 are important in connection with the current multilateral trade negotiations since their estimates of the costs of contemporary protectionism are helpful in identifying industries where priorities should be given to a liberalisation effort.

Table 5.37 Studies which derived analytical evidence on the incidence and effects of nontariff barriers

Study	Product–industry	Importing country sector	Comments
Glismann and Neu (1971)	Pit coal, coal briquettes and coke	Fed. Rep. of Germany	Employed domestic–international price differences to estimate nominal protection coefficients for the German coal industry. Rates of over 100 per cent are recorded against products originating in Poland and the United Kingdom.
Havrylyshyn (1988)	All sectors	All developing	Presents results from an inventory study of nontariff measures applied in 33 major developing countries in 1986. Over 40 per cent of all four-digit CCCN products encounter NTMs in these markets with the share for food reaching 54 per cent. Import licensing is the most frequently used measure.
Hindley (1985)	Automobiles	United Kingdom	Quantified the distributional price effects of UK VERs by comparing list prices of Japanese cars sold in Britain with those sold in Japan. The greatest differences occur for lower priced models. Overall this study suggests (p. 74) that the VER increased the prices of low-to-medium-cost Japanese cars by 20 to 25 per cent.
Hindley (1985)	Video cassette recorders	United Kingdom	Analysed the price-increasing effect of a 1983 VER in which Japan agreed to limit certain types of VCRs exported to the EEC. Concluded that the agreement raised prices by 15 per cent and cost consumers an additional 174 million pounds.

(continued on page 226)

Table 5.37 continued

Study	Product–industry	Importing country sector	Comments
Hufbauer *et al.* (1986)	Selected agricultural and manufactured goods	United States	Presents detailed estimates of consumer costs (in total and in terms of the cost per job saved) from US protection for 31 industries. The costs per job saved often range from $100 000 to $200 000 and higher. The case studies present tariff rates and some estimates of NTB *ad valorem* equivalents.
Jager and Lanjouw (1977)	Newsprint	Netherlands	The authors test a regression model for quantifying the impact of a tariff-free quota on imports of newsprint, using data for 1951–74. The results suggest the quota had a tariff equivalent of 10 to 15 per cent on average and that the quantity of imports was reduced by 10 per cent below unrestricted values.
Lawrence (1987)	All sectors	All developing	Employs an intra-industry regression model to assess Japanese relative import levels. Concluded that Japanese manufactured imports are unusually low, and that Japan has different tastes and displays an abnormal bias for home products.
Munger (1984)	Television sets	United States	Compiled quantitative evidence on the cost of 1980 VERs and tariffs on 11 different product sectors. The annual cost to the consumer per job saved varied between $74 000 and $110 000 with the ratio of this cost to average labour compensation in the industry ranging from three (carbon steel) to nine times (footwear).

Saxonhouse (1983)	All manufactures	Japan	Employing a Hecksher–Ohlin framework this study attempted to determine whether factors influencing Japan's foreign trade are distinctive in comparison to other major countries. Saxonhouse's results indicate that less than 5 per cent of Japan's trade falls outside a range predicted by this country's factor endowments.
U.S. House of Representatives (1980)	Automobiles	Japan	Compiled detailed statistics on the additional costs US automobile producers incur when exporting to Japan. Japanese standards and higher dealer margins increase the price of a subcompact model by 48 per cent; for a sports car by 75 per cent; and a compact by 82 per cent.
World Bank (1987)	Selected manufactured goods	United States, EEC, Canada and United Kingdom	Compiled information on the consumer costs of contemporary protection for industries experiencing structural adjustment problems (see table 8.11 on p. 150) US losses of \$2 to \$12 billion are estimated for textiles, clothing, steel and automobiles.
Yeats (1982)	All manufactures	Socialist Europe	This study develops comparative measures of countries' import performance. The results show that the USSR and other socialist countries' imports from developing countries fall far below the worst performing OECD nation. Socialist imports from developing countries would have to increase by \$7 billion to reach OECD norms.

Appendix 1: Country–Product Classifications for Trade-Barrier Analysis

Research studies or policy analyses involving trade barriers often require that some aggregation procedures be employed for products or countries. For the latter, a distinction is often made between developed, developing and socialist countries, but institutions such as the World Bank, International Monetary Fund, GATT and the United Nations utilise independent country classifications that have important differences. Similarly, trade policy analyses often make a distinction between broad classes of goods such as manufactures, agricultural raw materials or foodstuffs. While the existing product classifications are normally based on the Standard International Trade Classification (SITC) system, there are important differences between the groupings employed by organisations like UNCTAD and UNIDO. In both the formulation of policy studies, and the interpretation of published results, it is important to realise how the product or country classifications employed can influence empirical results.

PRODUCT CLASSIFICATION SCHEMES

Perhaps the most widely used product classification scheme is that employed by the United Nations Conference on Trade and Development for preparation of its *Handbook of International Trade and Development Statistics*. The UNCTAD scheme, outlined in Table A1.1, distinguishes between five broad groups of products: agricultural raw materials, foodstuffs, ores and metals, fuels and manufactured goods. The table indicates the major subgroups of products that comprise each of the five broad classes, and also shows their corresponding SITC numbers.[1] Table A1.2 gives a second product classification system employed by the World Bank in which the major distinction is between agricultural and manufactured goods. Here, the component products are identified in terms of four-digit CCCN headings or United States TSUSA groups. The latter is a system developed by the USA for classification of its national trade statistics.

For many policy studies involving trade barriers, interest centres on the incidence of restrictions on products at different levels of fabrication. For these analyses, UNCTAD developed a commodity processing chain classification system that distinguishes between primary, semi-fabricated, and processed stages of a specific commodity. This system will, for example, trace the transformation of (say) cocoa from cocoa beans (primary stage), to cocoa

Table A1.1   The UNCTAD product classification scheme for traded goods

Product group	Included items		Less: Excluded items	
	SITC	Description	SITC	Description
Agricultural raw materials	2	Crude materials, inedible	22	Oilseeds, oil nuts and oil kernels
			27	Crude fertilisers and minerals
			28	Metalliferous ores and scrap
All food items	0	Food and live animals		
	1	Beverages and tobacco		
	22	Oilseeds, oil nuts and oil kernels		
	4	Animal and vegetable oil and fats		
Ores and metals	27	Crude fertilisers and minerals		
	28	Metalliferous ores and scrap		
	67	Iron and steel		
	68	Non-ferrous metals		
Fuels	3	Mineral fuels and lubricants		
Manufactured goods	5	Chemicals	67	Iron and steel
	6	Manufactures classified by material	68	Non-ferrous metals
	7	Machinery and transport equipment		
	8	Miscellaneous manufactured articles		

Note: The above classification is based on the Standard International Trade Classification, revised as published in Statistical Office of the United Nations (1961).

powder and butter (intermediate stage products), to chocolate and products (final stage items). Table A1.3 provides details on these processing chains for commodities that accounted for over 90 per cent of developing countries' export earnings in 1984.[2] This classification has been used for analysing the structure of protection against primary and processed commodities, or for analysing biases in the structure of trade between different groups of countries. It has also been employed in most empirical analyses of trade-barrier escalation (see UNCTAD, 1983a, for an example of one such application).

Related empirical studies have attempted to analyse trade barriers facing goods with different product and production characteristics. One such useful scheme was developed by Bela Balassa who distinguished between the following four classes of manufactured goods. (i) Semi-manufactures whose main inputs are natural raw materials are classified as 'intermediate products I'.[3] (ii) Manufactured goods at higher levels of production are classified in 'intermediate products II'.[4] Additional categories in the Balassa scheme include (iii) consumer goods and (iv) investment goods.[5] In a US National

Table A1.2 World Bank definitions of product and country groups

Product	TSUSA headings	CCCN 4-digit headings
All items	10001–87045	0101–9906
All items, less fuels	10001–47462, 48005–52121 52141–87045	0101–2604, 2801–9906
Agricultural goods	10001–19324	0101–2402
Manufactured goods	20003–47462, 48005–49520, 53101–54805, 60502–87045	2801–9906
of which:		
textiles	30010–39060	5001–6302
footwear	70005–70095	6401–6406
iron and steel	60600–61081	7300–7399
electrical machinery	68205–68847	8501–8528
vehicles	69202–69260	8701–8714

Major exporters of manufactures: Argentina, Brazil, China (Taiwan Province), Hong Kong, Israel, Rep. of Korea, Philippines, Portugal, Singapore, Rep. of South Africa, Thailand, Yugoslavia.

Major Borrowers: Argentina, Brazil, Chile, Egypt, India, Indonesia, Israel, Rep. of Korea, Mexico, Turkey, Venezuela, Yugoslavia.

Bureau of Economic Research study, Hal Lary developed a useful classification for goods manufactured by labour-intensive production processes. The component items are identified at the three- and four-digit level of the SITC and United States SIC system.[6] Finally, Kojima (1964) develops a useful classification scheme for trade-barrier analysis in which three-digit SITC products are grouped into one of the following general categories: staple foods, other foodstuffs; agricultural raw materials; minerals, metals and fuels; labour-intensive goods of light industry; labour-intensive final goods of heavy and chemical industry origin; capital-intensive intermediate goods; capital-intensive heavy machines and equipment.

COUNTRY CLASSIFICATION SYSTEMS

Aside from the analysis of trade barriers on different products, studies have also examined the incidence of restrictions on countries which are at different levels of economic development, or whose exports are concentrated in products like petroleum or manufactured goods. Table A1.4 identifies countries in terms of a commonly used United Nations classification scheme for developed, developing and socialist countries of Europe and Asia. Other international organisations have employed country classifications that differ in important respects. For example, in the World Bank classification scheme Portugal, Spain, Greece and Israel are grouped with developing rather than developed countries.[7]

In some trade policy studies, the incidence of tariffs and nontariff barriers on developing countries classified by income levels has been examined. Table

A1.4 gives a classification employed by UNCTAD which groups developing countries whose 1980 per capita gross domestic product exceeded $1500, countries for which it fell between $1500 and $500, and countries whose GDP per capita fell short of $500. Table A1.4 also provides details of three other United Nations country classifications: developing countries that are major petroleum exporters, those that are major exporters of manufactures, and the least developed of the developing countries. As was the case with the other groupings, other international organisations have independently developed classifications that differ from those of the United Nations. For example, the World Bank's grouping of major developing-country exporters of manufactures also includes Israel, Philippines, Portugal, Republic of South Africa and Thailand, as well as the UNCTAD group. The World Bank also has a classification of major developing-country borrowers with more than $15 billion in long-term debt at the end of 1983 (Argentina, Brazil, Chile, Egypt, India, Indonesia, Israel, Republic of Korea, Mexico, Turkey, Venezuela, and Yugoslavia) that has been employed for trade policy analysis.

Table A1.3 The UNCTAD classification scheme for analysis of trade barriers over commodity processing chains

Commodity	Primary stage item		Intermediate stage(s)		Final stage(s)	
	SITC	Description	SITC	Description	SITC	Description
Meat	011	Fresh and frozen	–	none identified	013	Meat preparations
Fish	031	Fresh and frozen	–	none identified	032	Fish preparations
Fruit	051	Fresh fruit	–	none identified	053	Preserved fruit
Vegetables	054	Fresh vegetables	–	none identified	055	Preserved vegetables
Cocoa	072.1	Cocoa beans	072.2	Cocoa powder	073	Chocolate and products
			072.3	Cocoa butter		
Coffee	071.1	Green or roasted beans	–	none identified	071.3	Coffee extracts
Groundnuts	221.1	Groundnuts	421.4*	Crude groundnut oil	421.4*	Refined groundnut oil
			081.3*	Groundnut oil cake		
Copra	221.2	Copra	422.3*	Crude coconut oil	422.3*	Coconut oil, refined
			081.3*	Copra cake		
Palm kernel	221.3	Palm kernel	422.4*	Crude Palm kernel oil	422.4*	Palm kernel oil, refined
			081.3*	Palm kernel cake		
Palm oil	–	none identified	422.2*	Crude Palm oil	422.2*	Refined palm oil
Leather	211	Hides and skins	611	Leather	612	Leather goods
					831	Leather manufactures
					851	Shoes
Rubber	231.1	Natural rubber	–	none identified	629	Rubber products

Wood	242.2	Rough wood	243	Wood, simply worked	632	Wood manufactures
			631.2	Plywood		
Paper and pulp	242.1	Pulpwood	251	Woodpulp	641	Paper
					642	Paper articles
Wool	262.1	Raw wool	651.2	Wool yarn	653.2	Wool fabrics
Cotton	263.1	Raw cotton	651.3	Cotton yarn	652	Cotton fabrics
Jute	264	Raw jute	653.4	Jute fabrics	656.1	Jute sacks and bags
Sisal and Henequen	265.4	Sisal and henequen	–	none identified	655.6	Cordage
Iron	281.3	Iron ore	671	Pig iron	672	Steel ingots
					673	Rolling mill products
					676	Rolling mill products
					677	Other steel products
Copper	283.1	Copper ore	682.1	Unwrought copper	682.2	Wrought copper
Aluminium	283.3	Bauxite	513.6	Alumina	684.1	Aluminium unwrought
					684.2	Aluminium, wrought
Lead	283.4	Lead ore	685.1	Lead, unwrought	685.2	Lead, wrought
Zinc	283.5*	Zinc ore	686.1	Zinc, unwrought	686.2	Zinc, wrought
Petroleum	331	Crude petroleum	–	none identified	332	Petroleum products

* The processing-chain item constitutes part of the three- or four-digit SITC group.

Source: Compiled from various UNCTAD publications.

Table A1.4   The United Nations country classification scheme by major categories or income levels

Country/categories	Countries included
A. *By economic group*	
Developed market economy countries	Australia, Austria, Belgium, Canada, Denmark, Faeroe Island, Finland, France, Germany (Fed. Republic), Gibraltar, Greece, Iceland, Ireland, Israel, Italy, Japan, Luxembourg, Netherlands, New Zealand, Norway, Portugal, South Africa, Spain, Sweden, Switzerland, United Kingdom and United States.
Socialist countries of Europe	Albania, Bulgaria, Czechoslovakia, German Democratic Republic, Hungary, Poland, Romania and USSR.
Socialist countries of Asia	China, Democratic Peoples Republic of Korea, Mongolia and Viet Nam.
Developing countries and territories	All other countries and territories in Africa, America, Asia, Europe and Oceania not mentioned above.
B. *By income level*	
Developing countries with 1980 per capita GDP over $1500	Algeria, American Samoa, Argentina, Bahamas, Bahrain, Barbados, Bermuda, Brazil, British Virgin Islands, Brunei Darussalam, Cayman Islands, Chile, Costa Rica, Cuba, Cyprus, Fiji, French Guiana, French Polynesia, Gabon, Greenland, Guam, Hong Kong, Iran, Iraq, Kuwait, Libya, Macau, Malaysia, Malta, Martinique, Mexico, Nauru, Netherlands Antilles, New Caledonia, Oman, Panama, Panama Canal Zone, Puerto Rico, Qatar, Reunion, Republic of Korea, Saint Pierre and Miquelon, Saudi Arabia, Sechelles, Singapore, Suriname, Taiwan (Provnce of China), Trinidad and Tobago, U.S. Virgin Islands, United Arab Emirates, Uruguay, Venezuela, Wake Island, Yugoslavia.
Developing countries with 1980 per capita GDP between $500 and $1500	Angola, Antigua and Barbuda, Belize, Bolivia, Botswana, Cameroon, Christmas Island, Colombia, Congo, Cook Islands, Cote d'Ivoire, Dominica, Dominican Republic, Ecuador, El Salvador, Falkland Islands, Grenada, Guatemala, Guyana, Honduras, Jamaica, Jordan, Lebanon, Liberia, Mauritius, Montserrat, Morocco, Namibia, Nicaragua, Nigeria, Pacific Islands, Papua New Guinea, Paraguay, Peru, Philippines, Saint Christopher and Nevis, Saint Lucia, Saint Vincent and the Grenadines, Somoa, Sao Tome and Principe, Senegal, Solomon Islands, Swaziland, Syrian Arab Republic, Thailand, Tonga, Tunisia, Turkey, Turks and Caocos Islands, Tuvalu, Vanuatu, Wallis and Futuna Islands, Yemen, Zambia, Zimbabwe.
Developing countries with 1980 per capita GDP under $500	Afghanistan, Bangladesh, Benin, Bhutan, Burkina Faso, Burma, Burundi, Cape Verde, Central African Republic, Chad, Comoros, Democratic Kampuchea, Democratic Yemen, Djibouti, East Timor, Egypt,

Table A1.4 *continued*

Country/categories	Countries included
	Equatorial Guinea, Ethiopia, Gambia, Ghana, Guinea, Guinea-Bissau, Haiti, India, Indonesia, Kenya, Kiribati, Lao People's Democratic Republic, Lesotho, Madagascar, Malawi, Maldives.
C. *By major categories*	
Major petroleum exporting countries	Algeria, Angola, Bahrain, Brunei Darussalam, Congo, Ecuador, Gabon, Indonesia, Iran, Iraq, Kuwait, Libya, Mexico, Nigeria, Oman, Qatar, Saudi Arabia, Syria, Trinidad and Tobago, United Arab Emirates, Venezuela.
Major developing country exporters of manufactures	Argentina, Brazil, Hong Kong, Republic of Korea, Singapore, Taiwan Province of China, Yugoslavia.
Least developed countries	Afghanistan, Bangladesh, Benin, Bhutan, Botswana, Burkina Faso, Burundi, Cape Verde, Central African Republic, Chad, Comoros, Democratic Yemen, Djibouti, Equatorial Guinea, Ethiopia, Gambia.

Note: For trade and other economic statistics for the above country groupings see United Nations Conference on Trade and Development, *Handbood of International Trade and Development Statistics*, various issues (New York: United Nations).

Appendix 2:
Approximating the
Effective Rate of Protection

Since several empirical procedures or studies discussed in this book employ effective rates of protection rather than nominal rates for evaluating the influence of trade barriers, it is important to understand the relationship between these two measures. It is also important to realise why some seemingly low rates of nominal tariff or NTB protection become very large when translated into effective rates (see, for example, the study by Wipf, 1971, or Baldwin, 1970, reviewed in Chapter 5). To illustrate these relationships, Figure A2.1 shows effective rates of protection (ERP) that would occur under different levels of nominal protection for a product, different levels of protection for its production inputs, and the product's 'free trade' value-added coefficient. In the figure, the ratio of effective to nominal protection for a specific product (E_j/t_j) is shown on the vertical scale while the estimated free trade value-added coefficient is on the horizontal.[1] The curves in the four quadrants trace out the relation between these variables at different ratios (α) of nominal protection for production inputs to nominal protection for the manufactured (final) product.[2]

An example will show how the figure approximates effective rates. Assume a manufactured product has a free trade value-added coefficient of 11 per cent (represented by $0C$ in the figure). Nominal protection of 8 per cent is then afforded its production inputs, either through tariffs or NTBs, while nominal protection of 10 per cent is placed on the final product (i.e., α equals .08/.10 or 0.8). Figure A2.1 shows that the ERP would be close to 30 per cent, or three times ($0A$) the nominal rate of protection for the manufactured product. However, if the value-added coefficient were under 4 per cent ($0F$ in the figure), the effective rate would be 70 per cent, or seven times ($0C$) the rate of nominal protection.[3]

Using the nominal protection rate for the final product, the nominal rate for inputs, and the estimated free trade value-added coefficient, ERPs can be estimated in the above manner for individual products. Although the estimates are subject to some degree of error, due for example to problems in approximating the free trade value-added coefficient, Figure A2.1 also illustrates the relationships between different parameters that influence rates of protection. This can be useful for assessing results of some of the studies surveyed in Chapter 5. The figure can also be used, with rough estimates for some of the parameters, to approximate effective rates that are implied by nominal protection coefficients.

What are the major implications of Figure A2.1 for the empirical procedures outlined in Chapter 2 for estimating nominal equivalents for non-tariff barriers? First, the figure shows that equal rates of nominal protection

236

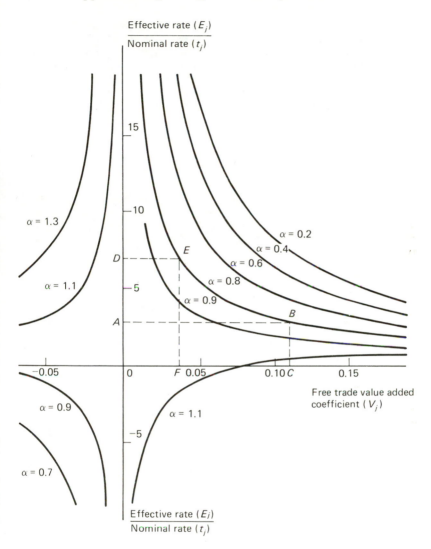

Figure A2.1   Analysis of the relation between the effective rate of protection, the value added coefficient, and nominal rates of protection

for different products may be a misleading gauge of (true) effective rates if either (free trade) value-added for the manufacturing process, or nominal protection rates for production inputs differ. Second, with given nominal rates of protection effective rates tend to increase rapidly as value-added decreases. Seemingly low nominal protection rates can mask very high effective rates of protection when value-added coefficients are low. Third, effective protection can be negative if nominal protection on inputs exceeds that for the final product. In this situation, the structure of protection implies a tax on the manufacturing process. Finally, Figure A2.1 has important implications for multilateral negotiations such as the Uruguay Round, since it shows that relatively larger proportionate cuts in nominal protection for production inputs than for the final product will raise effective rates of protection.

Appendix 3: Tariff Protection in Developed and Developing Countries

Several empirical procedures discussed in this book for quantifying trade barriers incorporate the joint protective effects of different forms of restrictions. Domestic–world price differentials will, for example, reflect the combined influence of tariffs and nontariff barriers. However, many policy or research studies require some indication of the relative importance or incidence of nontariff restrictions in total protection for a product or sector. The need to 'decompose' total protection into a tariff and NTB element has been increased by the fact that some developed countries' pre-Uruguay Round tariffs are quite high in sectors like textiles, clothing, footwear and agriculture where they range from 10 to 30 per cent, or more.[1] If one had independent estimates of nominal tariff protection for specific countries and items these rates could be 'subtracted' from estimates of total protection to approximate an NTB residual. This appendix will summarise basic information on pre-Uruguay tariffs in order to assist in assessing the importance of import duties and NTBs in total protection. In addition, it contrasts the level of tariff protection in different industries and countries. Where an empirical procedure discussed in Chapter 2 only provides *ad valorem* equivalents for the nontariff element, the tariff rates shown in this appendix can be added to the NTB nominal equivalent to approximate total protection levels.

For an initial assessment of the importance of pre-Uruguay Round tariffs, Table A3.1 provides statistics on their level in selected developed and developing countries. These tariff averages were computed using three systems of trade weights: those based on imports from developing countries, on imports from developed countries, and world trade weights in order to determine if import duties incorporate a systematic bias against different exporters. In addition, both MFN and 'applied' average tariff rates have been calculated. The latter reflect the trade-weighted average of the MFN, GSP, Lome Convention, preferential EFTA-EEC tariff rate, or other special preference import duty actually assessed on tariff-line-level imports.[2]

From the standpoint of estimating total rates of protection from both tariffs and NTBs, the divergences in developed-country tariff levels are important since there are relatively high and low tariff countries. In the United States, Japan, Switzerland and Sweden, MFN tariffs average under 4 per cent which is less than half the corresponding rates for Australia, Austria and New Zealand. Even greater diversity is reflected in the developing-country tariff statistics, however, where MFN tariff averages range from 1.3 per cent in Singapore to over 40 per cent in Bangladesh, Pakistan and India.[3] Empirical research that attempted to determine if NTBs offset or reinforce these variations in tariff protection would be useful for many policy purposes.

Appendix 3

Table A3.1   Trade-weighted average MFN and applied tariffs in selected developed and developing countries

| Country/country group[1] | Trade-weighted tariff average | | | | | |
| | Developing country trade weights | | Developed country trade weights | | World trade weights | |
	MFN	Applied	MFN	Applied	MFN	Applied
Developed countries						
Australia	8.3	4.8	14.0	9.4	12.4	8.2
Austria	5.5	5.6	10.5	1.5	9.9	2.0
Canada	6.1	4.6	6.6	4.5	6.5	4.5
European Community[2]	3.2	2.1	4.8	2.8	4.2	2.5
Finland	6.7	4.6	4.7	0.7	4.8	1.0
Japan	3.0	2.4	4.2	4.0	3.5	3.0
New Zealand	5.2	3.3	16.0	13.0	13.6	10.9
Norway	3.2	2.8	4.9	0.8	4.8	1.0
Sweden	3.1	2.5	3.6	0.7	3.5	0.8
Switzerland	2.7	2.5	3.0	0.9	3.0	1.0
United States	4.9	4.5	3.4	3.4	3.9	3.8
Developing countries						
Algeria (1982)	11.0	–	11.9	11.9	11.7	–
Bangladesh (1983)	69.3	–	68.3	68.3	68.8	–
CARICOM (1979)	7.7	–	18.7	18.7	17.0	–
CEUCA (1977)	12.5	–	18.3	18.3	17.2	–
Egypt (1981)	35.5	–	22.8	22.8	24.2	–
India (1984)	26.9	–	60.2	60.2	44.8	–
Indonesia (1980)	20.2	–	24.7	24.7	23.0	–
Cote d'Ivoire (1980)	37.3	–	33.6	33.6	34.9	–
Kenya (1982)	37.5	–	31.8	31.8	34.0	–
Korea, Rep. of	6.9	–	16.2	16.2	13.0	–
Malaysia (1981)	6.6	–	14.3	14.3	11.6	–
Mexico (1984)	19.3	–	20.2	20.2	20.0	–
Morocco (1982)	33.2	–	36.7	36.7	35.7	–
Nigeria (1982)	29.3	–	22.1	22.1	23.1	–
Pakistan (1982)	30.3	–	54.7	54.7	43.4	–
Philippines (1985)	17.5	–	21.5	21.5	19.9	–
Saudi Arabia (1980)	5.5	–	11.9	11.9	10.9	–
Singapore (1983)	0.4	–	2.1	2.1	1.3	–
Sri Lanka (1983)	19.7	–	23.8	23.8	21.8	–
Tanzania, United Rep. (1981)	12.5	–	15.9	15.9	15.1	–
Thailand (1981)	6.1	–	20.5	20.5	14.5	–
Tunisia	14.5	–	18.9	18.9	18.5	–
Yugoslavia (1980)	4.5	–	12.1	12.1	10.0	–

[1] The dates shown in parentheses show the year for which the tariff data were drawn. Since the UNCTAD data base did not contain information on developing-country preferential arrangements, 'applied' tariff averages could not be computed.
[2] The trade-weighted rates are based on the external trade of the EEC.
Source: Developed-country tariff averages have been computed from data in the GATT Tariff Study. Developing-country tariffs have been computed from data in the UNCTAD Trade Information System.

One potentially important point concerns the sizeable differences between some of the European countries' MFN and applied tariff averages. For example, Table A3.1 shows the average MFN rate in Norway and Finland is 4.8 per cent, yet the average applied tariff in both countries is about one-fifth this figure. Similarly, for the EEC the applied rate (2.5 per cent) is approximately 40 per cent lower than the average MFN duty. Analysis of the underlying tariff statistics shows the major factor accounting for these differences is an EEC-EFTA protocol that allows duty-free trade in most manufactured goods and some agricultural products between countries in these groups.[4] From the standpoint of estimating total rates of protection from tariffs and NTBs, these statistics have important implications. Specifically, if the incidence (*ad valorem* equivalents) of nontariff barriers are constant over all exporters then the underlying differences in tariff rates will cause total protection to vary proportionately against individual country exporters. What is not known, however, is whether discriminatory NTBs generally reinforce or offset tariff protection. This point accents the need for further research aimed at determining how tariff and NTB protection interact.

While Table A3.1 shows that wide variation exists in tariffs across countries, Table A3.2 indicates that considerable differences also exist across industry sectors. While many sectors have tariffs that average under 2 per cent, most-favoured-nation duties on clothing in the United States, Canada and Austria range from 20 to 50 per cent, while import tariffs average about 93 per cent in New Zealand. Japan's tariffs on footwear average 14 per cent, while MFN duties of 40 per cent or more face these products in Australia and New Zealand. Aside from demonstrating that current MFN tariffs are still a major trade barrier in some sectors (apart from NTB protection), Table A3.2 provides further information on the importance of existing deviations from the MFN principle, particularly in Europe. As an example, Finnish MFN tariffs on footwear average about 16 per cent, but due to multiple special trading arrangements the average 'applied' tariff is about 4 per cent. In Norway, most-favoured-nation tariffs on clothing average 20 per cent, while applied tariffs are only 3 per cent. Perhaps the key point that follows from Table A3.2 is that empirical procedures that only yield *ad valorem* equivalents for nontariff barriers could be misleading as a guide to total protection for some sectors. Also, the statistics shown in Table A3.2 accent the importance of decomposing total protection into a tariff and NTB element so any liberalisation effort could be directed at measures which have a maximum trade restrictive effect.

Table A3.2 The level of post-Tokyo MFN, applied and GSP tariffs in selected developed countries

Product/group	Australia	Austria	Canada	EEC	Finland	Japan	Norway	New Zealand	Sweden	Switzerland	USA	All developed
Average MFN tariff rates												
All food items	4.9	8.0	6.2	3.7	8.9	9.7	2.8	9.7	1.6	10.0	4.1	6.4
Food and live animals	2.8	5.9	6.8	3.2	9.3	10.0	3.0	5.7	1.4	9.0	3.8	6.5
Oilseeds and nuts	4.1	1.9	6.0	10.3	7.9	5.6	4.5	0.9	3.3	7.5	1.4	5.3
Animal & vegetable oils	2.0	0.8	0.0	0.1	0.8	0.3	0.0	0.0	0.0	0.2	0.9	0.1
Agricultural raw materials	5.1	2.3	0.6	3.4	1.1	0.7	0.6	1.0	1.7	1.9	0.3	0.8
Ores and metals	10.2	5.6	2.1	2.8	1.9	2.5	1.5	6.0	2.5	1.4	1.9	2.3
Iron and steel	17.2	8.4	5.4	5.5	3.9	5.0	1.8	8.8	4.8	2.0	4.3	5.1
Non-ferrous metals	3.9	6.1	2.2	3.2	1.2	5.5	1.9	4.0	1.0	1.2	0.7	2.3
Fuels	0.0	2.1	1.4	0.1	0.1	1.5	0.0	0.2	0.0	0.0	0.4	1.1
Chemicals	5.4	6.3	6.4	8.4	2.4	5.5	5.9	6.7	5.0	0.9	3.7	5.8
Manufactures exc. chemicals	17.7	14.1	7.0	8.1	8.2	5.7	6.1	22.6	5.4	3.3	5.6	7.0
Leather	17.8	5.3	3.8	10.2	11.8	11.9	4.7	20.9	4.1	1.8	4.2	5.1
Textile yarn & fabrics	15.3	18.2	9.4	17.3	22.7	8.6	12.8	16.2	10.6	6.0	10.6	11.7
Clothing	49.3	30.2	12.6	19.9	32.0	15.0	20.3	93.0	13.6	8.6	20.3	17.5
Footwear	43.9	25.9	11.9	22.5	16.0	14.2	11.2	40.3	14.3	9.6	11.7	13.4
Other items	0.2	3.3	0.1	4.8	1.3	2.3	2.0	1.2	1.8	0.4	4.2	3.8
All products	12.4	9.9	6.5	4.2	4.8	3.5	4.8	13.6	3.5	3.0	3.9	4.1
Average applied tariff rates												
All food items	3.1	6.8	3.0	4.4	5.2	9.4	1.4	7.8	0.8	9.1	3.5	5.3
Food and live animals	1.7	4.9	2.9	4.8	5.7	9.7	1.5	3.9	0.8	8.4	3.2	5.3
Oilseeds and nuts	2.0	1.5	4.6	4.9	5.5	4.8	4.3	0.7	2.2	7.4	1.0	4.0
Animal & vegetable oils	2.4	0.8	0.1	0.0	0.8	0.3	0.0	0.0	0.0	0.2	1.0	0.2
Agricultural raw materials	0.7	1.6	3.7	0.4	1.0	0.3	0.4	0.7	1.4	0.7	0.3	0.5
Ores and metals	4.3	0.3	2.7	0.7	0.1	1.8	0.4	4.2	0.2	0.1	2.2	1.5
Iron and steel	7.3	0.5	5.6	2.3	0.1	2.9	0.7	6.4	0.4	0.1	5.0	3.4
Non-ferrous metals	2.4	0.2	2.8	0.5	0.0	4.3	0.1	2.1	0.1	0.1	0.7	1.3

Fuels	0.0	1.5	0.2	0.3	0.0	1.2	0.0	0.0	0.0	0.0	0.4	0.6
Chemicals	4.0	0.5	3.0	3.4	0.1	4.8	0.4	4.9	0.4	0.1	3.9	3.1
Manufactures exc. chemicals	11.5	2.0	6.2	4.6	1.3	4.6	1.3	18.3	1.4	0.4	4.9	4.7
Leather	10.9	0.9	11.0	2.1	2.3	10.7	0.8	21.4	0.3	0.1	2.7	3.1
Textile yarn & fabrics	11.3	2.0	18.3	5.3	1.0	7.1	1.6	10.9	1.7	0.6	12.1	7.9
Clothing	35.6	5.1	17.2	7.3	7.7	10.0	3.0	75.6	4.8	1.7	18.1	11.9
Footwear	27.9	1.2	23.4	6.5	3.8	12.5	2.4	28.4	2.8	0.6	9.5	9.0
Other items	0.1	1.1	4.7	0.1	0.1	0.7	0.4	0.9	0.1	0.2	3.6	3.3
All products	8.3	2.0	4.4	2.5	1.0	3.1	1.0	11.0	0.8	1.0	3.4	3.0
Average tariff for GSP beneficiaries												
All food items	1.3	9.0	1.5	5.0	7.0	11.1	0.3	6.2	0.4	6.3	3.6	5.5
Food and live animals	1.0	8.9	1.3	5.1	7.2	11.7	0.3	0.8	0.4	6.5	3.4	5.6
Oilseeds and nuts	0.7	0.1	5.6	6.2	8.8	5.0	3.2	0.0	1.7	9.0	0.3	4.5
Animal & vegetable oils	0.3	0.3	0.0	0.0	10.7	1.2	0.0	0.0	0.0	0.1	0.1	0.4
Agricultural raw materials	0.1	1.4	3.1	0.5	5.5	0.5	0.5	0.0	2.1	0.3	0.1	0.5
Ores and metals	1.6	0.9	0.5	0.5	0.1	1.3	0.3	0.2	0.1	0.4	1.1	0.9
Iron and steel	4.9	2.9	4.0	3.3	0.4	2.0	0.4	2.3	1.0	0.4	3.5	3.0
Non-ferrous metals	0.3	1.1	0.9	0.5	0.0	3.1	1.7	0.5	0.1	0.9	0.3	1.1
Fuels	0.0	1.5	0.0	0.2	0.0	1.3	0.0	0.0	0.0	0.0	0.3	0.6
Chemicals	4.2	4.0	6.1	4.1	0.1	5.1	0.2	1.1	0.6	0.4	1.0	3.7
Manufactures exc. chemicals	11.4	18.9	13.8	6.4	9.3	4.2	5.9	14.3	6.9	2.7	6.6	6.7
Leather	9.6	6.6	9.6	2.8	6.1	8.4	5.5	18.0	1.2	1.1	1.4	3.2
Textile yarn & fabrics	6.3	17.5	19.8	7.6	6.0	6.1	11.0	8.5	6.8	2.7	9.0	8.4
Clothing	35.1	27.2	16.2	9.3	23.6	8.6	18.9	82.8	13.2	7.6	17.8	14.6
Footwear	25.6	24.4	23.3	9.1	14.8	7.9	11.6	22.1	13.4	4.4	9.4	10.1
Other items	0.0	5.3	5.6	0.1	0.1	1.0	0.1	1.7	0.0	0.4	4.0	3.8
All products	4.3	4.9	4.4	2.1	4.6	2.3	2.8	3.3	2.3	2.3	3.6	2.7

Source: Calculations on the basis of the GATT Tariff Study and UNCTAD Series D Trade Tapes.

Appendix 4: A Glossary of Nontariff Measures

This appendix presents a glossary of nontariff measures included in the UNCTAD Data Base on Trade Policy Measures.[1] At present, trade measures are classified under more than 100 different codes. This high level of detail permits, to a large extent, maintenance of the terminology used in the corresponding trade regulations of countries applying these measures. In this appendix, measures are only classified under broad groups. When analysing the statistics in the UNCTAD Data Base, any subset of individual measures can be selected and regrouped according to the specific purposes of each analysis. Chapter 4 provides examples of some of the most commonly used groups of nontariff barriers.

TARIFF MEASURES WHICH CONSTITUTE 'QUASI-NTMs'

Information on 'tariff-type' trade control measures are included in the Data Base when they involve limitations on the application of 'normal' MFN rates. The most common forms are tariff quotas and seasonal tariffs.

Tariff quotas

Tariff quotas constitute a limitation (quota) on the quantity (or value) of imports of specific products allowed, for a given time-period, under the 'normal' tariff rate, whereas higher tariff rates are charged on imports which exceed the quota. The Data Base records the existence of a tariff quota, but does not register the different tariff rates which are applied.

Seasonal tariffs

Seasonal tariffs are different tariff rates applied to a given product depending on the time of year. They are normally used for agricultural products with the highest import duties applied during the period of the domestic harvest.

Increased tariffs

Temporary increase of tariffs on specific articles above the 'normal' rates of duty. These increases may be retaliatory tariffs or tariff increases for import relief (safeguard actions).

ADDITIONAL TAXES, CHARGES AND FEES

Fixed charges, special levies and other duties

Fixed charges, special levies and other duties (excluding tariffs) include additional fiscal charges and service charges, which can be *ad valorem* (on the basis of the value declared by the importer or derived from standard customs valuation procedures), specific or combined. These charges have the net effect of increasing the domestic price of imported articles, but no target price is set. A distinction is generally made between these charges and European variable import levies.

Domestic taxes levied on imports

Border tax adjustments and domestic taxes levied on imports at higher rates (on a comparable basis) than charged against domestic products or their substitutes. If imports are not subjected to special adverse treatment these measures are not included in the Data Base.

Variable levies

Variable levies are special charges imposed on imports of certain goods with the purpose of increasing their price to a domestic target price. Variable levies are entered in the Data Base for all tariff lines which are subject to them, even if the measure might not be in operation at a particular point of time (no levy will be collected when the international price of a given product is above its domestic target price). These measures are extensively applied to agricultural imports of the EEC and some EFTA countries (particularly Sweden). See Sampson and Yeats (1976; 1977) for analyses of their importance and incidence.

ANTI-DUMPING AND COUNTERVAILING DUTIES

Anti-dumping duties

Duties levied on certain goods originating in (a) specific trading partner(s) to offset the effects of dumping. Duty rates may be enterprise-specific (i.e., levied only on products from certain enterprises) or may be applied on a country-wide basis.

Countervailing duties

Countervailing duties are special charges levied on certain goods to offset the effect of any bounty or subsidy granted directly or indirectly on the manufacture, production or export of these goods. In most developed countries, a formal administrative process is generally required before these charges (and anti-dumping duties) can be applied.[2]

QUANTITATIVE RESTRICTIONS AND RESTRICTIVE LICENSING

These are measures intended to restrain the volume or value of imports of any particular good from all sources, or from specific sources of supply, either to a predetermined level (quotas) or through restrictive licensing. They are generally considered to have far more detrimental trade and welfare effects than tariffs (see Yeats, 1979, for a discussion of this point).

Prohibitions

Prohibitions can apply under all circumstances or may be dependent on certain conditions. In some countries there are widely applied prohibitions, but imports may be permitted in special cases. The suspension of the issuing of import licences in countries where licensing is required is recorded as a *de facto* import prohibition. In the case of conditional prohibitions, the import-ation of certain goods may be prohibited under certain circumstances, e.g. prohibition for certain use and prohibition except for certain purchasers.

Global quotas

Global quotas are restrictions, for a given period of time, of the quantity (or value) of imports of specific products originating in all foreign sources of supply. Global quotas can be unallocated, that is administered on a 'first come first served' basis, or allocated to suppliers.

Bilateral quotas

Bilateral quotas are restrictions on the quantity or value of imports of specific products originating in specified (country) foreign sources of supply.

Seasonal quota

These measures are restrictions on the quantity or value of imports of specific products, especially agricultural products, for a given period of the year.

Quota (Unspecified)

Restrictions on quantity and/or value of imports of specific products for a given period of time, the allocation of which is not specified clearly in national customs schedules.

Non-automatic licensing

This NTM involves requirements that, as a prior condition to importation, an approval must be given which is not granted freely or automatically (in terms of the GATT licensing code). Licensing which is known to be used to administer a quota is included in the Data Base under that category (i.e. quotas) only. There are two distinct categories of non-automatic licensing. First, non-automatic licensing not subject to specific conditions is used to restrain the volume of imports when quotas have not been fixed in advance, or used for unspecified purposes. The Data Base includes various terms used by different authorities to describe non-automatic licensing regimes, such as discretionary licensing or liberal licensing.[3] Second, non-automatic licensing subject to specific conditions is licensing which is intended to ensure that certain specific conditions are met – for example, minimum export perform-ance, authorised use of the imported goods or purchase of domestic pro-ducts.

Import authorisations

These measures are non-automatic import certifications (authorisations) to be issued by a special agency such as a specific ministry. Their economic effects are generally similar to non-automatic import authorisation regu-lations.

'Voluntary' export restraints (VERs)

VERs are informal agreements between an exporter and an importer whereby the former agrees to limit, for a certain period of time, the exports of certain goods to the market of the importer to avoid the imposition of formal import restrictions. Although the restraints are administered by the exporter, VERs are included in the Data Base as NTMs applied by the importer, as the restrictions are imposed on the exporter by the importer. For various reasons (see Chapter 2) it is felt that the Data Base understates the number of VERs actually applied.

Orderly marketing arrangements

'Voluntary' export restraint agreements, other than textiles, concluded at the government level, are sometimes referred to as 'orderly marketing arrange-ments' or OMAs. Their economic effects are probably similar to those of VERs.

Multi-fibre arrangement (MFA)

The MFA, under its formal name the Arrangement Regarding International Trade in Textiles, was negotiated as a temporary exception to the GATT in 1973, and renewed three times since then, to provide for special rules governing trade in textiles and clothing. Governmental actions that can be taken under the Arrangement comprise mainly quantitative restrictions on imports of particular products from particular sources, which may take the form of import quotas or 'voluntary' export restraints implemented by the exporting country.

MFA restraint agreements

These are bilateral arrangements under the MFA which set quantitative restrictions for certain textile categories, while remaining articles are subject to consultation provisions.

MFA quota

Quantitative restriction, to a preset level, established for certain textile articles through bilateral agreement under the MFA. They include bilateral agreements under the MFA which have not set quantitative restraints at the moment of its signature, but which includes provisions for consultation with a view to introducing quantitative restrictions under certain circumstances.

MFA administrative co-operation agreement

These NTMs are arrangements between two MFA signatories, which provides for administrative co-operation with a view to avoiding disruptions in bilateral textile trade.

Other textile agreements

Agreements regarding trade in textiles between an importer and an exporter, the latter not being a signatory of the MFA. The specific measures under these agreements are recorded in the same way as MFA agreements.

Quantitative restrictions, unspecified

Quantitative restriction, the method of which (e.g. quota or non-automatic licensing) is not specified. These entries are often made when national customs documents fail to clearly indicate the nature of a quantitative restriction.

AUTOMATIC LICENSING AND IMPORT SURVEILLANCE

Automatic licensing

In the Data Base, automatic licensing is recorded where it is applied in a way consistent with its definition in the provisions of the GATT licensing code.

Import surveillance

Monitoring of imports, generally through the issuance of automatic licences. There are several codes used to reflect the terms used by the authorities to describe their surveillance systems, such as surveillance licence, monitoring, retrospective surveillance and community surveillance. In GATT and UNCTAD there has been considerable controversy about whether or not these NTMs have trade restrictive effects.

MONEY AND FINANCE MEASURES

These general measures are regulations and practices which may increase the financial costs of imports or restrain access to foreign exchange for import purposes.

Advance payment requirements

These measures take two forms. Import deposits are obligations to deposit some proportion of the value of imports for a given time-period in advance of the imports, with no allowance for interest on the deposit. Advance payments of customs duties are requirements that tariffs and other duties be paid in advance with no allowance made for interest to be accrued.

Regulations on the terms of payment of imports

These NTMs are special regulations regarding the terms of payments of imports and the obtaining and use of credit (foreign or domestic) to finance imports.

CONTROL OF THE PRICE LEVEL

Minimum pricing

Decreed target price for imported articles. Actual import prices below the minimum price may trigger action in the form of compensatory duties or price investigations when the actual import price falls below the target price. The Data Base includes different terms used by relevant authorities to describe systems of minimum pricing, such as minimum import price, reference import price, and basic import price.

'Voluntary' export price restraint

This is an undertaking by an exporter, accepted by the authorities in the importing country, to take actions which neutralise price effects of subsidies and/or dumping so that countervailing duty and/or anti-dumping actions will be suspended.

Price investigations

These actions generally attempt to determine whether imported articles are offered at allegedly unfair low prices due to subsidisation by foreign governments or because of dumping. If affirmative, the agency in charge of the investigation must also determine the subsidy or dumping margin. The price investigations are normally complemented with an investigation to determine whether domestic industry is injured through losses of sales due to underpricing of subsidised or dumped imports.

Anti-dumping investigation

An investigation to determine whether imported articles are offered at less than their fair value due to dual price policies of foreign firms. Their economic effects are thought to closely parallel those of 'price investigations'.

Countervailing duty investigation

An investigation to determine whether imported articles are underpriced relative to similar domestically produced goods as a result of subsidies granted by foreign governments.

Price surveillance

Surveillance of import prices. These actions can be intended to ensure that possible injury by low-priced, but not subsidised or dumped, imports is detected at an early stage.

SINGLE CHANNEL FOR IMPORTS

Government actions which may result in trade distortions, such as state monopolies and government-sanctioned private monopolies and exclusive transport and/or insurance. Such measures are often applied by the socialist countries of Eastern Europe.

State monopoly of imports

Under this measure, exclusive rights to import are granted to a state agency.

Sole importing agency

This measure involves government-sanctioned exclusive rights to import certain commodities. The right may be granted to either a government-controlled or private agency.

OTHER IMPORT MEASURES AND MISCELLANEOUS REGULATIONS

Special entry procedures

Special administrative procedures applied to imports as a condition for entry into the domestic market. They may involve carriage by the national fleet of the importing country, or entry through a specific port or customs station.

Additional customs formalities

Formalities other than those normally required by customs administrations for the clearance of imports.

Customs valuation procedures

Use of decreed price, rather than the invoice or transaction price, as a basis for the calculation of import duties to be levied on products subject to '*ad valorem*' duty rates.

Standards and regulations

Technical regulations and standards to be met by products for sale on the domestic market. The requirements apply, in principle, both to imports and to domestically produced goods. The principle Data Base entries are: technical standards; health, sanitary and safety regulations; and marketing and packaging requirements.

Measures to assist domestic industries

Measures which may distort international trade flows by providing assistance to import competing industries. Only such measures applied at the border are currently included in the Data Base.

Local content requirements

These NTNs involve the requirement that an imported product should have a minimum domestic or local content (the value added or the proportion that has been domestically or locally produced).

Appendix 5: The Punta del Este Ministerial Declaration

Meeting in Punta del Este (Uruguay) from 15–20 September on the occasion of the special session of the GATT Contracting Parties, ministers of GATT member countries adopted a Declaration launching a new round of multilateral trade negotiations – the Uruguay Round. The Declaration falls into two parts.

As contracting parties, the ministers adopted Part I of the declaration regarding trade in goods. It establishes the objectives and principles of the negotiations, and the launch of issues on which negotiations will take place. The Declaration provides for a standstill and rollback on trade restrictive or trade distortive measures under which governments undertake not to increase existing levels of protection and to phase out their existing breaches of GATT disciplines.

As representatives of governments meeting on the occasion of the Session, the ministers further decided to launch a negotiation on trade in services, and adopted Part II of the Declaration in that regard. It has been agreed that these negotiations will not be placed within the legal framework of GATT, but that GATT practices and procedures will nevertheless apply to them.

Ministers then adopted the Ministerial Declaration as a whole as a single policy commitment launching the Uruguay Round. The negotiations are to extend over four years.

Ministerial Declaration on the Uruguay Round

Ministers, meeting on the occasion of the Special Session of Contracting Parties at Punta del Este, have decided to launch Multilateral Trade Negotiations (The Uruguay Round). To this end, they have adopted the following Declaration. The Multilateral Trade Negotiations (MTN) will be open to the participation of countries as indicated in Parts I and II of this Declaration. A Trade Negotiations Committee (TNC) is established to carry out the Negotiations. The Trade Negotiations Committee shall hold its first meeting not later than 31 October 1986. It shall meet as appropriate at Ministerial level. The Multilateral Trade Negotiations wil be concluded within four years.

Part I – Negotiations on trade in goods

The Contracting Parties meeting at Ministerial level
Determined to halt and revise protectionism and to remove distortions to trade

Reprinted from GATT *Focus*, 8 October 1986.

Determined also to preserve the basic principles and to further the objectives of the GATT

Determined also to develop a more open, viable and durable multilateral trading system

Convinced that such action would promote growth and development

Mindful of the negative effects of prolonged financial and monetary instability in the world economy, the indebtedness of a large number of less-developed contracting parties, and considering the linkage between trade, money, finance and development

Decide to enter into Multilateral Trade Negotiations on trade in goods within the framework and under the aegis of the General Agreement on Tariffs and Trade.

A. Objectives

Negotiations shall aim to

(i) bring about further liberalization and expansion of world trade to the benefit of all countries, especially less-developed contracting parties, including the improvement of access to markets by the reduction and elimination of tariffs, quantitative restrictions and other non-tariff measures and obstacles;

(ii) strengthen the role of GATT, improve the multilateral trading system based on the principles and rules of the GATT and bring about a wider coverage of world trade under agreed, effective and enforceable multilateral disciplines;

(iii) increase the responsiveness of the GATT system to the evolving international economic environment, through facilitating necessary structural adjustment, enhancing the relationship of the GATT with the relevant international organizations and taking account of changes in trade patterns and prospects, including the growing importance of trade in high technology products, serious difficulties in commodity markets and the importance of an improved trading environment providing, inter alia, for the ability of indebted countries to meet their financial obligations;

(iv) foster concurrent co-operative action at the national and international levels to strengthen the inter-relationship between trade policies and other economic policies affecting growth and development, and to contribute towards continued, effective and determined efforts to improve the functioning of the international monetary system and the flow of financial and real investment resources to developing countries.

B. General principles governing negotiations

(i) Negotiations shall be conducted in a transparent manner, and consistent with the objectives and commitments agreed in this Declaration and with the principles of the General Agreement in order to ensure mutual advantage and increased benefits to all participants.

(ii) The launching, the conduct and the implementation of the outcome of the negotiations shall be treated as parts of a single undertaking. However, agreements reached at an early stage may be implemented on a provisional or a definitive basis by agreement prior to the formal conclusion of the negotiations. Early agreements shall be taken into account in assessing the overall balance of the negotiations.

(iii) Balanced concessions should be sought within broad trading areas and subjects to be negotiated in order to avoid unwarranted cross-sectoral demands.

(iv) Contracting Parties agree that the principle of Differential and More Favourable Treatment embodied in Part IV and other relevant provisions of the General Agreement and in the Decision of the Contracting Parties of 28 November 1979 on Differential and More Favourable Treatment, Reciprocity and Fuller Participation of Developing Countries applies to the negotiations. In the implementation of standstill and rollback, particular care should be given to avoiding disruptive effects on the trade of less-developed contracting parties.

(v) The developed countries do not expect reciprocity for commitments made by them in trade negotiations to reduce or remove tariffs and other barriers to the trade of developing countries, i.e. the developed countries do not expect the developing countries, in the course of trade negotiations, to make contributions which are inconsistent with their individual development, financial and trade needs. Developed contracting parties shall therefore not seek, neither shall less-developed contracting parties be required to make, concessions that are inconsistent with the latter's development, financial and trade needs.

(vi) Less-developed contracting parties expect that their capacity to make contributions or negotiated concessions or take other mutually agreed action under the provisions and procedures of the general agreement would improve with the progressive development of their economies and improvement in their trade situation and they would accordingly expect to participate more fully in the framework of rights and obligations under the General Agreement.

(vii) Special attention shall be given to the particular situation and problems of the least-developed countries and to the need to encourage positive measures to facilitate expansion of their trading opportunities. Expeditious implementation of the relevant provisions of the 1982 Ministerial Declaration concerning the least-developed countries shall also be given appropriate attention.

C. Standstill and rollback

Commencing immediately and continuing until the formal completion of the Negotiations, each participant agrees to apply the following commitments:

Standstill

(i) not to take any trade restrictive or distorting measure inconsistent with the provisions of the General Agreement or the Instruments negotiated within the framework of GATT or under its auspices;

(ii) not to take any trade restrictive or distorting measure in the legitimate exercise of its GATT rights, that would go beyond that which is necessary to remedy specific situations, as provided for in the General Agreement and the Instruments referred to in (i) above;

(iii) not to take any trade measures in such a manner as to improve its negotiating positions.

Rollback

(i) that all trade restrictive or distorting measures inconsistent with the provisions of the General Agreement or Instruments negotiated within the framework of GATT or under its auspices, shall be phased out or brought into conformity within an agreed timeframe not later than by the date of the formal completion off the negotiations, taking into account multilateral agreements, undertakings and understandings, including strengthened rules and disciplines, reached in pursuance of the Objectives of the Negotiations;

(ii) there shall be progressive implementation of this commitment on an equitable basis in consultations among participants concerned, including all affected participants. This commitment shall take account of the concerns expressed by any participant about measures directly affecting its trade interests;

(iii) there shall be no GATT concessions requested for the elimination of these measures.

Surveillance of standstill and rollback

Each participant agrees that the implementation of these commitments on standstill and rollback shall be subject to multilateral surveillance so as to ensure that these commitments are being met. The Trade Negotiations Committee will decide on the appropriate mechanisms to carry out the surveillance, including periodic reviews and evaluations. Any participant may bring to the attention of the appropriate surveillance mechanism any actions or omissions it believes to be relevant to the fulfilment of these commitments. These notifications should be addressed to the GATT secretariat which may also provide further relevant information.

D. Subjects for negotiations

Tariffs

Negotiations shall aim, by appropriate methods, to reduce or, as appropriate, eliminate tariffs including the reduction or elimination of high tariff and tariff escalation. Emphasis shall be given to the expansion of the scope of tariff concessions among all participants.

Nontariff measures

Negotiations shall aim to reduce or eliminate non-tariff measures, including quantitative restrictions, without prejudice to any action to be taken in fulfilment of the rollback commitments.

Tropical products

Negotiations shall aim at the fullest liberalization of trade in tropical products, including in their processed and semi-processed forms and shall cover both tariff and all non-tariff measures affecting trade in these products.

Contracting Parties recognize the importance of trade in tropical products to a large number of less-developed contracting parties and agree that negotiations in this area shall receive special attention, including the timing of the negotiations and the implementation of the results as provided in B(ii).

Natural resource-based products

Negotiations shall aim to achieve the fullest liberalization of trade in natural resource-based products, including in their processed and semi-processed forms. The negotiations shall aim to reduce or eliminate tariff and non-tariff measures, including tariff escalation.

Textiles and clothing

Negotiations in the area of textiles and clothing shall aim to formulate modalities that would permit the eventual integration of this sector into GATT on the basis of strengthened GATT rules and disciplines, thereby also contributing to the objective of further liberalization of trade.

Agriculture

Contracting Parties agree that there is an urgent need to bring more discipline and predictability to world agricultural trade by correcting and preventing restrictions and distortions including those related to structural surpluses so as to reduce the uncertainty, imbalances and instability in world agricultural markets. Negotiations shall aim to achieve greater liberalization of trade in agriculture and bring all measures affecting import access and export competition under strengthened and more operationally effective GATT rules and disciplines, taking into account the general principles governing the negotiations, by:

(i) improving market access through, inter alia, the reduction of import barriers;

(ii) improving the competitive environment by increasing discipline on the use of all direct and indirect subsidies and other measures affecting directly or indirectly agricultural trade, including the phased reduction of their negative effects and dealing with their causes;

(iii) minimizing the adverse effects that sanitary and phytosanitary regulations and barriers can have on trade in agriculture, taking into account the relevant international agreements.

In order to achieve the above objectives, the negotiating group having primary responsibility for all aspects of agriculture will use the Recommendations adopted by the Contracting Parties at their Fortieth Session, which were developed in accordance with the GATT 1982 Ministerial Programme and take account of the approaches suggested in the work of the Committee on Trade in Agriculture without prejudice to other alternative that might achieve the objectives of the Negotiations.

GATT Articles

Participants shall review existing GATT articles, provisions and disciplines as requested by interested contracting parties and, as appropriate, undertake negotiations.

Safeguards

(i) A comprehensive agreement on safeguards is of particular importance to the strengthening of the GATT system and to progress in the MTNs.

(ii) The agreement on safeguards:

-shall be based on the basic principles of the General Agreement;

-shall contain, inter alia, the following elements: transparency, coverage, objective criteria for action including the concept of serious injury or threat thereof, temporary nature, degressivity, and structural adjustment, compensation and retaliation, notifications, consultation, multilateral surveillance and dispute settlement; and

-shall clarify and reinforce the disciplines of the General Agreement and should apply to all contracting parties.

MTN agreements and arrangements
Negotiations shall aim to improve, clarify, or expand, as appropriate, agreements and arrangements negotiated in the Tokyo Round of multilateral negotiations.

Subsidies and countervailing measures
Negotiations on subsidies and countervailing measures shall be based on a review of Articles VI and XVI and the MTN agreement on subsidies and countervailing measures with the objective of improving GATT disciplines relating to all subsidies and countervailing measures that affect international trade. A negotiating group will be established to deal with these issues.

Dispute settlement
In order to ensure prompt and effective resolution of disputes to the benefit of all contracting parties, negotiations shall aim to improve and strengthen the rules and then procedures of the dispute settlement processs, while recognizing the contribution that would be made by more effective and enforceable GATT rules and disciplines. Negotiations shall include the development of adequate arrangements for overseeing and monitoring of the procedures that would facilitate compliance with adopted recommendations.

Trade-related aspects of intellectual property rights, including trade in counterfeit goods
In order to reduce the distortions and impediments to international trade, and taking into account the need to promote effective and adequate protection of intellectual property rights, and to ensure that measures and procedures to enforce intellectual property rights do not themselves become barriers to legitimate trade, the negotiations shall aim to clarify GATT provisions and elaborate as appropriate new rules and disciplines. Negotiations shall aim to develop a multilateral framework of principles, rules and disciplines dealing with international trade in counterfeit goods, taking into account work already undertaken in the GATT.

These negotiations shall be without prejudice to other complementary initiatives that may be taken in the World Intellectual Property Organization and elsewhere to deal with these matters.

Trade-related investment measures
Following an examination of the operation of GATT articles related to the trade restrictive and distorting effects of investment measures, negotiations should elaborate, as appropriate, further provisions that may be necessary to avoid such adverse effects on trade.

E. Functioning of the GATT system
Negotiations shall aim to develop understandings and arrangements:
(i) to enhance the surveillance in the GATT to enable regular monitoring of trade policies and practices of contracting parties and their impact on the functioning of the multilateral trading system;
(ii) to improve the overall effectiveness and decision-making of the GATT as an institution, including, inter alia, through involvement of Ministers;
(iii) to increase the contribution of the GATT to achieving greater coherence in global economic policy-making through strengthening its relationship with other international organizations responsible for monetary and financial matters.

F. Participation
(a) Negotiations will be open to:
(1) all contracting parties
(2) countries having acceded provisionally,
(3) countries applying the GATT on a de facto basis having announced, not later than 30 April 1987, their intention to accede to GATT and to participate in the negotiations,
(4) countries that have already informed the Contracting Parties, at a regular meeting of the Council of Representatives of their intention to negotiate the terms of their membership as a contracting party, and
(5) developing countries that have, by 30 April 1987, initiated procedures for accession to the GATT, with the intention of negotiating the terms of their accession during the course of the negotiations.
(b) Participation in negotiations relating to the amendment or application of GATT provisions or the negotiations of new provisions will, however, be open only to contracting parties.

G. Organization of the negotiations
A Group of Negotiations on Goods (GNG) is established to carry out the programme of negotiations contained in this Part of the Declaration. The GNG shall, inter alia:
(i) elaborate and put into effect detailed trade negotiating plans prior to 19 December 1986;
(ii) designate the appropriate mechanism for surveillance of commitments to standstill and rollback;
(iii) establish negotiating groups as required. Because of the interrelationship of some issues and taking fully into account the general principles governing the negotiations as stated in B(iii) above it is recognized that aspects of one issue may be discussed in more than one negotiating group. Therefore each negotiating group should as required take into account relevant aspects emerging in other groups;
(iv) also decide upon inclusion of additional subject matters in the negotiations;
(v) coordinate the work of the negotiating groups and supervise the progress of the negotiations. As a guideline not more than two negotiating groups should meet at the same time;
(vi) the GNG shall report to the Trade Negotiations Committee.
In order to ensure effective application of differential and more favourable treatment the GNG shall, before the formal completion of the negotiations, conduct an evaluation of the results attained therein in terms of the Objectives and General Principles Governing Negotiations as set out in the Declaration, taking into account all issues of interest to less-developed contracting parties.

Part II – Negotiations on trade in services

Ministers also decided, as part of the Multilateral Trade Negotiations, to launch negotiations on trade in services. Negotiations in this area shall aim to establish a multilateral framework of principles and rules for trade in services, including elaboration of possible disciplines for individual sectors, with a view to expansion of such trade under conditions of transparency and progressive liberalization and as a means of promoting economic growth of all trading partners and the development of developing countries. Such framework shall respect the policy objectives of national laws and regulations applying to services and shall take into account the work of relevant international organizations.

GATT procedures and practices shall apply to these negotiations. A Group on Negotiations on Services is established to deal with these matters. Participation in the negotiations under this Part of the Declaration will be open to the same countries as under Part I. GATT secretariat support will be provided, with technical support from other organizations as decided by the Group of Negotiations on Services.

The Group of Negotiations on Services shall report to the Trade Negotiations Committee.

Implementation of results under Parts I and II

When the results of the Multilateral Trade Negotiations in all areas have been established, Ministers meeting also on the occasion of a Special Session of Contracting Parties shall decide regarding the international implementation of the respective results.

Notes

Chapter 1 Policy Issues Involving Nontariff Trade Barriers

1. The MFN principle guarantees equal treatment to a country's trading partners and requires that concessions negotiated on a bilateral basis be extended to all GATT members. It also prohibits discrimination or differential treatment of GATT members. See Evans (1971) for an early preceptive analysis of the problems posed by NTBs and departures from the MFN principle. Lloyd (1974) also argues that nontariff barriers are an important factor dividing the world economy into trading blocks which increase the danger of trade wars. The Commonwealth Secretariat (1982) provides a comprehensive analysis and policy discussion of the adverse consequences of an increasing resort to nontariff protection.

2. Nontariff barriers authorised under GATT provisions may take several forms. First, the GATT's 'grandfather clause' (The Protocol of Provisional Application) permits countries acceding to the General Agreement to continue pre-existing practices and trade restrictions. Second, international trade in textiles is regulated by the Multifibre Arrangement which was negotiated under the auspices of GATT. This arrangement sets limits on the permissible volume of textile exports from developing to developed countries. GATT provisions also allow quantitative restrictions for balance-of-payments problems and for agriculture, but it was intended that they should be used infrequently.

3. In contrast, information on nominal tariff rates are readily available from national customs schedules. Prior to the Kennedy and Tokyo Round, GATT compiled detailed records on member countries' tariff schedules and made these records available to all states participating in the negotiations. In this effort, several technical problems were encountered. First, there was the problem of how to achieve data comparability, as some countries like the United States, Canada and Australia apply tariffs to the f.o.b. value of imports while others like the EEC and Japan employ a c.i.f. valuation base. Specific tariffs (i.e. those expressed as a fixed charge per unit of import) also caused problems since their incidence or nominal equivalents may vary considerably for different countries exporting a specific product. See Yeats (1976) for empirical information relating to this point.

4. A growing number of studies indicate many policy objectives of NTBs could be achieved by alternative instruments that have less onerous national and international effects. For example, after a detailed analysis of agricultural trade barriers in developed countries UNCTAD (1983) concluded that

> the specific national policies adopted to achieve certain goals are far from optimal from either a national or international standpoint. In part, this may be due to a failure to consider international responsi-

260

bilities when adopting national policies. It may also be due to a failure to adopt domestic policies that have clear and consistent long-term objectives. That the policies being pursued are not the most efficient is apparent when one considers some of their serious adverse effects. These include: (i) greater instability in world agricultural markets; (ii) welfare losses due to the misallocation of both domestic and international resources; (iii) displacement of traditional suppliers in third markets; (iv) adverse price and consumption effects in both producing and consuming countries; and (v) lower prices and foreign exchange earnings for agricultural exporters.

The UNCTAD report advocated the adoption of selective income maintenance schemes to replace many of the non-selective price support programmes as a means of improving transparency and also reducing the protectionist measures' most harmful effects.

5. Incentives for shifting from primary to processed exports include: employment creation associated with the processing function, greater stability in export earnings due to less volatile prices for processed commodities, the realisation of linkage effects between the processing industry and other sectors of the economy, and learning effects associated with the processing and export of fabricated goods. Since further processing often extends the useful lifetime of most food products, it is viewed as a way of reducing food spoilage in developing countries. For a more complete discussion of the potential advantages and constraints to commodity processing in developing countries, see Roemer (1979).

6. GATT provisions (article VII, 1(a)) require that the dutiable value of a product 'should be based on the actual value of the imported merchandise or like merchandise, and should not be based on the value of merchandise of national origin or on arbitrary or fictitious values'. However, under the American Selling Price system tariffs on US imports of benzenoid chemicals, rubber footwear, canned clams and low-value knitted woollen gloves were assessed on the value of domestically produced equivalent goods. Since US production costs for these items were generally far higher than foreign producers this resulted in tariffs of over 170 per cent on the actual import value of some products.

7. The Punta del Este (Uruguay Round) Declaration (see Appendix 5 in this book) established specific objectives for liberalising agricultural nontariff barriers in stating 'contracting parties agree that there is an urgent need to bring more discipline and predictability to world agricultural trade by correcting and preventing restrictions and distortions including those related to structural surpluses so as to reduce the uncertainty, imbalances and instability in world agricultural markets'. As far as NTBs are generally concerned, the Uruguay Round Declaration states 'negotiations shall aim to reduce or eliminate nontariff measures, including quantitative restrictions, without prejudice to any action to be taken in fulfilment of the rollback commitments'. Olechowski (1987) provides a useful analysis of NTB policy issues that need to be addressed in the negotiations.

8. See Stern (1976) for a discussion of these approaches. Essentially they

project the trade response to a tariff cut through the use of a partial equilibrium model where the trade change is a multiplicative function of the initial level of imports, the import demand elasticity for the products, and the percentage change in the tariff rate. See Chapter 3 in this book for a description of such a model and how it may be used for policy studies. If *ad valorem* equivalents were available, similar approaches could be employed for simulating the effects of a nontariff barrier liberalisation.

9. In the Tokyo Round, several general formulae were considered for an across-the-board reduction in tariffs. One of the simplest achieved a linear cut in which all tariffs are lowered by the same percentage. If T_0 is the initial tariff rate and T_1 is the duty after the cut this formula can be represented by:

$$T_1 = \alpha T_0, \tag{1.1}$$

where $(1 - \alpha)$ indicates the percentage reduction in duties and α is a constant between zero and one. As alternatives, several proposals sought to achieve tariff harmonisation (that is, to have the highest tariffs experience the largest percentage cuts). Here, a Swiss proposal was considered and generally applied:

$$T_1 = \alpha \, T_0 / (\alpha + T_0). \tag{1.2}$$

The formulae was intended to significantly reduce tariff disparities between countries and industries. For example, on the basis of a proposed coefficient (α) of 16, an initial tariff of 10 per cent would be reduced to $(16 \times 10)/(16 + 10)$, or to about 6.15 per cent. A higher tariff would be reduced by a greater proportion, a lower tariff by a smaller one. For a more detailed analysis of the tariff-cutting formulae that were proposed during the Tokyo Round, see Laird and Yeats (1987b).

10. If a nontariff barrier (say a quota) is applied in a market where trade was formerly unrestricted, the domestic price will rise from a free trade level (p_d) to some higher level ($p_d{}^*$). The difference between the two ($p_d{}^* - p_d$) will accrue to exporters or importers in the form of 'rents' with their respective proportions determined by factors like relative bargaining power or how the quota is administered. In cases where exporters secure the rents, they would logically work against a conversion to tariffs unless compensation were offered. See Chapter 2 for a more complete analysis of the rent-creating effects of nontariff barriers.

11. In United Nation debates, the socialist countries argue that they should not be expected to match the trade performance of the developed market economy countries since they have not had colonial relationships, which are taken to foster trade. If one accepts this line of reasoning, it would be best to choose countries like Norway, Finland, Sweden and Denmark as the control group since they have not had colonies. According to Yeats (1982), if the SCEEs matched the Scandinavian countries' imports per capita or imports relative to GDP this would increase their imports from developing countries by between $3 to $5 billion per year.

Chapter 2   Quantitative Approaches to Trade-Barrier Analysis

1. Lloyd (1974, p. 201) proposed the following definition which would include a somewhat different subset of measures from Ingo Walter's approach:

   > nontariff barriers is an omnibus term for the set of government policy instruments and practices which operate directly, or sometimes only incidentally, to restrain imports or distort exports. It is conventional to exclude from the broad meaning of the term only exchange rate changes and other monetary and fiscal measures which affect all export and import-competing goods and are designed, moreover, to maintain external balance rather than to give selective protection.

2. For details concerning the classification schemes and applications in tabulating statistics on nontariff measures, see UNCTAD (1983a). UNCTAD's attempts at quantification show that the determination of the precise effects of any nontariff measure at any point in time, or in any country, can be extremely difficult. This has led UNCTAD to put the emphasis in its policy analysis on nontariff measures, without entering into judgements as to whether any particular measure is operating as a barrier. In cases, measures in certain countries do not always operate with restrictive effects, but in other countries the same measures are applied in a way that they restrict trade.

3. A logical extension would be to collect information from exporters on measures they perceive to affect trade and cross-check this with information compiled from official government sources. The US Tariff Commission experimented with this approach during the Tokyo Round but concluded that exporters had difficulties in identifying many nontariff measures affecting their trade, and in cases reported measures that had non-discriminatory effects on foreign and domestic producers. Still the approach was useful in identifying restrictions like 'voluntary' export restraints that are often not recorded in official GATT or national sources. For a full account see US Tariff Commission (1974).

4. This measure suffers from the familiar problem of any 'own' trade-weighted index in that products facing very restrictive NTMs will enter the calculation with zero or low weights. The index is, therefore, downward biased in that it fails to properly account for the most restrictive trade measures. An alternative to weighting nontariff measures by a country's own imports would be to employ OECD trade weights. Such an index is defined by,

$$O_j = (M_{r;w} \div M_{j;w}) \times 100 \tag{2.3}$$

where $Mr{:}w$ represents the sum of OECD imports to which the country applies its NTMs, while $Mj{:}w$ indicates total OECD imports of commodity group j. This index can be biased since the same sectors in OECD countries (e.g. agriculture, ferrous metals, textiles, clothing, etc.) generally have the highest levels of NTM protection.

5. These indices can be computed for any single measure or subgroup of NTMs in the Data Base. For example, many previous analyses that utilised equations (2.1) and (2.2) focused on the following nontariff measures: variable import levies and product-specific charges; quotas; prohibitions; non-automatic import authorisations; 'voluntary' export restraints (VERs); and trade restraints under the Multifibre Arrangement. These NTMs are included in the coverage and frequency ratios in Table 2.2.

6. Up to 1985 the United States maintained an import licensing and surveillance system for energy imports. Although there is no evidence that the system was used to distort trade, licensing regulations have been employed in other countries for this purpose, i.e., they operate as barriers and not measures. This example underscores a basic problem with the inventory approach, e.g. that some included measures may not restrain trade. They have been included since they can have trade distorting effects depending on how they are applied. Other cases where a related problem may arise include unfilled quotas, variable levies for products where the world price is above the domestic target price, or state trading systems where there is no bias against foreign suppliers.

7. Apart from its records on NTMs, UNCTAD maintains extensive files on tariffs in developed and developing countries. These computerised files, available at the tariff line, record the pre- and post-Tokyo Round MFN tariff rates, generalised system of preference (GSP), Lome Convention or other special preferential tariff rates (including EFTA-EEC preferences). In cases where some exports face 'general' tariffs that are above MFN rates, such as the USSR's exports to the United States, these duties are also recorded. Specific tariffs have been converted to *ad valorem* equivalents by taking their ratio to the average unit value of all products in the tariff line (see Yeats, 1976, for discussion of the potential biases in this approach). Finally, the UNCTAD records also indicate whether the tariff is legally bound under provisions of GATT or if it has some other contractual status.

8. In Figure 2.1a, a variable import levy has the same effect although it operates in reverse fashion to a quota. While the latter fixes the permissible quantity of imports a variable levy fixes their permissible price. If this target price is P_r, and world prices fall below this level, the levy will constantly fluctuate to keep landed prices of the foreign good at P_r. As such, no matter how far world prices fall the quantity of imports would not increase above O_r. If the world price of the good falls to P_b then P_bP_r is the variable levy which represents a premium that will be collected by the importer, exporter or government depending on how the system is administered.

9. While it may be argued that barriers causing equal percentage reductions in imports are equivalent, this need not be the case when viewed from the exporter's side. Holzman notes that it is necessary to evaluate the barrier for its impact on world trade. For example, France typically imports about 25 times as much cocoa as Greece, so any given percentage reduction in imports by both countries involves an absolute reduction by France 25 times larger than by Greece. From the point of

view of world trade in cocoa, the French barrier is much more significant. If the French and Greek barriers reduced trade in cocoa by 10 per cent, 9.6 per cent of the decline in trade would be attributed to France and only 0.4 per cent to Greece.

10. Quantification of other nontariff-barrier effects may also be a key concern. For example, NTBs may cause trade to be diverted to alternative markets and lead to disruption there. There is some evidence that US restrictions in the 1980s against Japan caused exports to be diverted to the EEC, and it would be useful to develop quantitative measures of such diversion. There would also be considerable utility in developing measures of 'uncertainty' for NTBs. Indeed, some practices have been identified as NTBs almost entirely because of the uncertainties that they cause traders. Deardorff and Stern (1985) suggest that much of the NTB negotiating effort in the Tokyo Round was devoted not so much to preventing certain actions by governments, but regularising them so that traders would know what they had to contend with. Even barriers which are clearly restrictive, however, can become more so if their implementation is uncertain. For example, a quota which may appear to be non-binding may be quite restrictive if potential traders fail to fill it because of uncertainty as to who is entitled to import. Specially designed surveys of exporters' problems may be a useful way of gathering empirical information on the 'uncertainty' aspects of NTBs' application. Olechowski and Yeats (1982) also develop an 'uncertainty measure' for the potential spread of NTBs that warrants further testing (see Chapter 5 for details).

11. See the studies by Saxon and Anderson (1982), Pryor (1966), Cline *et al.* (1978) and the UN Food and Agricultural Organization (1987) for examples of investigations that have employed this approach. Figure 2.1 suggests that there would be merit in also defining equations (2.4) and (2.5) in terms of the 'free trade' import price (P_0), that is,

$$R_p' = (P_r \div E_{xi}P_0) \times 100 \tag{2.4'}$$

$$T_e' = ((P_r \div E_{xi}P_0) - 1) \times 100 \tag{2.5'}$$

However, the problem connected with this measure is to derive meaningful estimates for P_0. Except when the export supply curve is perfectly elastic Figure 2.1 shows that these price impact measures will always take smaller values than those derived from equations (2.4) and (2.5).

12. In general, it may be assumed that transactions are denominated in the exporting country's currency, and there is considerable supporting empirical evidence. For example, Grassman (1973) concluded that 'empirical evidence for countries where data on actual currency of foreign transactions are available show that most transactions are settled in the seller's currency' and provided empirical information in support of this point. The same conclusion was reached in an IMF (1982) survey which also found (p. 31) that 'the additional uncertainties arising from recent fluctuations in exchange rates have strengthened the preferences of exporters for using their own domestic currencies for trade invoicing and payment'.

13. Data collected in surveys on international living costs, like those conducted annually by management consulting firms such as Business International, are useful for the analysis of NTBs in that they employ a specification pricing approach. That is, the characteristics of the products are specified in detail before price collection starts. This should hold the influence of quality or product variations on prices to a minimum. For an illustration of how data drawn from such a survey can be employed to estimate price impact measures for nontariff barriers, see Roningen and Yeats (1976).

14. The basic data employed in this analysis were drawn from a 'specification' price survey undertaken by the firm Business International, so quality variations were assumed to have a minimum influence on observed price differences.

15. The international price comparison approach has been facilitated by the fact that a sizeable body of information on international transport costs became available in the 1970s and 1980s. For example, since 1973 the United States publishes the transport and insurance costs for imports (by country of origin) down to the level of the tariff line. Other countries like Australia, Brazil, Panama, Philippines, etc. now compile and publish similar information. For details on the available statistics, see Yeats (1981).

16. A quantity impact measure (M_q) could be defined in a way that corresponds directly to the NTB price impact measures. If Q_f and Q_r are the quantities imported under free trade and under the NTB, respectively, the following could be employed,

$$M_q = (Q_f - Q_r) \div Q_f \qquad (2.6)$$

Standardising the quantity difference $(Q_f - Q_r)$, i.e., dividing this term by variables such as population or gross national product, would also facilitate cross-country comparisons. As noted, the major difficulty associated with empirical estimation of quantity impact measures is to derive meaningful estimates for Q_f.

17. Expanded versions of equation (2.7) included explanatory terms such as: dummy variables taking a value of unity if special preferential trade arrangements existed between two countries and zero otherwise, a dummy variable for neighbouring countries which were expected to have more intense trade contacts, and a measure (the Gini Concentration Ratio) of the degree of diversification in each country's export structure. Illustrative examples of studies that tested gravity-flow trade models include Linnemann (1966) Tinbergen (1962) and Pulliainen (1963).

18. Since the general and specific restriction indices were only simple counts of the number of restrictions they do not reflect the severity or intensity with which the measures are applied. A second point is that the IMF sources provide a very incomplete tabulation of the restrictions used to control trade. As an example, Roningen's index for restrictions affecting trade regimes was based solely on three measures: import surcharges, advanced import deposits, and whether export earnings must be surrendered to the government. These measures constitute only a small part of

the types of restrictions that can influence trade regimes (see Table 2.1 for a broader listing). There would appear to be considerable merit in testing some of the more comprehensive indices shown in Chapter 4 in a model similar to that used by Roningen.

19. With textiles and clothing designated as the 'affected' group, Hamilton (1984a) employed all other manufacturers as the control group to analyse the influence of Swedish nontariff barriers on the rate of growth in imports of textile and clothing products. Using this procedure, it was possible to demonstrate that a major shift away from developing country imports occurred with this trade diverted to producers not affected by the NTBs.

20. Symbolically, equation (2.10), below, shows the target price is established at level k while equation (2.11) expresses the relation between the intervention and target price. Equation (2.12) indicates the threshold price equals the target price less internal EEC transport charges. The key to the system, equation (2.13), shows the variable levy fluctuates to maintain equality between world and EEC prices,

$$P_t = k, \tag{2.10}$$
$$(P_i - 0.1) \leq P_i \leq P_t \tag{2.11}$$
$$P_h = P_t - T_d, \tag{2.12}$$
$$L_i = P_t - (P_w + T_d) \tag{2.13}$$

where L_i can be greater than, less than or equal to zero. It should be noted (see Figure 2.1) that there are potentially important operational differences between variable import levies and quotas. If the demand curve for imports were to shift to the right, a quota would hold the quantity of imports constant while domestic price would increase. A variable import levy would hold the domestic price constant and permit the full increase in demand to be imported.

21. There are other ways a quota could be administered with each having different economic effects. Deardorff and Stern (1985) note that if the allocation is made on a political basis importing firms will have an incentive to bid for licences by lobbying or use other 'political' mechanisms. If the allocation is based on some economic criteria there is an incentive for firms to distort the factor used as an indicator. For example, if allocations are based on firms' size as measured by the book value of capital stocks, then the quota rents become part of their return to capital and firms have an incentive to over-invest. Or if allocations are on the basis of domestic sales, and if firms have access to a domestic source of supply, then they will expand their domestic supplies beyond even what would be indicated by the elevated domestic price in order to acquire larger quota rents. Numerous other examples could be given as to the types of distortions that would be created by alternative mechanisms of allocating the quota.

22. The extent to which such product 'upgrading' occurs within quantitative import restrictions has been documented in a number of empirical investigations. See, for example, Yan and Roberts (1986) or Feenstra (1985; 1988). In some cases, exporting-country governments actively

encouraged such upgrading. The Japanese government, for example, has allocated quotas on the basis of the price exporters charge for textile products and on the total value of a firm's textile exports, thereby penalising suppliers of low-price, low-quality goods.

23. For a description of these limit pricing models, see Scherer (1970) or Bain (1964). If the models are to be extended to analysis of nontariff barriers it will be necessary to distinguish between the threat of entry into an industry from (a) other domestic as opposed to (b) foreign firms which are affected by the restriction.

24. For example, the comparison used in the quota price approach is,

$$(P_2 - P_1) \div P_1 = (P_2 \div P_1) - 1. \tag{2.16}$$

while the 'true' implicit tariff is,

$$(P_2 - P_0) \div P_0 = (P_2 \div P_0) - 1. \tag{2.17}$$

Relating the two through inequalities,

$$P_2 \div P_1 \geqslant P_2 \div P_0 \tag{2.18}$$

since the above is equal to,

$$P_2 \div P_1 \geqslant P_2 \div (P_1 + P_0 P_1) \tag{2.19}$$

with $P_0 P_1$ being non-zero if input supply is not perfectly elastic.

25. An anti-dumping action is a specialised procedure intended to offset import prices that are lower than the prices the foreign seller charges in its domestic market. Similarly, a countervailing duty procedure is intended to offset a foreign subsidy on imports. See Finger (1987) for an analysis of the use of these procedures and a discussion of possible directions for change in GATT regulations concerning their use. Annex 8 in Finger and Olechowski (1987) provides detailed statistical information on the countries most often affected by these measures and those that most frequently resort to their use. Details are also provided on the final outcome of cases initiated over the period 1980–6. See Appendix 4 in this book for a glossary of terms relating to anti-dumping and countervailing duties as well as other nontariff measures.

26. Information on the imposition of anti-dumping duties is available from semi-annual reports submitted by the contracting parties to the GATT Committee on Anti-Dumping Practices, under Article 14:9 of the Agreement on Implementation of Article VI (the Anti-dumping Code), and to the Committee on Subsidies and Countervailing Measures under Article 2:16 of the Agreement on Interpretation and Application of Articles VI, XVI, and XXIII (the Subsidies Code). Relevant data, including information on actions not reported in the GATT submissions, were drawn from the following sources: the Official Journal of the European Communities, the United States Federal Register, the reports of the Trade Action Monitoring System of the Office of the United States Trade

Representative, and the Australian Customs Notice published by the Department of Industry and Commerce. See Olechowski and Finger (1987) pages 258–69 for additional details on the use of anti-dumping and countervailing duties over 1980–6.

27. Messerlin utilises an 'exposure' ratio in his analysis which is useful for analysing the initiation patterns of anti-dumping cases. This ratio is defined as the share of an exporting country in the number of cases initiated by an importing country divided by the share of exports of the exporting country in the total imports of the importing country. An exposure ratio equal to one means that a country share in anti-dumping actions corresponds exactly to its share in the imports of the country using anti-dumping procedures. If the ratio exceeds one it implies that the exporting countries is involved in a disproportionately high share of anti-dumping actions.

28. This approach is outlined more fully in Deardorff and Stern (1985). The estimated elasticity of import demand for product i in country $j(d_{ij})$ could be expressed as a function of m explanatory variables (X_1, X_2, X_m),

$$d_{ij} = f(X_1, X_2, \ldots X_m) \qquad (2.24)$$

and regression methods employed to fit the model with elasticity estimates drawn from existing surveys. (See, for example, Robert Stern *et al.*, 1976.) Projections from equation (2.24) could be compared with the estimates taken from the previously published sources, and those sectors where major differences occur 'flagged' for further analysis.

29. As an illustration, Glismann and Neu (1971) employed the following equation for German pottery imports from Japan which were subject to a changing bilateral quota,

$$\log Y = 1.2 - 0.45\log X_1 + 0.83\log X_2 \qquad (R^2. = 0.81) \qquad (2.25)$$

where Y was an index of import prices, X_1 is an index of quota levels, and X_2 was an index of domestic consumption of the product. A second regression employed the domestic wholesale price index as X_2,

$$\log Y = -3.2 - 0.58\log X_1 + 3.17\log X_2 \qquad (R^2. = 0.76) \qquad (2.26)$$

In the two regressions the quota-elasticity (i.e. the regression coefficient for X_1) hardly changed, while the influence of the ratio of domestic to import prices was higher than the influence of domestic consumption. The fact that quota elasticities indicate a decline in import prices as quotas are liberalised suggested that important 'rents' were associated with the restriction.

30. See Collyns and Dunaway (1987) for an example of how this approach can be applied. The authors construct an econometric model of the US automobile market and fit the basic equations using data from a period (1968–80) prior to the imposition of export restraints on Japan. Projections of prices, quantities purchased, and total expenditures were then made for the period when these restrictions were operative (1981–4) with

the differences between actual and estimated values attributed to the NTBs.

31. One would expect, *ceterus paribus*, a difference (d) in the unit values to occur that reflected the rent associated with the restriction, i.e., d equals ($x_{ij} - x_{ik}$) where x_{ij} is the unit value of shipments to the restricted market and x_{ik} is the unit value of similar goods exported to an unrestricted market. If statistical tests showed that d was approximately of the same order-of-magnitude as independently collected statistics on export quota prices these findings would support further use of export unit value differentials as proxies for NTB rents. In undertaking any empirical tests on this relationship, an effort would have to be made to ensure that the unit value differences were not influenced by other factors like product or quality differences.

32. A useful conceptual framework for studies attempting to quantify economic costs of trade restrictions can be found in Bhagwati (1987). According to Bhagwati the 'deadweight loss' results from distorting production and consumption decisions from what they would be if the economic agents taking these decisions faced international prices. The deadweight loss consists of two elements: costs to consumers and costs to producers. Most existing empirical studies (see the survey in Chapter 5) have examined consumer costs of trade restrictions.

33. The producer subsidy equivalent is considered to be a measure of the financial transfer necessary to leave the position of the producer unchanged were the trade-distorting and other measures terminated. The concept shares the shortcomings typical of static partial equilibrium measures and assumes the 'small-country' case of international trade theory. Nevertheless, it provides some useful approximations of the magnitude of the distortion associated with trade barriers and other related policy measures. An analogous measure, the consumer's subsidy equivalent, is a measure of the burden imposed on consumers by policies which distort domestic prices from their border equivalents.

34. The OECD (1987a) provides an algebraic framework for measuring producer and consumer subsidy equivalents. If Q is the level of production; C the level of consumption; P_d is the domestic producer price; P_c is the domestic consumer price; P_w is the reference price; D represents direct payments; L is producer levies and fees; B is other budget payments, direct or implicit; and G is budget payments to consumers, then:

$$\text{Total PSE} = Q(P_d - P_w) + D - L + B \tag{2.27}$$
$$\text{Per Unit PSE} = \text{Total PSE} \div Q \tag{2.28}$$
$$\%\ \text{PSE} = 100(\text{Total PSE}) \div Q(P_d) + D - L \tag{2.29}$$
$$\text{Total CSE} = -C(P_d - P_w) + G \tag{2.30}$$
$$\text{Per Unit CSE} = \text{Total CSE} \div C \tag{2.31}$$
$$\%\ \text{CSE} = 100(\text{Total CSE}) \div C(P_c) \tag{2.32}$$

In these equations, the reference price (P_w) may refer either to a world price or to a domestic price (in the case of two price systems). Implicit budgetary payments refer to the various cost-reducing measures from which producers benefit.

35. Underlying this definition are the basic assumptions of the effective protection model: (i) all production functions are of a fixed coefficient form with zero elasticity of substitution between intermediate inputs and primary factors (labour and capital), (ii) primary factors are internationally immobile, and (iii) import supply is perfectly elastic whereas the demand for exports is infinite. For an excellent non-technical discussion of the implications of these assumptions, as well as other points concerning the effective protection model, see Grubel (1971).

36. Assume an NTB with a 20 per cent *ad valorem* equivalent is applied to a product which sells for $10 on the world market while its raw material inputs, which account for 60 per cent of the free trade production value, do not face any tariffs or NTBs. Since the NTB raises the domestic price of the product, protection permits the producer to operate with a value added to $6 as opposed to a value added of $4 under free trade. The effective rate of protection would be 50 per cent ($6 − $4) ÷ $4 as opposed to the nominal rate of protection of 20 per cent from the NTB.

$$V_j = 1 + t_j - \Sigma a_{ij} \tag{2.35}$$

37. Continuing with the previous example, if an NTB with an *ad valorem* equivalent of 10 per cent is applied to the material inputs for product j, production costs could rise by 60 cents. However, as indicated by equation (2.27) the effective rate accounts for the combined effects of nontariff barriers on inputs and the final product. While the NTB on the final good adds $2 to free trade value added, the NTB on inputs lowers this by 60 cents. Thus, the joint effect of the two NTBs results in a value added of $5.40 which is 35 per cent (the effective protection rate) above the free trade value. It should be noted that the effective rate can be negative. This situation may occur when the weighted NTB *ad valorem* equivalents on inputs exceeds that on final products.

Chapter 3   Simulating the Effects of Trade Liberalisation

1. For a full technical description of the model, see Laird and Yeats (1986). Illustrations of empirical research and policy studies which employed the model include Laird and Yeats (1987a; 1987c) and Karsenty and Laird (1986). UNCTAD has employed the model in numerous policy studies including assessments of the impact of trade liberalisation on developing-country export earnings. See UNCTAD (1985), particularly pages 119–25 for an illustration.

2. See Cline *et al.* (1978), International Monetary Fund (1984), or Sapir and Baldwin (1983) for examples of previous work. For a non-technical discussion of the use of partial equilibrium models for evaluating the effects of trade liberalisation, see Stern (1976).

3. One widely utilised general equilibrium model has been developed at the University of Michigan, a description of which can be found in Deardorff and Stern (1986). For an example of the use of this model to examine the

impact of complete elimination of post-Tokyo Round tariffs, see Dear-dorff and Stern (1983).

4. As an example, if the United States extended a 5 per cent preferential tariff on products imported from developing countries, while all other exporters of the good face a 10 per cent MFN duty, this would cause some trade to be diverted to developing countries since their goods are more competitively priced than before. In other words, US importers would switch some purchases from (say) the EEC to developing countries since the latter's goods have fallen in relative price. This substitution is the trade diversion effect of the tariff preference. In addition, the lower prices of (preference receiving) imported goods would cause the overall level of imports to increase. This latter effect is trade creation. The operation of many NTBs could be altered to provide trade preferences. For example, quotas could be differentially liberalised in favour of developing countries, or these countries could be exempted from the full payment of variable import levies. For some concrete proposals for the creation of trade preferences through alteration of NTBs, see Murray and Walter (1977).

5. For most countries, these are comparable at the 4-digit level of the Customs Cooperation Council Nomenclature (CCCN), sometimes known under the name of the earlier Brussels Tariff Nomenclature (BTN). From 1988, most countries will record data using the Harmonized Commodity Coding and Classification System – the Harmonized System (HS) – and this will be comparable across countries at the 6-digit level. However, data will still be recorded at a much lower level of aggregation for most countries.

6. These files – known as the GATT Tariff Study – have been made available to the World Bank by the GATT Secretariat, with the consent of governments. These files are not publicly available.

7. The tariff statistics for the EEC countries are exceedingly complex as these nations have adopted multiple preference schemes for both developed and developing countries. Aside from the GSP, the EEC extends additional preferences to certain African, Caribbean, and Pacific (ACP) developing countries under the provisions of the Lome Convention. Other preferences are also extended to certain North African and Mediterranean developing countries. Finally, under the terms of an EEC-EFTA protocol almost all manufactured goods exchanged between these two country groups are traded free of import duties.

8. As an example, Japan has made numerous cuts in its post-Tokyo Round MFN tariffs in an attempt to reduce persistent trade surpluses with other OECD countries and these 'applied' tariffs are recorded on the GATT tapes as well as in official Japanese customs documents. While most MFN tariffs have legal bindings under GATT provisions, and cannot be raised above these ceilings, some tariffs (particularly in agriculture) are not legally bound and can easily be increased. A GATT report, *Basic Documentation for Tariff Study*, is useful in that it provides extensive information on tariffs compiled by CCCN headings. The Brussels – based International Customs Tariff Bureau's publication *International Customs Journal* translates national tariff schedules into five major languages.

9. However, as Chapter 2 shows, a liberalisation of nontariff barriers may merely reduce rents that accrue to foreign producers with the result that domestic prices are relatively unaffected. Given the state of current empirical analysis of NTBs it has not proved possible to isolate 'rent-reduction' effects from their influence on consumer prices.

10. For example, some studies suggest that the average *ad valorem* equivalent of United States NTBs on clothing and textile imports are in the range of 40 to 50 per cent. Obviously, this is an aggregate figure that differs considerably against individual producers. The NTB equivalent for a high labour cost country (say Germany) would probably be lower while for countries like Singapore or Hong Kong it would be higher. This point illustrates an important difference between nominal tariffs and nominal equivalents for nontariff barriers. While a given nominal tariff rate is the same for all exporters, the nominal equivalent of a given NTB may be quite different for individual exporting countries.

11. The Series D files are trade tapes that record imports and exports for a given country, by product and by trading partner, down to the four- and five-digit level of the SITC. For most developed (and many developing) countries these records extend back to the early 1970s or late 1960s. For researchers who do not have access to these computer files, the trade data are also published in a soft-cover book format. See United Nations, *Commodity Trade Statistics, Series D, Commodity by Country* (New York: United Nations, various countries and various years). The same data are available on-line in Geneva and New York and access can be gained by subscribers through public switch networks in their own countries.

12. See Cline *et al.* (1978), and Langhammer (1983b). Additional elasticity estimates can be found in Goldstein and Khan (1984). In cases, the elasticity estimates are only available at fairly high levels of detail. Here it is necessary to assume that all component (tariff-line) products have the same elasticity value.

13. See Armington (1969) for an elaboration of the theoretical foundation for this proposition.

14. Equation (12) in the annex to this chapter gives the formula for computing trade diversion from the import penetration ratio.

15. For those who wish to test the Baldwin and Murray approach, import penetration ratios are compiled by OECD (for details, see Brodin and Blades, 1986). An additional source of import-consumption ratios for developed countries is UNCTAD (1987), particularly table 7.1 on pages 518 to 525. Previous issues of the UNCTAD *Handbook* contain import-consumption ratios for earlier years. For most developing countries import-penetration ratios are not available and this necessitates an alternative procedure be used for estimating trade diversion (see equation (14) in the annex).

16. For a concordance between the SITC and CCCN systems, see *United Nations Statistical Papers, Series M, No. 34*, 'Standard International Trade Classification Review' (United Nations, New York, 1961). For a concordance between the SITC and ISIC, see United Nations, 'Classification of Commodity by Industrial Origin-Links between the Standard International Trade Classification and the International Standard Indus-

trial Classification', *Statistical Papers*: *Series M, No. 43, Rev. 1* (United Nations, New York, 1971).

17. This study used the earlier Baldwin–Murray (1977) methodoloy. Subsequent unpublished analysis with explicit elasticities of substitution did not yield significantly differently results, despite the questioning of the assumptions of Baldwin and Murray's model by Pomfret, as discussed earlier.

18. The developed-country simulation results presented in this chapter are all based on tariff-line-level projections that have been aggregated to higher levels of detail. In cases, some of the NTB *ad valorem* equivalents used in the simulations were derived for products at the four- and five-digit levels of the SITC. Here it was necessary to assume that all component tariff-line products had the same NTB nominal equivalent.

19. These calculations employ a discount rate of 5 per cent which approximated the existing spread between internationally competitive interest rates and rates of inflation in OECD countries. This figure was chosen under the assumption that the future value of increased exports will rise in line with the general rate of inflation. The present value estimate is influenced by biases associated withe exchange rate effects or resource costs of additional exports, yet it is more useful than annual figures as a gauge of debt relief associated with trade policy initiatives since it corresponds to the (stock) measure of the level of existing debt. The rationale for selecting the spread between interest and inflation rates is that the latter would be a factor working to increase the value of future developing countries' exports.

20. The authors conduct sensitivity tests on these simulations by inserting different supply elasticity values and note how they influenced the projections. See Erzan *et al.* (1986) for details. It should be noted that there have been extensive applications of these models in assessing effects of the Generalised System of Preferences (GSP), i.e., tariff preferences on specific products that developed countries have extended to developing countries since the early 1970s. Major efforts have been made to quantify the value of the GSP to developing countries and the adverse effects of reduced (eroded) preferential margins due to MFN tariff reductions in the Tokyo and Uruguay Round. See Karsenty and Laird (1986), Baldwin and Murray (1977) and Sapir and Baldwin (1983) for illustrative examples.

21. Valdes and Zietz do not derive new NTB *ad valorem* equivalents, but draw this material from published studies. See their report's appendix 1 (pp. 44–5) for details. In appendix 2, the authors project the price effects associated with the OECD liberalisation (50 per cent reduction in barriers) and indicate this could raise international prices of some commodities by as much as 15 per cent. These findings, which would be correspondingly greater for a full liberalisation, suggest that considerable biases may exist in domestic–'world' price measures for NTBs since international protectionism has a major depressant effect on world prices. Koekkoek and Mennes (1986) conduct a related simulation study involving removal of trade barriers facing textile and clothing products.

22. For several reasons, Valdes and Zietz acknowledge their projections may be downward biased. For many commodities, especially semi-

processed products, bilateral trade is so distorted by protectionism that the base year trade levels, on which the simulations are based, are not representative. Also, nominal equivalents for some nontariff barriers were not available so the products encountering these measures had to be excluded from the analysis. Furthermore, some gains such as the development of new export products, including the expansion of commodity processing, are not accounted for in the basic simulations. Finally, partial equilibrium simulations do not quantify gains such as those associated with increased trade's effects in reducing the power of domestic monopolies in importing countries.

Chapter 4 The Implications of NTB Inventory Studies

1. There is obviously an important judgemental element in defining 'hard core' restrictions and in some studies measures like tariff quotas, seasonal tariffs and minimum import price regulations have been added to the group. In sectors where they are important, this chapter analyses the use of these additional measures. Also, for some policy purposes inventory studies of measures not included in the 'hard core' group may be important. For example, during the Kennedy and Tokyo Round Multilateral Trade Negotiations efforts were made to achieve uniformity in national product standards, technical regulations and certification systems for domestic and traded goods. Data drawn from GATT and UNCTAD nontariff measure inventories played a key role in negotiating a 'code of conduct' for these measures in the Tokyo Round.

2. See equations (2.1) and (2.2) in Chapter 2 for the formulas employed in calculating the NTM frequency and coverage indices. Since year-to-year trade changes can affect NTM coverage indices an attempt was made to hold this factor constant. Specifically, the 1981, 1983 and 1986 calculations were made using a constant 1981 trade base. In other words, the 'hard core' nontariff measures actually operational in the three years (1981, 1983 and 1986) were applied to 1981 imports in the calculation of the NTM coverage indices. As such, changes in the indices reflect changes in nontariff measure usage while holding the influence of trade changes constant. This is like using a fixed basket of goods for the computation of price indices. In this case, changes can only occur because the product or country coverage of the nontariff measures have been extended or reduced. However, it takes no account of changes in the restrictiveness of specific NTMs, e.g. like changes in quota limits.

3. The results are somewhat sensitive to the treatment of petroleum. If these products are included in the product base 15.7 per cent or about $130 billion of OECD 1981 trade encounters 'hard core' nontariff measures. If the 15.7 per cent OECD coverage ratio also holds at the global level, about $200 billion in world trade encountered hard-core nontariff measures in 1981. This value estimated probably is low since nontariff measures seemingly are more frequently applied in developing as opposed to developed countries (see Table 4.10).

4. Official government sources report that Japan's imports of coal and coke (SITC 32) were subject to quantitative controls throughout 1981–6. The

1981 value of affected coal trade due to these restrictions (approximately $5.5 billion) represented about one-quarter of all Japanese imports which encountered hard-core NTMs. Excluding coal, the Japanese hard-core trade coverage ratio would be more than five points lower, or 18.7 per cent. Aside from these measures, most of the other important Japanese trade restrictions are concentrated in foodstuffs (SITC 0), beverages and tobacco (SITC 1), and textile yarns (SITC 65).

5. The perverse movement of the frequency and trade coverage ratios for Britain can be largely traced to two or three specific product sectors. A new 'voluntary' export restraint on automobile imports (SITC 73) caused the NTM trade coverage index for this sector to rise by four percentage points even though the frequency index was virtually unchanged (only one tariff line was affected). During the 1981 to 1986 period some relatively unimportant textile exporting countries and products were excluded from MFA quotas, a development which caused Britain's frequency ratio for this sector (SITC 84) to fall by over 20 points (from 58.7 to 38.3 per cent), while the extension of the MFA restrictions to other important products and countries (particularly the socialist countries of Eastern Europe) left the trade coverage ratio virtually unchanged.

6. The very low (1.1 per cent) trade coverage ratio for socialist countries' exports to Britain is due to a high trade concentration in relatively few products that do not face NTMs. Over 40 per cent of socialist exports consist of crude fertilisers and non-metallic mineral manufactures (SITC 27 and 66 respectively), while an additional 32 per cent consists of transport equipment (SITC 73). Britain does not apply nontariff restrictions to any of the tariff-line products exported by socialist countries in these groups.

7. The trade coverage figures in Table 4.3 relate to developing countries as a whole, but Laird and Yeats (1987a) show that the incidence of nontariff restrictions on some highly indebted industrialised developing countries is far greater due to the concentration of labour-intensive manufactures and/or agricultural products in their total exports. The Laird–Yeats study compiled *ad valorem* equivalents for NTBs facing indebted countries' major exports and then (using techniques discussed in this book, Chapter 3) simulated the effects of their (and post-Tokyo Round tariffs) removal. The value of the resulting trade expansion covered one-third or more of Argentina, Brazil, Colombia, Venezuela, Republic of Korea, Morocco, Pakistan, Philippines, Turkey and Yugoslavia's outstanding external debt, and covered at least one-fifth the debt of Chile and Ecuador.

8. Table A4.1 in the annex to this chapter provides 1986 NTM trade coverage ratios for each EEC(10) country and it is useful to compare these figures with the aggregate community data. There are two factors which can produce important differences between these statistics and the overall EEC averages shown in Table 4.4. First, aside from the common EEC-wide nontariff measures, individual countries often have different barriers that are applied at the national level. Estimates by the authors suggest that roughly 15 per cent of all EEC barriers are applied at the national level. Second, even with just the common EEC-wide barriers, differences in imports would produce variations in NTM trade coverage

ratios. As such, national differences in the statistics in Table A4.1 reflect both national differences in the use of nontariff measures, and import-mix differences from EEC country to country.

9. Table A4.7 in the annex to this chapter illustrates the discriminatory effects of the restrictions as MFA quotas are applied to 50 per cent of EEC textile imports, and to approximately 66 per cent of EEC clothing imports from developing countries. In addition, approximately 15 per cent of EEC imports from developing countries were subject to textile quotas negotiated outside the Multifibre Arrangement. In contrast, Table A4.7 shows that imports of these products from other developed countries are generally traded free of nontariff measures. An important exception occurs in the United States where some quantitative limits, which had their origin in the Short and Long-Term Textile Arrangement, are used against Japan. A final point is that studies surveyed in Chapter 5 suggest textile and clothing barriers often have *ad valorem* equivalents ranging from 25 to 50 per cent and that these barriers have a major cost-raising effect for consumers in developed countries. See Hamilton (1984a; 1984b), Hufbauer *et al.* (1986), and Jenkins (1980) among others.

10. Time-series analysis of NTM coverage ratios up to 1985 almost completely fail to reflect the liberalisation in New Zealand's trade barriers. This is due to the fact that NTM inventories merely recorded the existence of a trade restraint, but tell nothing about the intensity with which the measure is applied. See Chapter 2 for a discussion of this drawback in the inventory approach to trade-barrier analysis. There appears to be relatively few attempts to systematically estimate *ad valorem* equivalents for New Zealand's quotas, but several studies suggest they increased the cost of some consumer durables by 50 to 75 per cent.

11. Analysis of the underlying statistics shows that the United States' VERs with developed countries are exclusively concentrated in two areas: iron and steel (SITC 67) and transportation equipment (SITC 73). Approximately 77 per cent of US iron and steel imports and 43 per cent of transport equipment imports from developed countries encountered 'voluntary' restraints in 1986. The reader should recall the problems associated with compiling accurate information on VERs since these measures may not be recorded in official government documents (see Chapter 2 for a discussion of this point). As such, there is some reason to believe that the statistics in Tables 4.6 and 4.7 on VER use may be biased downward.

12. In 1986 quotas were applied to about 26 per cent of Japanese meat (SITC 01) imports from developed countries and to almost one-third of cereal imports (SITC 04). The highest coverage of quotas is on dairy products (SITC 02) where almost 74 per cent of all imports from developed countries encountered these barriers. In the manufacturing sector, between 18 to 25 per cent of Japan's imports of leather goods (SITC 61), transport equipment (SITC 73), and footwear (SITC 85) also face quotas.

13. There have been a number of attempts to derive *ad valorem* equivalents for these VERs and to measure their trade and other economic effects.

See, in particular, studies by Greenaway and Hindley (1985), Hufbauer *et al.* (1986), Hamilton (1984c), OECD (1985a) among others which are reviewed in Chapter 5 in this book.

14. Laird and Yeats (1987c) identify several developing countries whose tariffs are equal to or lower than post-Tokyo Round duties in developed countries. In Singapore, for example, tariffs average less than half a percentage point while import duties in Saudi Arabia average about one to two per cent. As a group, the Middle-East oil-exporting countries generally have relatively low levels of tariff protection and also do not rely heavily on nontariff barriers.

15. The NTM information used in preparing Table 4.10 is stored at the tariff-line level according to national classifications and these data were concorded to the four-digit CCCN level. If an NTM affected only (say) two tariff lines in a CCCN containing ten lines, then only 0.2 per cent of the four-digit CCCN is considered to be covered. The resulting statistics closely resemble NTM frequency indices (see equation 2.1) in Chapter 2. Since tariff-line-level import statistics are generally not available for developing countries, NTM trade coverage indices could not be computed.

16. The statistics presented in Table 4.10 relate only to product-specific NTMs and do not include general across-the-board measures such as foreign exchange restrictions for balance-of-payments purposes. Another point is that a more detailed analysis of the underlying NTM data shows these measures are generally not biased in favour of particular sectors, but are widespread through agriculture and manufacturing. In about one-half of the countries listed in Table 4.10, however, NTMs were applied to a relatively high share of foodstuff imports and manufactures excluding transport equipment (STIC 6 + 8 less 67 and 68).

17. Two factors can produce differences in individual EEC country NTM trade coverage ratios. First, most countries have various national nontariff measures as well as the common NTMs which operate at the Community level. Second, the import structures of individual EEC countries differ considerably with some having relatively high concentrations of imports that face nontariff measures. Even without differences in NTM use by individual countries these import-mix differences would cause nontariff measure trade coverage indices to vary.

Chapter 5   Findings of Empirical Studies of Nontariff Barriers

1. Although these analyses generally show that protectionism involves major costs for society, it is felt that they often understate these costs. The problem lies partly with the partial equilibrium models used to simulate protectionism's effects (see Chapter 3). These models do not generally account for economies of scale, the costs of lobbying for protection, the costs of diminished competition, the costs of discretionary interventionism, effects on national terms-of-trade or linkages to other sectors. For an analysis that attempts to quantify these additional costs, see Harriss (1984).

2. Since their conclusions parallel those of other studies surveyed in this

chapter, or results presented in Chapter 4, several important inventory studies are not examined in detail. These include, among others, B. Balassa and C. Balassa (1984), Cline (1985), Finger and Olechowski (1986), Laird and Finger (1986) and UNCTAD (1985).

3. Aside from the standard frequency and 'own' trade-weighted NTB coverage indices, Nogues *et al.* develop a coverage measure based on 'world' trade weights. This index substitutes the shares of four-digit SITC products in world trade for a country's actual imports in our equation (2.2). Shifting to such a measure has the potential advantage of reducing biases in 'own' trade-weighting procedures. In the latter, very restrictive NTMs may enter into the overall calculation with zero or low weights since they reduce actual imports well below potential levels or, in cases, restrict all trade. Unless the level and structure of NTMs in all countries is closely correlated the potential for such bias is smaller using world trade weights. (See appendix 1 on pages 35 to 37 of the Nogues *et al.* study for details on how the world trade-weighted index was constructed.)

4. In a related analysis, Olechowski (1987) documents continued marked differences in NTM use among industrial countries. Japan, for example, resorts almost exclusively to traditional NTMs such as quotas, prohibitions, and licensing. The United States is the largest user of VERs and anti-dumping and countervailing measures. The European nations (particularly Switzerland and the EEC) are the main users of administrative controls. Another interesting difference is that Japan and the United States almost exclusively use duties and volume restrictions while the EEC relies heavily on price controls. For example, minimum (or reference) prices and variable levies cover some 29 per cent of EEC agricultural imports, while price controls and price undertakings cover 37 per cent of iron and steel imports.

5. Two other important studies provide information on the proliferation of NTBs in the 1980s. Laird and Finger (1986) used constant 1981 trade weights and found that import coverage of hard-core NTMs (quantitative restrictions, 'voluntary' export restraints, and measures to encourage decreed import prices) increased some ten percentage points between 1981 and 1985. In other words, NTMs in 1985 affected 10 per cent more of developed-country imports than five years earlier. The increase in coverage of non-fuel imports was even greater: nineteen points for all NTBs and fifteen points for the hard-core measures. Finger and Olechowski (1986) document a smaller, but significant growth of NTMs by decomposing the change in current (rather than constant) indices of import coverage in 1981 and 1984 into several elements.

6. Empirical analyses show tariffs in developed countries have a common structure. Typically, zero or very low import duties are applied to primary (unprocessed) commodities and these tariffs increase or 'escalate' as goods undergo further processing. Developing countries regard escalating tariffs as a major barrier to local processing of domestically produced primary commodities and an important constraint to their industrialisation effort. The UNCTAD study shows nontariff barriers tend to behave in the same manner as tariffs, and that the effects of the

two types of trade restrictions may be mutually reinforcing. For a related policy analysis of the importance of these issues and empirical evidence, see Yeats (1987).

7. Empirical evidence developed by Laird and Yeats (1987c) suggests this latter conclusion may have to be re-examined since tariffs in many developing countries escalate to a far higher degree than do import duties in developed countries. These authors conclude that developing countries seem to extend equal (or higher) protection to local processing industries, but do this through tariffs rather than through nontariff measures.

8. Other inventory studies include Walter (1969; 1971). Walter's classification scheme places nontariff measures in the following three categories: Type I – policies and practices designed specifically to expand or restrict exports or impede imports; Type II – measures intended to deal primarily with problems not related to trade, but which are from time to time purposely used for trade restriction; Type III – measures intended to deal only with non-trade-related problems, but whose effects unavoidably spill over into the trade sector. These classifications are further subdivided as to whether they operate: (a) by quantitatively limiting exports or imports, or (b) by imposing costs on those engaged in trade, thereby affecting prices and competitive conditions.

9. Walter's analysis is based on the concept of 'affected' products which is normally no longer employed in inventory studies. A four-digit SITC product is considered to be 'affected' by NTBs if one or more component tariff-line products encounter these restrictions. Studies that employ this concept typically report higher NTB indices than those which reflect actual trade coverage.

10. The uncertainty index is based on the proposition that if any tariff-line item within a four-digit CCCN is covered by NTBs similar restrictions could easily spread to other items in the group, particularly if they are close substitutes. This index (U_j) is defined by,

$$U_j = (\Sigma D_i N_i \div N_t) \times 100 \tag{5.1}$$

where N_i is a four-digit CCCN product, D_i is a dummy variable that takes a value of unity if any tariff-line-level product within the CCCN encounters a nontariff barrier, and N_t is the total number of four-digit CCCNs in the product group under investigation.

11. These findings are at obvious odds with the empirical results presented in Chapter 4 which indicate that the NTB coverage ratios in Europe are lowest for the CPC countries. Since the Olechowski–Yeats study was published there has been a major shift in the composition of socialist country exports to the EEC with energy products becoming increasingly important. Since energy products do not encounter NTBs this has caused the overall trade coverage ratios to fall. In other words, the decline in the CPC nontariff barrier coverage ratios primarily reflect trade shifts rather than any liberalisation of NTBs.

12. These data show that Hungarian exports to the West are the most heavily restricted. As much as 97.8 per cent of Hungary's trade is subject to at

least one of the nine types of NTBs, with over one-third of the restraints taking the form of quotas or restrictive licensing arrangements. These barriers are applied with the highest frequency in the EEC where minimum price restrictions and variable import levies are applied to 25 per cent and 14 per cent of total exports. For full details see Olechowski and Yeats (1982), particularly table 3 on p. 13. It should be noted that there have been sizeable shifts in the structure of some CPC exports since the Olechowski–Yeats study was completed, with energy products comprising a much higher share of the total. This trade shift has significantly altered the NTM coverage indices.

13. For a concise discussion of the main agricultural policy issues to be addressed in the Uruguay Round, see Fitchett (1987). UNCTAD (1983b) and Yeats (1982) take a somewhat broader perspective and consider how major agricultural problems could also be addressed both within and outside the GATT negotiations.

14. In addition to the Saxon and Anderson study, several other analyses combine to provide fairly detailed and comprehensive statistics on the level and trend in Japanese agricultural protection. The OECD (1987a; 1987b) estimates producer and consumer subsidy equivalents for major agricultural products imported into other developed countries and Japan during 1979–81, while Fitchett (1988) updates the Japanese data to 1985. Studies such as Cline *et al.* (1978), Commonwealth Secretariat (1982), and IMF (1982) estimate support levels in earlier years. See the reviews of these investigations in this chapter. Finally, Otsuka and Hayami (1985) provide additional estimates of the deadweight loss associated with Japan's 1980 price support and acreage controls for rice.

15. While Table 5.4 shows ratios of domestic to border prices, Saxon and Anderson also compute ratios of producer to border prices. These latter figures are generally far higher than the ratios shown in Table 5.4. For example, in 1979 Japanese producer prices for rice were 414 per cent above border prices, while the corresponding figures for wheat and barley were 411 per cent and 515 per cent respectively. The differences between these and consumer prices were maintained by government assistance programmes to producers and the payment of direct subsidies.

16. The domestic prices are compiled at different points in distribution chains. The price of beef is the general wholesale price of domestically produced beef while the domestic price of yellowtails is the wholesale price of fresh yellowtails, including both domestic and imported products. For herring, squid, and cuttlefish the domestic prices are the wholesale prices of frozen goods that are principally imported. The domestic price of oranges is the wholesale price of the imported product. All the wholesale prices cited are those of the Tokyo wholesale market. For all other items the domestic prices are official producer's prices.

17. Gulbrandsen and Lindbeck present estimates of relative levels of protection for agricultural and industrial goods that differ in concept and must be viewed as very rough. Protection for agriculture is measured by differences between domestic and world prices, an approach that incorporates the effects of tariffs and NTBs, while protectionism for manufactured goods is only measured by tariffs. Failure to incorporate protection

from NTBs imparts a downward bias in the results for manufactured products, but it is difficult to quantify the magnitude of error that is introduced.

18. Starting with the Swedish government's official crisis diet (a daily caloric consumption of milk, cheese, butter, margarine, sugar, beef, pork, poultry, eggs, wheat, rye and potatoes is specified), Hamilton estimates the costs of maintaining Swedish agricultural production above official levels for these products over 1976–80. Costs are measured by the difference between Swedish domestic agricultural production, valued in local prices, and the same output valued in world prices. Since domestic Swedish prices do not reflect costs of surplus production, Hamilton recognises that his procedure understates the cost to the Swedish economy. His analysis indicates that the 'excess production' cost was highest for beef, pork and grains totalling approximately US$ 4.5 million (1980 prices) for these items. For all agricultural commodities in the crisis diet the cost of surplus production is put at about US$ 6.5 million annually.

19. Bale and Lutz (1979a) calculate 1976 nominal protection coefficients for agricultural products in France, Federal Republic of Germany, United Kingdom, Japan, Yugoslavia, Argentina, Egypt, Pakistan and Thailand. Differences between these figures and those reported in the IMF study appear to be due to variations in the product priced, or the fact that prices were drawn from different points in the distribution chain. Other important sources of nominal protection coefficient derived from world–domestic-price differentials include World Bank (1986) and UN Food and Agricultural Organization (1987). Monke and Salam (1986) provide detailed statistics on 1975–80 nominal protection coefficients for wheat, maize and rice in most developed and developing countries (see, in particular, their table 6, pp. 250–2).

20. The actual formula employed was $P_d Q_w / P_w Q_w R$, where R equals 1 plus the ratio of net sales taxes to net material production in each country. This adjustment is necessary since a 'neutral' sales tax will raise prices of both imports and domestic products above world prices by the same proportion. In such a case, domestic–world price differential would provide an inaccurate indication of trade barriers since the sales taxes do not discriminate against foreign products.

21. In evaluating the figures in Table 5.14 a point to note is that protection afforded by EEC levies may vary significantly from year to year as 'world' and domestic EEC prices change. For example, UNCTAD estimated that over 1975–81 *ad valorem* equivalents for EEC levies ranged from 22 to 143 per cent for wheat, 4 to 150 per cent for oats, 13 to 120 per cent for maize, and from 3 to 217 per cent for raw sugar. As such, it is very difficult to determine what constitutes an 'average' level of protection from levies. For empirical information on the level of EEC agricultural protection in different years, see UN Food and Agricultural Organization (1979) or UNCTAD (1983b).

22. In a related study FAO (1981) estimated that if OECD countries reduced protection for oilseeds and products by 50 per cent the potential increase in export revenues of developing countries would be about $400, a rise of some 7 to 10 per cent, and that world trade in these products would increase by about $1 billion (in 1977 prices).

23. Article 3 of the MFA specifies conditions under which trade restrictions can be imposed. Restrictions on trade should be resorted to sparingly and 'limited to the precise products and to countries whose exports of such products are causing market disruption'. Consultations on trade problems are required along with a detailed factual statement of reasons and justification for any request for consultations. If a mutually agreed restriction is necessary 'the level of restriction shall be fixed no lower than the level roughly equal to the previous year's imports'. If no agreement is reached within 60 days, however, unilateral action is available to limit imports to the previous (annual) level.

24. See Cable (1987) for a concise analysis of the MFA and an evaluation of issues regarding textiles and clothing trade to be addressed in the Uruguay Round. A plank in the Punta del Esta Ministerial Declaration establishes objectives for a new round: 'Negotiations in the area of textiles and clothing shall aim to formulate modalities that would permit the eventual integration of this sector into GATT on the basis of strengthening GATT rules and disciplines, thereby also contributing to the objective of further liberalization of trade' (see Appendix 5 in the present volume for the full text of the declaration). Many developing countries have serious problems with this proposal since it seemingly shifts resolution of major textile and clothing trade issues to some undetermined point after the Uruguay Round negotiations.

25. The 'basket extractor' and the 'anti-surge' provisions were controversial new elements at the time of their introduction, but they appear to have been less important than originally feared. The anti-surge procedures can be applied to regulate the level of imports in previously under-utilised quotas for highly sensitive produce in such a manner that sharp and substantial increases in imports are prevented. Under the provisions of the basket extractor, if exports from a given country reach a specified percentage of the total EEC imports of the product in the previous year, the EEC can call for consultations so as to arrive at an agreed quota level; in the absence of agreement a quota may be imposed unilaterally.

26. In the projections, four key assumptions are made: imports become more expensive under protection, but British producers do not respond by raising prices to increase profit margins; workers do not attempt to restore real-wage levels if these are reduced by protection; there is no reaction to the British trade restraints in foreign countries; and economies of scale associated with new protectionist measures will be roughly patterned after those achieved in the past. If any of these propositions are incorrect, the Cambridge Model projections could be substantially in error. A further required assumption was that any UK tariffs or nontariff barriers will be applied equally against all exporters and not on a selective (discriminatory) basis. There would be obvious practical problems with such general trade intervention measures as they would require raising restraints against other EEC member countries.

27. Arrangements for allocation and transfer of quotas are organised by the Department of Trade in Hong Kong with quotas granted on the basis of a firm's past exports. Thus, when a restraint agreement is concluded with an importing country, quotas are allocated in proportion to previous shipments to the restricted market. Once a quota has been awarded

there are rules governing its renewal and transfer. When a quota is transferred, a price (the quota 'premium') is normally paid to the seller. Greenaway suggests this premium can be taken as an indication of the scarcity value of the quota and the difference between the price of restricted supplies in the United Kingdom and the cost of production in Hong Kong (after allowing for the cost of transportation and insurance).

28. The total loss to the UK economy (£68.4 million) was lower since protection increased tariff revenues (by £53 million) and profits of domestic firms (£49.1 million). The £68.4 million economy-wide loss provides a basis for computing the cost of jobs saved by the trade restrictions. Estimates place the 'saved' jobs at between 8000 to 16 000 for the three clothing categories. Thus, if the domestic supply elasticity is equal to unity the cost per job saved is £8500 which is far above the average wage in the industry. However, this figure is for one year only and as long as the protection remains these costs are incurred. For instance, if protection remains permanently (assuming a 5 per cent discount rate) the cost per job saved would be approximately £171 000.

29. During the 1970s there was a sharp trend in Europe towards increased economic integration measured by the share of imports from partners in domestic demand. This also applies to manufactures other than textiles and clothing with their particular barriers against imports from developing countries. To study the effects of quantitative restrictions on the pattern of trade, adjustment must be made for this general underlying trend. This has been done in Table 5.25 by grouping 'other manufactures' together and using them as a control group. Hamilton refers to this procedure as 'normalising' changes in the pattern of trade.

30. Koekkoek and Mennes indicate they will provide details on the model employed in the simulations upon request. Textiles are taken to consist of SITC groups 26 and 65 while clothing is represented by SITC 84. The projections are based on 1983 trade data. It should be noted that the range in MFA tariff equivalents employed in this study (i.e., 5 to 15 per cent) appears low in comparison to the findings of other studies. See, for example, the Cable and Weale study surveyed in this chapter.

31. Based on data for a subset of all apparel consumed, the Council estimated that the consumer cost of US apparel tariffs is approximately $2700 million. Of this total, about $260 million goes to the government as tariff revenue, $2200 million goes to domestic producers, and about $210 million is a deadweight loss. If the same cost ratios apply to all apparel products consumed in the United States the costs for consumers would be about $9000 million annually. Peltzman (1983) provides a useful assessment of the Council's report and other analyses of US textile and clothing restrictions.

32. That is, a nominal protection coefficient (N_i) was estimated for each textile product (i) in each market (j) using the following formula:

$$N_i = (U_{ij} - U_{ir}) \div U_{ir} \qquad (5.2)$$

where U_{ij} is the domestic producer cost of product (i) in the home (European) market and U_{ir} is the average landed cost of the product from the four restricted developing countries. Roningen and Yeats (1976) employ a similar approach for quantifying trade barriers, but use comparative price information rather than data on production costs.

33. Hufbauer *et al.* (1986) estimate that any induced price increase in carbon steel imports by trade restrictions results in an increase in domestic steel prices which average 40 per cent of the increase in imported steel. For ball-bearings Hufbauer estimates this coefficient of price response takes a value of 20 per cent, while it is estimated to be 60 per cent for speciality steels.

34. Apparent consumption is defined as production minus exports plus imports of a specific product or industry. Since statistics on inventory change are generally not available, they are normally not accounted for in most empirical estimates of apparent consumption. The OECD currently conducts detailed cross-country studies of apparent consumption for industries defined at fairly low levels of aggregation. For details see Brodin and Blades (1986). These OECD studies also show the share of imports (in total and from various country groups) in apparent consumption. According to estimates published by UNCTAD (1988b, p. 525) imports of ferrous metals constituted 8.1 per cent of EEC apparent consumption in 1984–5, while the corresponding ratios were 6.1 per cent for the United States and Canada and 4.8 per cent for Japan.

35. Hufbauer *et al.* suggest that the price elasticity of US import demand for carbon steel products is approximately 2.5, while it is 0.25 for ball-bearings and 1.5 for speciality steels. Supply elasticities are estimated to be 2.0 for domestic production of ball-bearings and carbon steel products and unity for speciality steels. Crandall (1982) provides additional information on supply and demand parameters for steel while Stern *et al.* (1976) compiles estimates of import demand elasticities for steel and a wide range of industries in developed and some developing countries.

36. There would be obvious merit in testing separate regressions for socialist countries' imports from the world, from developed, and from developing countries. In the latter, an attempt should be made to include measures of colonial ties as dependent variables since the SCEEs have argued that the lack of these items is a major obstacle to the expansion of East–South trade. A crude, but possibly useful measure, might be a dummy variable for OECD countries that had established specific trade levels with developing countries prior to (say) the early 1900s.

37. The United States is not alone in restricting the sale of imported cars. In 1976, Italy limited Japanese imports to 2200 cars per year; in July 1986, it raised the limit to 3300 cars. France does not permit Japanese imports to exceed 3 per cent of domestic new car sales. Both Spain and the United Kingdom have had restraint agreements with Japan to limit Japanese auto exports. Because sales of Japanese cars in other European markets have been increasing, the EEC has prevailed upon Japan to limit voluntarily its car exports to Europe beginning in 1987. Representative studies that attempted to quantify the impact of US automobile restrictions include: Crandall (1984); Hunker (1984); and U.S. International Trade Commission (1985). An Australian Industries Assistance Commission (1980) report provides useful contrasting information on procedures

employed for Australian car protection and their effects.

38. The footwear industry received considerable tariff protection in the United Kingdom since The Second World War, and in the early 1980s average tariffs ranged from 8 per cent on leather shoes to 20 per cent on non-leather shoes. These were supplemented by restrictions on imports from Taiwan which started in August 1977 when the Commission of the European Community sanctioned a formal quota on imports of non-leather footwear. The quota was set at an annual rate of 5.5 million pairs for 1978 and 1979 was renewed for 1980. During 1980, however, a VER was negotiated with Taiwan which limited imports into the United Kingdom to 7 950 000 pairs in 1981. The VER was subsequently renewed for 1982 and the limit extended to 9 260 000 pairs.

39. This is a potentially important methodological approach for NTB quantification that warrants further research. If it can be verified that unit value differences do accurately reflect VER (and other NTB premiums), quantitative evidence could be derived on the incidence of a wide rage of trade restrictions for which we now have only 'inventory' tabulations. See the discussion relating to this point in Chapter 2. A key point is whether the unit value differences reflect the influence of VERs, or whether they are distorted by factors such as product-mix differences. In cases where VER auction prices are available, a useful test would be to compare these statistics with the unit value difference to determine if similar orders of magnitude were involved.

40. In March 1977, the US International Trade Commission determined that imports of colour television receivers were a substantial cause of serious injury to the domestic industry and recommended an average tariff increase of 16 per cent for five years. Rather than increase tariffs, the executive office instructed the US Special Trade Representative to negotiate an orderly marketing agreement. On 20 May 1977, Japan agreed to a VER on exports of complete and incomplete colour television sets from July 1977 to June 1980. The restraint agreement limited Japanese exports to 1.75 million units annually, which was about 30 per cent below the 1976 Japanese export level.

41. Several related studies applied similar empirical techniques for estimating NTB nominal equivalents in developing countries, although these findings have by now become somewhat dated. For example, Baldwin (1975, p. 102) presents data on US and Philippine wholesale prices for various goods between 1949 and 1965. Allowing for an average 25 per cent freight factor, he interprets the remaining price differences as measures of Philippine restrictions affecting imports. Bhagwati and Srinivasan (1975) estimate implicit tariff rates in India for 69 products for the years 1963–5 and 1968–9, while UN Economic Commission for Asia and the Far East (1972) derived similar estimates for various Asian countries.

42. There are several reasons why unit values for tariff-line-level imports from developing countries may be generally lower than similar goods from developed countries. First, these products may be of lower quality and therefore warrant a lower price. Second, developing countries may

often lack countervailing power in dealing with importers and may be forced to accept lower prices. Third, due to factors such as an adverse geographic location they may have to absorb generally higher freight costs in the price of their imports. There are, of course, some speciality items (like Turkish tobacco) where developing-country tariff-line products are more highly priced, but these run counter to the general trend.

Appendix 1   Country–Product Classifications for Trade-Barrier Analysis

1. In some variations of this scheme, iron and steel products (SITC 67) are excluded from the ores and metals group and are included with manufactured products. UNIDO has employed an alternative product classification scheme for some studies that places many processed foodstuffs in SITC 0 in the manufactured products group. For details see United Nations Industrial Development Organization (1982).
2. It is recognised that the problem of leakages may become increasingly important as one moves up the processing chains. That is, the processed commodity may be directed to some uses for which it is important, but not the major input, and hence would be lost from the chain. Some cotton thread, for example, may be employed in the production of rubber manufactures and would not show up in the cotton fabric stage.
3. Primarily thread and yarn; wood products; paper and paper products; leather; synthetics; other chemical products; non-metallic mineral products; glass; pig-iron and wrought non-ferrous metals. For details of the classification, see Balassa (1965).
4. The items include textile products; rubber goods; plastic articles; miscellaneous chemical products; ingots and other primary forms of steel; rolling mill products; other steel products and metal manufactures.
5. Consumer goods include hosiery; clothing; other textile articles; shoes and other leather goods; cleansing agents and perfumes; bicycles and motorcycles; precision instruments; toys; sporting goods and jewellery. Investment goods include items like electrical machinery and railway vehicles.
6. See Lary (1968), particularly appendix C entitled 'The Selection of Labor-Intensive Products', pp. 188–213. Tuong and Yeats (1980) updated Lary's results to the late 1970s and concluded that there had been no major changes in the labour-intensive product list.
7. GATT employs another definition of 'industrial' countries that has significant differences from either the World Bank or United Nations definitions of 'developed' countries. According to GATT, 'industrial' countries include the United States, Canada, Japan, the member countries of the EEC (10) and EFTA, Gibraltar, Malta, Spain, Turkey and Yugoslavia. Excluded from this listing are Australia, New Zealand, South Africa, the socialist countries of Eastern Europe (Albania, Bulgaria, Czechoslovakia, German Democratic Republic, Hungary, Poland, Romania and the USSR), China, Mongolia, North Korea, and Vietnam as well as all developing countries.

Appendix 2 Approximating the Effective Rate of Protection

1. Free trade value-added coefficients can be derived by deflating production shares observed in input–output tables by protection for inputs
   and the final product,

$$a_{ij} = a_{ij}'((1 + t_j)/(1 + t_i)) \qquad (A2.1)$$

where a_{ij} is the approximated free trade production coefficient and t_j and
t_i are nominal protection rates for the final product and production inputs
respectively.

2. In this formulation it is assumed that an average tariff for all production
   inputs has been computed and is represented by the value t_i. Ideally, this
   average should be computed using weights based on the cost of each
   production input.
3. Such low coefficients occur for products like vegetable oils where crush-
   ing only raises value-added by small amounts. The curves in Figure A2.1
   are derived from the following equation,

$$E_j/t_j = (1 - \alpha)/V_j + \alpha \qquad (A2.2)$$

where α is the ratio of nominal protection for inputs to that for the final
product. A major source of information on production costs and value
added for many processed commodities is the United States Census of
Manufactures which is published every three of four years. National
input–output tables have also been used for this information.

Appendix 3 Tariff Protection in Developed and Developing Countries

1. See Laird and Yeats (1987b) for statistics on pre-Uruguay Round tariff
   protection in developed and selected developing countries. The authors
   also summarise and discuss the major issues involving tariffs that should
   be addressed in the multilateral trade negotiations.
2. Applied rates for regional groupings of developing countries that have
   exchanged tariff preferences (like ASEAN or CARICOM) are no doubt
   lower than the MFN averages shown in Table A3.1. Difficulties encountered in tabulating these preferential tariff rates prevented the calculation of applied tariffs. The tariff averages for the EEC are based on
   external trade of the Community and do not reflect duty-free intra-trade.
   Some of the 'applied' MFN rates incorporated in the averages shown in
   Table A3.1 may be lower than the legally bound MFN rates. These
   divergences are especially important for Japan where major unilateral
   reductions have recently been made in MFN tariffs during the 1980s.
3. The 'own' trade weights employed in the developing-country tariff averages may incorporate a major bias in the resulting statistics. The problem
   is that high tariffs restrain (or prohibit) imports with the result that
   products covered by these duties enter the calculation of an overall
   average with low (or zero) trade weights. It has not proved possible to
   quantify the magnitude of this bias, but considerable evidence of prohibi-

tive tariffs (i.e., those of over several hundred per cent) have been found in some developing countries listed in Table A3.1 that have relatively low overall trade-weighted averages.

4. Under the protective wall of the common external tariff of the EEC and national tariffs of EFTA, some intra-European trade occurs that would otherwise not be competitive with outside suppliers. If MFN rates were reduced, this would lower European margins of preference, and trade would be diverted to (more competitive) non-European suppliers. For example, existing trade between (say) Sweden and France, Italy and Germany, or England and Norway would be diverted to outside suppliers like the United States and Japan that presently face (often high) MFN tariffs. It should be noted that developed countries that maintain Commonwealth Preferences like Canada, Australia and New Zealand would experience similar trade diversion.

Appendix 4   A Glossary of Nontariff Measures

1. In preparing this glossary, we have utilised two similar reports by UNCTAD (1988a) and Finger and Olechowski (1987) that provided clear definitions of different types of nontariff measures.
2. See annex 8 in Finger and Olechowski (1987) for a detailed tabulation of anti-dumping and countervailing duty actions filed in selected developed countries during the 1980s. This source also provides annual information on the number of cases that were dismissed and the number where duties were officially applied.
3. Various entries in the Data Base involving this term and automatic licensing have proved very controversial, particularly in countries like Switzerland where licensing procedures are extensively employed. The major point of contention is whether they have any trade restrictive effects or are primarily used for other purposes such as improving the quality of import statistics.

Bibliography

Agarwala, R. (1983) 'Price Distortions and Growth in Developing Countries', *World Bank Staff Working Paper No. 575* (Washington: World Bank).

Anderson, J. (1985) 'The Relative Inefficiency of Quotas: The Cheese Case', *American Economic Review*, vol. 75, pp. 178–90.

Anderson, Kym (1982) 'Northeast Asian Agricultural Protection in Historical and Comparative Perspective: The Case of South Korea', *Research Paper No. 82* (Canberra: Australian-Japan Research Centre).

Anderson, K. and R. Tyers (1983) *European Community's Grain and Meat Policies and U.S. Retaliation: Effects on International Prices, Trade and Welfare* (Canberra: Australian National University).

Anjaria, S. and Z. Iqbal, N. Kirmani and L. Perez (1982) 'Developments in International Trade Policy', *Occasional Paper No. 16* (Washington: International Monetary Fund).

Armington, P. (1969) 'A Theory of Demand for Products Distinguished by Place of Production', *IMF Staff Papers*, vol. 16 (Washington: IMF).

Australian Bureau of Agricultural Economics (1985) *Agricultural Policies in the European Community* (Canberra: Australian Government Publishing Service).

Australian Industries Assistance Commission (1980) *Report on Textiles, Clothing and Footwear* (Canberra: Industries Assistance Commission).

Bain, Joe (1964) 'Economies of Scale, Concentration and the Condition of Entry in Twenty Manufacturing Industries', *American Economic Review*, vol. 44, pp. 297–301.

Balassa, Bela (1965) 'Tariff Protection in Industrial Countries: An Evaluation', *Journal of Political Economy* (December) pp. 573–89.

Balassa, Bela (1982) 'Disequilibrium Analysis in Developing Countries: An Overview', *World Development* (December) pp. 153–82.

Balassa, Bela (1983) 'Exports, Policy Choices and Economic Growth in Developing Countries After the 1973 Oil Shock', *Discussion Paper Number 48* (Washington: World Bank Development Research Department).

Balassa, B. (1986) 'Japan's Trade Policies', *Weltwirtschaftliches Archiv*, Band 122, Heft 4, pp. 745–90.

Balassa, Bella and associates (1971) *The Structure of Protection in Developing Countries* (Baltimore: Johns Hopkins University Press).

Balassa, B. and C. Balassa (1984) 'Industrial Protection in the Developed Countries', *The World Economy* (June) pp. 176–96.

Baldwin, Robert (1970) *Nontariff Distortions of International Trade* (Washington: The Brookings Institution).

Baldwin, Robert (1975) *Foreign Trade Regimes and Economic Development* (New York: National Bureau of Economic Research).

Baldwin, Robert and Tracy Murray (1977) 'MFN Tariff Reductions and Developing Country Benefits Under the GSP', *The Economic Journal*, vol. 87 (March) pp. 30–46.

290

Bale, M.D. and E. Lutz (1979a) 'Price Distortions in Agriculture and Their Effects: An International Comparison', *World Bank Staff Working Paper No. 359* (Washington: World Bank).

Bale, M. and E. Lutz (1979b) 'The Effects of Trade Intervention on International Price Instability', *American Journal of Agricultural Economics*, vol. 61 (August).

Bale, M. and E. Lutz (1981) 'Price Distortions in Agriculture and Their Effects: An International Comparison', *American Journal of Agricultural Economics*, vol. 63, pp. 8–22.

Bayard, Thomas (1980) *Comments on the Federal Trade Commission Report on Effects of Restrictions on United States Imports: Five Case Studies and Theory* (Washington: Office of Foreign Economic Research of the Department of Labour).

Bell, Harry (1971) 'Some Domestic Price Implications of U.S. Protective Measures', in Commission on International Trade and Investment Policy, *United States International Economic Policy in an Interdependent World* (Washington: Government Printing Office).

Bergsten, C., Fred and William R. Cline (1987) *The United States–Japan Economic Problem*, 'Policy Analyses in International Economics, Number 3' (Washington: Institute for International Economics, October).

Bertrand, T. (1980) 'Thailand: Case Study of Agricultural Input and Output Pricing', *World Bank Staff Working Paper No. 385* (Washington: World Bank).

Bhagwati, Jagdish (1987) 'Economic Costs of Trade Restrictions', in J. Michael Finger and Andrzej Olechowski (eds), *The Uruguay Round: A Handbook on the Multilateral Trade Negotiations* (Washington: World Bank) pp. 29–36.

Bhagwati, Jagdish and T.N. Srinivasan (1975) *Foreign Trade Regimes and Economic Development: India* (New York: National Bureau of Economic Research).

Boyce, Patricia and Hayden Llewellyn (1982) *World Trade Distortions: A Study in Modern Trade Practice* (Melbourne: A.I.D.A. Research Centre).

Breckling, J., S. Thorpe and A. Stoeckel (1985) 'A Skeletal Version of a General Equilibrium Model for the European Community', Bureau of Agricultural Economics, Canberra, Australia, presented to the 1986 Australasian meeting of the Econometric Society, University of Melbourne, 28–30 August 1986.

Brodin, A. and D. Blades (1986) 'The OECD Compatible Trade and Production Data Base, 1970–1983', Department of Economics and Statistics, *OECD Working Papers, Number 21* (Paris: OECD).

Buckwell, A.E., D. Harvey, K. Thomson and K. Parton (1982) *The Costs of the Common Agricultural Policy* (London: Croom Helm).

Burniaux, J. and J. Waelbroeck (1985) 'The Impact of the CAP on Developing Countries: A General Equilibrium Analysis', in C. Stevens and J. Verloren van Themat (eds), *Pressure Groups, Policies and Development* (London: Hodder & Stoughton).

Cable, Vincent (1987) 'Textiles and Clothing', in J. Michael Finger and Andrzej Olechowski (eds), *The Uruguay Round: A Handbook on the Multilateral Trade Negotiations* (Washington: World Bank).

Cable, Vincent and Martin Weale (1985) 'The Economic Costs of Sectorial Protection', *The World Economy*, vol. 8, pp. 421–38.

Canto, Victor (1984) 'The Effect of Voluntary Restraint Agreements: A Case Study of the Steel Industry', *Applied Economics*, vol. 16 (April) pp. 175–86.

Carliner, Geoffrey (1985) 'Patterns in Japanese and American Trade', paper presented at the International Symposium on *Current Policy Issues in the United States and Japan*, Tokyo, 21–22 October.

Chenery, Hollis (1960) 'Patterns of Industrial Growth', *American Economic Review*, vol. 50, pp. 624–54.

Cline, William (1985) *Imports of Manufactures from Developing Countries: Performance and Prospects for Market Access* (Washington: The Brookings Institution).

Cline, William (1987) *The Future of World Trade in Textiles and Apparel* (Washington: Institute of International Economics).

Cline, William, Noboru Kawanabe, T.O.M. Kronsjo and Thomas Williams (1978) *Trade Negotiations in the Tokyo Round: A Quantitative Assessment* (Washington: The Brookings Institution).

Collyns, Charles and Steve Dunaway (1987) 'The Cost of Trade Restraints: The Case of Japanese Automobile Exports to the United States', *International Monetary Fund Staff Papers*, vol. 34, no. 1 (March) pp. 150–75.

Commonwealth Secretariat (1982) *Protectionism: Threat to International Order* (London: Commonwealth Secretariat).

Consumers Association of the United Kingdom (1979) *The Price of Protection: A Study of the Effect of Import Controls on the Cost of Imported Clothing* (London: Consumers Association).

Council of Economic Advisors (1988) *Economic Report of the President* (Washington: Government Printing Office) pp. 149–50.

Council on Wage and Price Stability (1978) *Textile & Apparel: A Study of the Textile and Apparel Industries* (Washington: United States Government Printing Office).

Crandall, R. (1982) *The U.S. Steel Industry in Recurring Crisis: Policy Options in a Competitive World* (Washington: The Brookings Institution).

Crandall, R. (1984) 'Import Quotas and the Automobile Industry: The Costs of Protectionism', *Brookings Review*, vol. 2 (Summer) pp. 8–16.

Cuddihy, W. (1980) 'Agricultural Price Management in Egypt', *World Bank Staff Working Paper No. 388* (Washington: World Bank).

Deardorff, Alan and Robert Stern (1983) 'The Economic Effects of the Complete Elimination of Post-Tokyo Round Tariffs', in W.R. Cline (ed.), *Trade Policy in the 1980s* (Washington: Institute for International Economics).

Deardorff, Alan and Robert Stern (1985) *Methods of Measurement of Non-tariff Barriers* (Geneva: UNCTAD).

Deardorff, Alan and Robert Stern (1986) *The Michigan Model of World Production and Trade: Theory and Applications* (Cambridge, Mass.: MIT Press).

Erzan, Refik, Sam Laird and Alexander Yeats (1986) 'On the Potential for Expanding South–South Trade Through the Extension of Mutual Preferences Among Developing Countries', UNCTAD Discussion Paper No. 16 (Geneva: UNCTAD).

Evans, John (1971) *The Kennedy Round in American Trade Policy, The Twilight of the GATT* (Cambridge, Mass.: Harvard University Press, 1971).

Feenstra, Robert (1985) 'Automobile Prices and Protection: The U.S. Japan Trade Restraint', *Journal of Policy Modelling*, vol. 7 (Spring) pp. 49–68.

Feenstra, Robert (1988) 'Quality Change in U.S. Autos', in Jagdish Bhagwati (ed.), *International Trade: Selected Readings*, 2nd edn (Cambridge, Mass.: M.I.T. Press).

Finger, J. Michael (1981) *The United States Trigger Price Mechanism for Steel Imports* (Washington: The World Bank).

Finger, J. Michael (1987) 'Antidumping and Antisubsidy Measures', in J. Michael Finger and Andrzej Olechowski (eds), *The Uruguay Round: A Handbook on the Multilateral Trade Negotiations* (Washington: The World Bank) pp. 153–61.

Finger, J. Michael and Andrzej Olechowski (1986) 'Trade Barriers: Who Does What to Whom', Paper presented at the *Conference on Free Trade in the World Economy – Toward an Opening of Markets*, Kiel, Germany, 23–26 June.

Finger, J. Michael and Andrzej Olechowski (eds) (1987) *The Uruguay Round: A Handbook on the Multilateral Trade Negotiations* (Washington: The World Bank).

Fitchett, Delbert (1987) 'Agriculture', in J. Michael Finger and Andrzej Olechowski (eds), *The Uruguay Round: A Handbook on the Multilateral Trade Negotiations* (Washington: The World Bank) pp. 162–70.

Fitchett, Delbert (1988) 'A Sunset Industry in the Land of the Rising Sun: Agriculture and Agricultural Trade Protection in Japan – A Survey Paper', *World Bank Staff Working Paper* (Washington: World Bank, mimeo).

Gardner, B. (1986) 'Economic Consequences of U.S. Agricultural Policies', *World Development Background Report Paper*, The World Bank, Washington.

General Agreement on Tariffs and Trade (1971) *Import Measures: Variable Levies and Other Special Charges* (COM. AG/W/68/Add.3) (Geneva: GATT, April).

Glismann, Hans and Axel Neu (1971) 'Towards New Agreements on International Trade Liberalization: Methods and Examples of Measuring Nontariff Trade Barriers', *Weltwirtschaftliches Archiv*, Band 107, pp. 235–71.

Goldstein, Morriss and Mohsin Khan (1984) 'Income and Price Effects in Foreign Trade', in Ronald Jones and Peter Kenen (eds), *Handbook of International Economics*, vol. II (North Holland: Amsterdam).

Gotch, C. and G. Brown (1980) 'Prices, Taxes and Subsidies in Pakistan Agriculture', *World Bank Staff Working Paper No. 387* (Washington: World Bank).

Grassman, Sven (1973) 'A Fundamental Symmetry in International Payment Patterns', *Journal of International Economics* (May) pp. 106–16.

Greenaway, David (1985a) 'Clothing from Hong Kong and Other Developing Countries', in David Greenaway and Brian Hindley (eds), *What*

Britain Pays for Voluntary Export Restraints, Thames Essay No. 43 (London: Trade Policy Research Centre).

Greenaway, David (1985b) 'Non-Leather Footwear from Taiwan and Korea', in David Greenaway and Brian Hindley (eds), *What Britain Pays for Voluntary Export Restraints*, Thames Essay No. 43 (London: Trade Policy Research Centre).

Greenaway, David and Brian Hindley (1985) *What Britain Pays for Voluntary Export Restraints*, Thames Essay No. 43 (London: Trade Policy Research Centre).

Grubel, Herbert (1971) 'Effective Tariff Protection: A Non-Specialist Introduction to the Theory, Policy Implications and Controversies', in Herbert G. Grubel and Harry G. Johnson (eds), *Effective Tariff Protection* (Geneva: GATT).

Gulbrandsen, Odd and Assar Lindbeck (1973) *The Economics of the Agricultural Sector* (Stockholm: Almqvist & Wiksell).

Hamilton, Carl (1984a) 'Swedish Trade Restrictions on Textiles and Clothing', *Skandinaviska Enskilda Banken Quarterly Review*, no. 4, pp. 103–12.

Hamilton, Carl (1984b) 'Voluntary Export Restraints on Asia: Tariff Equivalents, Rents and Trade Barrier Formation', *Seminar Paper No. 276* (Stockholm: Institute for International Economic Studies).

Hamilton, Carl (1985) 'ASEAN Systems for Allocation of Export Licenses Under VERs', in C. Findlay and R. Garnaut (eds), *The Political Economy of Manufacturing Sector Protection in ASEAN and Australia* (London: Allen & Unwin.

Hamilton, Carl (1986) 'Agricultural Protection in Sweden 1970–1980', *European Review of Agricultural Economics*, vol. 13, no. 1, pp. 75–87.

Harling, K. and R. Thompson (1985) 'Government Interventions in Poultry Industries: A Cross-Country Comparison', *American Journal of Agricultural Economics*, vol. 67, pp. 243–9.

Harriss, Richard (1984) 'Applied General Equilibrium Analysis of Small Open Economies and Imperfect Competition', *The American Economic Review*, vol. 74, no. 5 (December) pp. 1016–32.

Havrylyshyn, O. (1988) *Trade Control Measures and Developing Country Trade: An Analysis Using the UNCTAD Trade Information (TIS) Data Base* (UNCTAD/ECDC/TA/21) (Geneva: UNCTAD).

Hayami, Y. and Honma M. (1983) 'The Agricultural Protection Level of Japan in an International Comparative Perspective', *The Forum for Policy Innovation*, Research Report No. 1 (Tokyo).

Hindley, Brian (1985) 'Motor Cars from Japan', in David Greenaway and Brian Hindley, *What Britain Pays for Voluntary Export Restraints*, Thames Essay No. 43 (London: Trade Policy Research Centre).

Holzman, Franklyn (1969) 'Comparison of Different Forms of Trade Barriers', *Review of Economics and Statistics* (May) pp. 159–65.

Hufbauer, Gary, Diane Berliner and Kimberly Elliott (1986) *Trade Protection in the United States: 31 Case Studies* (Washington: Institute for International Economics).

Hunker, J.A. (1984) *Structural Change in the U.S. Automobile Industry* (Lexington: Lexington Books).

International Monetary Fund (1982) *Some Aspects of Using the SDR to*

Invoice Private International Goods and Services Transactions (DW/82/29) (Washington: IMF, April).

International Monetary Fund (1984) *Effects of Increased Market Access on Selected Developing Countries Export Earnings: An Illustrative Exercise* (DM/84/85) (Washington: IMF).

Jackson, John (1984) 'Perspectives on the Jurisprudence of International Trade', *The American Economic Review* (May) pp. 277–81.

Jages, M. and C.J. Lanjuan (1977) 'An Alternative Method for Quantifying International Trade Barriers', *Weltwirtschaftliches Archiv*, 113 (Heft 4), pp. 719–40.

Japan Economic Institute (1983) *Agricultural Protectionism* (Tokyo: Japan Economic Institute).

Jenkins, Glen (1980) *Costs and Consequences of the New Protectionism: The Case of Canada's Clothing Sector* (Ottawa: The North South Institute).

Jondrow, M. (1978) 'Effects of Trade Restrictions on Imports of Steel', in *The Impact of International Trade on Investment and Employment* (Washington: US Government Printing Office).

Karsenty, Guy and Sam Laird (1986) 'The Generalized System of Preferences – A Quantitative Assessment of the Direct Trade Effects and Policy Options', *UNCTAD Discussion Paper No. 19* (Geneva: UNCTAD).

Keesing, Donald (1967) 'Outward-Looking Policies and Economic Development', *Economic Journal* (June) pp. 303–20.

Koekkoek, K.A. and L.B.M. Mennes (1986) 'Liberalizing the Multifibre Arrangement', *Journal of World Trade Law*, vol. 20, no. 2 (March: April) pp. 142–69.

Koester, U. (1982) 'Policy Options for the Grain Economy of the European Community: Implications for the Developing Countries', *International Food Policy Research Institute Report No. 35* (Washington: IFPRI).

Koester, U. and M. Bale (1980) 'Agricultural Protection in Industrialized Countries and its Global Effects: A Survey of Issues', *Aussenwirtschaft*, vol. 35, no. 4, pp. 331–54.

Kojima, Kiyoshi (1964) 'The Pattern of International Trade Among Advanced Countries', *Hitotsubashi Journal of Economics*, vol. 5, no. 1 (June) pp. 16–36.

Laird, Sam and J. Michael Finger (1986) 'Protection in Developed and Developing Countries', paper presented at the *Conference on the Role and Interests of the Developing Countries in the Multilateral Trade Negotiations*, Bangkok, Thailand, 30 October to 1 November.

Laird, Sam and Alexander Yeats (1986) 'The UNCTAD Trade Policy Simulation Model: A Note on the Methodology, Data and Uses', *UNCTAD Discussion Paper Number 19* (Geneva: UNCTAD).

Laird, Samuel and Alexander Yeats (1987a) 'On the Potential Contribution of Trade Policy Initiatives for Alleviating the International Debt Crisis', *Journal of Economics and Business*, vol. 39, no. 3 (August) pp. 209–24.

Laird, Samuel and Alexander Yeats (1987b) 'Tariff Cutting Formulas – And Complications', in J.M. Finger and Andrzej Olechowski (eds), *The Uruguay Round: A Handbook on the Multilateral Trade Negotiations* (Washington: World Bank) pp. 89–100.

Laird, Samuel and Alexander Yeats (1987c) 'Empirical Evidence Concerning the Magnitude and Effects of Developing Country Tariff Escalation', *The Developing Economies*, vol. 25, no. 2 (June) pp. 99–123.

Langhammer, Rolf (1983a) 'Sectoral Profiles Import Licensing in Selected Developing Countries and Their Impact on North–South and South–South Trade Flows', *Konjunkturpolitik*, 29 Jahrg. H. 1, pp. 21–32.

Langhammer, Rolf (1983b) 'Problems and Effects of a Developing Countries' Tariff Concession on South–South Trade', *Kiel Working Paper Number 167* (Kiel: Institute for World Economics).

Lary, Hal (1968) *Imports of Manufactures from Less Developed Countries* (New York: National Bureau of Economic Research).

Lawrence, Robert Z. (1987) 'Imports in Japan: Closed Markets or Minds?', *Brookings Papers on Economic Activity*, no. 2, pp. 517–54.

Linnemann, Hanns (1966) *An Econometric Study of International Trade Flows* (Amsterdam: North-Holland Publishing Co.).

Lloyd, Peter (1974) 'Strategies for Modifying Nontariff Distortions', in Hugh Corbet and Robert Jackson (eds), *In Search of a New World Economic Order* (London: Croom Helm) pp. 199–209.

Lowinger, Thomas (1976) 'Discrimination in Government Procurement of Foreign Goods in the U.S. and Western Europe', *Southern Economic Journal*, vol. 42, no. 3 (January) pp. 451–60.

Lutz, E. and P. Scandizzo (1980) 'Price Distortions in Developing Countries: A Bias Against Agriculture', *European Review of Agricultural Economics*, vol. 7, no. 1.

MacPhee, C. (1974) *Restrictions on International Trade in Steel* (Lexington: D.C. Heath).

McNamara, Robert (1979) 'The High Cost of Protectionism', *Institutional Investor* (September) pp. 15–20.

McCulloch, Rachel and R. Spence Hilton (1983) 'Identifying Nontariff Distortions of U.S. Merchandise Trade', *Research Paper No. 8310* (New York: Federal Reserve Bank of New York).

Messerlin, Patrick (1988) *Experiences of Developing Countries with Anti-dumping Laws* (Washington: The World Bank).

Miller, Geoffrey (1986) *The Political Economy of International Agricultural Policy Reform* (Canberra: Australian Government Publishing Service).

Monke, Eric and Salah Salam (1986) 'Trade Policies and Variability in International Grain Markets', *Food Policy*, vol. 11, no. 3 (August) pp. 238–52.

Moreci, P. and L.L. Megna (1983) *United States Policies Affecting Industrial Trade* (Washington: US Federal Trade Commission).

Morkre, M.E. and D.G. Tarr (1980) *Effects of Restrictions on United States Imports: Five Case Studies*, Federal Trade Commission Staff Report (Washington: US Government Printing Office).

Munger, Michael (1984) 'The Costs of Protectionism', *Challenge* (January–February) pp. 54–8.

Murray, Tracy and Ingo Walter (1977) 'Quantitative Restrictions, Developing Countries and GATT', *Journal of World Trade Law*, vol. 11 (September: October) pp. 391–421.

Nogues, Julio, Andrzej Olechowski and L. Alan Winters (1985) *The Extent of Nontariff Barriers to Industrial Countries' Imports* (Report No.

DRD115) (Washington: Development Research Department of the World Bank, January).

Noland, Marcus (1987) *An Econometric Analysis of International Protection* (Washington: Institute for International Economics, September).

Olechowski, Andrzej (1987) 'Nontariff Barriers to Trade', in J.M. Finger and Andrzej Olechowski (eds), *The Uruguay Round: A Handbook on the Multilateral Trade Negotiations* (Washington: World Bank) pp. 121–6.

Olechowski, Andrzej and Alexander Yeats (1982) 'The Incidence of Nontariff Barriers on Socialist Country Exports', *Economia Internazionale*, vol. 35, no. 2 (May) pp. 3–21.

Organization for Economic Cooperation and Development (1985a) *Costs and Benefits of Protection* (Paris: OECD).

Organization for Economic Cooperation and Development (1985b) 'Econometric Annex to Chapter 6 – Textiles and Clothing', in *Costs and Benefits of Protection* (Paris: OECD).

Organization for Economic Cooperation and Development (1985c) 'Steel', in *Costs and Benefits of Protection* (Paris: OECD).

Organization for Economic Cooperation and Development (1985d) 'Econometric Annex to Chapter 8 – Consumer Electronics: The Case of Colour Television Receivers', in *Costs and Benefits of Protection* (Paris: OECD).

Organization for Economic Cooperation and Development (1987a) *National Policies and Agricultural Trade* (Paris: OECD).

Organization for Economic Cooperation and Development (1987b) *National Policies and Agricultural Trade: Country Study Japan* (Paris: OECD).

Organization for Economic Cooperation and Development (1987c) *National Policies and Agricultural Trade: Study on the European Economic Community* (Paris: OECD).

Otsuka, K. and Y. Hayami (1985) 'Goals and Consequences of Rice Policy in Japan, 1965–80', *American Journal of Agricultural Economics*, vol. 67, pp. 529–38.

Parikh, K., G. Fischer, K. Frohberg and O. Gulbrandsen (1986) 'Towards Free Trade in Agriculture', *Draft Report of the Food and Agricultural Program of the International Institute of Applied Systems Analysis* (Vienna: IIASA).

Peltzman, J. (1983) 'Economic Costs of Tariff and Quotas in Textile and Apparel Products Imported into the United States: A Survey of the Literature and Implications for Policies', *Weltwirtschaftliches Archiv*, Band 119, Heft 3, pp. 523–41.

Pomfret, Richard (1986) 'Effects of Trade Preferences for Developing Countries', *Southern Economic Journal*, vol. 53, pp. 18–26.

Pryor, Frederic (1966) 'Trade Barriers of Capitalist and Communist Nations Against Foodstuffs Exported by Tropical Underdeveloped Nations', *Review of Economics and Statistics*, vol. 47, no. 4 (November) pp. 406–11.

Pulliainen, K. (1963) 'A World Trade Study: An Econometric Model of the Pattern of Commodity Flows in International Trade', *Ekonomiska*, no. 2, pp. 78–91.

Roemer, Michael (1979) 'Resource Based Industrialization in Developing Countries: A Survey of the Literature', *Harvard Institute for International Development: Discussion Paper Number 21* (Cambridge, Mass.: HIID).

Roningen, Vernon (1978) 'The Effects of Exchange Rate, Payments and Trade Restrictions on Trade Between OECD Countries, 1967–1973', *Review of Economics and Statistics* (August) pp. 471–5.

Roningen, Vernon and Alexander Yeats (1976) 'Nontariff Distortions of International Trade: Some Preliminary Empirical Evidence', *Weltwirtschaftliches Archiv*, Band 112, Heft 4.

Sampson, G. and R. Snape (1980) 'Effects of the EEC's Variable Levies', *Journal of Political Economy*, vol. 88, no. 5.

Sampson, Gary and Alexander Yeats (1976) 'Do Import Levies Matter? The Case of Sweden', *Journal of Political Economy* (August) pp. 881–92.

Sampson, Gary and Alexander Yeats (1977) 'An Evaluation of the Common Agricultural Policy as a Barrier Facing Agricultural Exports to the European Economic Community', *American Journal of Agricultural Economics* (February) pp. 99–106.

Sapir, Andre and Robert Baldwin (1983) 'India and the Tokyo Round', *World Development*, vol. 2, no. 2, pp. 30–46.

Sarris, A. (1985) *Domestic Price Policies and International Distortions: The Case of Wheat and Rice* (Rome: FAO, unpublished).

Sarris, A. and J. Freebairn (1983) 'Endogenous Price Policies and International Wheat Prices', *American Journal of Agricultural Economics*, vol. 65, no. 2, pp. 214–24.

Saxon, Eric and Kym Anderson (1982) 'Japanese Agricultural Protection in Historical Perspective', *Pacific Economic Papers No. 92* (July).

Saxonhouse, Gary (1983) 'The Micro- and Macroeconomics of Foreign Sales to Japan', in William Cline (ed.), *Trade Policy in the 1980s* (Washington: Institute for International Economics).

Scandizzo, P. and C. Bruce (1980) 'Methodologies for Measuring Agricultural Price Intervention Effects', *World Bank Staff Working Paper No. 394* (Washington: World Bank).

Scherer, Frederick (1970) *Industrial Market Structure and Economic Performance* (New York: Prentice Hall).

Schiff, M. (1985) *An Econometric Analysis of the World Wheat Market and Simulation of Alternative Policies, 1960–80* (Washington: US Department of Agriculture, International Economics Division).

Silberston, Z.A. (1984) *The Multi-Fibre Arrangement in the U.K. Economy* (London: HMSO).

Snape, Richard (1981) 'A Foreigner's View of Import Restrictions', paper presented at a *Conference on the United States and Asia Economic Relations*, New Jersey, Rutgers University, 16–18 April.

Spencer, J. (1985) 'The European Economic Community: General Equilibrium Computations and the Economic Implications of Membership', in J. Piggot and J. Whalley (eds), *New Developments in Applied General Equilibrium Analysis* (Cambridge: Cambridge University Press).

Statistical Office of the United Nations (1961) *Standard International Trade Classification, Revised* (Series M, no. 34) (New York: United Nations Department of Economic and Social Affairs).

Stern, Robert (1976) 'Evaluating Alternative Tariff Cutting Formulae', *Journal of World Trade Law* (January: February) pp. 50–64.

Stern, Robert *et al.* (1976) *Price Elasticities in International Trade* (London: Macmillan Press).

Stoeckel, A. (1985) *Intersectoral Effects of the CAP: Growth, Trade and Unemployment*, Occasional Paper 95 (Canberra: Bureau of Agricultural Economics).

Tackacs, W. (1975) 'Quantitative Restrictions in International Trade', unpublished Ph.D. Dissertation (Baltimore: Johns Hopkins University).

Tarr, David and Morris Morkre (1984) *Aggregate Costs to the United States of Tariffs and Quotas on Imports: General Tariff Cuts and Removal of Quotas on Automobiles, Steel, Sugar and Textiles*, Staff Report to the Federal Trade Commission (Washington: Federal Trade Commission).

Thomson, K. (1985) 'A Model of the Common Agricultural Policy', unpublished paper presented at the March meeting of the UK Agricultural Economic Society.

Tinbergen, Jan (1962) *Shaping the World Economy: Suggestions for an International Economic Policy* (New York: The Twentieth Century Fund).

Tuong, Ho Dac and Alexander Yeats (1980) 'On Factor Proportions as a Guide to the Future Composition of Developing Country Exports', *Journal of Development Economics*, vol. 7 (Fall) pp. 521–39.

Tyers, R. (1982) 'Effects on ASEAN of Food Trade Liberalization in Industrial Economies', paper presented at the Second Western Pacific Food Trade Workshop, Jakarta, August.

Tyers, R. and K. Anderson (1986) 'Distortions in World Food Markets: A Quantitative Assessment', *World Development Report Background Paper*, The World Bank, Washington.

UNCTAD (1968) *The Kennedy Round Estimated Effects on Tariff Barriers* (TD/6/Rev. 1) (New York: United Nations).

UNCTAD (1972) *Agricultural Protection and the Food Economy*, Research Memo. No. 46 (Geneva: UNCTAD).

UNCTAD (1979) *The Processing Before Export of Primary Commodities: Areas for Further International Cooperation* (Manila: UNCTAD).

UNCTAD (1983a) *Nontariff Barriers Affecting the Trade of Developing Countries and Transparency in World Trading Conditions* (TD/B/940) (Geneva: UNCTAD, February).

UNCTAD (1983b) *Protectionism and Structural Adjustment in Agriculture* (TD/B/939) (Geneva: UNCTAD, March).

UNCTAD (1984) *Anti-Dumping and Countervailing Duty Practices* (TD/B/979) (Geneva: UNCTAD, 20 January).

UNCTAD (1985) *Trade and Development Report, 1985* (Geneva: UNCTAD).

UNCTAD (1987) *Handbook of International Trade and Development Statistics* (New York: United Nations).

UNCTAD (1988a) *Consideration of the Questions of Definition and Methodology Employed in the UNCTAD Data Base on Trade Measures* (TD/B/AC. 42/5) (Geneva: UNCTAD).

UNCTAD (1988b) *Handbook of International Trade and Development Statistics* (New York: United Nations).

United Nations (1961) *Standard International Trade Classification, Revised*, series M, number 34 (New York: United Nations).

United Nations (various issues) *Commodity Trade Statistics: Series D, Commodity by Country* (New York: United Nations).

United Nations Economic Commission for Asia and the Far East (1972)

Intraregional Trade Projections: Effective Protection and Income Distribution, vol. 2 (Bangkok: United Nations).

United Nations Food and Agricultural Organization (1979) *Commodity Review and Outlook, 1979–1980* (Rome: FAO).

United Nations Food and Agricultural Organization (1980) *Protectionism in the Livestock Sector* (Rome: FAO).

United Nations Food and Agricultural Organization (1981) *Protectionism in the Oilseeds, Oils and Oilmeals Sector* (CCP:OF 81/82) (Rome: FAO).

United Nations Food and Agricultural Organization (1983) *Expert Consultation on Agricultural Price Policies* (Rome: FAO).

United Nations Food and Agricultural Organization (1984) *Agricultural Price Policies in Africa* (Rome: FAO).

United Nations Food and Agricultural Organization (1985) *Agricultural Protection and Stabilization Policies: A Framework of Measurement in the Context of Agricultural Adjustment* (C75/LIM/1) (Rome: FAO).

United Nations Food and Agricultural Organization (1987) *Agricultural Price Policies: Issues and Proposals* (Rome: FAO).

United Nations Industrial Development Organization (1982) *Changing Patterns of Trade in World Industry: An Empirical Study on Revealed Comparative Advantage* (New York: United Nations).

United States Department of Agriculture (1981) *Sugar and Sweetener: Outlook and Situation* (Washington: Department of Agriculture).

United States Federal Trade Commission (1977) *Staff Report on the United States Steel Industry and Its International Rivals* (Washington: US Government Printing Office).

United States House of Representatives (1980) *Auto-Situation, 1980*, Sub-Committee on Trade of the Committee on Ways and Means (Washington: US Government Printing Office).

United States International Trade Commission (1985) *A Review of Recent Developments in the U.S. Automobile Industry Including an Assessment of the Japanese Voluntary Restraint Agreements*, USITC Publication No. 1648 (Washington: USITC).

United States Tariff Commission (1974) *Trade Barriers: An Overview* (Washington: US Tariff Commission).

Valdes, Alberto and Joachim Zietz (1980) *Agricultural Protection in OECD Countries: Its Cost to Less-Developed Countries* (Washington: International Food Policy Research Institute).

Walter, Ingo (1969) 'Nontariff Barriers and the Free Trade Area Option', *Banca Nazionale del Lavoro Quarterly Review* (March) pp. 16–45.

Walter, Ingo (1971) 'Nontariff Barriers and the Export Performance of Developing Countries', *American Economic Association Papers and Proceedings*, vol. 61 (May) pp. 195–205.

Walter, Ingo (1972) 'Nontariff Protection Among Industrial Countries: Some Preliminary Empirical Evidence', *Economia Internazionale*, vol. 55 (May) pp. 335–54.

Westlake, M. (1987) 'The Measurement of Agricultural Price Distortion in Developing Countries', *The Journal of Development Studies*, vol. 23, no. 3 (April) pp. 367–81.

Winters, L. Alan (1987) *The Economic Consequences of Agricultural Support: A Survey*, OECD Economic Studies Number 9 (Paris: OECD).

Wipf, Larry (1971) 'Nontariff Distortions and Effective Protection in U.S. Agriculture', *American Journal of Agricultural Economics* (August) pp. 423–30.

Wolf, Martin (1983) 'Managed Trade in Practice: Implications of the Textile Arrangements', in W. Cline (ed.), *Trade Policies in the 1980s* (Washington: Institute for International Economics).

Wolf, Martin, Hans Hinrich Glismann, Joseph Pelzman and Dean Springer (1984) *Costs of Protecting Jobs in Textiles and Clothing*, Thames Essay No. 37 (London: Trade Policy Research Centre).

World Bank (1980) *Philippines: Industrial Development Strategy and Policy* (Washington: World Bank).

World Bank (1981) *World Development Report, 1982* (New York: Oxford University Press for the World Bank).

World Bank (1982) *Turkey: Industrialization and Trade Strategy* (Washington: World Bank).

World Bank (1983) *Yugoslavia: Adjustment Policies and Development Perspectives* (Washington: World Bank).

World Bank (1985) 'The Costs of Protecting Sugar and Beef', *World Development Report, 1985* (Washington: World Bank).

World Bank (1986) *World Development Report, 1986* (New York: Oxford University Press for the World Bank).

World Bank (1987) *World Development Report, 1987* (New York: Oxford University Press for the World Bank).

Yan, Aw Bee and Mark J. Roberts (1986) 'Measuring Quality Change in Quota-Constrained Import Markets: The Case of U.S. Footwear', *Journal of International Economics*, vol. 21, pp. 45–60.

Yeats, Alexander (1976) 'An Analysis of the Incidence of Specific Tariffs on Developing Country Exports', *Economic Inquiry* (March) pp. 71–80.

Yeats, Alexander (1979) *Trade Barriers Facing Developing Countries: Commercial Policy Measures and Shipping* (London: Macmillan Press).

Yeats, Alexander (1981a) 'Agricultural Protectionism: An Analysis of its International Economic Effects and Options for Institutional Reform', *Trade and Development* (Winter) pp. 1–30.

Yeats, Alexander (1981b) *Shipping and Development Policy: An Integrated Assessment* (New York: Praeger Scientific Publishers).

Yeats, Alexander (1982) 'Development Assistance: Trade Versus Aid and the Relative Performance of Industrial Countries', *World Development*, vol. 10, no. 10 (October) pp. 863–70.

Yeats, Alexander (1987) 'The Escalation of Trade Barriers', in J. Michael Finger and Andrzej Olechowski (eds), *The Uruguay Round: A Handbook on the Multilateral Trade Negotiations* (Washington: The World Bank) pp. 110–20.

Index

302